Great Moments
In
Penn State Football

This book begins at the beginning of Football and goes to the James Franklin era

> The book is written for those of us who love Penn State Football. Those who hate PSU football will also want this book so they can get a leg up on the facts missing from the bookshelves of those PSU fans who do not have this book.
>
> The book first tells the story about Penn State's founding in 1855 and quickly gets to the first American football game in 1867. From there, the progression leads, to the Penn State's first football game in 1881, then to the first Penn State Football coach George Hoskins in 1892, and of course to the great immortal Penn State coaches—Hugo Bezdek, Bob Higgins, Rip Engle, and Joe Paterno—to the current season Coach James Franklin.
>
> This book captures the great moments in Penn State Football. It takes the reader through stories about Penn State's 17 coaches to great stories about 127 seasons worth of great games (1280 games). The book often stops in time and talks about a particular player such as John Cappelletti, Franco Harris, Chuck Fusina, Jack Ham, Jimmy Cefalo, Todd Blackledge, and Lydell Mitchell.
>
> You will not be able to put this book down.

Brian Kelly

Copyright © July 2016, Brian W. Kelly   Editor: Brian P. Kelly
Great Moments in Penn State Football   Author Brian W. Kelly
All rights reserved: No part of this book may be reproduced or transmitted in any form, or by any means, electronic or mechanical, including photocopying, recording, scanning, faxing, or by any information storage and retrieval system, without permission from the publisher, LETS GO PUBLISH, in writing.

Disclaimer: Though judicious care was taken throughout the writing and the publication of this work that the information contained herein is accurate, there is no expressed or implied warranty that all information in this book is 100% correct. Therefore, neither LETS GO PUBLISH, nor the author accepts liability for any use of this work.

Trademarks: A number of products and names referenced in this book are trade names and trademarks of their respective companies.

Referenced Material: *Standard Disclaimer: The information in this book has been obtained through personal and third party observations, interviews, and copious research. Where unique information has been provided or extracted from other sources, those sources are acknowledged within the text of the book itself or in the References area in the front matter. Thus, there are no formal footnotes nor is there a bibliography section. Any picture that does not have a source was taken from various sites on the Internet with no credit attached. If resource owners would like credit in the next printing, please email publisher.*

Published by: .... LETS GO PUBLISH!
Editor in Chief ....Brian P. Kelly
Email: .... info@letsgopublish.com
Web site .... www.letsgopublish.com

Library of Congress Copyright Information Pending
Book Cover Design by Michele Thomas--Offset Production Supervisor - Arlene O'Malley
Editor—Brian P. Kelly

ISBN Information: The International Standard Book Number (ISBN) is a unique machine-readable identification number, which marks any book unmistakably. The ISBN is the clear standard in the book industry. 159 countries and territories are officially ISBN members. The Official ISBN For this book is

978-0-9962454-8-7

The price for this work is:......							$ 24.50 USD	
10	9	8	7	6	5	4	3	2	1

Release Date: July 2016

Penn State Season Records from 1887 through 2015

Year	Coach	Record	Champs	Year	Coach	Record	Champs	Bowl col 2
1887	No coach	2-0		1952	Rip Engle	7–2–1		
1888	No coach	0–2-1		1953	Rip Engle	6-3		
1889	No coach	2.2		1954	Rip Engle	7-2		
1890	No coach	2-2		1955	Rip Engle	5-4		
1891	No coach	6-2		1956	Rip Engle	6-2		
1892	George Hoskins	5-1		1957	Rip Engle	6-3		
1893	George Hoskins	4–1		1958	Rip Engle	6–3-1		
1894	George Hoskins	6-0-1		1959	Rip Engle	9-2		Won Liberty
1895	George Hoskins	2-2-3		1960	Rip Engle	7-3		Won Liberty
1896	Samuel B. Newton	3-4		1961	Rip Engle	8-3		Won Gator
1897	Samuel B. Newton	3-6		1962	Rip Engle	9-2		Won Gator
1898	Samuel B. Newton	6-4		1963	Rip Engle	7-3		
1899	Sam B. Boyle	4-6-1		1964	Rip Engle	6-4		
1900	WM Pop Golden	4-6-1		1965	Rip Engle	5-5		
1901	WM Pop Golden	5-3		1966	Joe Paterno	5-5		
1902	WM Pop Golden	7-3		1967	Joe Paterno	8–2-1		Tied Gator
1903	Daniel A. Reed	5-3		1968	Joe Paterno	11-0		Won Orange
1904	Tom Fennell	6-4		1969	Joe Paterno	11-0		Won Orange
1905	Tom Fennell	8-3		1970	Joe Paterno	7-3		
1906	Tom Fennell	8-1-1		1971	Joe Paterno	11-1		Won Cotton
1907	Tom Fennell	6-4		1972	Joe Paterno	10-2		Lost Sugar
1908	Tom Fennell	5-5		1973	Joe Paterno	12–0		Won Orange
1909	Wm. Hollenback	5-0-2		1974	Joe Paterno	10–2		Won Cotton
1910	Jack Hollenback	5-2-1		1975	Joe Paterno	9-3		Lost Sugar
1911	Wm. Hollenback	8-0-1		1976	Joe Paterno	7-5		Lost Gator
1912	Wm. Hollenback	8-0		1977	Joe Paterno	11–1		Won Fiesta
1913	Wm. Hollenback	2-6		1978	Joe Paterno	11-1		Lost Sugar
1914	Wm. Hollenback	5-3-1		1979	Joe Paterno	8–4		Won Liberty
1915	Dick Harlow	7–2		1980	Joe Paterno	10-2		Won Fiesta
1916	Dick Harlow	8–2		1981	Joe Paterno	10-2		Won Fiesta
1917	Dick Harlow	5-4		1982	Joe Paterno	11-1	Champs	Won Sugar
1918	Hugo F. Bezdek	1-2-1		1983	Joe Paterno	8-4-1		Won Aloha
1919	Hugo F. Bezdek	7-1		1984	Joe Paterno	6–5		
1920	Hugo F. Bezdek	7-0-2		1985	Joe Paterno	11-1		Lost Orange
1921	Hugo F. Bezdek	8-0		1986	Joe Paterno	12-0	Champs	Won Fiesta
1922	Hugo F. Bezdek	8–1–1	L. Rose	1987	Joe Paterno	8–4		Lost Citrus
1923	Hugo F. Bezdek	6-4-1		1988	Joe Paterno	5-6		Won Fiesta
1924	Hugo F. Bezdek	6-3	Champs	1989	Joe Paterno	8-3		Won Holiday
1925	Hugo F. Bezdek	4-4-1		1990	Joe Paterno	9–3		Lost Champs
1926	Hugo F. Bezdek	5-4		1991	Joe Paterno	11–2		Won Fiesta
1927	Hugo F. Bezdek	6-2-1		1992	Joe Paterno	7-5		Lost Champs
1928	Hugo F. Bezdek	3-5-1		1993	Joe Paterno	10-2		Won Citrus
1929	Hugo F. Bezdek	6-3-0	Champs	1994	Joe Paterno	12-0		Won Rose
1930	Bob Higgins	3-4-2	Champs	1995	Joe Paterno	9–3		Won Outback
1931	Bob Higgins	2-8		1996	Joe Paterno	11-2		Won Fiesta
1932	Bob Higgins	2-5		1997	Joe Paterno	9-3		Lost Citrus.
1933	Bob Higgins	3–3–1		1998	Joe Paterno	9-3		Won Outback

Year	Coach	Record	Notes	Year	Coach	Record		Bowl
1934	Bob Higgins	4-4		1999	Joe Paterno	10-3		Won Alamo
1935	Bob Higgins	4-4		2000	Joe Paterno	5-7		
1936	Bob Higgins	3-5		2001	Joe Paterno	5-6		
1937	Bob Higgins	5-3		2002	Joe Paterno	9-4		Lost Cap "1"
1938	Bob Higgins	3-4-1		2003	Joe Paterno	3-9		
1939	Bob Higgins	5-1-2		2004	Joe Paterno	4-7		
1940	Bob Higgins	6-1-1		2005	Joe Paterno	11-1		Won Orange
1941	Bob Higgins	7-2		2006	Joe Paterno	9–4		Won Outback
1942	Bob Higgins	6-1-1		2007	Joe Paterno	9-4		Won Alamo
1943	Bob Higgins	5-3-1	Champs	2008	Joe Paterno	11-2		Lost Rose
1944	Bob Higgins	6-3		2009	Joe Paterno	11-2		Won Cap "1"
1945	Bob Higgins	5-3		2010	Joe Paterno	7–6		
1946	Bob Higgins	6-2	Champs	2011	Joe Paterno	8-1		
1947	Bob Higgins	9-0 T Cottn	Champs	2011	Tom Bradley	1-3		Lost TickC
1948	Bob Higgins	7-1-1		2012	Bill O'Brien	8-4		Ineligible
1949	Joe Bedenk	5-4	Champs	2013	Bill O'Brien	7-5		Ineligible
1950	Rip Engle	5-3-1		2014	James Franklin	7-6		Lost Pinstripe
1951	Rip Engle	7–2–1		2015	James Franklin		7-6	Lost FTaxS
Total: 856 Wins		382 L	42 Ties					

Total Wins   856
Total Losses   382
Total Ties   42   * Prior to Overtime Rules
Stats from   1887   *** Through August 2016**

LETS GO PUBLISH!

Dedication

Monsignor Joseph G. Rauscher

Because he is such a great human being and a caring, dedicated instrument of God, who has tended his flock ahead of his own needs, I dedicate this book to Monsignor Joseph G. Rauscher, for his wonderful 27 years of shepherding of St. Nicholas Parish in Wilkes-Barre. The good Monsignor, who is known as Wyoming Valley's pastor, is a man who has touched thousands of lives and even he admits that the interactions "can blow me away some times."

He has most recently been the pastor of St. Nicholas Church, Wilkes-Barre, and in this role has counseled and assisted people across all boundaries — faith, race, ethnicity, social standing — and all by the standards of an Old Testament, Book of Micah injunction, "Do justly, love mercy, walk humbly with thy God."

"He is a wonderful guy. He is extremely kind. We just love him," said John Anstett, a high school classmate, longtime friend and parishioner at St. Nicholas where the 75-year-old priest has served since 1989. "Even in high school, he cared about everyone, about feelings," Anstett said.

Asked his greatest joy as a priest, Monsignor Rauscher said, "It is how privileged I feel the way so many people trust me, confide in me."

"I see him as the community's priest," said Rabbi Larry Kaplan of Temple Israel. "He is there for anyone in need, and he's always smiling. He makes you feel comfortable."

Monsignor Jack Bendik, pastor of St. John the Evangelist Church in Pittston and a seminary classmate of Monsignor Rauscher, said, "He is the most dedicated priest that I ever met. He has a very inclusive nature. He may be in pain, but he is a great inspiration to me and others."

In addition to his pastoral accomplishments, Monsignor Rauscher is one of the most avid Penn State Football fans. He gets to games whenever he can. He loves the Nittany Lions. He and two of his best friends, and high school classmates, John Anstett and Bill Desciak love sharing great stories at their annual luncheon renewals. Of course Penn State and its wonderful football program from over the years is often a main topic. God bless the good Monsignor in his retirement.

Acknowledgments:

I appreciate all the help that I received in putting this book together, along with the 66 other books from the past.

My printed acknowledgments were once so large that book readers needed to navigate too many pages to get to page one of the text. To permit me more flexibility, I put my acknowledgment list online at www.letsgopublish.com. The list of acknowledgments continues to grow. Believe it or not, it once cost about a dollar more to print each book.

Thank you all on the big list in the sky and God bless you all for your help.

Please check out www.letsgopublish.com to read the latest version of my heartfelt acknowledgments updated for this book. Thank you all!

In this book, I received some extra special help from many avid Penn State supporters including Bruce Ikeda, Dennis Grimes, Gerry Rodski, Wily Ky Eyely, Angel Irene McKeown Kelly, Angel Edward Joseph Kelly Sr., Angel Edward Joseph Kelly Jr., Ann Flannery, Angel James Flannery Sr., Mary Daniels, Bill Daniels, Robert Gary Daniels, Angel Sarah Janice Daniels, Angel Punkie Daniels, Joe Kelly, Diane Kelly, Brian P. Kelly, Mike P. Kelly, Katie P. Kelly, Ben Kelly, and Budmund (Buddy) Arthur Kelly.

References

I learned how to write creatively in Grade School at St. Boniface School on Blackman Street. I even enjoyed reading some of my own stuff.

At Meyers High School and King's College and Wilkes-University, I learned how to research, write bibliographies and footnote every non-original thought I might have had. I learned to hate ibid, and op. cit., and I hated assuring that I had all citations written down in the proper sequence. Having to pay attention to details took my desire to write creatively and diminished it with busy work.

I know it is necessary for the world to stop plagiarism so authors and publishers can get paid properly, but for an honest writer, it sure is annoying. I wrote many proposals while with IBM and whenever I needed to cite something, I cited it in place, because my readers, IT Managers, could care less about tracing the vagaries of citations. I always hated to use stilted footnotes, or produce a lengthy, perfectly formatted bibliography. I bet most bibliographies are flawed because even the experts on such drivel do not like the tedium.

I wrote 66 books before this book and several hundred articles which were published by many magazines and newspapers. I choose to cite only when an idea is not mine or when I am quoting, and again, when I cite, I choose to cite in place. The reader does not have to trace strange numbers through strange footnotes and back to bibliography elements that may not be readily accessible or available.

Yet, I would be kidding you, if in a book about the great moments in Penn State Football, I tried to bluff my way into trying to make you think that I knew everything before I began to write anything in this book. I spent as much time researching as writing. I might even call myself an expert of sorts now for all the facts that I have uncovered.

Without any pain on your part you can read this book from cover to cover to enjoy the stories about the many great moments in Penn State Football—and there ae many!

This book is not intended for historians but it does teach a lot of history. It is for regular people of all levels of intelligence. It is for people that want to have a fun read, who like smiling when Penn State Football is the topic. It is for people who love Penn State and perhaps for some PSU haters who want some more facts to bolster their arguments.

There are lots and lots of facts in this book. This book is not for sticklers about the mundane aspects of writing that often cause creative writers to lay bricks or paint houses instead. It is for everyday people like you and I who enjoy Penn State because it is Penn State and who enjoy football because it is football. It is that simple.

When The Nittany Lions play a team and they win or lose, that is a historical fact. To discover such facts, it does not require fundamental or basic research. The University itself copyrights its material but only so it can say "no" if somebody else's creativity affects the university negatively. Even Penn State Dame does not own well-known facts that are readily available about legacies such as John Cappelletti, Bob Higgins, Joe Paterno and championship seasons.

The championships and the coaches are well known and well defined. So what? As the author of this book, I care but it is a sports book. I use a judicious approach to assure that I am not throwing the bull when I was present facts.

Nonetheless, this is not a book about heavy math algorithms, or potential advances to the internal combustion engine, or space travel, or the eight elements necessary to find a cure for cancer. So, I refuse to treat this book 100% seriously. If you find a fault with this book, I will fix it. Just tell me about it.

This is a book about sports and sports legends and stories about sporting events that have been recorded seven million times already someplace else. Though I tried for sure to get it all right and I used the work of others to assure so, I bet I made a mistake or two.

What is my remedy for the *harmed* if I have made a mistake? I did not write this book to harm anybody. If I did not write this book, would the *harmed individuals* from the book be unharmed. So, at the very least, I can *unpublish* those parts of the book. If any reader is harmed, let me know, and I will do whatever must be done for all to be OK. There is so much to write about Penn State football that if I must remove a story or two the ones that replace it them will be better.

If somehow, I did not cite a fact that a person owns or a quote somebody once spoke first, it surely was not my intention. If you find any such instances in this work, I will do my best to cite in place before the next printing or take the offensive fact or quote out of the book completely at your pleasure. Just let me know. This book is built for fun, not to create anybody any angst.

It took me about three months to write because I had to research and come to some conclusions about the Sandusky travesty. I take a position. If I were to have made sure a thought that I had was not a thought somebody else ever had, this book never would have been completed or the citations pages would exceed the prose.

I used PSU Season summaries from whatever source I could to get the scores of all the games. I verified facts when possible. There are many web sites that have great information and facts. Ironically most internet stories are the same exact stories regardless of who the author might be. While I was writing the book, I wrote down a bunch of Internet references that I show you below and when you finish reading this book, you may click and enjoy them.

My favorite source has been the **Penn State Student Magazine** called the Collegian, which has been published in one way or another under different names from day one at the university.

While I was writing this book, because I was not sure that my citations within the text would be enough, and I was not producing a bibliography, I copied URLs of areas on the Internet in which I had read articles or had downloaded material and had brought articles or pieces of articles into this book. Hopefully, this will satisfy any request for additional information. Here are the URLs used as references or used for information that I have read that helped me write the book. These are not in any particular sequence:

http://espn.go.com/colleges/psu/notebook/_/page/pennstatealltimefantasydraft

http://www.cbsnews.com/news/has-media-ignored-sex-abuse-in-school/

http://shoebat.com/2014/05/06/sexual-abuse-protestant-churches-catholic/

https://www.pinterest.com/pin/9570217928134808/

http://www.salon.com/2011/11/22/alan_dershowitz_thinks_joe_paterno_was_treated_unfairly/

http://www.statecollege.com/news/local-news/the-origins-of-happy-valley,1466515/

http://usatoday30.usatoday.com/sports/college/football/2012-01-26-1060933973_x.htm

http://articles.mcall.com/2012-01-01/sports/mc-penn-state-1231-20120101_1_wally-triplett-chima-okoli-joe-paterno

http://www.centredaily.com/news/local/education/penn-state/jerry-sandusky/article42834075.html

Jack Ham references

- Didinger, Ray. *Pittsburgh Steelers*. New York: Macmillan Co., Inc., 1974.
- "Dobre Shunka." *Official Site of Pro Football Hall of Fame*. 2007. Pro Football Hall of Fame. 30 Sept. 2007. <http://www.profootballhof.com/history/release.jsp?release_id=765>.
- "Hall of Famers." *National Football Foundation's College Football Hall of Fame*. 2007. College Football Hall of Fame. 28 Oct. 2007. <http://www.collegefootball.org/famersearch.php?id=60020>.
- "Jack Ham." *Official Site of Pro Football Hall of Fame*. 2007. Pro Football Hall of Fame. 30 Sept. 2007. <http://www.profootballhof.com/hof/member.jsp?player_id=86>.

- McCullough, Bob. *My Greatest Day in Football: the Legends of Football Recount Their Greatest Moments.* St. Martin's P, 2001.
- O'Toole, Andrew. *Smiling Irish Eyes, Art Rooney and the Pittsburgh Steelers.* Haworth, NJ: St. Johann P, 2004.
- Rappoport, Ken. *The Pennsylvania State University Nittany Lions, Where Have You Gone?* Champaign, IL: Sports LLC, 2005.
- Russell, Andy. *A Steeler Odyssey.* Champaign, IL: Sports LLC, 1998.

http://www.blackshoediaries.com/2007/6/10/214341/999

http://www.sports-reference.com/cfb/players/franco-harris-1.html

http://www.pennlive.com/sports/index.ssf/2013/10/top_10_penn_state_football_games.html

http://www.collegefootballpoll.com/bowl_history_penn_state.html

http://bleacherreport.com/articles/1066020-penn-state-football-10-greatest-nittany-lions-players-in-nfl-history/page/2

https://en.wikipedia.org/wiki/Lombardi_Award

http://www.nytimes.com/1981/11/29/sports/penn-state-routs-no-1-pitt-48-14-bryant-sets-mark-blackledge-leads-lions.html

http://espn.go.com/colleges/psu/notebook/_/page/pennstateallti mefantasydraft

http://abcnews.go.com/US/joe-paterno-biography-reveals-penn-state-coach-despised/story?id=17043830
http://www.blackshoediaries.com/2007/5/13/221130/292

http://www.framingpaterno.com/betrayal-joe-paterno-chapter-ten-conclusions

Preface:

This book is all about Penn State Football; its founding; its struggles; its greatness; and its long-lasting impact on American life. I love Penn State and I especially love Penn State football from the days of Rip Engle when I was coached by my older brother Ed (RIP) about the PSU nuances to the takeover of the program by the one and only Joe Paterno.

People like me, who love Penn State, will not be able to apply any other emotion to this book but love. You will love this book. If you hate Penn State, and you read this book, you may develop a deep affinity for the Blue and White that you will have to explain to you friends.

I like to say that Penn State haters will want their very own copy of this book just for additional ammo to verify the PSU faithful braggadocio. No matter what, PSU as an entity will survive, because its greatness transcends the humans that have helped move it forward. Go Lions!

James Franklin is now the head coach of the Nittany Lions. Franklin is a great coach and I wish him well. Joe Paterno had been Penn State everything for 46 years plus 15 as an assistant. Looking at the records of coaches before and after Paterno, he is clearly in a league by himself. If you take Paterno's record and superimpose it upon any great NCAA program, Penn State will dominate.

Season after season from pre-teen to current age status, I rooted for the Nittany Lions to be National Champions. They had five undefeated seasons along the way in which they were not declared the champs. To the faithful, they were the champs in those years. Who knows why they were not selected? In 1982 and 1986, PSU won the big one—the National Championship. They earned it.

This book walks you through the whole PSU journey minus 6 years. Yes, even before PSU's first official game, the Lions had played an unofficial game in which they were victorious in 1881. We tell you about it early in the book. Then, the first season without coaches was in 1887. Think about the struggle without even having a coach.

Few of the PSU seventeen coaches took the team for more than five years but eventually, coaches like Bob Higgins and Rip Engle and finally Joe Paterno came along and together they put lots of years in their tenure and they put PSU on the football map.

Penn State is a long-time football power

One hundred thirty years is a long time to be playing football. The Penn State Nittany Lions football team was established in 1887. This great and storied football powerhouse represents the Pennsylvania State University in college football. The moniker *Nittany Lions* comes from the notion of the Nittany Mountain Lions, which were once thought to have roamed Mount Nittany, the famous local landmark. In addition to the great teams spanning well over 100 years, we will also stop to talk about PSU traditions such as the Nittany Lion.

Today, the Penn State football team competes in the Big Ten Conference, in the NCAA Division I Football Bowl Subdivision. Coach Joe Paterno worked on the arrangements for PSU to join the Big Ten in 1993 after playing as an Independent college football team from its founding through the 1992 season.

You are going to love this book because it is the perfect read for anybody who loves Penn State and Penn State Football and wants to know more about the most revered athletic program of all time.

Few sports books are a must-read but Brian Kelly's *Great Moments in Penn State Football* will quickly appear at the top of

Americas most enjoyable must-read books about sports. Enjoy!

Who is Brian W. Kelly?

Brian W. Kelly is one of the leading authors in America with this, his 70th published book. Brian is an outspoken and eloquent expert on a variety of topics and he has also written several hundred articles on topics of interest to Americans.

Most of his early works involved high technology. Later, Brian wrote a number of patriotic books and most recently he has been writing human interest books such as The Wine Diet and Thank you, IBM. His books are always well received.

Brian's books are highlighted at www.letsgopublish.com. They are for sale at www.bookhawkers.com

The best!

Sincerely,

Brian P. Kelly, Editor in Chief
I am Brian Kelly's eldest son.

Table of Contents

Chapter 1---Introduction to Penn State Football 1
Chapter 2---The Founding of Penn State University 15
Chapter 3---Penn State's Mission 23
Chapter 4 — Penn State Launches its First Official Football Team ... 27
Chapter 5---The Evolution of Modern Football 39
Chapter 6—Nittany Legacies & Lore 59
Chapter 7—Jerry Sandusky: A Story that Teaches Big Lessons 71
Chapter 8 — Penn State Football's Highlights 1881 through 2016 97
Chapter 9—Penn State Football – The First Six Years 161
Chapter 10 — Penn State Football First Coach -- George Hoskins . 167
Chapter 11 — Penn State Football – the Sam Newton Era 175
Chapter 12 — PSU Football – the Pop Golden Era.......................... 181
Chapter 13 — Penn State Football – Tom Fennell Era 187
Chapter 14—The Hollenback Era 193
Chapter 15—The Dick Harlow Era... 209
Chapter 16—The Hugo Bezdek Era 213
Chapter 17—The Bob Higgins Era 229
Chapter 18 — The Rip Engle Era 259
Chapter 19 — The Joe Paterno Era from 1966 to 1980 281
Chapter 20 — The Joe Paterno Era from 1981 to 1995 329
Chapter 21 — The Joe Paterno Era From 1996 to 2011 405
Chapter 22 — The Bill O'Brien Era From 2012 to 2013 489
Chapter 23 — The James Franklin Era From 2014 to 2016 505
Chapter 24 — Joe Paterno: Fine Man, Great Coach, Legend! 511
Chapter 25 --- The First Family of Nittany Lion Football................... 555
Chapter 26 --- Joe Paterno: A Life - He was Penn State 589
Chapter 27— Penn State's Best Linebackers from 1965 to 2015 605
Chapter 28---Penn State's Greatest Running Backs 1909-2012...... 617
LETS GO PUBLISH! Books by Brian W. Kelly 635

About the Author

Brian Kelly retired as an Assistant Professor in the Business Information Technology (BIT) Program at Marywood University, where he also served as the IBM i and Midrange Systems Technical Advisor to the IT Faculty. Kelly designed, developed, and taught many college and professional courses. He continues as a contributing technical editor to a number of technical industry magazines, including "The Four Hundred" and "Four Hundred Guru," published by IT Jungle.

Kelly is a former IBM Senior Systems Engineer. His specialty was problem solving for customers as well as implementing advanced operating systems and software on his client's machines. Brian is the author of 66 books and hundreds of magazine articles. He has been a frequent speaker at technical conferences throughout the United States.

Brian was a candidate for the US Congress from Pennsylvania in 2010 and he ran for Mayor in his home town in 2015. He loves Penn State Football and has been a fan all his life. .

Chapter 1 Introduction to Penn State Football

PSU football celebrates 130 Years in 2016!

This book celebrates Penn State Football; its founding; its struggles; its greatness; and its long-lasting impact on American life. People like me, who love Penn State, will love this book. Penn State Haters will want their own copy just for additional ammo. Yet, it won't help them! Hah!

James Franklin, PSU Head Coach Leading the Nittany Lions

We begin the rest of the Penn State football story in Chapter 2 with the founding of the Penn State institution and we continue in subsequent chapters, right into the founding of the PSU football program in 1887.

In defining the format of the book we chose to use a timetable that is based on a historical chronology. Within this framework, we discuss the great moments in Penn State football history, and there are many great moments. No book can claim to be able to capture them all, as it would be a never ending story, but we sure try.

John Cappelletti exemplifies PSU football

John Cappelletti was a great Penn State running back and he is the university's only Heisman trophy winner. He was recruited and mentored by Joe Paterno. Cappelletti was not only a great PSU and Pro football player, he is a wonderful man.

Penn State's only Heisman Trophy winner, John Cappelletti, and members of the 1973 team were honored on the 40th anniversary of their undefeated season, at halftime Saturday at Beaver Stadium. Cappelletti's number 22 was retired.

His younger brother Joey, with whom he had a deep relationship, died of leukemia on April 8, 1976. The bond between the brothers was so strong that they made a TV movie about it called "Something for Joey." Cappelletti was played by Marc Singer. This is a great football story that demonstrates the hugeness of the brothers' bond.

In his senior year. Penn State was scheduled to play West Virginia in late October. The morning of the game, Cappelletti was with his little brother Joey and he asked him what he wanted for his upcoming 11th birthday. Joey replied "I want you to score three touchdowns for me. No, four." In the movie, we learn a lot more than the humble Cappelletti would be telling even his closest friends.

Cappelletti did reveal to a teammate before the game his concerns about his brother's wish: "How am I going to score four touchdowns?" Yet, at the end of the 1st half, he had already scored 3 touchdowns. He had four in the bag.

Coach Paterno was not known for running up the score or padding an individual's already impressive stats. Before John went back on the field, the Coach told him that he had played enough and that he would be on the bench for the second half.

Cappelletti said nothing. He quietly took his seat on the bench like a man. Late in the third quarter, a teammate whispered to Paterno, Joey's wish. Joe Paterno, a softie at heart, shouted "22" on the next PSU possession, and Cappelletti took the field. Cappelletti scored his 4th touchdown on the same possession. John Cappelletti pointed to his brother Joey as he ran off the field.

Joe Paterno loved to help build character as well as skill in his players. And, so he was not much for retiring football jerseys. When Bill O'Brien took over the team, during the 2013 season O'Brien made a big change. While Penn State's only Heisman Trophy winner, John Cappelletti, and members of the 1973 team were honored on the 40th anniversary of their undefeated season, at halftime September 7 at Beaver Stadium, Cappelletti's number 22 was retired.

Having to be a Heisman may be a future prerequisite to get a jersey retired at PSU but regardless, the bar at Penn State for retired jerseys is now set very high.

One would expect that if he were asked for his opinion after this commemorative event with Penn State defeating Eastern Michigan 45-7, Joe Paterno would not have blessed it just because that wasn't Joe. One could understand his rationale as being that PSU jerseys could not be retired because with all of the history of Penn State football, there would be no numbers left.

I am using this same Paterno idea to help promulgate the notion that nobody can write a book about Penn State football that is all inclusive, because even if it can be written, it would be too big to ever be read. I hoped this book would come in at a little over 200 pages, but if it had, you would not have liked it. Read what you can when you can. If you love Penn State, it will be a fun experience.

Penn State has been playing football longer than a whole world of people have been alive. During this period, many long and storied rivalries have been formed on the gridiron. For example, the Nittany Lions have played 18 teams 20 or more times in the 130-year history of the program.

Penn State has fared very well in these rivalries. The Nittany Lions own a winning record against 14 of the 18 team's that they have met 20 or more times.

Seven of those 18 teams were on the 2015 schedule; including Temple (43 meetings), Maryland (37), Ohio State (30), Michigan State (28), Army West Point (25), Rutgers (25) and Illinois (22).

Six of those 18 teams are current members of the Big Ten: Illinois, Iowa, Maryland, Michigan State, Ohio State and Rutgers. Eight teams are/were among the opponents on the 2015 and 2016 schedules.

Penn State has played since 2012 or has a future meeting scheduled with 11 of the 18 teams (all of the FBS teams except Navy). Those opponents include: Army West Point (2015), Illinois (2014-15, '18), Iowa (2016-18), Pitt (2016-19), Syracuse (2012), Temple (2014-16) and West Virginia (2023-24), while the Nittany Lions will meet yearly with Big Ten East Division opponents Maryland, Michigan State, Ohio State and Rutgers.

Thirteen of the 18 programs are currently members of NCAA Division I FBS. Bucknell, Lehigh and Penn are among NCAA Division I FCS, while Gettysburg and Lebanon Valley are Division III programs.

We Are... Penn State!

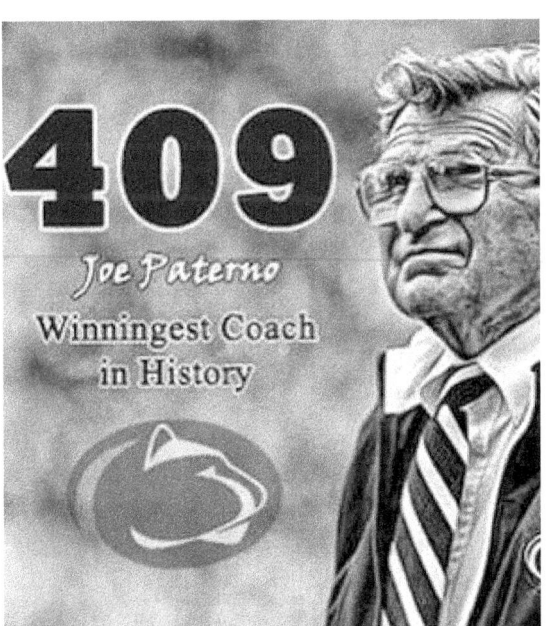

"We Are...Penn State!" These words are what you hear loud and proud during the whole game. As one side of Beaver Stadium exclaims "WE ARE," the other side responds "PENN STATE!" Some say that this chant, which has become the emblem that embodies Penn State, began in 1948 when the Penn State football team was set to play against the Southern Methodist University at the Cotton Bowl.

Before game day, SMU wanted to meet with PSU to protest having Penn State's black players play in the game. In response to this request, Penn State Guard and Team Captain Steve Suhey came to the defense of his teammates proclaiming, "We are Penn State. There will be no meetings." Today, the slogan is everywhere in the Penn State community as a sign of strength and pride.

There is another story about the origin of the cheer. Cheerleaders from the 1970 / 1980 period were looking for a lively chant such as Ohio State's and USC's great cheers. They adopted "We Are Penn State" as their beat-all, end-all cheer. From the late 1940's to the 1970's the chant was not a mainstay. Thus, Penn State Historian Lou Prato says it was the latter, not the former that brought us the famous chant. All I know is "We Are Penn State!" Either way it is a fine legacy!

Penn State is a long-time football power

One hundred thirty years is a long time to be playing football. The Penn State Nittany Lions football team was established in 1887. This great and storied football powerhouse represents the Pennsylvania State University in college football. The moniker *Nittany Lions* comes from the notion of the Nittany Mountain Lions, which were once thought to have roamed Mount Nittany, the famous local landmark. Soon, we'll tell you more about the Nittany Lion.

Today, the Penn State football team competes in the Big Ten Conference, in the NCAA Division I Football Bowl Subdivision. Coach Joe Paterno worked on the arrangements for PSU to join the Big Ten in 1993 after playing as an Independent college football team from its founding through the 1992 season.

At the present time, there are only three independent teams left in the NCAA Division I—the Army Black Knights, the BYU Cougars, and the Notre Dame Fighting Irish. The UMass Minuteman team is expected to go independent very soon. So there will be just three independents from a time in 1978, less than 40 years ago, when there were 54 independent teams playing college football.

PSU is proud of its closeness to the beautiful Mount Nittany and it celebrates the landmark often at its sporting events by playing a special song on campus entitled "The Nittany Lion." Fans know this song as Hail to the Lion, even though that is not technically the name of the song. The song is reprinted at the end of this chapter for your enjoyment.

As an aside, all PSU sports teams are known as the Nittany Lions except the ladies basketball team which goes by "The Lady Lions."

Penn State: A great football legacy

Established in 1887, the Nittany Lions football team have achieved numerous on-field successes, the most notable of which include four consensus national championships (in 1911, 1912, 1982 and 1986); three Big Ten Conference Championships (in 1994, 2005 and 2008); and 45 appearances in college bowl games, with a postseason bowl record of 28–15–2. You cannot get much better than that.

The team is also #8 all-time in total-wins, one game behind Oklahoma and Alabama. The Nittany Lions play their home games at Beaver Stadium, which is located on-campus in University Park, Pennsylvania. With an official seating capacity of 106,572, Beaver Stadium is worth talking about all by itself. It is a fitting playing venue for a great football program, and a great university. The team is currently coached by James Franklin

Summary of PSU football:

Penn State's intercollegiate football team was established at a time that American Football was just being shaped. The first official PSU football game was played in 1887 but unofficially, the students had managed to slip in an intercollegiate game of their own in 1881. Football became a permanent part of Penn State life in 1887 but the student players had no coaches. They relied on team captains. The desire to play football helped make all the seasons successful.

The first of seventeen Penn State football coaches was George Hoskins, who was hired in 1892. Having been undefeated in its first unofficial season (2-0), the Penn State team soon became a collegiate powerhouse and football became a part of campus life.

The team made numerous bowl appearances and came to national prominence in the 1950s and 1960s under Coach Rip Engle. Joe Paterno took over as coach in 1966, and guided the Nittany Lions to the most wins by any coach in Division I history, as well as the most bowl appearances, and most bowl wins.

Under Coach Paterno, the squad has won two consensus national championships, in 1982 and 1986, three Big Ten titles, and completed five undefeated seasons. Penn State competed as an independent before joining the Big Ten in 1993. On November 22, 2008, Penn State became the sixth Division I program to win 800 games. Four Penn State coaches -- Dick Harlow, Hugo Bezdek, Bob Higgins, and Joe Paterno -- are in the Football Hall of Fame.

Spring 2016 Press Conference

At his March press conference in spring 2016, Coach Franklin, who took over the team in 2014, got a question, which helped him sum up the notion of expectations and results. The Coach is ready and he is convinced the team is ready but he does not want to appear too optimistic. Here it is right from the Coach's mouth

Press Question for Coach Franklin in March 2016: You said the biggest challenge since you've been here is managing expectations. Is that still a challenge and what level will that be in the coming year? [From http://www.gopsusports.com/]

JF: I think it is. I think it's been our biggest challenge. I think it's still our challenge moving forward, because there's still work to be done. I think it's something when you're at a place like Penn State, you have to embrace. I love the fact that we have such high expectations, I do. I love that.

You know, I think obviously me coming in in the opening press conference and even moving forward, I've heard from a number of people that I've been too positive. But I think there's that fine line of, we have to build excitement for the direction of the program and we have to build excitement of where we're going because we're going there. There's signs of it all over the place.

But as fans and as coaches and as players, it doesn't always happen at the rate we want it to happen. And again, at a place like Penn State with the history and the traditions and everything we've been through -- I think that's part of it. I think everything that we've been through over the last five years, everybody's ready to get back, and I get that, and I appreciate that and I respect that and our players do and our coaches do, as well.

There's so many signs and so many great things heading in the right direction for this program and getting back to the Penn State that everybody wants to see on Saturdays and everybody wants to see at the spring game.

It's going to continue to be a challenge of that fine line of getting people excited and stating all the different things that people should be excited about, and also educating.

Also educating what's going on in our country and the game of college football what's going on all across the country when it comes to facilitates and recruiting and all those things. It's that fine line between educating where we're at, where we're going and how we're going to get there.

I do know this: The only way we're going to get where we're going is all of us together; that's the players; that's the coaches; that's the campus; that's the community; that's the alumni; that's everybody doing it together. And to be honest with you, 99 percent of everybody has been great. The one percent that isn't, they are loud. They are loud. But that's anywhere. I've had that in every college I've been at.

Our thanks to PSU Sports for the facts.

Some thoughts on April 2016 Blue / White game

With Christian Hackenberg hoping to land an NFL spot, PSU's Spring Blue and White Game was a competition between Trace McSorley and Tommy Stevens to run Penn State's revamped offense. McSorley took the first team and did quite well while Stevens got the second team and played one set of downs with the Blue Team.

Of course, the pundits were asking Coach Franklin about who would be named the starter. Franklin responded:

"I don't think it's fair to our football team and I don't think it's fair to Tommy right now to name a starter when I think Tommy can really close the gap from now and (fall)...That's also going to create a competitive edge in our locker room and keep Trace working because he's got a lot of areas to improve as well."

McSorley was nearly flawless in the classic 2016 Blue-White game, though analysts have suggested, in picking sides, McSorley had the benefit of the better players.

McSorley, played all but one series with the first team in the scrimmage. He completed 23 of 27 passes for 281 yards and four touchdowns. The first-team "Blue" scored a 37-0 win over the Stevens led "White." McSorley played a fine game deciding on targets quickly, throwing well on the run and spreading the ball around.

He made one big error early on an intermediate throw to tight end 6 foot 6 Mike Gesicki. He overshot the big guy and his pass was snatched away by White Team player Amani Oruwariye.

There is reason to be encouraged as the offense did a real good job of moving the ball with last year's maligned offensive line doing much better. "The Blue made successful plays and successful drives, finishing drives with touchdowns...I think we were real happy with how this day went. I think I did well. There's definitely some things I could do better," McSorley said.

Meanwhile, Stevens did not do too badly for being on the second team. He completed 7 of 14 passes for 48 yards. Let's hope we see some of this good stuff in the fall.

The Nittany Lion fight song

"The Nittany Lion" is a the PSU unofficial fight song heaped in Penn State tradition but it is not the official PSU fight song. It is, however, played by the Penn State Blue Band at football games and other sporting events.

During the pre-game show of home football games at Beaver Stadium, it has become part of the traditional Lion fanfare and downfield activities. This song is one of the songs most widely associated with the university. Though it is The Nittany Lion, it is often incorrectly referred to as "Hail to the Lion" (or Lions).

Like clock-work, literally, on Fridays and Saturdays, the clock tower in Penn State's Old Main plays a line of the chorus music at the fifteen-minute mark of each hour, and it adds a line every 15 minutes until the whole chorus is played on the completion of the hour. Such great traditions are a part of the Penn State experience.

The song was composed by 1914 Penn State graduate and former Glee Club member James Leyden in 1919. Leyden also wrote the "Victory" song which is the official PSU fight song. *The Nittany Lion* is a classic number with four verses (with the potential for a fifth verse as Nebraska enters the conference) talking about each of the teams Penn State has played or plays in sports.

The first verse talks solely about Penn State and its mascot, the Nittany Lion, while the second verse (older teams like Pitt, Harvard, Cornell, Princeton, and Penn) and third verse (half of the Big Ten) talk about each of the other schools' mascots and how they pale in comparison to the "mighty Nittany Lion."

Realizing that the song left out Wisconsin, Minnesota, Iowa and Illinois, retired Penn State Alumni Association. Director Roger Williams added a fourth verse this millennium.

Here is the song:
Every college has a legend, *Verse I*

Passed on from year to year.
To which they pledge allegiance

And always cherish dear.
But of all the honored idols,

There's but one that stands the test,
It's the stately Nittany Lion,

The symbol of our best.

This is the Chorus -
Hail to the Lion, Loyal and True.

Hail Alma Mater. with your White and Blue.
Penn State forever, Molder of men,

Fight for her honor, Fight, and Victory again.

Indiana has its Hoosiers, *Verse II*

Purdue its gold and black.
The Wildcats of Northwestern

And Spartans on attack.
Ohio State has its Buckeyes,

Up north the Wolverines.
But the mighty Nittany Lion's,

The best they've ever seen. ---*Now, sing the chorus again*

There's Pittsburgh with its Panther, *Verse III*

And Penn her Red and Blue,
Dartmouth with its Indian,

And Yale her Bulldog. too.
There's Princeton with its Tiger,

And Cornell with its Bear.
But speaking now of victory,

We'll get the Lion's share. ---*Now, sing the chorus again*

Roger Williams' verse is commonly sung by the Penn State Glee Club, but is not typically played on the field by the Penn State Blue Band, making it much less known than the previous three.

Minnesota has its Gophers, *Verse IV*

The Illini with the Spear.
The Badgers of Wisconsin,

And Iowa--never fear!
The Big Ten is our conference:

The nation's best by far.
And the Penn State Nittany Lions,

The Big Ten's shining star! ---*Now, sing the chorus again*

Chapter 2   The Founding of Penn State University

Beautiful PSU Main Building and Flowers

As Pennsylvania's only land-grant university, Penn State has a broad mission of teaching, research, and public service. But that mission was not so grandly conceived in 1855, when the Commonwealth chartered it as one of the nation's first colleges of agricultural science, with a goal to apply scientific principles to farming.

Please note that a land-grant university (also called land-grant college or land-grant institution) is an institution of higher education in the United States designated by a state to receive the benefits of the Morrill Acts of 1862 and 1890. The purpose of the acts were to educate citizens in the fields of Agriculture, Home Economics, the Mechanic Arts, and other useful professions. Thus, Penn State's humble beginning was for very practical reasons.

Centre County became the site of the new college in response to a gift of 200 acres from gentleman farmer and ironmaster James Irvin of Bellefonte. Founding President Evan Pugh drew on the scientific education he had received in Europe to plan a curriculum that combined theoretical studies with practical applications.

Pugh and similar visionaries in other states championed Congressional passage of the Morrill Land-Grant Act in 1862. The act enabled states to sell federal land, invest the proceeds, and use the income to support colleges "where the leading object shall be, without excluding scientific and classical studies ... to teach agriculture and the mechanic arts [engineering] ... in order to promote the liberal and practical education of the industrial classes in all the pursuits and professions of life." The state legislature designated Penn State the land-grant institution of Pennsylvania.

But not until the 1880s, shortly before the introduction of football to the institution, under the leadership of President George W. Atherton, did the college expand its curriculum to match the Land-Grant Act's broad mandate. From that time onward, curriculums in engineering, the sciences, the liberal arts, and more began to flourish. In the early 1900s, Penn State introduced cooperative extension and additional outreach programming, extending the reach of its academic mission.

An even greater segment of the Commonwealth's population had opportunities for engagement in the 1930s when Penn State established a series of undergraduate branch campuses, primarily to meet the needs of students who were location-bound during the Great Depression. Those campuses were predecessors of today's system of 24 Penn State campuses located throughout the Commonwealth.

Penn State began offering systematic advanced-degree work in 1922 with the formation of the Graduate School. Graduate education and research evolved hand in hand. By 1950 the University had won international distinction for investigations in dairy science, building insulation, diesel engines, and acoustics, and other specialized fields.

A college of medicine and teaching hospital were established in 1967 with a $50 million gift from the charitable trusts of renowned chocolate magnate Milton S. Hershey. In 1989 the Pennsylvania College of Technology in Williamsport became an affiliate of the University. In 2000, Penn State and the Dickinson School of Law merged. In 2015, two Penn State law schools, known as Dickinson Law (in Carlisle, Pennsylvania) and Penn State Law (on University Park campus) will be in operation. Penn State's online World Campus graduated its first students in 2000 and now enrolls more than 12,000.

Introduction to Penn State 2016

Pennsylvania State University, a great university which the people of PA affectionately call Penn State, is a public research university that awards associate, bachelor's, master's, doctoral, and professional degrees and offers continuing education programs.

Penn State has many campuses across Pennsylvania, including one in everybody's back yard. Its main campus is located in the city of University Park. Its nineteen branch campuses are spread throughout the state. There is also a medical school in Hershey, a law school in Dickinson, a school of graduate and professional studies in Malvern, and the Pennsylvania College of Technology in Williamsport. Penn State is about education, and oh, did I mention, football.

The university's mission is one "that improves the lives of the people of Pennsylvania, the nation, and the world through integrated, high-quality programs in teaching, research, and service."

History / Review
Although the school was not officially established until 1863, the idea of it was born in the 1850's. Like many land grant universities, the school began as an agricultural college.

Over the decades, Penn State grew as an agricultural research institution while developing a respected scientific research community. The United States' involvement in the space race, along with national concerns for the quality of education, among other hot topics, have guided the fledgling college to develop leading educational and research programs. The school received full university status in 1953.

Academics
The university's strongest academic programs are in the technical and scientific fields, primarily life sciences, engineering, agriculture, and the earth sciences. As an IT guy myself with 23-years with IBM, and as a professor in the Business Information Technology program at Marywood University and Penn State, I know first-hand that Penn State has always been much respected in the technological sciences area.

These are also some of the tougher disciplines on campus. Other quality programs include geography, chemistry, mathematics, and business. Some of the more popular lectures can have class sizes of 300 or more. Overall, Penn State offers more than 225 programs of study for undergraduates. Universities are comprised of two or more colleges, which specialize in specific areas of endeavor.

The University Park Campus is comprised of several different schools and colleges:

- College of Agricultural Sciences
- College of Arts and Architecture
- Smeal College of Business
- College of Communications
- College of Earth and Mineral Sciences
- College of Education
- College of Engineering
- College of Health and Human Development
- School of Information Sciences and Technology
- College of the Liberal Arts
- College of Medicine
- College of Nursing
- Eberly College of Science
- School of Law
- Schreyer Honors College
- The Graduate School
- Pennsylvania College of Technology
- Division of Undergraduate Studies

Bachelor's degrees are awarded in a number of different disciplines, including of accounting, administration of justice, agriculture, a wide range of the sciences and humanities, classics and ancient Mediterranean studies, creative writing, business, engineering, education, forensic science, hotel restaurant and institutional management, information sciences and technology, mathematics, music, nursing, plastics engineering technology, psychology, Russian, statistics, theatre, and women's studies.

Graduate programs at the University Park campus also cover a wide range of fields, including acoustics, apply statistics, as your biology, counselor education, educational leadership, fuel science, health policy and administration, industrial engineering, mathematics, music, nursing, plant pathology, world sociology, teacher certification, wildlife and fisheries science, and youth and family education. There are graduate minor programs in gerontology, high-performance computing, language acquisition, linguistics, literary theory, criticism and aesthetics, medieval studies, religious studies, science, technology, and society, and social thought.

Graduate programs are also offered at the Erie campus, the Harrisburg campus, the School of Graduate and Professional Studies campus, and the College of Medicine. A few graduate programs, primarily in education, are also available through the online world campus. The law school is a partnership with the Dickinson school of Law.

Unique Programs
The meteorology program is home to AccuWeather, a system used to make accurate weather forecasts. In fact, the system's designer is an alum. Other unique academic programs include Industrial Health and Safety and a focus on electrical engineering.

One beneficial offering is the L.E.A.P. (Learning Edge Academic Program). This intensive program immerses freshmen in the lifestyle of a large university, but teams them with like-minded students who have similar interests. Students study and attend class together and, in some cases, even live together. They also have access to career counselors to determine exactly how their degree can be put to use.

Athletics
The athletic department fields twenty-nine varsity teams in CAA Division I, with baseball, basketball, cross-country, diving, fencing, football, golf, gymnastics, lacrosse, soccer, swimming, tennis, track & field, volleyball, and wrestling for

men and basketball, cross-country, diving, fencing, field hockey, golf, gymnastics, lacrosse, soccer, softball, swimming, tennis, track & field, and volleyball for women. Besides football, national titles have been captured in field hockey, fencing, and volleyball.

Sports facilities include Beaver Stadium, which, with the modifications for the physically challenged now has capacity of 106,572 seats, a multipurpose building, golf courses, baseball and softball fields, a tennis center, and a center for basketball. (The Jordan Center also hosts entertainment and other activities.) The University has a sports museum with 10,000 square feet.

We thank Lou Prato, a noted Penn State Historian for this chronology of significant dates in Penn State University History, as noted below:

February 22, 1855 — Pennsylvania Governor James Pollock signs the charter creating the Farmers' High School of Pennsylvania with its location to be determined.

September 1855 — Two-hundred acres of farm land outside the village of Centre Furnace in Centre County are chosen as the location of the Farmers' High School after a review committee, headed by Governor James Pollock, visits other proposed sites in Allegheny, Butler, Erie and Perry counties.

February 16, 1859 — Sixty-nine students show up for the first day of classes at the new Farmers' High School of Pennsylvania.

1861 — Penn State graduated its first class, marking the first graduates of a baccalaureate program at an American agricultural college.

1862 — The Farmers' High School of Pennsylvania is given a new name as the Agriculture College of Pennsylvania in anticipation of being given official recognition as a land grant college under the federal Morrill Act.

1874 — The name of the college is officially changed to Pennsylvania State College. The town's post office takes the name State College.

1953 — Penn State officially became a university. Branch campuses offered associate degrees.

Chapter 3 Penn State's Mission

The Pennsylvania State University, University Park, PA

Mission Description

Penn State is a multi-campus public research university that educates students from Pennsylvania, the nation and the world, and improves the wellbeing and health of individuals and communities through integrated programs of teaching, research, and service.

Our instructional mission includes undergraduate, graduate, professional, and continuing education offered through both resident instruction and online delivery. Our educational programs are enriched by the cutting edge knowledge, diversity, and creativity of our faculty, students, and staff.

Our research, scholarship, and creative activity promote human and economic development, global understanding, and progress in professional practice through the expansion of knowledge and its applications in the natural and applied sciences, social sciences, arts, humanities, and the professions.

As Pennsylvania's land-grant university, we provide unparalleled access and public service to support the citizens of the Commonwealth. We engage in collaborative activities with industrial, educational, and agricultural partners here and abroad to generate, disseminate, integrate, and apply knowledge that is valuable to society.

Public Character

Penn State, founded in 1855 as an agricultural college, admitted its first class in 1859. The Pennsylvania legislature designated Penn State as the Commonwealth's sole land-grant institution in 1863, which eventually broadened the University's mission to include teaching, research, and public service in many academic disciplines. Penn State has awarded more than a half-million degrees, and has been Pennsylvania's largest source of baccalaureate degrees at least since the 1930s.

Although the University is privately chartered by the Commonwealth, it was from the outset considered an "instrumentality of the state," that is, it carries out many of the functions of a public institution and promotes the general welfare of the citizenry. The governor and other representatives of the Commonwealth have held seats on Penn State's Board of Trustees since the University's founding, and the legislature has made regular appropriations in support of the University's mission since 1887.

Today Penn State is one of four "state-related" universities (along with the University of Pittsburgh, Temple University, and Lincoln University), institutions that are not state-owned and -operated but that have the character of public universities and receive substantial state appropriations. With its administrative and research hub at the University Park campus, Penn State has twenty-three additional locations across Pennsylvania. While some of these locations, such as the Penn State Milton S. Hershey Medical Center, have specialized academic roles, they all adhere to a common overall mission and set of core values.

Leadership et al.

Penn State is a leader in higher education and carries out its mission of teaching, research, and service with pride and focus on the future.

Our leadership in administration, faculty, and staff make our mission come alive every day. The Board of Trustees reviews and approves the budget of the University and guides general goals, policies, and procedures from a big-picture perspective. The President's office ensures that all aspects of the University are running smoothly and promotes overall principles that students, faculty, and staff abide by for the long term. The University Faculty Senate represents the Penn State faculty with legislative authority on all matters regarding the University's educational interests.

We strive to celebrate diversity in all aspects of our educational and operational activities. Our strategic plans are designed to result in ongoing improvements that help prepare future generations of leaders. Our budget is an integral part of our strategic process.

In addition to student life and education, these are the areas in which we concentrate to being about the best result in educating our students across the full spectrum of ideas.

- Board of Trustees
- President's Office
- University Faculty Senate
- Diversity and Inclusion
- University Strategic Plan
- Strategic Plan for Diversity and Inclusion
- Budget

Through these bodies, this great institution thrives and grows and does its good!

Chapter 4 — Penn State Launches its First Official Football Team

The image above is a team photo from Penn State's first football team in 1887

1887: Nearly 33 years from the founding

Penn State played its first unofficial football game November 12, 1881 against Lewisburg University in Lewisburg, PA. The Nittany Lions were not yet the Nittany Lions yet they played like they were. Penn State won the makeshift game with rules that were part American football, part rugby, and part soccer as the rules were being incrementally formed. The score was W (9-0).

It was six years later in September (1887) that the School administration gave its approval under President George Atherton. With the top brass's OK; a group of Penn State freshmen organized its first official football team. The architects were freshman George "Lucy" Linsz along with classmate Charles Hildebrand.

Just a month later the storied Penn State tradition began putting notches in its story. Penn State played its first official game November 12, 1887 against Bucknell (formerly Lewisburg) at Lewisburg winning, 54-0. The rules had improved somewhat since 1881 but they were still not the rules of which we are familiar today.

To make it a season and not a shot-in-the dark on-time game as in 1881, Penn State engaged again just one week later on November 19). A mascot-less Penn State played its first home game using a makeshift field on the Old Main lawn. Penn State won the game 24-0 over "rival" Bucknell. Penn State finished its first competitive football season with a 2-0 record. Wins have been the big story in the Penn State football story from 1887 on, and if I may be so bold, unofficially the wins began in 1881.

The notion of college football was just beginning as other Eastern teams such as Harvard and Princeton were also just getting it going. Notre Dame also had its first game in 1887. In 1881, there was a desire to play the evolving game of American football and so the students did it themselves in much the way teams play sandlot football today.

Penn State Students organized a football team without administration support and as noted they scheduled and played a game against a close-by school that at the time was known as the University of Lewisburg (renamed Bucknell University in 1896). The "kids" had to do some research just to know the rules and Penn State learned quite well as it defeated Lewisburg 9-0, in a cold, sleet-like drizzle.

As time moved on from this first encounter with football, there were no more formal games until September 1887 when George "Lucy" Linsz arrived on campus as a freshman and, with the help of a fellow freshman Charles Hildebrand, he managed to get approval from President George Atherton to organize the first official football team for Penn State College.

There was no coach and would be no coach for this team until 1894.

As hard as it is to believe back in the fall 1887, Penn State chose Pink and Black as the team colors. They changed the colors to blue and white the following year.

Penn State of course won its first game W (54-0) at Bucknell on the Lewisburg campus. It was the Penn State's first official game. A week later, with no field to speak of, Penn State hosted a home game on the Old Main Lawn. Team Captain and quarterback Lucy Linsz scored three second-half touchdowns to lead Penn State to a 24-0 win over Bucknell. And thus ended Penn State's first football season.

From the Lawn to the Field to the Stadium

Beaver Stadium, the home of the Nittany Lions, is one of the nation's premier football venues. An expansion and renovation prior to the 2001 season added more than 12,000 seats, increasing the stadium's capacity to 106,572 and easing the waiting list for season ticket requests from Penn State fans.

When you graduate more than 13,500 students per year university-wide, all of whom love Penn State, is it possible that a stadium holding as many as 500,000 might be insufficient? There are a lot of students and each year, the alumni pool increases by about 13,500. PSU's stadium must be big enough to fit huge crowds

In early 2016, while I was writing this book, Penn State expected to award over 13.500 diplomas to students University-wide who are completing over 500 associate, over 11,000 baccalaureate, over 1,500 master's, over 200law, over 275 doctoral and about 150 medical degrees, bringing the University's total number of graduates to an estimated total of more than 775,000.

At University Park alone, about 9,000 students are expected to be awarded baccalaureate degrees. Approximately 1000 master's degree students are expected to graduate, as are approximately 300 doctoral degree candidates.

Penn State is a fine academic institution and having so many smart people on campus bolsters the opportunity to have a smart football team. PSU football players love playing at Beaver Stadium almost as much as the opposition hates the deafening roar of the eternally optimistic average Penn State fan with a Saturday football ticket.

Beaver Stadium – A Great Football Venue

Beaver Stadium is the second-largest stadium in the nation and the third largest in the world. Renovations and expansions over the years have added rest rooms and concession facilities, new scoreboards with instant-replay capability, and improved handicap access and pedestrian circulation patterns. The most noticeable recent changes are 60 enclosed skyboxes in a three-level structure above the East stands and an 11,500-seat upper deck in the South end zone.

Today's Beaver Stadium

Beaver Stadium has more than doubled in size since it was relocated from its former site northeast of Rec Hall on the west side of campus to the east end of the campus in 1960. The addition of a 10,033-seat upper deck in the north end zone in 1991 and portable seats on the north end zone concourse increased the stadium's capacity to 93,967.

In 1980, an expansion raised the capacity to 83,770. Lights were added in 1984. In 1985, the addition of walkways around the tops of the end zones and entry ramps at the four corners resulted in lowering the capacity to 83,370.

Penn State dedicated the newly moved and expanded Beaver Stadium with a 20-0 win over Boston University on Sept. 17, 1960. Nittany Lion halfback Eddie Caye scored the stadium's first touchdown at 10:45 of the first quarter.

Early Beaver Stadium

Built in a horseshoe configuration seating 46,284 in 1960, the stadium now towers 110 rows on the east side, 100 rows on the west, 60 in the lower end zones, 35 in the north upper deck, 20 in the club seating level and 25 in the south upper deck. Most reasonably large cities cannot hold the capacity of Beaver Stadium.

Working from the 1960 move and expansion forward, additions of over 2,000 seats in 1969 and more than 9,000 in 1972 increased the capacity to 57,538. Expanded bleachers in the south end zone in 1976 raised the capacity to 60,203.

A uniquely engineered expansion during the winter, spring and summer of 1978 added more than 16,000 seats, bringing the growing capacity to 76,639. To make this happen, the stadium was cut into sections, raised eight feet by hydraulic jacks and precast concrete seating forms inserted within the inner circle of the stadium, where a running track previously had been located. I bet that one kept the architects and engineers busy figuring out that one.

Before Beaver Stadium, PSU was playing football. Penn State's first permanent home for football was Beaver Field, which stood between the present-day Osmond and Frear laboratories in center campus. Before that, games were played on the Old Main lawn. How about that for scrapping it out?

Old Beaver Field

The first game at 500-seat Beaver Field was played on Nov. 6, 1893 against Western University of Pittsburgh (later to become the University of Pittsburgh). The 32-0 Penn State victory was delayed two days because of bad weather and played on a Monday afternoon.

New Beaver Field, located near Rec Hall, was dedicated in 1909 with a 31-0 win over Grove City. Originally constructed of wood, the stadium was converted to steel in 1936. The area also contained facilities for baseball, lacrosse, soccer and track.

New Beaver Field was the Lions' home through the 1959 season, after which the 30,000-seat stadium was dismantled and moved in 700 pieces one mile to the east side of campus. The old stadium was reassembled with 16,000 additional seats to form Beaver Stadium.

New Beaver Field

The stadium was and is still named in honor of James A. Beaver. Mr. Beaver was a lawyer in nearby Bellefonte at the outbreak of the Civil War. He enlisted in the Union Army as a second lieutenant and rose to the rank of brigadier general prior to his discharge in 1864. Beaver, who died in 1914, served as a superior court judge, governor of Pennsylvania and president of the University's Board of Trustees. He is credited with being among the most influential leaders in the development of the University at the turn of the century.

Though the field officially holds just under 107,000, the game gatekeepers have been able to cheat a bit in permitting more than the stadium's capacity in to see special games. Well, not exactly! Beaver Stadium's official attendance figures include the press box, suites, bands, ushers and other stadium personnel. Here are the top ten games according to attendance.

Top 10 Beaver Stadium Crowds

#	Attend.	Date	Outcome
1.	110,753	Sept. 14, 2002	Penn State 40, Nebraska 7
2.	110,134	Oct. 27, 2007	Ohio State 37, Penn State 17
3.	110,078	Sept. 8, 2007	Penn State 31, Notre Dame 10
4.	110,033	Nov. 7, 2009	Ohio State 24, Penn State 7
5.	110,017	Oct. 18, 2008	Penn State 46, Michigan 17
6.	110,007	Oct. 14, 2006	Michigan 17, Penn State 10
7.	109,865	Nov. 5, 2005	Penn State 35, Wisconsin 14
8.	109,845	Nov. 22, 2008	Penn State 33, Northwestern 7
9.	109,839	Oct. 8, 2005	Penn State 17, Ohio State 10
10.	109,754	Oct. 13, 2007	Penn State 38, Wisconsin 7

2016 Beaver Stadium Expansion
Thoughts from Pennlive.com

November 5, 2015 STATE COLLEGE, Pa. (AP) — Penn State's athletic director says she would prefer to renovate the university's aging icon, Beaver Stadium, rather than build a new one on campus.

The announcement came Wednesday after Sandy Barbour addressed the Nittany Lion faithful during a town hall meeting organized by Penn State's athletic program.

Barbour also said she wasn't opposed to reducing Beaver -- Stadium's seating capacity as part of a future renovation.

[July 2016, Barbour is expected to make her announcement.]

Comments by PSU fans / alums

Here are two PSU fans / alums who offer their opinion on whether the university should invest in a new stadium or invest in an upgrade to the existing Beaver Stadium. These are comments from the Penn Live article snippet shown immediately above.

Kenneth Harper Nov 5, 2015
   PSU needs to take a very serious look at building a new stadium. PSU got 55+ years out of this one. In 1960 when the stadium was moved to its current location there was nothing around the stadium but plenty of parking. Over time many buildings, (baseball stadium, visitor center, arena and of course the BJC) were built around the stadium. A new stadium at a new location with plenty of parking, professional seating, modem bathrooms, food stands and even an all year round restaurant would be nice.

DTM26 Nov 5, 2015
   Having a 107,000 seat stadium is huge asset to this team. I know the critics will say "yeah but we only have ~98,000 a game." Yes but that will change when we start winning again. And look at games like Rutgers (stripe out) and all the whiteout games, those games make Beaver Stadium the best show in college football, and I'm sure some people won't want to hear this, but the high concentration of people is what makes the whiteouts and stripe outs look so good.

   It's a huge recruiting tool to say to a kid "you have a chance to play in the third largest stadium in the WORLD." These fans (all 107,000 of them) make this one of the toughest places to play. Lesser teams (like Rutgers this year) are shaken by the very sight of that many people in one place, they simply aren't prepared for it.

I have no problem upgrading Beaver Stadium, especially in the growing arms race that college football is becoming. Rest rooms, concessions, elevators, a new press box, and general sprucing up are all things that should be considered. If some people want individual seats fine, but do not decrease the capacity one person. I suggest we close the four corners of the stadium and add new seats in all 4 corners.

This will do 2 things: add more seats for the people who want more space (let's not forget that the massive south end zone expansion is made up entirely of individual seats as well), and it will also trap noise making it louder. ANY drop in capacity will be downgrade. And why would you pay hundreds of millions of dollars on a downgrade? This program is headed in the right direction; let's not go backwards now.

38　Great Moments in Penn State Football

Chapter 5 The Evolution of Modern Football

Yale vs. Columbia

Lots of playing before playing became official

The official agreed upon date for the first American-style college football game is November 6, 1869. If you can find a replay of this game someplace in the heavens, however, you would find it would not look much like football as we know it. But, it was not completely soccer or rugby either.

Before this game, teams were playing a rugby style similar to that played in Britain in the mid-19th century. At the time in the US, a derivative known as association football was also played. In both games, a football is kicked at a goal or run over a line. These styles were based on the varieties of English public school football games. Over time, as noted, the style of "football" play in America continued to evolve.

On November 6, 1869, the first football game in America featured Rutgers and Princeton. Before the teams were even on the field it was being plugged as the first college football game of all time. Penn State did not get a Rugby team until the early 1960's. Nobody at Penn State in 1869, from what I could find, was even thinking about the game of football.

The first game of intercollegiate football was a sporting battle between two neighboring schools on a plot of ground where the present-day Rutgers gymnasium now stands in New Brunswick, N.J. Rutgers won that first game, 6-4.

There were two teams of 25 men each and the rules were rugby-like, but different enough to make it very interesting and enjoyable.

Like today's football, there were many surprises; strategies needed to be employed; determination exhibited, and of course the players required physical prowess.

1st Game Rutgers 6 Princeton 4 College Field, New Brunswick, NJ

At 3 p.m. the 50 combatants as well as 100 spectators gathered on the field. Most sat on a low wooden fence and watched the athletes discard their hats, coats and vests. The players used their suspenders as belts. To give a unique look,

Rutgers wore scarlet-colored scarfs, which they converted into turbans. This contrasted them with the bareheaded boys from Princeton.

Two members of each team remained more or less stationary near the opponent's goal in the hopes of being able to slip over and score from unguarded positions. Thus, the present day "sleeper" was conceived. The remaining 23 players were divided into groups of 11 and 12. While the 11 "fielders" lined up in their own territory as defenders, the 12 "bulldogs" carried the battle.

Each score counted as a "game" and 10 games completed the contest. Following each score, the teams changed direction. The ball could be advanced only by kicking or batting it with the feet, hands, heads or sides.

Rutgers put a challenge forward that three games were to be played that year. The first was played at New Brunswick and won by Rutgers. Princeton won the second game, but cries of "over-emphasis" prevented the third game in football's first year when faculties of both institutions protested on the grounds that the games were interfering with student studies.

This is an excerpt of the Rutgers account of the game on its web site. A person named Herbert gave this detailed account of the play in the first game:

"Though smaller on the average, the Rutgers players, as it developed, had ample speed and fine football sense. Receiving the ball, our men formed a perfect interference around it and with short, skillful kicks and dribbles drove it down the field. Taken by surprise, the Princeton men fought valiantly, but in five minutes we had gotten the ball through to our captains on the enemy's goal and S.G. Gano, '71 and G.R. Dixon, '73, neatly kicked it over. None thought of it, so far as I know, but we had without previous plan or thought evolved the play that became famous a few years later as 'the flying wedge'."

"Next period Rutgers bucked, or received the ball, hoping to repeat the flying wedge," Herbert's account continues. "But the first time we formed it Big Mike came charging full upon us. It was our turn for surprise. The Princeton battering ram made no attempt to reach the ball but, forerunner of the interference-breaking ends of today, threw himself into our mass play, bursting us apart, and bowing us over. Time and again Rutgers formed the wedge and charged; as often Big Mike broke it up. And finally on one of these incredible break-ups a Princeton bulldog with a long accurate, perhaps lucky kick, sent the ball between the posts for the second score.

It was at this point that a Rutgers professor could stand it no longer. Waving his umbrella at the participants, he shrieked, "You will come to no Christian end!"

Herbert's account of the game continues: "The fifth and sixth goals went to Rutgers. The stars of the latter period of play, in the memory of the players after the lapse of many years, were "Big

Mike" and Large (former State Senator George H. Large of Flemington, another Princeton player)...

The University of Notre Dame did not get into the football act until the late 1880's. At this time, the rules of rugby kept changing to accommodate the infatuation for the Americanized style of "football" play that would ultimately become the American game of football.

Walter Camp: the father of American football?

Walter Camp was a very well-known rugby player from Yale. In today's world, he would have been characterized as a rugby hero. It was his love of the game, his knowledge of the game as it was played, and his innovative mind that caused him to take the evolution of football even further. He pioneered the changes to the rules of rugby that slowly transformed the sport into the new game of American Football.

The rule changes that were introduced to the rugby and association style of play were mostly those authored by Camp, who was also a Hopkins School graduate. For his original efforts, Walter Camp today is considered to be the "Father of American Football". Among the important changes brought to the game were the introduction of a line of scrimmage; down-and-distance rules; and the legalization of interference (blocking).

There was no such thing in those days as a forward pass and so the legalization of interference in 1880 football permitted blocking for runners. The forward pass would add another dimension to the game that made it much different than rugby or association football.

Soon after the early football changes, in the late nineteenth and into the early twentieth centuries, more game-play type developments were introduced by college coaches. The list is like a who's who of early American College Football. Coaches, such as Eddie Cochems, Amos Alonzo Stagg, Parke H. Davis, Knute Rockne, John Heisman, and Glenn "Pop" Warner helped introduce and then take advantage of the newly introduced forward pass. College football as well as professional football, were introduced prior to the 20th century. Fans were lured into watching again and again once they saw the game played.

College football especially grew in popularity despite the existence of pro-football. It became the dominant version of the sport of football in the United States. It was this way for the entire first half of the 20th century. Bowl games made the idea of football even more exciting in the college ranks. Rivalries grew and continued and the fans loved it! This great football tradition brought a national audience to college football games that still dominates the sports world today.

This book has little to do with pro-football or any other sport. However, there is no denying that the greatest college football players more often than not eventually found their fortunes in professional football. Pro football can be traced back to the season that Notre Dame brought forth a real football team after a two-year lapse from its last half-Rugby season in 1889. It was 1892 when William "Pudge" Heffelfinger signed a $500 contract to play for the Allegheny Athletic Association against the Pittsburgh Athletic Club.

Twenty-eight years later, the American Professional Football Association was formed. This league changed its name to the National Football League (NFL) just two years later. Eventually, the NFL became the major league of American football. Originally, just a sport played in Midwestern industrial towns in the United States, professional football eventually became a national phenomenon. We all know this because from August to February, in America, many of us are glued to our TV sets or chained to our seats in some of the most intriguing pro-football stadiums in America.

Rules and Penalties

The big problem players from different teams and different geographies had when playing early American-style football in college was that the style of play was not standardized. The rulebooks were not yet written or were at best incomplete and disputable.

A rule over here, for example, would be a penalty over there. And, so in the 1870's there was a lot of work to try to make all games to be played by the same rules. There were minor rule changes such as team size was reduced from 25 to 20 but of course over the years, this and all other rules continued to evolve. For years, there was no such thing as a running touchdown. The only means of scoring was to bat or kick the ball through the opposing team's goal.

Early rugby rules were the default. The field size was rugby style at 140 yards by 70 yards v 120 X 53 1/3 (including end zones) in today's football game. There was plenty of room to huff and puff and almost get lost. There were no breaks per se for long periods. Instead of fifteen minute quarters, the game was more like Rugby and Soccer with 45 minute halves played continuously.

In 1873 to put some order to the game, Columbia, Princeton. Rutgers, and Yale got together in a hotel in New York City and wrote down the first set of intercollegiate football rules. They changed a few things along the way but the end product was a much more standard way of playing football games. Rather than use the home team's rules, all teams then were able to play by the same rules

Harvard did not to comply with American rules

For its own reasons, Harvard chose not to attend the rules conference. Instead, it played all of its games using the Harvard code of rules. Harvard therefore had a difficult time scheduling games. In 1874, to get a game, Harvard agreed to play McGill University from Montreal Canada. They had rules that even Harvard had never seen. For example, any player could pick up the ball and run with it, anytime he wished.

Another McGill rule was that they would count tries (the act of grounding the football past the opponent's goal line. Since there was no end zone, which technically makes a football field of today 120 yards long, a touchdown gave no points. Instead, it provided the chance to kick a free goal from the field. If the kick were missed, the touchdown did not count.

In 1874 McGill and Harvard played a two-game series. Each team could play 11 men per side. This was in deep contrast to the even earlier days of college football before standard rules when games were played with 25, 20, 15, or 11 men on a side.

The first game was played with a round ball using what were known as the "Boston" rules (Harvard). The next day, the teams played using the McGill rules, which included McGill's oval ball which was much like an American football, and it featured the ability to pick up the ball and run with it. Harvard enjoyed this experience especially the idea of "the try" which had not been used in American football. Eventually, the try evolved into the American idea of a touchdown and points were given when a try was successful.

Not all the rules lasted the duration and some were very strange by today's standards. One of the most perplexing rules was that a man could run with the ball only while an opponent chose to pursue him. When a tackler abandoned the ball-carrier, the latter had to stop, and was forced to kick, pass or even throw away what was called "his burden."

McGill has a great account of this match on their web site. Type *McGill web site football against Harvard* into your search engine.

Their players wore no protective pads. Woolen jerseys covered the torso, while white trousers encased the players' legs. Some trousers were short and some were long. It did not seem to matter for the game. A number of the men wore what they called black "football turbans" which were the ancestors of the modern helmet; others chose to wear white canvas hats.

The Harvard players wore undershirts made of gauze. Think about that for a while. They also wore what were called *full length gymnasium costumes*. They also wore light baseball shoes. Most of the team wore handkerchiefs, which were knotted about their heads.

The gauze undershirts were a trick. There was strategy in this choice of top uniform. When a player was first tackled, the gauze would be demolished and the next opponent would have nothing to grab other than "slippery human flesh." Harvard won this game by a score of 3-0

The next go at playing by the rules was when Harvard took on Tufts University on June 4, 1875. This was the first American college football game played using rules similar to the McGill/Harvard contest. Tufts won this game. Despite the loss, Harvard continued pushing McGill style football and challenged Yale.

The Bulldog team accepted under a compromise rule set that included some Yale soccer rules and Harvard rugby rules. They used 15 players per team. It was November 13, 1875 for this first meeting of Harvard v Yale. Harvard won 4-0. Walter Camp attended the game and the following year he played in the game as a Yale Bulldog.

Camp was determined to avenge Yale's defeat. Onlookers from Princeton, who saw this Harvard / Yale game loved it so much, they brought it back to Princeton where it was quickly adopted as the preferred version of football.

Once Walter Camp caught onto the rugby-style rules, history says he became a fixture at the Massasoit House conventions. Here the rules of the game were debated and changed appropriately. From these meetings, Camp's rule changes as well as others were adopted.

Having eleven players instead of fifteen aided in opening the game and it emphasized speed over strength. When Camp attended in 1878, this motion was rejected but it passed in the 1880 meeting. The line of scrimmage and the snap from center to the quarterback also passed in 1880. Originally the snap occurred by a kick from the center, but this was later modified so the ball would be snapped with the hands either as a pass back (long snap) or a direct snap from the center.

It was Camp's new scrimmage rules, however, which according to many, revolutionized the game, though it was not always to increase speed. In fact, Princeton was known to use line of scrimmage plays to slow the game, making incremental progress towards the end zone much like today during each down.

Camp's original idea was to increase scoring, but in fact the rule was often misused to maintain control of the ball for the entire game. The negative effect was that there were many slow and unexciting contests. This too would be fixed with the idea of the first down coming into play.

In 1982, at the rules meeting, Camp proposed that a team be given three downs to advance the ball five yards. These rules were called the down and distance rules. Along with the notion of the line of scrimmage, these rules transformed the game of rugby into the distinct sport of American football.

Among other significant rule changes, in 1881, the field size was reduced to its modern dimensions of 120 by 53 1/3 yards (109.7 by 48.8 meters). Camp was central to these significant rule changes that ultimately defined American football.

Camp's next quest was to address scoring anomalies. His first cut was to give four points for a touchdown and two points for kicks after touchdowns; two points for safeties, and five points for field goals. The notion of the foot in football /rugby explains Camp's rationale.

In 1887, game time was fixed at two halves of 45 minutes each. Additionally college games would have two paid officials known as a referee and an umpire, for each game. In 1888, the rules permitted tackling below the waist and then in 1889, the officials were given whistles and stopwatches to better control the game.

An innovation that many list as most significant to making American football uniquely American was the legalization of blocking opponents, which back then was called "interference." This tactic had been highly illegal under the rugby-style rules and in rugby today, it continues to be illegal.

The more those who know soccer and football find rugby to be more like soccer.

Though *offsides* is a penalty infraction today, *offsides* in the 1880's in rugby was very much the same as *offsides* in soccer. The prohibition of blocking in a rugby game is in fact because of the game's strict enforcement of its *offsides* rule. Similar to soccer, this rule prohibits any player on the team with possession of the ball to loiter between the ball and the goal. Blocking continues as a basic element of modern American football, with many complex schemes having been developed and implemented over the years, including zone blocking and pass blocking.

Camp stayed active in rule making for most of his life. He had the honor of personally selecting an annual All-American team every year from 1889 through 1924. Camp passed away in 1925. The Walter Camp Football Foundation continues to select All-American teams in his honor.

With many rule changes as noted, as American style rugby became more defined as American football, more and more colleges adopted football as part of their sports programs. Most of the schools were from the Eastern US. It was not until 1879 that the University of Michigan became the first school west of Pennsylvania to establish a bona-fide American-style college football team.

Back then, football teams played whenever they could in the fall or the spring. For example, Michigan's first game was in late spring, near the end of what we would call the academic year. On May 30, 1879 Michigan beat Racine College 1–0 in a game played in Chicago. In 1887, Michigan and Notre Dame played their first football game, which did not benefit from Camp's rules.

The first night time game

It was not until September 28, 1892 that the first nighttime football game was played. Mansfield State Normal played Wyoming Seminary in Mansfield, Pennsylvania. These schools are close to where I live. The game ended at a "declared" half-time in a 0–0 tie. It had become too dark to play.

Wyoming Seminary was not a college and to this day it is not a college. I live about five miles from the school. It is a private college preparatory school located in the Wyoming Valley of Northeastern Pennsylvania. During the time period in which the game was played, it was common for a college and high school to play each other in football—a practice that of course has long since been discontinued.

The reason that it got too dark to play, ironically was not because the game began at dusk. Mansfield had brought in a lighting system that was far too inadequate for game play. This historical game lasted only 20 minutes and there were only 10 plays. Both sides agreed to end at half-time with the score at 0-0. Though it may seem humorous today, for safety reasons, the game was declared ended in a 0-0 tie after several players had an unfortunate run-in with a light pole.

Mansfield and Wyoming Seminary are thus enshrined in football history as having played in the first night game ever in "college football." History and football buffs get together once a year to celebrate the game in what they call "Fabulous 1890's Weekend." This historic game is reenacted exactly as it occurred play by play just as the actual game is recorded in history. Fans who watch the game are sometimes known to correct players (actually actors) when they deviate from the original scripted plays. Now, that shows both a love of the game and a love of history.

Mansfield and Wyoming Seminary's game added additional fame to both schools when the 100th anniversary of the game just happened to occur on Monday, September 28, 1992. Monday Night Football celebrated "100 years of night football" with its regularly scheduled game between the Los Angeles Raiders and the Kansas City Chiefs at Arrowhead Stadium. The Chiefs won 27–7 in front of 77,486 fans. How about that?

More football history was recorded when Army played Navy in 1893. In this game, we have the first documented use of a football helmet by a player in a game. Joseph M. Reeves had been kicked in the head in a prior football game. He was warned by his doctor that he risked death if he continued to play football. We all know how tough the Midshipmen and Black Nights (Cadets) are regardless of who they may be playing. Rather than end his football playing days prematurely. Reeves discussed his need with a shoemaker in Annapolis who crafted a leather helmet for the player to wear for the rest of the season.

Football conferences

Things were happening very quickly in the new sport of football. Organization and rules became the mantra for this fledgling sport. It was being defined while it was being played. Formal college football conferences were just around the corner. In fact, the Southeastern Conference and the Atlantic Coast Conference both got started in 1894.

The forward pass

None of Camp's rules for American Football included the most innovative notion of them all – the forward pass. Many believe that the first forward pass in football occurred on October 26, 1895 in a game between Georgia and North Carolina. Out of desperation, the ball was thrown by the North Carolina back Joel Whitaker instead of having been punted. George Stephens, a teammate caught the ball.

Despite what most may think or surmise, it was Camp again when he was a player at Yale, who executed the first game-time forward pass for a touchdown. During the Yale-Princeton game, while Camp was being tackled, he threw a football forward to Yale's Oliver Thompson, who sprinted to a touchdown. The Princeton Tigers naturally protested and there appeared to be no precedent for a referee decision. Like many things in football including a game-beginning coin-toss, the referee in this instance tossed a coin, and then he made his decision to allow the touchdown.

Hidden ball trick

Dome one-time tricks have not survived football. For example, on November 9, 1895 Auburn Coach John Heisman executed a hidden ball trick. Quarterback Reynolds Tichenor was able to gain Auburn's only touchdown in a 6 to 9 loss to Vanderbilt. This also was the first game in the south that was decided by a field goal.

The trick was simple but would be illegal today. When the ball was snapped it went to a halfback. The play was closely masked and well screened. The halfback then thrust the ball under the back of the quarterback's (Tichenor) jersey. Then the halfback would crash into the line. After the play, Tichenor "simply trotted away to a touchdown."

The end of college football?

Football was never a game for the light of heart. You had to be tough physically and tough mentally to compete. Way back in 1906, for example complaints were many about the violence in American Football. It got so bad that universities on the West Coast, led by California and Stanford, replaced the sport with rugby union. At the time, the future of American college football, a very popular sport enjoyed by fans nationwide was in doubt. The schools that eliminated football and replaced it with rugby union believed football would be gone and rugby union would eventually be adopted nationwide.

Soon other schools followed this travesty and made the switch. Eventually, due to the perception that West Coast football was an inferior game played by inferior men when compared to the rough and tumble East Coast, manhood prevailed in the West over the inclination to make the game mild. The many tough East Coast and Midwest teams had shrugged off the loss of the few teams out West and they had continued to play American style football.

And, so the available pool of rugby union "football" teams to play remained small. The Western colleges therefore had to schedule games against local club teams and they reached out to rugby union powers in Australia, New Zealand, and especially, due to its proximity, Canada.

The famous Stanford and California game continued as rugby. To make it seem important. The winner was invited by the British Columbia Rugby Union to a tournament in Vancouver over the Christmas holidays. The winner of that tournament was rewarded with the Cooper Keith Trophy. Nobody in America cared. Eventually the West Coast came back to football.

Nonetheless the situation of injury and death in football persisted and though there was a lot of pushback, it came to a head in 1905 when there were 19 fatalities nationwide. President Theodore Roosevelt, a tough guy himself, is reported as having threatened to shut down the game nationwide if drastic changes were not made. Sports historians however, dispute that Roosevelt ever intervened.

What is certified, however, is that on October 9, 1905, the President held a meeting of football representatives from Harvard, Yale, and Princeton. The topic was eliminating and reducing injuries and the President according to the record, never threatened to ban football. The fact is that Roosevelt lacked the authority to abolish football but more importantly, he was a big fan and wanted the game to continue. The little Roosevelts also loved the sport and were playing football at the college and secondary levels at the time.

Meanwhile, there were more rule changes such as the notion of reducing the number of scrimmage plays to earn a first down from four to three in an attempt to reduce injuries. The LA Times reported an increase in punts in an experimental game and thus considered the game much safer than regular play. Football lovers did not accept the new rule because it was not "conducive to the sport."

Because nobody wanted players injured or killed in a game, on December 28, 1905, 62 schools met in New York City to discuss major rule changes to make the game safer. From this meeting, the Intercollegiate Athletic Association of the United States, later named the National Collegiate Athletic Association (NCAA), was formed.

The forward pass is legalized

One rule change that was introduced in 1906 was devised to open up the game and thus reduce injury. This new rule introduced the legal forward pass. Though it was underutilized for years, this proved to be one of the most important rule changes in the establishment of the modern game.

Because of these 1905-1906 reforms, mass formation plays in which many players joined together became illegal when forward passes became legal. Bradbury Robinson, playing for visionary coach Eddie Cochems at St. Louis University, is recorded as throwing the first legal pass in a September 5, 1906, game against Carroll College at Waukesha.

Later changes were in the minutia category but they added discipline and safety to the game without destroying its rugged character. For example, in 1910, came the new requirement that at least seven offensive players be on the line of scrimmage at the time of the snap, that there be no pushing or pulling, and that interlocking interference (arms linked or hands on belts and uniforms) was not allowed. These changes accomplished their intended purpose of greatly reducing the potential for collision injuries.

As noted previously, great coaches emerged in the ranks who took advantage of these sweeping changes. Amos Alonzo Stagg, for example, introduced such innovations as the huddle, the tackling dummy, and the pre-snap shift. Other coaches, such as Pop Warner and Notre Dame's Knute Rockne, introduced new strategies that still remain part of the game.

Many other rules changes and coaching innovations came about before 1940. They all had a profound impact on the game, mostly in opening up the passing game, but also in making the game safer to play without diminishing its quality.

For example, in 1914, the first roughing-the-passer penalty was implemented. In 1918, the rules on eligible receivers were loosened to allow eligible players to catch the ball anywhere on the field. The previously more restrictive rules allowed passes only in certain areas of the field.

Scoring rules also changed which brought the scoring into the modern era. For example, field goals were lowered from five to three points in 1909 and touchdowns were raised from four to six points in 1912.

Jim Thorpe, Circa 1915

Star Players:

Star players emerged in both the collegiate and professional ranks including Jim Thorpe, Red Grange, and Bronko Nagurski were other stars. These three in particular were able to move from college to the fledgling NFL and they helped turn it into a successful league.

Notable sportswriter Grantland Rice helped popularize the sport of football with his poetic descriptions of games and colorful nicknames for the game's biggest players, including Notre Dame's "Four Horsemen" backfield and Fordham University's linemen, known as the "Seven Blocks of Granite".

Legends existed all during the formation of football. There was Stagg, Halas, Warner, Thorpe, Heisman, Grange, Rockne and The Four Horsemen, and of course Mr. 409 himself, Penn State's own modern legend. While the early legends forged the structure for football as it is known today, later legends such as Joe Paterno made football a great sport.

Before Paterno, of course there was Rip Engle, and the great Bob Higgins.

The Heisman

In 1935, New York City's Downtown Athletic Club awarded its first Heisman Trophy to University of Chicago halfback Jay Berwanger. He was also the first ever NFL Draft pick in 1936. The trophy continues to this day to recognize the nation's "most outstanding" college football player. It has become one of the most coveted awards in all of American sports.

Jay Berwanger, 1st Heisman Winner

New formations and play sets continued to be developed by innovative coaches and their staffs. Emory Bellard from the University of Texas, developed a three-back option style offense known as the wishbone. Bear Bryant of Alabama became a preacher of the wishbone.

The strategic opposite of the wishbone is called the spread offense. Some teams have managed to adapt with the times to keep winning consistently. In the rankings of the most victorious programs, Michigan, Texas, and Notre Dame are ranked first, second, and third in total wins.

And so that is as far as we will take it in this chapter about the early evolution of football. With so many conferences and sports associations as well as pro, college, high school, and mini sports, something tells me we have not yet seen our last rule change.

Chapter 6—Nittany Legacies & Lore

The Nittany Lion

The Nittany Lion mascot often pumps up the crowd at many a Penn State football game at Beaver Stadium. The mascot is not entirely fictional. It has some real and some fictitious parts. The legend of the mascot, however, is all real.

The Nittany Lion Shrine
The campus is home to the Nittany Lion Shrine, a likeness of the lion carved into limestone, where students gather for spirit events.

As the story goes The Nittany Lion as Penn State's mascot originated with Harrison D. "Joe" Mason, a member of the Penn State class of 1907. In 1904, while playing a baseball game v Princeton in 1904, Mason and other members of Penn State's baseball team were shown a statue of Princeton's famous Bengal tiger as an indication of the *merciless* treatment they could expect to encounter on the field.

At the time, Penn State had no mascot and so Mason replied to the challenge with an instant fabrication of the Nittany Lion, "fiercest beast of them all." Mason's tale suggested the Nittany Lion could overcome even the tiger. Penn State went on to defeat Princeton that day. Over the next few years, the idea of Mason's "Nittany Lion" caught on and won such widespread support among students, alumni, and fans that there was never any official vote on its adoption.

So the closest we can come to the truth is that The Nittany Lion is in essence an ordinary mountain lion who lived in the region by Mount Nittany. Ordinary mountain lions were tough beasts for sure and were also known as cougar, puma, panther, and catamount. Mountain lions are creatures that reportedly roamed central Pennsylvania until the 1930's, although unconfirmed sightings continue. By attaching the prefix "Nittany" to this beast, Mason gave Penn State a unique symbol that no other college or university could claim.

The Lion's primary means of attack against the Tiger would be its strong right arm, capable of slaying any foes. This fact is now traditionally exemplified through one-armed push-ups after the team scores a touchdown.

Upon returning to campus from this priceless baseball victory over Princeton, Mason set about making his *invention* a reality. In 1907, this graduating senior wrote the following piece in the student publication "*The Lemon:*"

"Every college the world over of any consequence has a college emblem of some kind—all but The Pennsylvania State College. Why not select for ours the king of beasts—the Lion!! Dignified, courageous, magnificent, the Lion allegorically represents all that our College Spirit should be, so why not 'the Nittany Mountain Lion'? Why cannot State have a kingly, all-conquering Lion as the eternal sentinel?"

Ironically, the Lion came from the mind of a Penn State baseball player, not a football guy. Nonetheless it caught on and has been the mascot for over 100 years. With the exception of the *Lady Lions* basketball team, the Nittany Lion moniker represents all sports at Penn State University.

Mount Nittany and *Happy Valley*

Penn State does not rest on the top of Mount Nittany. Quite the opposite. Penn State's University Park campus is situated at the approximate midpoint of the Nittany Valley. Penn State fans, however, like to suggest that the campus is located in "Happy Valley." The other high point creating the Nittany Valley is Muncy Mountain, which is more popularly known as Bald Eagle Ridge.

The Nittany Valley (Happy Valley) itself extends about 60 miles, spans four counties, and at some points is more than five miles wide. Farms and small towns characterize much of the valley's landscape, while the mountains on either side are densely forested.

State College is listed well at the top among popular college towns in America. Pennsylvania State University, with over 44,000 students lives in the middle of the valley, and so students are not a rare sighting.

The whole area around Penn State, including State College, is affectionately referred to as "Happy Valley" as previously noted. Locals revel in the inaccuracy of it all. A fictional lion and a brave Indian Princess are not enough for the locals. Mostly everybody is happy to be in Happy Valley for sure.

State College is a small, family friendly town that has what the pundits say, *multiple notches on its belt*, such as the fact that in 2010, State College was rated as the 3rd safest metropolitan area in the entire United States and in 2013, It was also rated the best college town in the U.S. State college, Pennsylvania has plenty of opportunities of employment for undergraduate and graduate students alike. Indeed.com notes 2334 jobs of all kinds available in April 2016.

Plus, whether you see it or not, there is always a big welcome sign, which in fact is the entire town. You are welcome to State College and Penn State so come on by!

Beaver Stadium is the University's popular football field. I suspect somebody, maybe one person, in State College may not have been to Beaver Stadium. The stadium has an official seating capacity of 106,572, thereby making it currently the second largest stadium in the Western Hemisphere and the third largest in the world. Rungrado May Day Stadium in Pyongyang Nth Korea is #1 in the world. Penn State's 2016 plans for the stadium are not complete and are again being reviewed for enhancements, with the plans to be announced in July.

Penn State University is located in University Park, which is another name for its campus located in State College. University Park PA is not really a city but it is the postal address used by the University.

Throngs of PSU fans from all over Pennsylvania have visited this PA landmark town. Some say that more often than not it has been to see a great Penn State football game in the rejuvenated and still massive Beaver Stadium. As of today, no other PSU sports team plays in Beaver Stadium but other teams play close by. For example, the Nittany Lions Baseball team plays in Medlar Field, which is just in the "shadow of Beaver Stadium." Beaver Stadium is reserved for Penn State Football.

This revered stadium, in which many of the greats played over the years is expected to get some additional uses built in soon with its seventh makeover. The University is considering modifying the stadium for the seventh time in history, though there is talk of a new stadium. Either way, this time it will be to make the facility more available for other events besides Nittany Lions football. It is reported that the *NHL,* for example has inquired about playing at Beaver Stadium.

The PSU athletic department also would like to host summer concerts, FIFA events and perhaps even bring Pennsylvania's high school football championships to the stadium. Wouldn't that be great! Athletic Director Sandy Barbour is all for the purpose of the changes. *"Where Beaver Stadium is today from an infrastructure standpoint, it would be very difficult to do that," Barbour said.* There's more on the history of Beaver Stadium in chapter 4.

Mount Nittany itself is very near Penn State. It is considered part of the global Penn State experience. The fame of the mountain begins with the legend of Princess Nittany, and of course as we Penn State fans like to say; it is a major landmark for the Pennsylvania State University. See below for more on the Princess. The PSU mascot, discussed above, the Nittany Lion, is named for both the Nittany Mountains and for Pennsylvania's one-time mountain lion population.

If you are interested in touring Mount Nittany when you have the opportunity to visit Penn State, there are many hiking excursions available. They are from 2-8 miles in length, depending on the path chosen. They say it takes no more than 4-5 hours to see the whole mountain, or under 2 hours to circle the top.

The Full Legend of Nittany Mountain

This original story is of unknown date and authorship, but is believed to be based on Henry W. Shoemaker's original folklore concerning Mount Nittany and Princess Nita-Nee. This legendary origin story appears in The Nittany Valley Society's 2013 book titled: "The Legends of the Nittany Valley," available in paperback, Kindle, Nook, and iBooks.

The famed Nittany Lion discussed above, still strides the ledges and vales of the legendary Mount Nittany. It is as though he embodied the restless spirit of the mysterious Indian Princess Nit-A-Nee who gave her name to the Mountain, the Valley, and the Lion.

Princess Nittany

According to legend an old Indian warrior and his squaw once lived in the broad valley between the Tussey and Bald Eagle Mountains. Each year the crops they planted were wrested from their fields by a wicked North Wind in the autumn before the harvest. The valley was being deserted in the face of this Wind until a mysterious Indian maiden appeared who taught the tribe to build shields to hold against the wicked winds of the North.

The appreciative Indian tribe called the maiden Nit-A-Nee, which means "wind-breaker," and made her their Princess.

This Indian Princess fell in love with a handsome Indian brave of the tribe called Lion's Paw. This fearless Brave was killed in a fierce battle with the wicked wind from the North after his shield was stolen from him while he slept.

When she heard of Lion's Paw's death, Princess Nit-A-Nee searched every hill and dale of the land until she found the fearless Indian Brave's body, still standing even after he had died. She enfolded him in her arms and carried his still erect body back to a place in the center of the Valley where she laid the strong Brave in his grave and built a mound of honor over his strength.

On the last night of the full moon, after she had finally raised the last of the soil and stone over his high mound, a terrible storm came up unleashing itself with thunder and lightning and the wailing of a horrendous wind from the depths of the earth. Every Indian in the Valley shuddered and all eyes were directed to the Indian Brave's high mound upon which the beautiful maiden Princess Nit-A-Nee was mounted with arms outstretched to touch the sources of the lightning bolts in the sky.

Through the night they watched with awe as the Indian Brave's burial mound grew and rose into a Mountain penetrating the center of the big valley between the two legs of the Tussey and Bald Eagle ridges. When the dawn finally came a huge Mountain was found standing erect in the center of the Valley.

A legend had been born. The mound and the maiden had given place to a Mountain, and standing on its summit was a Lion surrounded by eleven orphaned male cubs, each of whom had the courage of the fearless Indian Brave and the heart of the mysterious Indian Princess.

From that day forward every place in the valley was safe, and the wind wrested nothing from the fields on which these Lions strode as fearless heroes from the Mountain. The people of the Valley from that date forward knew only happiness and bounteous plenty.

In the fullness of time men came from across the farthest seas to build a college at the foot of this Mountain. The strength and courage of the students of this college became known far and wide. In memory of the fearless Indian Brave and the mysterious Indian Princess, the students of the college erected posts on a field and fought their way across this field as the North Wind had once ravaged the fields of the ancient Indian warrior and his squaw.

As each student learned the destructive power of the North Wind across the fields, he also learned the strength of the Princess known as Wind Breaker, called in her language Nit-A-Nee, and the courage unto death of the Indian Brave called Lion's Paw. As long as this strength and courage is known in the Valley, Mount Nittany will stand as a breaker against the wicked Wind of the North.

It is passed on from generation to generation that, as long as the fields of the Valley resound each year to the reenactments of the battles between the wicked North Wind and the Indian Brave, the people who live in the valley will be happy and prosperous and safe.

But if the reenactments ever stop, Mount Nittany will lose its strength and disappear, and the wicked Wind of the North will stream down through the valley between the legs of the Tussey and Bald Eagle ridges, searing the land, wresting away all that has been planted and grown there, and scattering the tribes who live there. All the warriors and squaws of the place will then have to abandon the Valley and seek their homes in other places and climes, and learn the customs and ways of strangers.

This is the legend of Mount Nittany. May it stand forever high and strong in our midst, our breaker against the harsh winds of destiny and fate which sweep down from the North, the source of fearless courage and deathless love, both father and mother of the games by which we live.

May Mount Nittany ever rise above us as the Guardian before the gates of Old Penn State. May the mysterious Indian Princess ever stand in our midst as breaker and shield against the destructive power of the winds of fate. And may the Nittany Lion's cubs forever join in the games which are the guarantee of the life of the land we love.

Nit-A-Nee Myth or Reality?

Myth: The word "Nittany" is derived from Princess Nita-nee, a member of the Native American tribes who once lived in central Pennsylvania.

Fact: Princess Nita-nee was "invented" by author and publisher Henry W. Shoemaker and has no basis whatever in fact. Shoemaker's mention of the princess first appeared in print in 1903. At that time he attributed the tale to "an aged Seneca Indian named Isaac Steele." Shoemaker, a well-known Pennsylvania folklorist, later admitted that both Steele and Nita-nee were "purely fictitious." It is a great story nonetheless.

Great place for visitors

For visitors to the university and the local community, the Nittany Lion Inn offers visitors a spirited and historic location with all the comforts of the northeast.

Pennsylvanians and others have a great reason to want to be part of Penn State, whether it is for a great education or a wonderful experience rooting for the Penn State football team.

Summary of the beginnings

Pattee library

Pennsylvania State University has an amazing 24 campuses in total, but the institution's biggest – and perhaps most beautiful—is its University Park location in State College. This 5,448-acre area includes the campus' famed Mall, through which students can amble to class from Pattee Library, down a walkway lined with elms that have earned their own spot in the U.S. National Register of Historic Places.

In the words of a Penn State Press university guide, during the summer and fall months "the elms' branches overhead create a dappled and leafy tunnel" – a lovely sight that may take the sting ever so slightly out of hitting the books.

If you want to read even more about Penn State, the university for students, feel free to take this link:
Pennsylvania State University-Main Campus (PSU, Penn State) Introduction and History - University Park, PA
http://penn.stateuniversity.com/#ixzz46EFxjzW1

Chapter 7—Jerry Sandusky: A Story that Teaches Big Lessons

Quick to judge; slow to learn

There was frustration, anger, & confusion following the tragic events at Penn State regarding child abuse and Jerry Sandusky In 2011. The situation, they say, had been ignored long enough and finally could be ignored no longer.

There is a lesson there someplace. It would have been easy to fall into the trap of finding blame without finding any real lessons for ourselves. We all sometimes are quick to judge and slow to learn.

This is not to say that the observations and judgments in the Sandusky case have all been appropriate or that all have beeb inappropriate. The majority of the discourse has been rightfully focused on the failures of the leadership at Penn State, why it happened, who was involved, and how severely they should be punished. And rightly so. Jerry Sandusky is already doing time for his gruesome deeds.

There are some stubborn souls who wonder that Second Mile, the Sandusky charity, was not the villain, and what about the PA state agencies that monitored this haven for unwanted children. What were they doing in their full time jobs when so many think that a full-time football coach should have been monitoring the safety of children in a network that had over 1000 protectors? Where was the state of PA in all of this? Second Mile did not reside on the PSU campus and Sandusky, when convicted at least, was not working for PSU. Why were *those he worked for* not charged?

Besides the abuse victims for which we continue to grieve, many other innocents at Penn State, including those in the surrounding communities, have suffered through this major disruption. Though the university made a lot of mistakes, it is now learning from the whole ordeal and it is gaining character. Others are learning also.

For everyone not directly involved in the proceedings, and perhaps even those who do not even live in Pennsylvania, there is another conversation that thankfully is also taking place. What can we all learn from this Penn State tragedy to help improve our organizations, our leaders, & ourselves?

Brian Kight from the Focus 3 Blog, wrote an outstanding teaching article, which he titled: "10 Leadership Lessons from the Penn State Scandal." Kight hits on all cylinders and nails down the big learning opportunities in his article. It is well worth the read. Without a doubt Kight points out that the most important element is leadership, which is point # 1 in this piece.

Kight also hits on culture, defining moments, circumstances, trust, accountability, status and position, minimum requirements, and consequences. I think we all would gain from a review of these points and their applicability to the current matter. I have taken the liberty to copy his point # 1 below from the article. It is very instructional.

Great leadership is rare & valuable

"Leadership is not "a" difference maker. It is "the" difference maker. The decisions and actions of leaders have a profound impact on the organization, its people, and its customers and constituents. For decades to come, Penn State will be defined not by what Jerry Sandusky did, but by what Penn State leaders, state leaders, and social agencies failed to do. For leaders everywhere, the question is not, "Will you make a difference?" The question is "What difference will you make?"

Some references

NPR pieces and CNN writings were used as reference sources for some information in this chapter chronology on Jerry Sandusky and Penn State

The chapter that should never need to be printed again.

I wrestled with including this chapter and several others such as this, in an upbeat book about Penn State Football. Yet, the last four years with Bill O'Brian, followed by James Franklin were as they were because of Jerry Sandusky and a number of people who failed to see the ugly side of reality or perhaps chose to ignore it or do the minimum. We know that many children were hurt and for their lack of guardianship for those children, many adults are now wishing their behavior had been much more appropriate for the circumstances.

This chapter presents the facts, mostly collected by NPR and then from the trial on, from work by CNN. Thank you to these sources for my permission to use your accounts and thank you to them for their vigilance in this travesty.

Michael Sokolove writing for the New York Times July 16, 2014, summarizes one of the predominant thoughts regarding how quickly the PSU board tried to dispose of the matter: It was a "rallying point for those who believe that a panic-driven response brought further disrepute to an already reeling university." Some say the rush of the board was to preserve the board, not to help the situation. You make the call.

We finish this chapter upbeat again with some excerpts from a positive piece from a hometown State College resident, Ethan Kasales. He lived through State College's and the University's many problems of the last five years.

When I write the next version of this book, perhaps five years from now, God willing, my wish is that whatever insights or lessons that are learned will have come about by telling this story again and again. Hopefully, the lessons will be so well learned by then that this chapter in edition # 2 will be 100% unnecessary. The chapter number will be there but the many pages will all be blank. Won't that symbolize the recovery of many of those from Penn State who were not victims per se but who have had a painful ordeal, nonetheless.

From having it all to messing it up for others

Penn State's former defensive coordinator Gerald "Jerry" Sandusky once seemed to have it made but he crossed the big line at Penn State and in his own personal charity. He was caught and he is being punished in jail. He was found guilty of sexual abuse, convicted of 45 out of 48 counts on Friday, June 22, 2012. He had been accused of sexually abusing 10 boys over a 15-year period in a scandal that rocked the university's community and quite frankly, the nation. Several alleged victims' stories of their particular abuse were heard in the trial, which began on June 11.

Sandusky, 72, (68 at the time of the trial) and his attorney continue to maintain his innocence of the charges. I wish I could buy his arguments as so many wished, but, like the jury, I cannot. The charges stem from a full and complete grand jury investigation. The former coaching assistant claims that he merely "horsed around" with the boys, all of whom he met through his "too convenient" Second Mile Charity.

Penn State University's Board of Directors took unprecedented action by firing long-time coach Joe Paterno and University President Graham Spanier on Nov. 9, four days after Sandusky was initially arrested. Two other school officials stepped down from their posts—Athletic Director Tim Curley and a vice president, Gary Schultz. Both were accused of perjury and failing to report suspected child abuse. Knowing the pain of the victims, these accused perpetrators could offer no plausible excuses.

When the investigation became public, Pennsylvania Attorney General Linda Kelly said that Paterno was "not regarded as a target." The former coach, distraught from not taking more action as he wished that he had, died of lung cancer on January 22, 2012. Many Penn State fans believe that the issues with Sandusky and the University's actions helped hasten Coach Paterno's demise. Joe felt he could have done more.

The individual people who were figures in the case against Jerry Sandusky are listed below. After Sandusky, they are presented in alphabetic sequence by last name.

Jerry Sandusky is the main alleged perpetrator in the case.

The former defensive coordinator was charged with sexually abusing 10 boys over a 15-year period. Sandusky, 72, maintains he is innocent. The defensive coach played football at Penn State and was a coach at the school for 32 years. He had experienced what otherwise might have been called a fine career as defensive coordinator. He and his wife, Dottie, raised six adopted children.

Other alleged perpetrators include the following:

Jim Calhoun

Calhoun was a temporary worker who served as a janitor at Penn State for just eight months. He had told co-workers and a supervisor in 2000 that he witnessed Sandusky engaging in sexual activity with a boy in a campus locker-room shower. Several staff members later said that Calhoun, a veteran of the Korean War, was visibly shaken by what he reported as seeing. In 2012, it was reported that Calhoun resided in an assisted living facility and reportedly was suffering from dementia.

Wendell Courtney

Wendell Courtney is the former general counsel for Penn State University is also the longtime lawyer for Sandusky's charity foundation, called *The Second Mile*. He was working for both organizations when, according to Schultz, he reviewed the 1998 university police report about Sandusky's behavior with boys.

Tim Curley

The Penn State athletic director, 61, Joe Paterno's immediate supervisor, denies being told of sexual misconduct by Sandusky in 2002. He is accused of covering up allegations tied to the scandal. He was named athletic director on Dec. 30, 1993. Curley chose to take an administrative leave the day before his Nov. 7 arraignment.

Ray Gricar

District Attorney DA Gricar went missing and was declared legally dead in July, 2012. He had been the Centre County district attorney from 1985 to 2005, at which time, he disappeared. He chose not to prosecute Sandusky in 1998, after allegations of inappropriate contact with young boys surfaced. The decision helped to end a police investigation into the report.

Mike McQueary

McQueary had offered to Coach Paterno in 2002, when he was a graduate assistant that he had witnessed Sandusky abusing a boy in a Penn State locker room shower. Paterno immediately informed Curley, who was Paterno's boss about what McQueary had seen. Paterno did not follow-up with his boss. Curley later met with McQueary and Schultz. McQueary later became an assistant coach at Penn State. He gave his statement to the grand jury. He reportedly said in testimony that he went to the police but the authorities dispute his claim. The school put him on administrative leave on Nov. 11, 2011.

Joe Paterno

Coach "Joe Pa," revered by many at Penn State University as well as a legion of fans, died on January 22, 2012 at age 85. Having planned to retire after the 2011 season, Paterno was fired from his job four days after Sandusky's arrest. Taking over from Rip Engle as head coach, he had been an assistant or head coach at Penn State since 1950. The scandal prompted Paterno's thoughts on retirement, but school trustees ended his tenure hours after the coach made that pledge.

In a statement before he was fired, Paterno said, "This is a tragedy. It is one of the great sorrows of my life. With the benefit of hindsight, I wish I had done more." Some of us wish that the coach had lived long enough to recover and become an advocate for the cause. Paterno was a good man who made a mistake.

Graham Spanier

Spanier, 67, was fired along with Coach Paterno on Nov. 9, 2011. He had become university president in 1995, after serving at universities in Oregon, Nebraska, and New York. He served on the faculty and as a staff member at Penn State from 1973 to 1982. Spanier's academic background is concentrated in sociology and family counseling.

Spanier had ruled over a veritable empire: about 45,000 students on a stately, sprawling main campus in State College; another 40,000 students at locations around the state; and an annual budget exceeding $4 billion. Spanier took none of the accusations lying down. Who really knows?

Gary Schultz

Schultz was the senior vice president for finance and business. In this capacity, he had oversight of the university police. He was charged with covering up abuse allegations. He served as Penn State's senior vice president and treasurer from 1993 to 2009, at which time he retired after nearly 40 years of service.

Before the huge publicity of the scandal, he was rehired for the same job in 2011, on a temporary basis. In late July, he was named interim senior vice president for Finance and Business while the university conducted a national search to fill the position. PSU had retained Brill Neumann Executive Search Consulting to assist in the national search for this position. In early 2010, the university named a campus child care center after Schultz, and later unofficially and very quietly renamed it as the Child Care Center at Hort Woods. Schultz retired for the second time on Nov. 6, 2011

This timeline of events is taken from work originally put together by NPR.

Chronology

1977
In 1977, Jerry Sandusky established *The Second Mile* in State College, Pa., "as a group foster home devoted to helping troubled boys," according to the grand jury's findings. The program evolved into a statewide charity whose honorary board members included Paterno and other sports figures.

1993
Tim Curley became Penn State's athletic director. That same year, Gary Schultz was named the school's treasurer and senior vice president.

1994

A boy identified as Victim 7 in the grand jury report meets Sandusky through the Second Mile program. Now 30, Victim 7 says that after a couple of years in the program, he often spent Friday nights at Sandusky's house and attended football games with him the next day. He says Sandusky touched him in ways that made him uncomfortable, primarily during car rides and when the two showered after a workout.

1998

An 11-year-old boy returned home with wet hair after an outing with Sandusky. Victim 6 tells his mother he took a shower with Sandusky and that the coach hugged him several times. The boy's mother contacts university police. This action triggered an investigation.

On May 13 and May 19, Det. Ronald Shreffler made a recording of a call of the boy's mother with Sandusky. Court papers say Sandusky acknowledged that he showered with the boy, as well as with others. When the mother cuts off contact with Sandusky after a second call, he tells her, "I wish I were dead," according to court papers.

On June 1, Jerry Lauro, an investigator from the Pennsylvania Department of Public Welfare, takes part in an interview of Sandusky by Shreffler. According to the grand jury report, Sandusky admits to hugging the boy in the shower, and says he will not shower with children again.

Det. Shreffler speaks to another boy who reports similar treatment to that reported by Victim 6. But the investigation ends after District Attorney Ray Gricar decides the case warrants no criminal charges. Shreffler tells the grand jury that Thomas Harmon, who headed the campus police, told him to close the inquiry.

1999
Sandusky retires from Penn State's football program. Because there had been "no" issues with his employment, the "revered," defensive coordinator gained an "emeritus" label. This permitted him full access to campus facilities, including the locker rooms and an office in the Lasch Football Building. Schultz testified that the timing of Sandusky's retirement was not related to the university police investigation a year earlier.

2000
Jim Calhoun, a janitor at the Lasch building, tells a co-worker and his supervisor that he saw Sandusky engaged in sexual activity with a boy in the assistant coaches' shower. The boy, referred to as Victim 8 in court papers, was never identified. Calhoun is devastated personally for having witnessed this act, and secondly for how willing the janitorial staff was to clam-up.

Calhoun's colleague Ronald Petrosky, who reported seeing Sandusky's car in the parking lot later that night in the fall of 2000, says that members of the janitorial staff were concerned that they might lose their jobs if they spoke out about what had happened.

After Calhoun told his supervisor, Jay Witherite, what he had seen, Witherite told him whom he could report the incident to, if he chose to do so. Everybody seemed scared, perhaps of Sandusky, but nobody seemed willing to go the full mile.

2002
A graduate assistant reports seeing Sandusky sexually assaulting a boy in the showers at Lasch Football Building on the Penn State campus, around 9:30 p.m. on Friday, March 1. The assault on the boy, who Kelly said "appeared to be about 10 years old," is reported to Paterno the next day. Paterno, in turn, passes the information to Curley one day later. Curley was Paterno's boss.

The graduate assistant, who has since been identified as Penn State assistant coach Mike McQueary, meets with Curley and Schultz, but not Paterno, some 10 days later. According to McQueary, he told them that he had seen Sandusky having sex with a boy in the showers. No report is made to police or to any child protection agency — a breach of state law, prosecutors say.

Two weeks later, Curley tells McQueary that Sandusky's keys to the locker room have been taken away and that the incident was reported to The Second Mile charity.

Sandusky is banned from bringing children onto the Penn State campus in a decision reviewed and approved by Spanier, the university president. Sandusky was not a PSU employee at the time.

2009
The mother of the boy identified by court papers as Victim 1 calls a high school in Clinton County to report that her son was sexually abused by Sandusky. The school district bans Sandusky from any of its campuses, and the police are notified.

2010
In December, the graduate assistant who had reported the 2002 assault testifies before a grand jury investigating Sandusky, detailing what he saw and what he told to Paterno, Schultz and Curley.

In 2010 or 2011, Victim 7 tells the grand jury that prior to his testimony, he received voice mails from Sandusky, his wife and a friend of Sandusky's. Victim 7 says he did not return any of the calls.

2011
In his Jan. 12 grand jury testimony, Curley says the graduate assistant reported only "inappropriate," not "sexual" conduct, calling the conduct "horsing around."

Also testifying on Jan. 12, Schultz says he met with Curley and Paterno about the abuse allegations. But he tells the grand jury that he was unsure about the details of what had happened and that he thought Sandusky and the boy might have been wrestling when the inappropriate contact occurred.

Saturday, Nov. 5: The investigation into Sandusky, Curley and Schultz becomes public, with prosecutors accusing Sandusky of making inappropriate sexual advances or assaults on eight boys, from 1994 to 2009.

Sun. Nov. 6: Curley and Schultz vacate their university posts following an emergency meeting with school officials.

Mon. Nov. 7: Curley and Schultz are arraigned on charges of making false statements to the grand jury and failing to report the possible abuse of a child.

Wed. Nov. 9: Paterno, coming under increasing criticism and pressure to resign in the wake of the Sandusky scandal, announces that he will retire at the end of the 2011 season, when his three-year contract expires. In a statement, Paterno said, "This is a tragedy. It is one of the great sorrows of my life. With the benefit of hindsight, I wish I had done more."

But hours after Paterno made his announcement, the Penn State Board of Trustees announced that it had fired both Paterno and school president Graham Spanier — "effective immediately," according to the board.

In their place, the trustees named executive vice president and Provost Rodney A. Erickson as the school's interim president, and assistant coach Tom Bradley as the interim head football coach.

Fri. Nov. 11: Penn State places McQueary on administrative leave. The move comes one day after the school announced it would be "in the best interest of all" if

McQueary did not attend the season's final home game, citing multiple threats made against him.

Sun. Nov. 13: The leader of The Second Mile, the charity Sandusky founded and, according to prosecutors, used to find his alleged victims, resigns. President and CEO Jack Raykovitz had held the post for 28 years.

Mon. Nov. 14: The ongoing child-abuse investigation discovered another ten other young men who may have also been abused, according to a report in *The New York Times*. In a telephone interview with Bob Costas, Jerry Sandusky admits to showering with boys, but he says he is innocent of the charges, and that he only "horsed around" with them.

Thurs. Nov. 17: City and university police dispute McQueary's claim that he had spoken with police and "made sure it stopped," after allegedly witnessing Sandusky abusing a boy in 2002 — claims McQuery had apparently made in an email to friends after the scandal had become public.

Mon. Nov. 21: Penn State announced that it had hired former FBI director Louis Freeh to investigate the abuse allegations.

Wed. Nov. 30: A civil lawsuit is filed against Sandusky, The Second Mile and Penn State, claiming that Sandusky sexually abused the plaintiff more than 100 times when he was between 10 and 14 years old. The plaintiff, identified only as John Doe, 29 [now 33] was not among the eight alleged victims in the grand jury's report. This news came just one day after Second Mile (Sandusky's charity) urged its supporters to make future donations to another charity, the Pennsylvania Coalition against Rape.

Wed. Dec. 7: Sandusky is arrested and charged with abusing two more boys. The new cases mean that the former coach at this time faced 52 charges in the abuse of more than 10 boys.

Like the other alleged victims, the young men say they first met Sandusky through his Second Mile charity.

Tues. Dec. 13: Sandusky waived his right to a Dec. 13 preliminary hearing to establish probable cause on the abuse charges. The move kept Sandusky's accusers from providing early testimony in this high-profile case. The former coach's next court date was set for Jan. 11, 2012.

Sections of the timeline as written by NPR, which I used as a reference were based on events as described by the investigating grand jury's findings.

2012

Fri. Jan. 6: Penn State hires Bill O'Brien as its new head football coach. Like Paterno, he is a graduate of Brown University.

Sun. Jan. 22:
Former coach Joe Paterno dies, (RIP) after a battle with lung cancer.

Tues. May 8:
At the prosecutors' request, Judge John Cleland allows documents related to some of McQueary's allegations against Sandusky to be altered. The revisions change the date of events McQueary had previously said happened in March of 2002; the papers now allege that the events occurred 13 months earlier, in February of 2001.

Tues June 5, former assistant coach Jerry Sandusky was photographed walking to the county courthouse for the first day of his trial on child sex abuse charges.

Wed. June 6:
A nine-member jury consisting of five men and seven women is chosen for Sandusky's trial in Pennsylvania's Centre

County. Several of the jurors have ties to Penn State, as either professors or students.

Mon. June 11:
As the trial opens, prosecutor Joe McGettigan tells the jury that Sandusky is a "serial predator," and shows them photos of the alleged victims, taken when they were children. Defense attorney Joe Amendola tells the jurors that the accusers in the case are seeking financial gain.

Mon. June 18:
After featuring the testimony of several alleged victims, the prosecution in the case rests. The defense begins with a successful request to remove one count, regarding victim 7, on the grounds that the charge was made under a statute that would not have applied at the specified time.

Wed. June 20:
Sandusky's defense team rests its case, one day after his wife, Dottie, took the stand. Other defense witnesses included friends and young men who said Sandusky had helped them personally and through his charity. Despite hints otherwise, the former coach did not testify on his own behalf.

Fri. June 22:
The jury finds Sandusky guilty of 45 out of 48 counts of sexual abuse.

Sat. June 30
Mike McQueary's contract as assistant football coach ends.

Thurs. July 5
McQueary learns that his contract has not been renewed.

Fri. July 6
Former Penn State President Graham Spanier tells investigators than he had never been informed of any incident involving Sandusky.

Thurs. July 12
Louis Freeh announces the findings of the investigation into Penn State's action concerning Sandusky and child abuse. The report accuses the former leaders at Penn State of showing "total and consistent disregard" for child sex abuse victims, while covering up the attacks of a longtime sexual predator.

Mon. July 23
The NCAA announces a $60 million fine against Penn State and bans the team from the postseason for four years. Additionally, the school must vacate all wins from 1998-2011, and will lose 20 football scholarships a year for four seasons.

- The Big Ten Conference rules that Penn State's share of bowl revenues for the next four seasons - roughly $13 million - will be donated to charities working to prevent child abuse.

Fri. Aug. 24
"Victim 1" files a lawsuit against Penn State.

Thurs. Sept. 20
Feinberg Rozen LLP (headed by Kenneth Feinberg who oversaw the 9/11 and BP oil spill victim's funds) is hired by Penn State.

Tues. Oct. 2
Mike McQueary files a whistleblower lawsuit against Penn State.

Mon. Oct. 8
An audio statement from Sandusky airs in which he protests his innocence and says he is falsely accused.

Tues Oct. 9
Sandusky is sentenced to no less than 30 years and no more than 60 years in prison. During the hearing, Sandusky is designated as a sexually violent offender.

Mon. Oct. 15
A lawsuit is filed by plaintiff "John Doe," a 21-year-old male. Defendants include Sandusky, Penn State, the Second Mile, Spanier, Curley, and Schultz. Doe alleges Sandusky sexually abused him and that he would not have been assaulted by Sandusky if officials who were aware that Sandusky was molesting boys had not covered up his misconduct.

Thurs. Oct. 18
Sandusky's lawyers file an appeal.

Tues. Oct. 23
Sandusky is transferred to a state prison facility located in Camp Hill, Pennsylvania.

Thurs. Nov. 1
The Commonwealth of Pennsylvania files eight charges against former Penn State President Graham Spanier in connection with the rape scandal. The charges include perjury and endangering the welfare of a child. Former university Vice President Gary Schultz and former Athletic Director Tim Curley face the same charges, according to Attorney General Linda Kelly.

Wed. Nov. 7
Graham Spanier is arraigned. His bail is set at $125,000 unsecured and he is ordered not to leave Pennsylvania without permission.

Thurs. Nov. 15
The Middle States Commission on Higher Education lifts its warning and reaffirms Penn State's accreditation.

Wed Dec. 5
The trial dates scheduled for January 07, 2013, for Tim Curley and for Gary Schultz are postponed until further notice.

2013

Wed. Jan. 30,
Judge John M. Cleland denies Sandusky's appeal for a new trial.

Tues. July 30,
A judge rules that Graham Spanier, Tim Curley and Gary Schultz will face trial on obstruction of justice and other charges related to the Jerry Sandusky child sex abuse scandal.

Mon. Aug. 26
Sandusky's adopted son and six other victims have finalized settlement agreements.

Wed. Oct. 2
Sandusky's appeal is denied by the Superior Court of Pennsylvania.

Mon. Oct. 28
Penn State announces that they have reached settlements with what it calls 26 victims of Jerry Sandusky, and the amount paid by the university totals $59.7 million.

2014

Wed. April 2
Sandusky's appeal is denied by the Supreme Court of Pennsylvania.

Mon. September 8
NCAA ends the Nittany Lions' postseason ban and scholarship limits. A $60 million fine and 13 years of vacated wins of renowned coach Joe Paterno remain in place.

2015

Fri. Jan. 16
The NCAA agrees to restore Joe Paterno's wins as part of a settlement of the lawsuit brought by State Senator Jake Corman and Treasurer Rob McCord. Also as part of the settlement agreement, Penn State agrees to commit $60 million to the prevention and treatment of child sexual abuse.

Penn State's football team got back its 112 hard-fought wins that had been wiped out during the Jerry Sandusky child molestation scandal, and the late Joe Paterno has been restored as the winningest coach in major college football history.

The NCAA announced the new settlement with the school Friday, weeks before a scheduled trial on the legality of the 2012 consent decree that the agreement replaced.

The new deal also directs a $60 million fine to address child abuse be spent within Pennsylvania and it resolves that lawsuit.

Most Penn State fans and supporters of the institution never believed that the NCAA should have punished the non-guilty in the Sandusky case. Adam Rittenberg wrote:

"Exposed yet again, the NCAA folded after reaching a settlement with Penn State and showed why it should have never been involved in this issue in the first place."

Sometimes even the big chiefs do not get it right! The NCAA's board of governors approved the settlement, association spokesman Bob Williams said. The Penn State board approved it Friday afternoon.

Wed. Dec. 23
A spokeswoman for the State of Pennsylvania employee retirement system says Sandusky will receive $211,000 in back payments and regular pension payments will resume. This is the result of a November 13 court ruling that reversed a 2012 decision to terminate Sandusky's pension under a state law that allows the termination of pensions of public employees convicted of a "disqualifying crime." The judge said in his ruling that Sandusky was not employed at the time of the crimes he was convicted of committing.

2016

Fri. Jan. 22
A three-judge panel reverses the obstruction of justice and conspiracy charges against Spanier, Curley and Schultz, and the perjury charges against Spanier and Curley.

Sun. Jan. 24, 2016
Summation of Dropped Charges
Philly.com by Susan Snyder and Craig R. McCoy, STAFF WRITERS

POSTED: JANUARY 24, 2016

"The Pennsylvania Superior Court scaled back the criminal case Friday against three former Pennsylvania State University administrators accused of conspiring to cover up Jerry Sandusky's child sex abuse, validating their assertion that it was unfair to let the university's former top lawyer testify against them.

"In three opinions, the judges reversed a lower-court ruling that upheld obstruction of justice and conspiracy charges against former Penn State president Graham B. Spanier, former vice president Gary Schultz, and former athletic director Tim Curley, as well as perjury charges against Spanier and Schultz.

"The judges left intact charges of child endangerment, a third-degree felony, and failure to report suspected child abuse, a summary offense, against all three men, as well as a perjury charge for Curley.

"But defense lawyers hailed the rulings, perhaps their biggest legal victory in a case that has languished for four years." We're elated that they threw out the most important charges," said Elizabeth Ainslie, an attorney for Spanier.

"A spokesman for Attorney General Kathleen G. Kane said her office would review the ruling and decide if it would appeal to the Pennsylvania Supreme Court.

"Prosecutors contend that Spanier, Curley, and Schultz either ignored signs that Sandusky, a longtime assistant to football coach Joe Paterno, was a sexual predator or covered it up.

"All retired, resigned, or were forced out in the wake of Sandusky's arrest. Each has denied the allegations."

Happy Valley had stopped smiling

Though not ever as much as the little ones affected by this travesty, all of Happy Valley and surrounds had a tough four to five years because of Jerry Sandusky and others. The locals lamented the wonderful times they had in the pre-Sandusky trial years and they all wished things could be brought back to normal.

Nobody wanted anything rushed but the penalties against the university, not the perpetrators, were not looked upon well by the townspeople. Closure came when the verdict was in and the guilty went to jail. The rest of State College could breathe easier as justice had been done. All pray for the little saints who live on but who were harmed and all hope they gain their freedom from this curse, which in some ways ended with the original verdict.

I selected excerpts from this healing piece for the people of Happy Valley and State College. God bless you all. Please check out this nice piece by Ethan Kasales and the excerpts I selected as part of the healing that all of us need. Amen!

"Four Years Later: A Townie's Take on Penn State's Past and Future"

BY ETHAN KASALES ON NOVEMBER 5, 2015 AT 4:04 AM

Excerpt:

"There is a remarkable amount of resiliency in Happy Valley, and it was put on full display in front of a global audience in the months and years following the scandal. Even after the NCAA overstepped its bounds, handing down perhaps the most severe sanctions on a college program ever, Penn State didn't crumble.

"Current New Orleans Saint and beloved Nittany Lion linebacker Michael Mauti said it best when he and teammate Michael Zordich gave brief, yet incredibly moving remarks outside of the Lasch Building on July 25, 2012. "We take this as an opportunity to create our own legacy. This program was not built by one man, and this program's sure as hell not gonna be torn down by one man. This program was built on every alumni, every single player that came before us; built on their backs."

"Critics called Penn State a university with a "culture problem" of putting football on a pedestal. But I would argue that this program will always serve as an example of the outstanding pride and dedication to "success with honor" both on and off the field.

"Then, when the sanctions were lifted midway through last season, the sky continued to clear. It's a process that is certainly ongoing, but the foundation is in place to reach greatness once again."

[At the point in last season when this was written,]...Penn State has gone a combined 29-17 since the start of 2012.

ESPN on-air personality Stephen A. Smith tweeted the following on July 13, 2012: "there's no future at Penn State for the foreseeable future. Minimum next five years."

"Well, the past four seasons have been unorthodox, that much is certain, but you simply can't call them a failure. In fact, the future is growing brighter each day...the optimism surrounding this team stretches far beyond the last three weeks of the 2015 regular season.

"This is not "just a football school," though. Of course, football is a big part of fall in Happy Valley, helping local businesses to flourish and providing an escape from the daily grind of classes and work for students, fans, and alumni. But the same can be said for countless Division I programs across the nation.

"What makes Penn State different is the compassion and connection with our peers that we're encouraged to enjoy. There is a niche where every student, faculty, and staff member alike can become involved and truly make a difference in the lives of others. The beauty of this place, both visceral and physical, is unlike anywhere else I've ever been. Sure, winters in State College provide a constant struggle in terms of motivating oneself to walk to class amid negative wind chills, but I'll gladly layer up in pursuit of a degree from what I believe is the greatest all-around university this country has to offer.

"Thankfully fall is still in full effect, though the gorgeous summer-like weather of late may beg to differ. The aura of tradition runs deep here, but like any great institution, students and community members alike are again in the midst of a shift toward the unexpected. Penn State's compass is dialed in on the future, but where will it lead next? That part is up to each and every one of us. How will you leave your mark on this place?

"Time will continue to press on, downtown will experience more changes as the skyline above State College evolves, but a few things will always remain constant here: the endless opportunities to find oneself, a chance to connect with the people and things that make one happy, and the feeling of camaraderie you're forever a part of as a member of the Penn State family."

This was a major trajedy from which PSU cannot escape. Nobody has the right key to open the lock behind which the truth hides undetected.

Joe Paterno did not like Jerry Sandusky as much as he liked the mosquito next door. Yet, his instincts never got up so high about a big bully of a guy who most of his coaches feared. How could this big moose mammoth bully ever like little boys? It had to hit those who even once considered it as a blind-hit between the eyes. How could a big surly, nasty, non-loving guy like Sandusky have liked little boys?

To repeat: How a big surly guy like Sandusky that most men did not even want to like—how could he like little boys? I suspect JoaPa dismissed it all for these reasons.

I suppose in his reflections, Joe Paterno had those thoughts also and so he did what he needed to do at minimum. It was a conundrum. He reported what had been told and then went on to coaching which was why he was being paid.

Chapter 8 — Penn State Football's Highlights from 1881 through 2016

Unofficial and Official Games

http://grfx.cstv.com/photos/schools/psu/sports/m-footbl/auto_pdf/2013-14/misc_non_event/12-Timeline.pdf

Information from the Penn State Football Encyclopedia by Lou Prato, a noted Penn State football historian, was used in the original compilation of this chronology by CBS, which is available on the Web. Our thanks to CBS for providing this to our readers, and for Lou Prato for compiling it.

The material we used was current as of March 11, 2013, and we provided additional research to bring this chronology current to the summer of 2016. This is an extremely impressive compendium of happenings in Penn State Football and thus this book is not about just the greatest moments in Penn State Football. It is about the great moments and even the contributing moments to Penn State's greatness.

Like all Penn State fans, I expect you to thoroughly enjoy whipping through this 130 years' worth of Penn State Football in this most efficient way. Enjoy! Then we will look at each season in detail, game, by game.

November 12, 1881 — Penn State College students organize a football team without administration support and play the first game against the University of Lewisburg (renamed Bucknell University in 1896) in Lewisburg. Penn State wins, 9-0, in a cold, sleet-like drizzle.

September 1887 — George "Lucy" Linsz arrives on campus as a freshman and, with the help of fellow freshman Charles Hildebrand, gets approval from President George Atherton to organize the first official football team for Penn State College

Fall 1887 — Pink and Black are picked as the team colors.

November 12, 1887 — The first official game is played against Bucknell at Lewisburg. Penn State wins, 54-0.

November 19, 1887 — The first home game is played with Old Main lawn used as the field. Captain and quarterback Lucy Linsz scores three second-half touchdowns to lead Penn State to a 24-0 win over Bucknell.

Fall 1888 — The team colors are changed to Blue and White. A Student Athletic Association is formed to help support athletics with three divisions, including football, baseball and general.

November 11, 1889 — Penn State is handed its worst all-time defeat, 106-0, by Lehigh at Bethlehem. Penn State plays the first half with only nine players; the referee mercifully stops the game with five minutes left to play.

March 18, 1890 — Blue and White are formally adopted as the college colors at a meeting of the Athletic Association.

November 7, 1891 — Penn State plays its biggest game since 1887 against Bucknell for the lead in the Pennsylvania Intercollegiate Foot-Ball Association and loses a mistake-prone game, 12-10.

January 9, 1892 — Penn State is awarded the first championship of the Pennsylvania Intercollegiate Foot-Ball Association after finishing with a 4-1 league record, edging out "bitter rival" Bucknell (3-1-1).

January 1892 — George "The General" Hoskins is hired as the first "official" head football coach and first director of physical training for the Athletic Association.

Spring 1892 — Football players participate in the first spring practice as George Hoskins stresses physical conditioning and teamwork.

November 6, 1893 — Beaver Field (later to be known as Old Beaver Field) is dedicated with General James Beaver and his wife present, as Penn State plays its first game against Pitt, then known as Western University of Pennsylvania, and wins easily, 32-0. Funding of $15,000 from the State Legislature helps in the construction of a field, including 500-seat grandstand.

October 13, 1894 — Charlie Atherton sets four all-time records that still stand in the opening game, a 60-0 win against Gettysburg. Atherton kicks 10-of-10 extra point attempts to set the game extra points record for accuracy, points and attempts, and also adds three touchdowns for the most points in a game by a senior (32).

November 10, 1894 — Bill Suter establishes a Penn State record that has never been broken for the longest touchdown run from scrimmage with a 90-yard dash around right end for the only Penn State touchdown in a 6-6 tie with Navy in Annapolis.

November 24, 1894 — Charlie Atherton kicks one of the first placements from scrimmage in the history of college football; his 25-yard boot in a 9-6 win over Oberlin is ignored by historians.

November 29, 1894 — Penn State finishes its first unbeaten season with a 14-0 win over the Pittsburgh Athletic Club and a final 6-0-1 record.

Summer 1896 — George Hoskins resigns as "head coach" to become coach at Pitt and Dr. Sam Newton is hired as his replacement.

September 1897 — "Henny" Scholl introduces the first helmet to Penn State football during fall practice. The helmet is really a derby hat with the brim cut off and rags stuffed inside for padding. It gets little usage. The Athletic Association sets a mandatory student fee of $2.00 to support athletic programs, including football.

October 30, 1897 — The "Hidden Ball Trick" is used for the first time in intercollegiate football by Cornell against Penn State in a game at Ithaca. Cornell wins, 45-0.

Summer 1898 — Dr. Sam Newton resigns as "head coach" to coach at Lafayette and Sam Boyle is hired as his replacement as coach and trainer. Fall 1898 — The school's loosely organized drum and bugle corps expands to create a full-sized Cadet Band, which later changes its name to the Blue Band.

December 1898 — Junior guard "Brute" Randolph becomes the first Penn State player named to the All-America team, when selected by Walter Camp for the 1898 third team.

Spring-Fall 1899 — Sam Boyle of the University of Pennsylvania is hired as "head coach" but leaves at the end of the season.

October 7, 1899 — Star quarterback Earl Hewitt runs back a punt 65 yards for the only touchdown, then makes a game-saving tackle on the Penn State six-yard line late in the game as Penn State upsets Army, 6-0, in the first meeting of the two teams at West Point. Penn State will not beat Army again for 60 years.

Winter 1900 — William "Pop" Golden is hired as head coach and director of physical training for the Athletic Association. October 1903 — Pop Golden is chosen as the school's first unofficial athletic director and gives up the position of head coach of the football team.

Dan Reed of Cornell is hired as head coach for the last month of the season and decides not to return in 1904.

October 24, 1903 — In the first game at Pitt, Carl Forkum scores 39 points on 5 TDs and 9-of-10 PATs and Irish McIlveen scores two touchdowns — one on a 56-yard run — as Penn State clobbers Pitt, 59-0, in what would be the biggest margin of victory in the series for 65 years.

Winter 1904 — Tom Fennell, Cornell star of the 1890s, is hired as the first full-time head coach.

October 1, 1904 — Carl Forkum sets the all-time kickoff return record with a 115-yard run back for a touchdown in a 50-0 win over Allegheny, but his feat is never listed in the Penn State record books.

November 3, 1905 — Penn State sets a team scoring record with a 73-0 win over Geneva at Beaver Field as nine players score touchdowns.

October 6, 1906 — Penn State wins one of its biggest games ever with a 4-0 victory over the Carlisle Indians before 4,000 fans at Williamsport as freshman "Bull" McCleary kicks a 35-yard field goal for the game's only points.

October 20, 1906 — Ed Cyphers runs the "wrong-way" after recovering a blocked kick during the big game with Yale in New Haven and his "bad luck" error helps lose the game, 10-0. It will be the only defeat of the season.

November 29, 1906 — The first of Penn State's outstanding teams finishes the season with an 8-1-1 record after beating Pitt, 6-0, on Thanksgiving Day in Pittsburgh on a touchdown in the last 30 seconds. The team sets a record of nine shutouts that remains the all-time best for the Nittany Lions.

December 1906 — Center William "Mother" Dunn becomes Penn State's initial first-team All-American when selected by Walter Camp. March 17, 1907 — Senior H.D. "Joe" Mason advocates adopting a Lion as the college mascot in an article in the humor magazine Lemon. Mason says the idea evolved when he was a freshman baseball player during a 1904 game with the Princeton Tigers, and that he answered taunts by Princeton players that the "king of the beasts" — Lions — roamed the Nittany Valley until becoming extinct from hunting by Indians and settlers. Penn State beat Princeton in baseball that day in 1904, 9-1. Students later vote to adopt a mountain Lion as the mascot and, thus, Penn State becomes the first college to use Lion as its symbol.

October 26, 1907 — Penn State sets a team scoring record with a 75-0 win over Lebanon Valley at Beaver Field. Sophomore "Bull" McCleary scores five touchdowns in the game, setting a season scoring record of 13 touchdowns (which remained the record until broken by Charlie Pittman in 1968).

November 28, 1907 — Penn State's former football captains and managers meet in Pittsburgh on Thanksgiving evening to form an organization that becomes the forerunner of today's Varsity Letterman's Club.

September 19, 1908 — Penn State loses its first and only game on Old Beaver Field in a shocking 6-5 upset by Bellefonte Academy.

November 7, 1908 — A record crowd of several thousand (exact figure unknown) turns out as Penn State plays the final game on Old Beaver Field, beating Bucknell, 33-6. The victory is the 48th against only one defeat on the playing field.

Spring-Summer 1909 — Tom Fennell resigns as head coach and Bill Hollenback, All American fullback and captain of the 1908 University of Pennsylvania team, is hired as his replacement with the title of "advisory coach." Former Penn State player and then current baseball coach, "Irish" McIlveen, is given the title of "head coach."

September 1909 — Penn State's first great recruiting class enters school and starts football practice. The recruits include two future members of the College Football Hall of Fame — Pete Mauthe and Dex Very.

October 2, 1909 — Two major milestones in Penn State football history take place as Penn State records its 100th all-time victory and the first game is played at New Beaver Field. A crowd of 500 sees Penn State beat Grove City, 31-0, with Captain Larry Vorhis, the quarterback, scoring the first touchdown and kicking a field goal.

October 9, 1909 — Penn State gives up the lead on a two-point safety in the last minute to allow Pop Warner's Carlisle Indians to gain 8-8 tie before 10,000 at the neutral site of Wilkes-Barre. A major brawl breaks out after game when Penn State and Carlisle players fight over which team gets the "victory" ball.

October 23, 1909 — After 15 consecutive defeats since the series began in 1890, Penn State ties Penn, 3-3, at Franklin Field. The Nittany Lions go on to finish the year at 5-0-2 for their second undefeated season in history.

Summer 1910 — Bill Hollenback resigns to accept a one-year position as head coach at Missouri. Hollenback's older brother, Jack, takes over as "advisory coach" and McIlveen continues as "head coach."

November 12, 1910 — An admission fee is charged at a home game for the first time as Penn State beats Bucknell, 45-3.

Summer 1911 — Bill Hollenback returns from Missouri to again become coach, still with the title of "advisory coach."

Former star running back and 1908 captain "Bull" McCleary is named "head coach."

October 14, 1911 — Penn State pulls off a major upset over Cornell, 5-0, in Ithaca, touching off a riot back in State College that has been called the worst in history following a football game. Students and townspeople fight with fists, clubs and shovels throughout the streets and alleys of the borough after which school officials apologized.

October 28, 1911 — Penn State beats Pennsylvania for the first time, 22-6, as "Shorty" Miller shocks the crowd of 15,000 at Franklin Field by running back the opening kickoff 95 yards for a touchdown.

December 12, 1911 — New eligibility rules are adopted by the Athletic Association requiring athletes to finish their education in four years and eliminating rules that allowed athletes to take less credit hours than the minimum requirements for a freshmen.

Spring 1912 — Pop Golden resigns as unofficial athletic director to enter private business.

Summer 1912 — Bill Hollenback is formally given the title "head coach."

October 12, 1912 — The largest crowd at New Beaver Field since its opening in 1909 — 4,000 fans — watches as Penn State beats Washington & Jefferson, 30-0. Pete Mauthe kicks three field goals to set the record for most field goals in a game.

November 16, 1912 — Penn State "upsets" Ohio State at Columbus in the first game between the two teams by the unofficial score of 37-0. The Buckeyes walk off the field with nine minutes left to play claiming "unnecessary roughness" and the score is officially recorded as a 1-0 forfeit.

November 28, 1912 — Penn State's greatest team to date beats Pitt, 38-0, on Thanksgiving Day at Forbes Field to finish with an 8-0 record, outscoring opponents 256-6 and ending a two-year run of 16-0-1. Pete Mauthe sets the record for the longest field goal with a 51-yard boot. The kick remains the record until broken by Chris Bahr in 1975. Mauthe scores a total of 20 points, with two touchdowns and five extra points. Mauthe also sets an individual season scoring record of 119 points that is not broken until 1971, with 11 touchdowns, 8 field goals and 29 PATs.

February 5, 1913 — A rule is adopted by the Athletic Association requiring athletes to "be in good standing for a four-year collegiate course." This tightened eligibility requirement eliminated the so-called "tramp athlete" who would be on a campus for only one year to play a specific sport while taking a few courses and then move on to another college.

Fall 1913 — A new fight song called "Victory" ("Fight, Fight, Fight, For the Blue and White") is introduced by its author, undergraduate Jimmy Leydon, and sung at all football games.

October 4, 1913 — "Shorty" Miller sets the game rushing record that lasts 68 years with 250 yards, including five touchdowns on runs of 23, 55, 47, 37 and 40 yards as Penn State beats Carnegie Tech, 49-0, at Beaver Field in the 1913 season-opener.

November 8, 1913 — Penn State loses its first game at New Beaver Field before a record crowd of "several thousand" in its first ever major intersectional game and first game against Notre Dame. The Fighting Irish win, 14-7, in a game that ends with a controversial referee decision nullifying a Penn State touchdown. Knute Rockne catches a touchdown pass from Gus Dorais for Notre Dame that helps end Penn State's 20-game home unbeaten streak.

October 25, 1914 — Penn State stops Harvard's 22-game winning streak with a 13-13 tie at Cambridge, as Harvard, considered the best team in the country, rallies on a trick-play touchdown in the last minutes of the game. A celebration on campus two days later causes injuries and major damage to school buildings as a bonfire explodes.

November 13, 1914 — A record crowd of 10,000, including Governor John K. Tener, watch on Pennsylvania Day as Penn State loses its second major intersectional game at Beaver Field in its first game with Michigan State, 6-3.

December 1914 — Bill Hollenback resigns as head coach to enter private business in Philadelphia. January 2, 1915 — Assistant coach Dick Harlow becomes the first former Penn State player to be named an official head coach of the football team.

December 1, 1915 — Sophomore end Bob Higgins becomes the first Penn State underclassman to earn first-team All-American honors when picked by International News Service.

November 4, 1916 — Penn State breaks a nine-year old scoring record with a 79-0 rout over Geneva at Beaver Field.

October 6, 1917 — Junior Harry Robb sets a record — that has never been broken — for most touchdowns in a game with six in an 80-0 rout of Gettysburg at Beaver Field, as the team again shatters the game scoring record.

October 13, 1917 — Penn State breaks its one-week old team scoring record with a 99-0 win over St. Bonaventure at Beaver Field. Nine players score touchdowns, including three by Harry Robb. November 17, 1917 — Harry Robb ties "Bull" McCleary's season record for touchdowns with 13 by scoring three TDs as Penn State plays Maryland for first time and wins, 57-0, at Beaver Field.

July 1918 — Dick Harlow asks out of his contract as head coach to enter military service. He says he will return.

July 18, 1918 — Lt. Levi Lamb, a star lineman on the teams of 1912-14, is killed near Soissons, France, while leading his army platoon against a German stronghold. He is one of two former players to die in World War I as 1912 teammate Red Bebout is killed on a French battlefield on Sept. 29, 1918.

August 25, 1918 — Hugo Bezdek, manager of the Pittsburgh Pirates Baseball Club, is hired as head football coach and director of physical education with supervision over intercollegiate sports.

November 27, 1918 — Penn State completes an unusual season because of World War I by losing, 28-6, at Pitt and finishing with a 1-2-1 record.

Fall 1919 — Dick Harlow returns to Penn State to serve as assistant coach to Hugo Bezdek.

October 4, 1919 — A new tune — "The Nittany Lion" — is introduced at the opening game against Gettysburg at Beaver Field. The first words, "Hail to the Lion, Loyal and True," written by Jimmy Leyden, will become familiar to generations of Penn State fans.

November 27, 1919 — End Bob Higgins takes a flat-pass near his own goal line from Bill Hess on a fake punt and officially runs 92 yards for a touchdown for the longest pass play in Penn State history (historians say it should have been recorded as 95 yards). The surprise play helps Penn State down Pitt, 20-0, to finish with its best season since 1912, but Penn State will not beat Pitt again for 20 years.

September 25, 1920 — New wood grandstands are added to Beaver Field's East side, raising the seating capacity to 5,500, but only 2,500 show up for the season-opening 27-7 victory over Muhlenberg. October 9, 1920 — On the first alumni

"Home-Coming" day, a record standing-room crowd of 12,000 turns out to see Penn State beat Dartmouth, 14-7.

October 16, 1920 — In only the third major intersectional game at Beaver Field, and the first since 1914, Penn State clobbers North Carolina State, 41-0.

October 23, 1920 — Penn State sets the all-time team scoring record with 109-7 win over Lebanon Valley at Beaver Field, coming back from a 7-0 first-quarter deficit. Charlie Way scores three touchdowns in the first quarter to lead the rout.

November 6, 1920 — Penn State wins its fourth major intersectional game at Beaver Field in its first game against Nebraska, 20-0, on Pennsylvania Day. Glenn Killinger and Charlie Way combine to lead the victory as each scores a touchdown and Killinger passes for another.

September 24, 1921 — New Beaver Field opens its first press box, located atop the West stands. The press box is used for the first time in a 53-0 season-opening win over Lebanon Valley.

October 22, 1921 — Penn State gives up a touchdown in the fourth-quarter darkness at Cambridge as heavily favored Harvard manages to come back for a 21-21 tie in a game many sportswriters at the time called "one of the greatest football games ever."

October 29, 1921 — In the first Penn State game played in New York City, Penn State easily beats national power Georgia Tech, 28-7, at the Polo Grounds as Glenn Killinger's 85- yard kickoff return for a touchdown breaks open the game and helps make him a first-team All American.

December 3, 1921 — Penn State plays its first game on the West Coast, beating Washington, 21-7, before 35,000 in Seattle to complete an 8-0-2 season and its 24th straight game without a defeat.

Spring 1922 — Dick Harlow quits as assistant coach after a final dispute with Hugo Bezdek and becomes head coach at Colgate.

September 23, 1922 — The New Beaver Field seating capacity is increased to 12,000 as the 1922 season opens with a 54-0 victory over St. Bonaventure. October 27, 1922 — Ten surviving members of the first official team in 1887 are honored in New York City by the Alumni Association as the "founders" of Penn State football.

October 28, 1922 — The Nittany Lion mascot makes its first appearance on the field dressed in an African Lion uniform during Penn State's first game against Syracuse played at New York's Polo Grounds. Dick Hoffman, Class of '23, dresses in the uniform of a maned African Lion that he had worn while appearing in the Penn State Players' production of George Bernard Shaw's "Androcles and the Lion." Penn State and Syracuse battle to a 0-0 tie before a crowd of 25,000.

November 3, 1922 — Navy uses a fake punt and fumble recovery to end Penn State's 30- game unbeaten streak, 14-0, before 35,000 spectators at Washington's American League Park. Dozens of congressional, government and foreign leaders and many of college football's leading coaches, players and sportswriters are in attendance.

January 1, 1923 — Penn State plays in its first bowl game, the 1923 Rose Bowl at Pasadena, and loses to Southern California, 14-7, but receives $21,350 for participating in the game. It is the first Rose Bowl played at its present site in Pasadena's Arroyo Seco area and the first appearance in the game by Southern California. The contest is the first radio broadcast of a Penn State game and any post-season game by Los Angeles radio station KHJ.

September 29, 1923 — Additional wooden bleachers are constructed at New Beaver Field, raising the seating capacity to 13,500. Only 3,000 turn out to see Penn State beat Lebanon Valley, 58-0, in the season-opener.

October 20, 1923 — A new Beaver Field attendance record of 20,000 was set as Penn State upset unbeaten Navy, 21-3, in the Homecoming game. "Light Horse" Harry Wilson has his greatest game, rushing for 123 yards and scoring all three Penn State touchdowns with a 55-yard interception return, a 95-yard kickoff return and a 72-yard run off a fake reverse.

Spring 1924 — Bas Gray becomes the first junior elected team captain.

September 15, 1924 — The football team moved into new Varsity Hall, across the street from New Beaver Field. Varsity Hall includes dormitory rooms, a training table and football locker room. The building name is later changed to Irvin Hall after athletes move out and now is an undergraduate residence hall.

October 25, 1924 — Penn State's 29-game winning streak at New Beaver Field comes to an end as Syracuse wins the Homecoming game, 10-6. The streak began after a loss to Rutgers during World War I in 1918.

November 7, 1925 — Penn State surprises Notre Dame by tying the Irish, 0-0, in driving rain and mud on Homecoming Day at New Beaver Field before a record breaking crowd reported as 25,000 by several newspapers. But official attendance is listed at 20,000.

November 14, 1925 — Penn State visits West Virginia for the first time to participate in dedication ceremonies for West Virginia's new Mountaineer Stadium, and loses, 14-0.

November 26, 1925 — The annual Thanksgiving Day game with Pittsburgh is played for the first time at new Pitt Stadium and Penn State loses, 23-7.

January 14, 1926 — The Penn State administration appoints an alumni committee to study football policies in the wake of allegations by the Carnegie Foundation and others that Penn State over-emphasizes sport to the detriment of educational goals of higher education.

October 9, 1926 — Penn State wins its 200th game by beating Marietta, 48-6, at New Beaver Field. Cy Lungren runs back a kickoff 95 yards for a touchdown to spark the win.

October 16, 1926 — Penn State loses its 100th football game as Notre Dame wins, 28-0, in the Nittany Lions' first visit to South Bend, Ind.

December 25, 1926 — Dr. Ralph Hetzel becomes the 10th president of Penn State and calls for stronger supervision of the athletic programs, especially football, by the administration.

February 26, 1927 — A blue ribbon committee known as the Beaver White Committee issues its final report recommending the elimination of all athletic scholarships and the creation of two separate bodies to supervise Penn State's athletic programs for athletes and students: the Board of Athletic Control and the Department of Physical Education.

August 10, 1927 — The newly organized Board of Athletic Control ends all financial aid to athletes beginning with 1928 incoming freshmen and recommends that Penn State athletic officials "not scout opponents' games regardless of scouting policies of opponents."

October 1, 1927 — The first radio broadcast of a Penn State football game is carried over the college station, WPSC. Assistant coach Larry Conover describes the action in a 34-13 win over Gettysburg. Conover goes on to broadcast four more games from Beaver Field in the 1927 season.

October 22, 1927 — Penn State beats Syracuse for the first time, after four defeats and a tie, as Captain Johnny Roepke shakes off an injury and sparks the team to victory by kicking a 21-yard field goal and making a game-saving tackle on the ensuing kickoff in a 9-6 victory at Archbold Stadium.

November 24, 1927 — The first away game is broadcast over radio by KDKA in Pittsburgh as undefeated Pitt scores the most points against Penn State in 11 years to win 30-0 at Pitt Stadium.

September 29, 1928 — The first radio broadcast of a Penn State game by students is done over the college station, WPSC. Sophomore Ken Holderman (later a university vice president and trustee) does play-by-play in a 25-0 victory over Lebanon Valley.

January 19, 1929 — A new athletic building, soon to be known as Recreation Hall, is used for the first time for "winter" football practice. The $600,000 building is dedicated on March 23, 1929 during the weekend of the Intercollegiate Boxing Championships.

October 26, 1929 — Cooper French and Frank Diedrich team for one of the greatest punt returns in history in an impromptu razzle-dazzle 60-yard lateral-and-run for a touchdown on the last play of the game to defeat Lafayette, 6-3, before a disbelieving but cheering Homecoming crowd of 10,000 at Beaver Field.

October 29, 1929 — The Carnegie Foundation releases a 383-page report on the Advancement of Teaching condemning Penn State and other colleges for dishonesty in over-emphasizing football and other intercollegiate sports by giving athletic scholarships and urged a return to amateurism. Carnegie later issues an addendum declaring Penn State had changed policies two years previously, but the addendum is virtually ignored by the public and press and Penn State's educational image is damaged. (The stock market crashes this same day, precipitating a nationwide depression.)

January 20, 1930 — Hugo Bezdek is relieved of his football head coaching duties and named the first director of the new School of Physical Education. March 27, 1930 — Former two-time All-American Bob Higgins is promoted from assistant coach to head coach of the football team.

October 31, 1931 — Pitt coach Jock Sutherland rests his first team and plays the scrubs the entire game as the Panthers clobber the Nittany Lions, 41-6, scoring the most points since the series began, then insults the Beaver Field Homecoming crowd by working out his first team for 15 minutes after game. Fans did not know that Sutherland had received Bob Higgins' approval before the game for the workout. This was Pitt's first visit to Penn State since 1902, and the teams did not play again until 1935.

November 28, 1931 — Penn State ends a seven-game losing streak, which remains the school record, by beating Lehigh, 31-0, in a post-season game for charity at Philadelphia's Franklin Field and ends the season with its worst record in history, 2-8.

October 14, 1933 — Penn State football hits a low point when Muhlenberg wins in a major upset, 3-0, at Beaver Field. The team goes on to a 3-3-1 record.

October 20, 1934 — Penn State wins its first regular-season road game in five years and the first away game in the Higgins era with 31-0 win over Lehigh in Bethlehem.

September 1, 1936 — Penn State opens preseason practice with its first all-alumni coaching staff: Bob Higgins ('20), head coach; Joe Bedenk ('24), Earle Edwards ('31) and Al

Michaels (Mikelonis) ('35), varsity assistants; and Marty McAndrews ('30), freshmen coach.

October 1, 1936 — Former head coach Hugo Bezdek agrees to a one-year leave of absence with pay from the position of director of Physical Education School, and resigns one year later.

October 6, 1936 — Four surviving members of the 1881 "forgotten pioneers" team are officially recognized as playing in Penn State's first intercollegiate football game and given Varsity "S" letters.

Fall 1937 — Dr. Carl P. Schott is hired as the director of Physical Education and de facto Dean of Athletics.

October 2, 1937 — The first game is filmed on request by the coaches to help the team during practice. Penn State beats Gettysburg, 32-6, at Beaver Field, but the film shot by student cameramen turns out too dark and Bob Higgins hires zoology instructor and part-time track coach Ray Conger to take charge of filming. Conger remains in the position for 39 years.

November 13, 1937 — Penn State clinches its first winning season since 1929 and the first in Bob Higgins' coaching regime by beating Maryland in the last minute at Beaver Field, 21-14, but loses the next week to National Champion Pitt and finishes with a 5-3 record. There is suspicion from this scribe that Penn State was playing with both hands tied as other schools paid athletes with scholarships to matriculate at their universities.

September 26, 1938 — Ridge Riley writes and publishes first "Football Newsletter" with a preseason analysis of the 1938 season.

October 1, 1938 — The first Penn State radio network is set up and starts broadcasting with an opening game against

Maryland at Beaver Field. KDKA Pittsburgh originates a broadcast with Bill Sutherland on play-by-play and Jack Barry doing color commentary as Penn State wins, 38-0.

October 29, 1938 — Two players each get 100 yards in one game for the first time as sophomore Chuck Peters (156 yards) and junior Steve Rollins (122 yards) help lead Penn State to 33-6 win over Syracuse at Beaver Field. November 20, 1938 — Penn State loses, 26-0, at Pitt to finish with 3-4-1 record that will be the last losing season for 49 years. Despite the record, the team sets three NCAA defensive records, including one for fewest yards passing allowed per game (13.1 yards average) that still stands.

November 25, 1939 — Future All-American Leon Gajecki leads Penn State to its first victory over Pitt in 20 years in a 10-0 upset before a record-tying crowd of 20,000 at Beaver Field and Penn State finishes the year with its best record since 1921 at 5-1-2.

November 9, 1940 — Juniors Bill Smaltz and Lenny Krouse team for the greatest passing day to date as Smaltz completes 14-of-21 passes (including 12 in succession that remained a record until 1994) for 193 yards and two touchdowns and Krouse catches 10 for two touchdowns and 155 yards (yardage is still the most in game by a junior).

November 16, 1940 — Chuck Peters sets the all-time kickoff return record with a 101-yard touchdown return on the opening kickoff of a 25-0 win over NYU. It's his second touchdown run back of the season (96 yards against Temple to open the second half) and sets the season record for kickoff touchdown returns that is now shared by Curt Warner (1980).

November 23, 1940 — Penn State loses its first and only game of the season and a chance for a bowl game when upset by Pitt, 20-7, at Pitt Stadium.

September 1941 — Dave Alston and his brother, Harry, of Midland, Pa., become the first African-American players on the football team. Dave becomes the star of the unbeaten freshman team and is selected by some preseason magazines as college football's "sophomore of the year."

September 1941 — The State College Quarterback Club organizes and meets for the first time to sponsor Wednesday luncheons with head football coach Bob Higgins, players and other assistant coaches.

September 10, 1941 — The Athletic Board authorizes freshmen to play on varsity teams for the duration of World War II

October 31, 1941 — Penn State plays its first night game, at New York's Polo Grounds, against New York University and wins, 42-0, in heavy rain on a sloppy field.

November 12, 1941 — Led by Dave and Harry Alston, Steve Suhey and Red Moore, the freshmen team goes unbeaten for the first time since 1916 with a 5-0 record. Dave Alston scores eight touchdowns, passes for four others and drop-kicks six extra points in one of the school's outstanding individual freshman performances ever.

August 15, 1942 — Freshman star Dave Alston, Penn State's first African-American player, dies in Bellefonte Hospital after a tonsillectomy operation, but his death is traced to injuries suffered in a spring practice scrimmage against Navy. (Brother Harry is so shaken he never returns to school.)

September 1, 1942 — The first radio network, organized by KDKA, dissolves because of World War II. A major gasoline sponsor can't get enough gas to sell.

October 24, 1942 — The Nittany Lion Shrine, created by famed sculptor Heinz Warneke, near the entrance of Beaver Field is dedicated during halftime of a 13-10 Homecoming win over Colgate. H.D. "Joe" Mason, Class of 1907, who instigated the move for a Lion as the mascot, is among the crowd of 11,510.

November 14, 1942 — In one of the biggest upsets of the Higgins era, Penn State shocks Penn, 13-7, before 50,000 at Franklin Field behind the punting of Joe Colone and the running and defensive play of Larry Joe, who is carried off the field at the end of the game.

November 30, 1942 — Penn State is ranked for the first time by the Associated Press at the end of the season, tying at No. 19 with defending National Champion Minnesota and Holy Cross, as a team dominated by sophomores and freshmen surprises the nation with a 6-1-1 record.

November 13, 1943 — Snow forces some officials to be late for the Temple game at Beaver Field as Doggie Alexander, owner of the Rathskeller Tvern, comes out of the grandstand to be the field judge and Philadelphia Inquirer sportswriter Stan Baumgartner leaves the press box to serve as the head linesman. Only one 15-yard penalty is called in Penn State's 13-0 victory.

October 21, 1944 — Larry Cooney, 16, of Pittsburgh becomes the youngest player ever to start a Penn State football game. He opens at right halfback against Colgate in the fourth game of season, when frosh were eligible because of World War II, and carries the ball five times for eight yards. Johnny Chuckran becomes the only freshman ever to serve as captain for a season, and runs back a punt 50 yards in the last minute to spark 6-0 upset win over Colgate in Hamilton, N.Y.

October 28, 1944 — For the first time in history, an all-freshmen starting lineup takes the field and loses a thriller to West Virginia, 28-27, at Beaver Field in the first defeat at home since 1938.

November 17, 1945 — Freshman Wally Triplett becomes the first African-American player to start a Penn State game when he takes the field at right halfback (the tailback position in the single-wing formation) against Michigan State at East Lansing, Mich. The Nittany Lions lose, 33-0, but Triplett is praised for his all-around play.

Summer 1946 — Jim O'Hora, a center at Penn State from 1933-35, and Earl Bruce, the high school coach from Brownsville, Pa., join Bob Higgins' coaching staff, O'Hora as assistant line coach and Bruce as freshmen coach based at California (Pa.) State Teachers College.

Summer 1946 — Casey Jones and other Pittsburgh area alumni raise $19,000 to buy an old fraternity house off campus to house football players. New assistant coach Jim O'Hora agrees to be "counselor" of the new facility and he and his family move in. All freshmen players are assigned to the campus of California State Teachers College, where they will train under the direction of Bruce.

November 9, 1946 — Penn State cancels the final game of season, set for Nov. 29, when University of Miami (Fla.) officials request that Penn State not bring its two African-American players, Wally Triplett and Dennie Hoggard, on the trip. Guard Steve Suhey earned first-team All-America honors in 1947 and was a member of arguably the most prominent family in Penn State football history. Suhey married a daughter, Ginger, of Penn State All American and future head coach, Bob Higgins, and three of their sons — Paul, Larry and Matt Suhey — played for Penn State in the 1970s. Kevin and Joe Suhey became fourth-generation members of the Higgins-Suhey family to play for the Nittany Lions during the 2000s.

November 16, 1946 — A U.S. President makes his first known attendance at a Penn State game as Harry Truman gives Navy a pep talk before the game and at halftime in Annapolis. Penn State upsets the heavily favored Middies,

12-7, as Elwood Petchel runs back a pass interception for one touchdown and scores another on a one-yard run.

October 18, 1947 — Penn State sets an NCAA defensive record for fewest total yards allowed in a game by holding Syracuse to a minus-47 yards in a 40-0 Homecoming victory at Beaver Field.

October 25, 1947 — In what was the key game of the 1947 season, Penn State comes from behind to beat undefeated West Virginia, 21-14, before the largest Beaver Field crowd (20,313) since the 1925 Notre Dame game and stays on track for its first bowl game in 25 years.

November 15, 1947 — Penn State wins its 300th game with a 20-7 conquest of Navy at Baltimore's Memorial Stadium. Fullback Jeff Durkota runs 48 and 42 yards for touchdowns on the identical inside-reverse play.

November 22, 1947 — Penn State beats Pitt, 29-0, to become the first Penn State squad in history to win all nine games of a regular-season and sets school records for giving up the least amount of points (27) and the most shutouts (6). The Nittany Lions also set NCAA defensive records for fewest rushing yards allowed per game (17) and per rush (0.64).

December 8, 1947 — Penn State finishes in the Top 10 for the first time when ranked fourth in the final Associated Press poll. The Nittany Lions also are awarded the Lambert Trophy as the best team in the East for the first time since the trophy's inception in 1936.

January 1, 1948 — Tailback Wally Triplett and end Dennie Hoggard become the first African-Americans to play in the Cotton Bowl game. Triplett scores a TD and plays an outstanding defensive game as Penn State and Doak Walker-led SMU battle to a 13-13 tie.

October 23, 1948 — A New Beaver Field attendance record of 24,579 is set during Homecoming as Penn State ties Michigan State, 14-14, in a game marked by controversy over a clipping penalty that nullified a Spartan 100-yard touchdown on an interception return.

November 6, 1948 — Penn State plays before the largest crowd to date — 71,180 — and defeats Penn at Franklin Field, 13-0, sparked by a razzle-dazzle touchdown run-and-pass play of Fran Rogel-to-Chuck Drazenovich-to-Elwood Petchel-to-Rogel.

November 27, 1948 — A Penn State team travels by airplane for the first time to play Washington State at Tacoma and wins the game, 7-0, to finish the season at 7-1-1 and achieve the No. 18 ranking in the Associated Press college football poll.

March 12, 1949 — Bob Higgins announces his resignation as head football coach and longtime assistant coach Joe Bedenk is named as his successor.

Spring 1949 — Earle Edwards resigns from the football coaching staff following spring practice and joins the Michigan State staff as an assistant coach. Joe Bedenk names former Penn State lineman Sever Toretti (1936-38) as line coach and ex-Pitt star Frank Patrick as defensive backfield coach. 1949 — Tuition scholarships for all sports are re-established by the Board of Trustees on the recommendation of the Athletic Board with 100 total scholarships approved.

September 1949 — The first class of scholarship players since 1927 enters Penn State but are sent to California State Teachers College because of crowded housing conditions on the main campus. Among the freshmen are future starters Joe Yukica, Don Barney, Jim Dooley and Joe Gratson.

October 1, 1949 — Penn State plays its 500th game since 1887 and loses, 42-7, to an Army team that would stay unbeaten and be rated No. 4 in the country. This contest also is the first known telecast of a Penn State football game. It is televised on WNBT-TV in New York City.

March 5, 1950 — Joe Bedenk resigns after one year as head football coach, but remains on the staff as an assistant coach.

March 31, 1950 — The Athletic Board sets 30 scholarships exclusively for football to include tuition, room and board.

April 22, 1950 — Charles A. "Rip" Engle, head coach at Brown University, is named head football coach by acting Penn State president James Milholland. May 27, 1950 — Rip Engle names Joe Paterno, his senior quarterback at Brown, to the coaching staff and assigns him to coach the quarterbacks.

October 14, 1950 — Penn State loses for the first time at night after four wins at night dating to 1941, all played in the rain, as Syracuse wins, 27-7, on a clear night away at Syracuse's Archbold Stadium.

November 11, 1950 — The first Band Day is held at Beaver Field, with nine Centre County high school bands participating as Penn State beats West Virginia, 27-0. Band Day was held annually for 25 years, with the final one taking place at the Nov. 16, 1974 game with Ohio University. Band Day was brought back for the Blue-White games from 1984-88.

December 2, 1950 — A major snow storm forces postponement of the final game of the season against Pitt at Pitt Stadium on November 25. The game is moved to Forbes Field one week later, where Penn State wins, 21-20, in what becomes known as "the Snow bowl."

December 1950 — The Athletic Board adds 15 scholarships for football, bringing the total to 45.

September 1, 1951 — The Athletic Board and Eastern Intercollegiate Athletic Conference agree to make freshmen eligible for varsity play because of the Korean War. The authorization only lasts one year before freshmen are banned again.

October 21, 1951 — Another New Beaver Field attendance record —30,321 — is set, again in a Homecoming game, against unbeaten (and eventual No. 2) Michigan State, but this time Penn State loses, 32-21.

July 1952 — Ernest "Ernie" McCoy, basketball coach at Michigan since 1948, takes over as Director of Athletics and Dean of the Physical Education Department.

September 20, 1952 — Former player and Coach Joe Bedenk watches his first game since 1917 as a spectator after stepping down as assistant coach. He sees a 20-13 win over Temple at Beaver Field.

September 27, 1952 — Junior Tony Rados surprises fans and makes national headlines by giving Penn State its greatest passing day in 12 years, completing 17-of-30 passes for 179 yards and one TD (and 2 interceptions), and out-dueling Purdue's All-American passing sensation, Dale Samuels, in leading Penn State to a surprising 20-20 tie at Beaver Field.

November 13, 1952 — Penn State goes over 100,000 in total season home attendance for the first time in history (103,751 in five games) as 15,957 at Beaver Field watch the Lions escape with a 7-6 win over underdog Rutgers.

November 22, 1952 — Penn State upsets Pitt, 17-0, to knock the Panthers from the Orange Bowl before 53,766 at Pitt Stadium. The Nittany Lions' defense, led by Jack Sherry's two interceptions, and Ted Kemmerer's punting throttles the Pitt attack, while Rados' passing sparks the Lions' offense.

October 17, 1953 — Mickey Bergstein, color man and engineer for Penn State's radio network, makes a spectacular debut as play-by-play announcer in a game against Syracuse at Beaver Field, when he takes over in the fourth quarter for regular announcer Bob Prince, who has to leave to broadcast a Steelers-Eagles NFL game in Philadelphia that night. Bergstein describes how the Nittany Lions score two touchdowns in the fourth quarter in a come-from-behind 20-14 win that ends with a full-fledged brawl at the Syracuse bench.

November 7, 1953 — Heavy snow blankets State College in a 24-hour period, forcing a major snow removal at Beaver Field for a game against Fordham. Kickoff is delayed by two hours because of the late arrival of the Penn State team, which was trapped in a Clinton County hunting camp known as "Camp-Hate-To-Leave-It." The Nittany Lions go on to win a 28-21 thriller before some 13,897 hearty fans.

November 13, 1953 — Penn State becomes The Pennsylvania State University and the next day the Nittany Lions play their first game as Penn State and come from behind from a 14-6 second-quarter deficit to whip Rutgers, 54-26, at New Brunswick.

December 1953 — The Levi Lamb Fund, named for the former Penn State star, is established at the suggestion of athletic director Ernie McCoy to assist in obtaining financial aid for athletes and the athletic department.

March 1, 1954 — J.T. White, who played on Michigan's 1948 National Champion team as well as at Ohio State as a center, joins Rip Engle's staff as an assistant coach.

September 25, 1954 — Underdog Penn State stuns preseason Big Ten Conference favorite Illinois, 14-12, in the opening game of the season played at Champaign, shocking the college football world and becoming an overnight front-runner to win the Lambert Trophy.

October 23, 1954 — Jesse Arnelle, Rosey Grier and Lenny Moore become the first African Americans to play college football in Fort Worth, Texas, but the Nittany Lions make too many mistakes and lose to Texas Christian, 20-7.

October 30, 1954 — Penn State plays its first game on national television and beats Penn, 35-13, at Franklin Field, scoring the most points in the long-time series against the Quakers. Lenny Moore rushes for 140 yards and scores three touchdowns.

September 1, 1955 — Penn State begins a year-long celebration of its Centennial Year with Navy scheduled to visit Beaver Field for the first time since 1923. A new dateline of "University Park" is established with the opening of a campus post office.

September 29, 1955 — The first game is televised from Beaver Field as CBS transmits the season-opener with Boston University to a limited region in the East. The Nittany Lions win, 35-0, as an unknown fifth-string sophomore fullback — Joe Sabol — scores two touchdowns to lead the team to victory.

November 5, 1955 — Syracuse's Jim Brown outgains PSU's Lenny Moore, 159 yards to 146, and scores all the Syracuse points on three touchdowns and two extra-point kicks, but Penn State comes back from a 20-7 deficit on the quarterbacking of Milt Plum to win a thrilling 21-20 Band Day contest in one of the greatest games ever played at New Beaver Field before a crowd of 30,321 and a CBS regional TV audience.

September 29, 1956 — The first all-Penn State alumni broadcasting team works its first game for the Nittany Lions football radio network as Mickey Bergstein ('43) moves from color commentary to play-by-play and Bob Wilson ('40) takes over color. Penn State beats Pennsylvania, 34-0, at Franklin Field in Philadelphia.

October 20, 1956 — Penn State stuns heavily-favored Ohio State, 7-6, in Columbus, winning on Milt Plum's extra point kick before the largest crowd to see a Penn State football game up to that time, numbering 82,584.

October 19, 1957 — Pete Mauthe, captain of the undefeated 1912 team, becomes the first Penn State player inducted into the College Football Hall of Fame during halftime ceremonies of the Homecoming game against Vanderbilt. The Nittany Lions squander a 13-point lead and are upset, 32-20.

October 26, 1957 — The third game of the Engle era is televised from Syracuse by CBS on a regional basis as Penn State beats the Orangemen, 21-12, behind the surprise quarterbacking of sophomore Richie Lucas, who was forced to take over for the injured starter, Al Jacks.

December 1957 — Outstanding freshman running back Robert "Red" Worrell, who was a potential varsity starter on the 1958 team, is electrocuted at his family home in Denbo, Pa., while helping his father erect a TV antenna. Athletic officials establish an award in his name to honor the most improved player after spring practice. Lineman Andy Stynchula wins the first award in 1958.

Spring 1958 — Former linebacker Dan Radakovich, one of the standouts in the 7-6 upset over Ohio State in 1956, becomes Penn State's first linebacker coach when hired as an undergraduate assistant. The next year, Radakovich continues coaching linebackers as a graduate assistant.

September 27, 1958 — Penn State ends the longest running series with one of its oldest opponents, Pennsylvania, with a 43-0 victory at Franklin Field. The series, which began in 1890, was never played outside of Philadelphia and finished with Penn State winning 18, losing 25 and tying 4. The team's first ever two-point conversion is scored when Al Jacks passes to end John Bozick after Penn State's second touchdown. Later in the game, Richie Lucas passes to Jim Schwab for a second two-point conversion.

December 19, 1959 — Penn State plays in the first Liberty Bowl and tackle Charlie Janerette becomes the first African-American to play against Alabama as the Nittany Lions beat the Crimson Tide, coached by Paul "Bear" Bryant, 7-0, in Philadelphia's Municipal Stadium.

April 1959 — The Nittany Lion Club is organized by 15 alumni who want to arouse interest in Penn State athletic affairs through contributions to the Levi Lamb Fund. Membership stipulated an annual contribution to the fund of at least $50 or at least $25 for graduates of less than 10 years. Members will receive "special consideration" on game tickets and "preferred parking" at the stadium.

November 7, 1959 — The all-time attendance record is set at New Beaver Field as 34,000 watch a memorable battle of unbeatens play with national rankings and bowl berths at stake. Syracuse edges Penn State, 20-18, despite an electrifying 100-yard kickoff return by sophomore Roger Kochman as the Nittany Lions fail to make an extra point kick and two two-point conversions.

November 14, 1959 — Penn State downs Holy Cross, 46-0, in the last game played at New Beaver Field as 20,000 spectators watch the final quarter in rain and heavy wind. The Nittany Lions end the 229th game played on the site with a record of 184-34-11.

January 2, 1960 — Dan Radakovich is hired as a fulltime assistant coach in charge of linebackers. He eventually will become known as "The Father of Linebacker U."

September 17, 1960 — Penn State opens Beaver Stadium before a less than capacity crowd of 22,559 as the Nittany Lions beat Boston University, 20-0. Lion senior halfback Eddie Caye scored the stadium's initial touchdown at 10:25 of the first quarter.

October 3, 1960 — What later becomes known as "Tailgating" is first suggested in a front-page column by Centre Daily Times Editor Jerry Weinstein after monumental traffic jams developed before and after the Homecoming game against Illinois at Beaver Stadium on Saturday, October 1. Weinstein advocates adoption of the Ivy League tradition of pregame "picnic lunches" and says Penn State fans should add "picnic suppers" for after the game while traffic disperses.

October 8, 1960 — The "hero" defensive back makes its debut in a 27-16 victory over Army at West Point. Senior Sam Sobczak is the first player designated as "Hero."

September 29, 1961 — The Athletic Department experiments with closed-circuit television by televising Penn State's first game ever against Miami (Fla.) from the Orange Bowl Stadium to Rec Hall and Schwab Auditorium on the Penn State campus. However, paid attendance is disappointing with less than 40 percent of the seating capacity filled.

November 4, 1961 — Maryland beats Penn State for the only time in the lengthy series, 21-17, at College Park behind the passing combination of Dick Shiner and Gary Collins.

December 30, 1961 — End Dave Robinson becomes the first African-American to play in the Gator Bowl and makes the defensive "play-of-the-game" with a quarterback sack and fumble recovery that helps the Nittany Lions beat Georgia Tech, 30-15.

Spring 1962 — Penn State joins Pitt, Syracuse and West Virginia in agreeing to forbid "redshirting," a practice that withholds athletes from competition for a year so they can "mature."

October 13, 1962 — Penn State becomes the first team to play three service academies in one season, losing to Army at West Point on this date, 9-6, after beating Navy, 41-7, and Air Force, 20-6, earlier in the season at Beaver Stadium.

October 27, 1962 — Assistant coach Joe Paterno is presented a game ball by the team for the first time since he joined Rip Engle's staff in 1950, when the Nittany Lions overcome the sensational debut of sophomore quarterback Craig Morton and defeat California, 23-21, in Berkeley.

December 1962 — End Dave Robinson becomes the first African-American player in Penn State's football history to be named first-team All-American when selected by the Associated Press, the Football Writers and others.

Summer 1963 — Penn State joins Pitt, Syracuse and West Virginia in a Letter of Intent agreement for incoming freshmen football players, obligating recruits to a specific school for at least one year. The national agreement under consideration also would include the Big Ten, Southwest, Southeastern, Atlantic Coast, Big Eight and Missouri Valley conferences. Lenny Moore was among the greatest players to wear the blue and white. In 1954, he became the first Nittany Lion to rush for more than 1,000 yards in a season, gaining 1,082 with 11 touchdowns. Moore was a dynamic runner, receiver and kick returner, accumulating 3,543 all-purpose yards from 1953-55. Moore was selected by the Baltimore Colts in the first round of the 1956 NFL Draft and had a brilliant 12-year career with the Colts, playing in seven Pro Bowls and gaining induction into the Pro Football Hall of Fame in 1975. 170

Summer 1964 — Joe Paterno is named associate coach and heir-apparent to succeed Rip Engle as head coach when Engle retires.

November 7, 1964 — Penn State, with a 3-4 record, shocks unbeaten No. 2 Ohio State, 27-0, in what the Associated Press calls the "college upset of the year." The Nittany Lions' defense limits the Buckeyes to 60 net yards, while the Lions' offense totals 341 yards.

November 24, 1964 — In a closed door meeting without coaches, players vote down the opportunity to play in the Gator Bowl after overcoming a 0-3 start and ending a 6-4 season with stunning shutout victories over Ohio State and Pitt and winning the Lambert Trophy. This will mark the last time that players are given the opportunity to vote on bowl games.

Fall 1965 — College football is changed forever with a rule change implementing unlimited substitution for the first time in the modern era.

December 4, 1965 — Rip Engle coaches his last game as Penn State beats Maryland, 19-7, at Byrd Stadium, in a game televised nationally by NBC, to finish a 5-5 season and wind up 16 years at Penn State with a 104-48-4 record and no losing seasons.

February 18, 1966 — Rip Engle officially announces his retirement as head coach, about one month from his 60th birthday (March 26).

February 19, 1966 — Associate head coach Joseph V. Paterno, 38, is named head football coach by University President Eric Walker and Director of Athletics and Dean of the Physical Education Department Ernest McCoy at an annual salary of $20,000.

September 17, 1966 — Joe Paterno wins his first game, 15-7, in the season-opener against Maryland at Beaver Stadium as sophomore middle guard Mike Reid sets a team record by scoring three safeties before a crowd of 40,911. The team presents Paterno with the game ball for only the second time in his coaching career.

September 24, 1966 — Joe Paterno suffers his first loss as then No. 1 Michigan State, led by All-Americans Bubba Smith and George Webster, whip the Nittany Lions, 42-8, before 65,763 at East Lansing.

September 29, 1967 — In what becomes the "turning point" game of Joe Paterno's career, he replaces several defensive veterans with untested sophomores, including future All American Dennis Onkotz, and tackle Steve Smear and Penn State beats Miami (Fla.), 17-8, in Orange Bowl Stadium behind the running of Bobby Campbell and pass receiving of another future All-American, Ted Kwalick. Among the 39,516 spectators on hand that night are 150 members of Penn State's first Alumni Holiday Tour.

October 7, 1967 — A new policy requires students to buy tickets (at $4 each) for home games as the University eliminates pre-paid activity fees for football. Several thousand students are among the 46,007 in attendance to watch Penn State lose, 17-15, to No. 3 UCLA. The loss is the Nittany Lions' last over the next 31 games, stretching into the 1970 season.

November 11, 1967 — A Paterno-coached team gains national recognition for the first time with a 13-8 upset over then # 3 North Carolina State after a fourth-down goal line stand in the last minute preserves the win at Beaver Stadium.

November-December 1967 — Junior tight end Ted Kwalick becomes the first first-team All American coached by Joe Paterno when named by the Newspaper Enterprise Association and the Football Coaches. Kwalick also is the first junior to win the honor and the first underclassman selected since Bob Higgins in 1915.

December 30, 1967 — Joe Paterno gains nationwide attention in the Gator Bowl by gambling for a first down on his own 15-yard line with a 17-0 third-quarter lead. When the gamble fails, Florida State rallies for a 17-17 tie in front of a record crowd of 68,019.

December 7, 1968 — The first Joe Paterno team to have a regular-season game televised nationally beats Syracuse, 30-12, at Beaver Stadium to become the first Penn State squad to be unbeaten in the regular-season since 1947 and the first one to win 10 games.

January 1, 1969 — With Chuck Burkhardt as QB, Joe Paterno's Penn State Nittany Lions completed a perfect 11-0 season and beats Kansas, 15-14, in a thrilling Orange Bowl game after the Jayhawks are penalized for having 12 men on the field. Though undefeated and untied, the team makes its highest ever finish in the final Associated Press poll after bowl games at No. 2 behind Ohio State, which beats previous No. 1 Southern California and Heisman Trophy winner O.J. Simpson in the Rose Bowl. July 1, 1969 — Ed Czekaj, placekicker and end on the undefeated 1947 team, becomes Athletic Director, succeeding the retiring Ernie McCoy.

September 27, 1969 — Some 2,000 seats and an enlarged press box are constructed at Beaver Stadium before a record crowd of 51,402 turns out to see Penn State beat Colorado, 27-3. Paul Johnson returns a kickoff 91 yards for a touchdown. Glenn

November 29, 1969 — Penn State completes a second straight unbeaten regular-season with its 21st straight win by beating North Carolina State, 33-8, in Raleigh as part of the second half of a ABC national television doubleheader following the Army-Navy game. All American Charlie Pittman scores two touchdowns to stretch his career touchdown record to 31, and break Pete Mauthe's 67-year-old career scoring record with 186 points.

December 31, 1969 — Earl Bruce, long-time assistant coach, retires. January 1, 1970 — Penn State's defense, led by Outland and Maxwell Trophy winner Mike Reid, sets an Orange Bowl record with seven intercepted passes as Penn State beats Missouri, 10-3, for its second consecutive 11-0 season, tying a 30-game school unbeaten streak set by teams from 1919-22, but again finishes No. 2 in the Associated Press (and UPI) poll to Texas, which beat Notre Dame in the Cotton Bowl.

September 19, 1970 — Penn State sets a record for consecutive games won (23) and unbeaten games in a row (31) with a 55-7 pasting of Navy in the season-opener at Beaver Stadium. Senior Mike Cooper of Harrisburg becomes the first African-American to start at quarterback for Penn State and throws for two touchdowns. The new six-station television network telecasts the first of five home games on a delayed basis at 11 p.m. The games are aired in Philadelphia, Altoona, Harrisburg, Scranton, Lancaster and York. Governor Ray Shafer helps do color commentary with Dick Scherr of WTAF (Philadelphia) and Dick Richards of WFBG (Altoona) handling play-by-play and other commentary, respectively.

September 26, 1970 — Colorado ends Penn State's consecutive game winning and unbeaten streaks by beating the Nittany Lions, 41-13, in Boulder before an ABC national television audience. September 18, 1971 — Albert Vitiello, a native of Naples, Italy, becomes the first junior college transfer to play for Penn State, the first placekicking specialist to be recruited and given a "grant-in-aid" and the first soccer-style placekicker for the Nittany Lions. He debuts by kicking eight extra points in a season-opening 56-3 win at Navy.

November 20, 1971 — Lydell Mitchell establishes an NCAA record for scoring and touchdowns and breaks Pete Mauthe's 59-year old season scoring record with 174 points and Charlie Pittman's career touchdown record with 29 by scoring three touchdowns in a 55-18 win over Pitt.

December 4, 1971 — In one of the most significant losses of the Paterno era, the Nittany Lions are upset by Tennessee, 31-11, in Knoxville, ruining another unbeaten season.

December 1971 — Tackle Dave Joyner becomes Penn State's first pure offensive interior lineman to be named a first-team All-American when selected by six organizations, including United Press International, the American Football Coaches and the Football Writers.

January 1, 1972 — Penn State rallies from a 6-3 halftime deficit to stun Texas, 30-6, in the Cotton Bowl in a game Joe Paterno said was one the Nittany Lions "had to win" more than any other in Penn State history. The victory helps quiet criticism of Penn State's football program and establishes the Lions solidly as a legitimate national power.

Spring 1972 — For the first time in history, the team elects four co-captains, choosing quarterback John Hufnagel and guard Carl Schaukowitch for offense and tackle Jim Heller and safety Greg Ducatte on defense.

September 23, 1972 — The Beaver Stadium seating capacity expands to 57,537 as 5,600 seats are added to the east side and 3,570 to the north end zone, but just 50,547 turn out to watch Penn State come from behind to beat four-touchdown underdog Navy, 21-10, in the season-opening game.

September 30, 1972 — The majorettes debut with the Blue Band as a corps of 12 coeds, led by junior Judy Shearer, before a record crowd of 58,065 at the Iowa game.

Fall 1972 — Freshman eligibility, which since the early 1900s had been allowed only in the war years of 1918, 1944-45 and 1951, is restored for Division I NCAA football teams. However, Coach Joe Paterno refuses to play freshmen until the 1973 season.

November 25, 1972 — Pitt announces it will no longer follow a mutual agreement with Penn State, Syracuse and West Virginia prohibiting "redshirting" and a maximum of 25 football grants-in-aid per year.

December 31, 1972 — Penn State plays in the first Sugar Bowl held on New Year's Eve and loses, 14-0, to second-ranked Oklahoma after star running back John Cappelletti is forced to miss the game with a virus. Oklahoma is later forced to forfeit the game to Penn State after the NCAA penalizes Oklahoma for using ineligible players.

September 1973 — Defensive tackle Randy Crowder becomes the first African-American elected captain when he is chosen as a defensive co-captain along with linebacker Ed O'Neil. Tailback John Cappelletti and center Mark Markovich are elected offensive co-captains.

September 22, 1973 — Dave Shukri and Brad Benson become the first freshmen to play varsity football since 1951 when they play in the second half of a 39-0 win at Navy.

September 19, 1973 — Women become members of the marching Blue Band as the band entertains a near record Homecoming crowd of 59,980 in the home season-opener with Iowa. The five coed pioneers include Debbie Frisbee, flag carrier; Carol Gable, alto horn; Linda Hall, clarinet; Kit Murphie, alto horn; and Susan Nowlin, drums.

December 13, 1973 — John Cappelletti becomes the first Nittany Lion to win the Heisman Trophy as college football's outstanding player and accepts the award with an emotional speech about his younger brother, stricken with leukemia, before Vice President Gerald Ford and 4,000 other dignitaries in New York.

January 1, 1974 — Penn State beats LSU, 16-9, in the Orange Bowl to become the first Nittany Lion team to win 12 games without a loss, but the squad is voted No. 5 by the

Associated Press and UPI. Joe Paterno calls the team "the best I've ever coached" and votes it No. 1 in the "Paterno Poll."

July 1, 1974 — Penn State withdraws from the Eastern College Athletic Conference in a dispute over financial arrangements with its 214 member schools. Penn State balks at paying 1/5th of the ECAC's total budget, plus 10 percent of television and bowl revenues.

September 21, 1974 — In what might have been the biggest upset of a Joe Paterno team ever, 24-point underdog Navy, coached by former Paterno assistant George Welsh, beats the Nittany Lions, 7-6, in rain and wind at Beaver Stadium.

October 12, 1974 — Tight end Randy Sidler becomes the first freshman to start since 1951 when two-year regular Dan Natale is sidelined by injury in the Homecoming game against Wake Forest. Sidler catches two passes for 41 yards, but another freshman wingback, Jimmy Cefalo from Northeastern PA thrills the crowd by scoring touchdowns on a 57-yard pass from Tom Shuman and a 39-yard run. Quarterback Chuck Burkhart directed Penn State to its first two undefeated seasons under Joe Paterno in 1968 and '69. In the 1969 Orange Bowl against Kansas (above), Burkhart ran for a three-yard touchdown with eight seconds left and Bob Campbell's two-point run gave Penn State one of its most thrilling victories in program history, 15-14, to cap an 11-0 season and No. 2 finish in the Associated Press poll.

November 16, 1974 — Penn State wins its 500th game by beating Ohio University, 35-16, at Beaver Stadium despite 85 yards in penalties and four lost fumbles as Tom Donchez scores three touchdowns.

December 31, 1975 — Penn State plays in the first Sugar Bowl held at the Louisiana Superdome and loses to Alabama, 13-6.

January 6, 1976 — Ridge Riley, creator of the alumni "Football Letter," dies of a heart attack in the kitchen of head coach Joe Paterno while interviewing Paterno for the final chapter of his soon-to-be-published book, "Road to Number One."

August 1976 — John Black takes over the alumni "Football Letter" and writes the first issue analyzing the team before fall practice.

September 18, 1976 — A record crowd of 62,503 and a regional TV audience watch as Ohio State visits Penn State for the first time in history and avenges four previous losses in five games at Columbus with 12-7 win.

November 6, 1976 — Joe Paterno wins his 100th game as a head coach as the Nittany Lions beat North Carolina State, 41- 20, before 60,462 at Beaver Stadium. July 1, 1977 — Assistant coaches Jim O'Hora and Frank Patrick retire; O'Hora after 31 years and Patrick after 24 years of coaching and three as athletic academic counselor.

September 19, 1977 — The last record crowd before another Beaver Stadium expansion — a standing room only gathering of 62,554 — turns out in the second game of the season to see Penn State beat Houston, 31-4. Junior quarterback Chuck Fusina hits 15-of-23 passes for 245 yards and a TD and All American Randy Sidler makes 11 tackles and causes one fumble to lead the victory.

October 15, 1977 — Joe Paterno misses the first game of his head coaching career when his 11-year old son, David, is severely injured in a trampoline accident. Paterno spends the day in a hospital in Danville, Pa., as his team, coached by offensive coordinator Bob Phillips and defensive coordinator Jerry Sandusky, staves off a fourth-quarter comeback at Syracuse and win the game, 31-24.

September 1, 1978 — The addition of 16,000 seats to Beaver Stadium is completed after lifting the existing stadium by hydraulic jacks, constructing 20 to 40 new rows of concrete stands, eliminating the track that had encircled the field, closing the south end of the horseshoe and expanding the press box.

September 11, 1978 — A Beaver Stadium record crowd of 77,154 sees Penn State beat Rutgers, 26-10, in the home season-opener. Matt Bahr ties his brother Chris's record of four field goals and Chuck Fusina hits Scott Fitzkee for a 53-yard touchdown pass in the first quarter to spark the win.

November 6, 1978 — In a watershed battle of unbeaten teams before another record crowd of 78,019 and a national TV audience, No. 2 Penn State defeated No. 5 Maryland, 27-3, limiting the Terps to minus-32 yards rushing, intercepting five passes (three by Pete Harris) and recording 10 quarterback sacks (three by Larry Kubin). Matt Bahr kicked two field goals and Chuck Fusina connected on a 63-yard TD pass to Tom Donovan. November 13, 1978 — For the first time in history, Penn State is voted No. 1 in the polls by the Associated Press and United Press International after beating North Carolina State, 19-10, thanks to another record four field goals by Matt Bahr.

November 16, 1978 — The Nittany Lion Shrine near Recreation Hall is damaged for the first time since it was dedicated in 1942, when vandals smash off the right ear.

January 1, 1979 — No. 1 ranked Penn State plays for the National Championship for first time and loses to No. 2 Alabama, 14-7, in the Sugar Bowl when Mike Guman is stopped on fourth-and-inches at the goal line in the fourth quarter in what was the biggest play of the game.

November 3, 1979 — Miami (Fla.) upsets Penn State, 26-10, at Beaver Stadium behind the passing of surprise starting freshman quarterback Jim Kelly. The Hurricanes' new coach

Howard Schnellenberger tells reporters, "This day will go down in the history of Miami football as the day we turned our football program around."

December 1, 1979 — The first Penn State punt to be blocked in 10 years occurs when Ralph Giacomarro's punt is blocked by Pitt after 629 consecutive successful kicks in a 29-14 loss to the Panthers at Beaver Stadium.

March 1, 1980 — Joe Paterno becomes Athletic Director succeeding Ed Czekaj, but Paterno remains head football coach. July 1, 1980 — J.T. White, the last assistant coach from the Rip Engle era except for Joe Paterno, retires after 26 years of coaching the defensive ends.

September 6, 1980 — Beaver Stadium's seating capacity increases to 83,600 with the addition of 7,000 seats. An electronic scoreboard also debuts as a record crowd of 78,926 watches Penn State whip Colgate, 54-10.

October 10, 1981 — A new Hall of Fame room and Indoor Sports Complex is dedicated at Homecoming festivities as the No. 2 Nittany Lions win their fourth straight by beating Boston College, 38-7, before a record crowd of 84,473.

October 20, 1981 — Penn State is voted No. 1 for only the second time in history after beating Syracuse, 41-16, in the Nittany Lions' first appearance at the Carrier Dome. Curt Warner breaks Shorty Miller's 69-year old rushing record with 256 yards and a touchdown on 26 carries. But with Warner sidelined by injury, the Lions lose two weeks later at Miami, 17-14, and drop to No. 6 as Pitt moves up to No. 1.

November 28, 1981 — Penn State pulls off one of its finest come from behind victories, snapping back from a 14-0 second-quarter deficit to rout No. 1 Pitt, 48-14, and end the national title chances of the Sugar Bowl-bound Panthers before a national television audience and 60,260 at Pitt Stadium. The victory was sparked by interceptions of Dan

Marino passes by Roger Jackson and Mark Robinson and the passing combination of Todd Blackledge to Kenny Jackson.

January 1, 1982 — Penn State plays in the first Fiesta Bowl held on New Year's Day and beats Southern California, 26-10, holding Heisman Trophy winner Marcus Allen to 85 yards as Curt Warner gains 145 yards on 26 carries. Penn State finishes No. 3 in the Associated Press and UPI rankings.

March 1, 1982 — Associate Athletic Director Jim Tarman succeeds Joe Paterno as Athletic Director as Paterno continues as head coach of the football team.

September 11, 1982 — Penn State wins its 100th game at Beaver Stadium in a 39-31 shootout with Maryland. Todd Blackledge passes for 262 yards and four touchdowns and Maryland's Boomer Esiason throws for 276 yards and two touchdowns before a sellout crowd of 84,567.

September 25, 1982 — In one of the most thrilling games ever played at Beaver Stadium, No. 8 Penn State comes from behind with a 65-yard drive in the last 1:18 to beat No. 3 Nebraska. Todd Blackledge throws the winning two-yard touchdown pass to tight end Kirk Bowman with four seconds left on the clock before record crowd of 85,304 and a national television audience.

November 26, 1982 — Curt Warner establishes the Penn State career rushing record of 3,398 yards and Todd Blackledge sets the career touchdown passing record of 41 as they lead the Nittany Lions to a 19-10 win over once-beaten Pitt at Beaver Stadium to take a No. 2 ranking to the Sugar Bowl. Warner gains 118 yards and Blackledge throws a 31-yard TD pass to Kenny Jackson to assure the victory.

January 1, 1983 — Penn State wins its first National Championship by beating previously No. 1 Georgia, 27-23, in the Sugar Bowl. Todd Blackledge passes 47 yards to Gregg

Garrity for a key fourth-quarter touchdown and Curt Warner out-duels Heisman Trophy winner Herschel Walker with 117 yards and two touchdowns.

August 29, 1983 — Penn State plays in the first Kickoff Classic at Giants Stadium in the New Jersey Meadowlands and loses to a Nebraska team that would finish the regular-season ranked No. 1.

September 9, 1983 — A new Penn State sports logo is introduced featuring a sleek, Lion head.

October 8, 1983 — Unranked Penn State upsets No. 3 Alabama, 34-28, at Beaver Stadium on two last-minute defensive plays that lead to one of the biggest controversies in Penn State history when the back judge nullifies an end zone pass reception by Alabama, ruling the receiver juggled the ball as he fell out of bounds.

November 19, 1983 — In one of most bizarre finishes in Penn State football history, Nick Gancitano kicks a 32-yard field goal to tie Pitt, 24-24, after most of the 60,283 spectators and TV viewers thought the game at Pitt Stadium had ended. The clock showed no time left after a Nittany Lion running play had been stopped, but officials said six seconds remained because of a penalty a few moments earlier. Players had to be called back from the dressing room and the field cleared for the game to finish. It was only the second tie game in Joe Paterno's coaching career.

Spring 1983 — Running backs coach Fran Ganter is promoted to offensive coordinator to succeed Dick Anderson, who takes the head coaching position at Rutgers.

September 8, 1984 — Former offensive coordinator Dick Anderson returns to Beaver Stadium as head coach of Rutgers and in the first game of his career, his team loses to Penn State, 15-12. The "Hawaiian Wave" makes its first appearance in Beaver Stadium as 84,409 fans help the "wave" roll around the stadium several times.

Fall 1984 — Permanent lights costing $575,000 are installed at Beaver Stadium after the U.S. Supreme Court rules against the NCAA's control of televised games and permits individual colleges to make their own arrangements.

September 14, 1985 — A new home team locker room and media room open at Beaver Stadium along with additional permanent seats in the North end zone for the handicapped and the visiting band. Four circular concrete ramps to help spectators reach their seats are part of the renovation.

October 26, 1985 — Penn State wins its 600th game by beating West Virginia, 27-0, before a sellout Homecoming crowd of 85,534 and an ABC regional TV audience. John Shaffer throws two touchdown passes and the defense limits the Mountaineers to 268 yards with three interceptions, two fumble recoveries and four sacks.

November 6, 1985 — Penn State is voted No. 1 for the fourth time in program history when the UPI coaches board selects the Nittany Lions first after a 16-12 come from behind fourth quarter win over Boston College. But, in the Associated Press poll, the Lions remained No. 2 behind Florida, coached by former Penn State quarterback Galen Hall.

November 13, 1985 — Penn State moves to No. 1 in the Associated Press rankings after beating Cincinnati, 31-10, in Riverfront Stadium, while Florida lost to Georgia. January 1, 1986 — Oklahoma beat the No. 1 Nittany Lions, 25-10, in the Orange Bowl to win the National Championship as two Penn State interceptions and a fumble helped the Sooners to victory.

September 6, 1986 — Penn State played the first night game at Beaver Stadium in the season-opener against Temple that helps launch the celebration of the first 100 years of Penn

State football. Quarterback John Shaffer passed for three touchdowns and ran for another in the 45-15 victory.

October 25, 1986 — The sixth-ranked Nittany Lions shocked the country with a dominating 23-3 upset win over No. 2 Alabama in Tuscaloosa behind a defense led by linebackers Shane Conlan and Trey Bauer and the running of D. J. Dozier. It was just the Crimson Tide's third loss in 25 years at Bryant-Denny Stadium. The victory pushed Penn State to No. 2 in the polls and on track to play No. 1 Miami (Fla.) for the national title.

January 2, 1987 — Penn State won its second National Championship in four years by upsetting previous No. 1 Miami, 14-10, in the Fiesta Bowl with a four-down goal line stand in the last minute of play behind a defense led by All-American Shane Conlan. The Nittany Lions flustered Heisman Trophy winner Vinny Testaverde with five sacks and five interceptions, including one by linebacker Pete Giftopoulos at the goal line on the game's last play.

September 5, 1987 — Joe Paterno picked up his 200th game in a 45-19 victory over Bowling Green in the season-opening game at Beaver Stadium and later he told the media, "I may live to be 100, but I'll never be around for another 100 victories." Gittyup Gittyup Gittyup 409!

October 1, 1988 — Tony Sacca becomes the first true freshman to start at quarterback in the Paterno and Engle eras and leads Penn State to 45-9 win over Temple at Veterans Stadium in Philadelphia.

November 19, 1988 — Penn State loses to Notre Dame, 21-3, in South Bend to finish with record of 5-6 and the Nittany Lions' first losing season in 49 years.

December 19, 1989 — Representatives of Penn State and the Big Ten Conference announce that an "invitation in principle" has been extended for Penn State to join the Big

Ten. The invitation is made formal on June 4, 1990 in a 7-3 vote of the Council of 10 ruling body and Penn State accepts. Penn State via Paterno decided to throw its hat into a great football conference—the Big Ten.

December 29, 1989 — In one of the zaniest games in Penn State history, the Nittany Lions best Brigham Young in a Holiday Bowl shootout, 50-39, scoring 21 points in a wild fourth quarter that includes two spectacular plays, one by All-American linebacker Andre Collins and another by defensive back Gary Brown. Collins scores Penn State's first ever two points off an opponent conversion attempt when he returns an interception 102 yards following a BYU touchdown. Moments later, Brown strips the ball from Cougars' quarterback Ty Detmer and runs 53 yards for another touchdown with 45 seconds remaining.

November 17, 1990 — Penn State pulls off one of the biggest upsets in program history as freshman Craig Fayak kicks a 34-yard field goal with 58 seconds left to give the 18th-ranked Nittany Lions a 24-21 victory at No. 1 Notre Dame after trailing at halftime, 21-7.

Spring 1991 — The Big Ten announces Penn State football will be fully integrated into the Big Ten for the 1993 season. Iowa becomes the first opponent on the schedule, fulfilling dates previously set with Notre Dame in 1993 and 1994. The new Big Ten schedule is expected to mark the end of games with traditional rivals Pitt and West Virginia.

September 7, 1991 — A 10,000-seat upper deck is added in the north end of Beaver Stadium and a new attendance record of 94,000 is set as Penn State beats Cincinnati, 81- 0, in the home-opener. The score is the largest winning point differential in the Paterno era.

January 1, 1992 — In the most bizarre and exciting four-minute span in program history, the Nittany Lions come back from a 17-7 third-quarter deficit with 28 points in less than four minutes to defeat Tennessee, 42-17, in the Fiesta Bowl. A crowd of 71,133 helps take Penn State's total season attendance over one million for the first time, with 1,017,843 attending the Lions' 13 games.

September 12, 1992 — A new policy is implemented banning smoking inside Beaver Stadium, starting with the season-opener against Temple. For just the second time in the Paterno era, a true freshman starts at quarterback as Wally Richardson leads the Nittany Lions to 49-8 victory over Temple.

October 10, 1992 — In what is the biggest game at Beaver Stadium in several years and a clash of unbeaten teams, No. 2 Miami (Fla.) beats No. 5 Penn State, 17-14, with the help of an interception return for a TD and sends the Nittany Lions into a tailspin for the season.

January 1, 1993 — Penn State loses to Stanford, 24-3, in the Blockbuster Bowl in Joe Robbie Stadium in its final game as an independent.

September 4, 1993 — Penn State ends 106 years of independence with a 38-20 win over Minnesota in its first game as a member of the Big Ten Conference. Redshirt sophomore wideout Bobby Engram catches four touchdown passes of 29, 31, 20 and 31 yards from junior quarterback John Sacca to set an all-time touchdown receiving record. Minnesota's Tim Schade sets two Penn State opponent records, completing 34-of-66 pass attempts.

September 18, 1993 — Joe Paterno wins his 250th game as head coach and receives the game ball from the players as the Nittany Lions shut out Iowa in Iowa City, 31-0, behind a defense that sets up three touchdowns with interceptions and sacks the Hawkeye quarterback nine times for 89 yards in losses.

October 16, 1993 — Penn State plays its 1,000th game in history and loses at Beaver Stadium in the first meeting with Michigan, 21-13, for its initial defeat in the Big Ten Conference.

November 27, 1993 — The Nittany Lions rally from a 37-14 deficit late in the third quarter on the passing of Kerry Collins to Bobby Engram to beat Michigan State, 38-37, at East Lansing and clinch third place in their first year of Big Ten conference play.

December 30, 1993 — Jim Tarman retires as Athletic Director and is succeeded by former football walk-on Tim Curley.

October 15, 1994 — Unbeaten Penn State beats Michigan, 31-24, in Ann Arbor before the largest crowd ever to see the Nittany Lions play, 106,832, and is voted No. 1 for the first time since the 1987 Fiesta Bowl victory over Miami (Fla.) in polls by both the Associated Press writers and broadcasters and the USA Today / CNN coaches.

October 29, 1994 — The Nittany Lions trounce Ohio State, 63-14, but still lose their No. 1 Associated Press ranking to previously No. 3 Nebraska. Ohio native Ki-Jana Carter scores four touchdowns and runs for 137 yards and quarterback Kerry Collins passes for 265 yards and two touchdowns as the defense limits the Buckeyes to 214 net yards, while intercepting three passes.

November 5, 1994 — The Nittany Lions lose their No. 1 USAToday/CNN ranking to Nebraska after two last-minute touchdowns by Indiana claim a 35-29 victory against the Nittany Lions in Bloomington which looked closer than it was.

November 12, 1994 — The Nittany Lions clinch their first Big Ten Championship by overcoming a 21-0 first-quarter deficit with one of the greatest clutch drives in school history, a 96-yard, 15-play march into the rain and wind late in the fourth quarter to beat Illinois, 35-31, at Champaign in a late afternoon game televised by ABC.

Ki--Jana Carter breaks away in Illinois Last-Minute Victory

The drive was engineered by passes from quarterback Kerry Collins to Bobby Engram and Kyle Brady and the running of Ki-Jana Carter and Brian Milne, who scored the winning touchdown on a two-yard plunge with 57 second left in game.

November 18, 1995 — The Centre Region was hit with a rare 18-inch snowfall three days before No. 12 Michigan came to Beaver Stadium. Volunteers, including some local inmates, gladly cleared the snow from the stands and an estimated 80,000 fans attended the "Snow Bowl." Joe Nastasi's run for a touchdown on a fake field goal late in the game sealed the Nittany Lions' 27-17 win.

November 25, 1995 — Wide receiver Bobby Engram climaxes his career and cements his standing as one of the greatest clutch players in Penn State history, scoring the winning touchdown with eight seconds left and no time outs on a four-yard flanker screen pass from Wally Richardson, ducking under two Michigan State tacklers, to give the Nittany Lions a thrilling 24-20 win over Michigan State at East Lansing. No rewards for long sentences!

January 2, 1995 — Penn State whipped Oregon, 38-20, to win the Rose Bowl, but, despite a 12-0 season, the Nittany Lions were ranked # 2 to Nebraska, which was named National Champion by the Associated Press and USAToday/CNN. The New York Times computer rankings listed Penn State No. 1 with a schedule rated the 19th toughest by the NCAA compared to Nebraska's 57th rating. But, there was no opportunity for judges and arguments.

August 25, 1996 — Penn State introduced a new logo with a Lion head looking even fiercer than the last as Penn State upset Southern California, 24-7, before a record Kickoff Classic crowd of 77,716. Tailback Curtis Enis came within 15 yards of Curt Warner's game rushing record with 241 yards and three touchdowns at Giants Stadium.

September 28, 1996 — Penn State became just the sixth school in college football history to win 700 games by beating Wisconsin, 23-20, at Madison in a last-second thriller.

October 12, 1996 — Tackle John Blick became the first true freshman to start in the interior offensive line in the Paterno era in a 31-14 Homecoming win over Purdue.

April 26, 1997 — A record crowd of 60,000 attended the annual intrasquad scrimmage [Blue – White game] at Beaver Stadium, beating the previous mark of 40,000 for the 1996 Blue-White game.

September 2, 1997 — For the first time ever, Penn State was rated No. 1 in the Associated Press preseason rankings. The USAToday / CNN coaches' poll rated the Nittany Lions No. 2 behind Washington.

September 20, 1997 — Penn State scored 50 points in the first half to tie the record of the unbeaten 1947 team in a 57-21 romp at Louisville. Nonetheless, it lost the No. 1 ranking in the bogus Associated Press poll to Florida, which beat Tennessee.

October 11, 1997 — The Nittany Lions came from behind to beat No. 7 Ohio State, 31-27, before a record crowd of 97,282 at Beaver Stadium and with that victory it moved to # 1 in the Associated Press and USAToday / CNN polls for the first time since October 23, 1994. LSU had upset previous No. 1 Florida and the Nittany Lions filled the void.

October 18, 1997 — Penn State had to come from behind to beat Minnesota, 16-15, and so it lost its # 1 ranking in both the Associated Press and USAToday / CNN polls to Nebraska, which had beaten Texas Tech. All-Americans Bobby Engram (left) and Kerry Collins celebrated Penn State's thrilling 31- 24 win at Michigan on October 15, 1994 in Penn State's first game in Ann Arbor. Engram and Collins were among five first-team All-Americans that led the Nittany Lions to Big Ten and Rose Bowl titles, becoming the first Big Ten team to finish 12-0. 175 S

September 12, 1998 — Joe Paterno got his 300th career victory on the field, becoming only the sixth coach in history to reach that milestone and the first to do it all at one college. On this day, the Nittany Lions beat Bowling Green, 48-3, before 96,291 in Beaver Stadium.

October 31, 1998 — Sophomore linebacker LaVar Arrington made one of the most spectacular defensive plays in program history, leaping over the Illinois center and guard as the ball was snapped and the stopped the runner cold just as he got the hand-off. Sports Illustrated later cited the "LaVar Leap" as college football's "defensive play of the year" as the Nittany Lions beat the Fighting Illini, 27-0.

September 30, 2000 — One week after freshman cornerback Adam Taliaferro suffered a career-ending spinal injury in a game at Ohio State, the Nittany Lions rallied to beat eventual Big Ten Champion Purdue, 22-20, in Beaver Stadium.

September 1, 2001 — Less than one year after suffering a serious spinal injury, Adam Taliaferro led the Nittany Lions onto the field against Miami (Fla.) in the first game in the newly-expanded Beaver Stadium, which had grown to a capacity of 107,282.

October 27, 2001 — Penn State rallied from a 27-9 deficit to score the final 20 points and defeat Ohio State, 29-27, giving Joe Paterno his 324th career victory on the field and moving him past Paul "Bear" Bryant and into the all-time victories lead among major college coaches. The comeback is then Penn State's greatest at home under Paterno. Quarterback Zack Mills gains a school-record 418 yards of total offense.

September 14, 2002 — The Nittany Lions buried unbeaten and No. 8 ranked Nebraska, 40-7, in a primetime meeting in front of a Beaver Stadium record crowd of 110,753.

November 16, 2002 — Senior tailback Larry Johnson rushed for a Penn State record 327 yards, scoring four touchdowns, to lead the Nittany Lions to a 58-25 win at Indiana.

November 23, 2002 — Larry Johnson rushed for 279 yards and four touchdowns against Michigan State to become the first Nittany Lion and only the ninth player in NCAA Division I-A history to gain 2,000 yards in a season. The Maxwell and Doak Walker awards winner, Johnson finished the season with 2,087 yards on 271 attempts, scoring 20 touchdowns.

October 9, 2004 — The first Penn State Student Whiteout made a strong and lasting impression on the Nittany Lions, the Beaver Stadium faithful and the opposition, as No. 9 Purdue escapes with a 20-13 win.

November 13, 2004 — The Nittany Lion defense stopped Indiana on four consecutive running plays from the Penn State one-yard line to preserve a dramatic 22-18 win in Bloomington. The victory began a streak that saw Penn State beat Michigan State at home the next week and post a 51-13 record through the end of the 2009 season.

September 24, 2005 — Penn State staged a critical come from behind 34-29 win at Northwestern in the Big Ten-opener. After falling behind, 23-7, and still trailing, 29-27, with less than 2:00 to play, the Nittany Lions converted a fourth-and-15 play from their own 15-yard line, gaining 20 yards on a pass from Michael Robinson to tight end Isaac Smolko. Robinson then threw his third touchdown pass of the game, connecting on a 36-yard strike to freshman Derrick Williams with 51 seconds remaining for the dramatic win. All-America linebacker Paul Posluszny made 22 tackles (14 solo).

October 1, 2005 — Paul Posluszny's leaping tackle at the goal line highlighted the Nittany Lions' 44-14 thumping of No. 18 Minnesota, lifting Penn State to 5-0 and back into the national rankings. Quarterback Michael Robinson (114) and tailback Tony Hunt (112) become the first Penn State tandem to gain 100 rushing yards in a Big Ten game.

October 8, 2005 — All-American Tamba Hali forces a fumble near midfield with 1:21 to play that Scott Paxson recovers to preserve the Nittany Lions' 14-10 win over No. 6 Ohio State in a primetime thriller. A crowd of 109,839 in Beaver Stadium helped will the Nittany Lions to the crucial win, which vaulted Penn State into the Top 10.

January 3, 2006 — Kevin Kelly's 29-yard field goal in the third overtime lifts Big Ten Champion Penn State to an exciting 26-23 victory over Florida State in the 2006 FedEx Orange Bowl. In a meeting of the two winningest major college coaches of all-time, the longest game in Penn State history ends at 12:57 a.m. The Nittany Lions (11-1) finish No. 3 in the final polls.

September 30, 2006 — Sophomore wide receiver Deon Butler makes 11 receptions for a school-record 216 yards, breaking O.J. McDuffie's mark of 212 (Boston College, 1992), to lead the Nittany Lions to a 33-7 win over Northwestern.

November 4, 2006 — Joe Paterno suffers serious leg and knee injuries in the third quarter at Wisconsin when two players tumble into him on the sideline. Paul Posluszny becomes Penn State's all-time leading tackler with 14 stops, passing Greg Buttle's mark of 343 that had stood since 1975. A two-time All-American and Bednarik Award winner, Posluszny finishes his career with 372 tackles.

November 11, 2006 — Joe Paterno misses just the third game in his Penn State coaching career, while recovering from surgery on his left leg six days earlier. The Nittany Lions limit Temple to two first downs and 74 yards in a 47-0 win in Beaver Stadium.

January 1, 2007 — Cornerback Tony Davis scoops up a fumble and returns it 88 yards to break a 10-10 fourth-quarter tie, lifting Penn State to a 20-10 win over No. 17 Tennessee in the Outback Bowl. Facing their fifth ranked opponent of the season, the Nittany Lions force three Volunteer turnovers and finish No. 24 in the final Associated Press poll.

September 1, 2007 — The Big Ten Conference launches its own network, the Big Ten Network, and Penn State makes its debut during the network's launch weekend, pounding Florida International, 59-0, in the season-opener in Beaver Stadium. The Big Ten Network would be available in more than 70 million homes by the end of its second year on the air.

September 8, 2007 — The first full stadium "Whitehouse" crowd of 110,078 sees Derrick Williams' punt return touchdown ignite the Nittany Lions to a 31-10 defeat of Notre Dame in front of an ESPN primetime audience.

November 3, 2007 — All-America linebacker Dan Connor records 11 tackles in the Nittany Lions' 26-19 Senior Day win over Purdue, moving him past Paul Posluszny to become Penn State's all-time leading tackler. A two-time All-American and winner of the 2007 Bednarik Award, Connor finishes his career with 419 tackles.

November 10, 2007 — Junior kicker Kevin Kelly becomes Penn State's all-time leading scorer in the Nittany Lions' 31-0 blanking of Temple in Philadelphia, kicking a 32-yard field goal and connecting on all four PAT attempts. Kelly surpasses Craig Fayak's total of 282 points from 1990-93.

December 4, 2007 — Joe Paterno becomes just the third active coach to be inducted into the National Football Foundation College Football Hall of Fame. Paterno is forced to delay his induction by one year due to leg injuries suffered in the 2006 game at Wisconsin. He had been scheduled to enter the Hall in 2006 with active coaches Bobby Bowden and John Gagliardi.

December 29, 2007 — Joe Paterno coaches his 500th game as head coach of the Nittany Lions. His team erases a 14-0 first-quarter deficit to defeat Texas A&M, 24-17, in the Valero Alamo Bowl. A diving 30-yard touchdown catch by Deon Butler and an 11-yard scoring run by Daryll Clark spark the win and a No. 25 ranking in the final USA Today Coaches poll.

September 27, 2008 — Kevin Kelly breaks the NCAA record for consecutive games with at least one field goal (25) when he connects on a 25-yarder in the third quarter of a 38-24 primetime victory over Illinois in Beaver Stadium. Kelly's streak would reach 31 games, ending when he did not attempt a field goal in the season-finale with Michigan State.

October 11, 2008 — Senior Derrick Williams becomes the first player under Joe Paterno to return five kicks for a touchdown in his career (three punts, two kickoffs) when he brings back a punt 63 yards for a score in Penn State's 48-7 win at Wisconsin.

October 18, 2008 — Jared Odrick records a safety on a sack to break a 17-17 third-quarter tie and spark the Nittany Lions' 46-17 Homecoming win over Michigan. The 46 points are the Lions' highest total in the series. Kevin Kelly becomes the Big Ten career kick scoring leader when he connects on a 32-yard field goal, giving Penn State a 29-17 lead.

October 25, 2008 — Penn State scores 10 points in the final 6:25 to record a 13-6 win over No. 10 Ohio State in a primetime game in Columbus. Mark Rubin records a career-high 11 tackles and forces a fumble in the fourth quarter, which Navorro Bowman recovers in Ohio State territory to set up the go-ahead score. Ohio State is held to its fewest points at home since a 6-0 loss to Wisconsin in 1982.

November 8, 2008 — Kevin Kelly becomes the Big Ten leader in field goals when he boots the 73rd of his career, a 23-yard kick in the first quarter of a 24-23 loss at Iowa that ends the Nittany Lions' unbeaten season. November 15, 2008 — Deon Butler becomes Penn State's career receptions leader with 172, surpassing Bobby Engram, when he makes five catches in a 34-7 win over Indiana at Beaver Stadium.

November 22, 2008 — Daryll Clark throws for 341 yards and four touchdowns to propel No. 8 Penn State past No. 15 Michigan State, 49-18, to clinch the Nittany Lions' second Big Ten Championship in four years. Penn State passes for a school-record 419 yards, improving to 11-1 and earning a Rose Bowl berth against Southern California. Penn State becomes the sixth school in the nation to win 800 games.

December 11, 2008 — Senior A.Q. Shipley is announced as Penn State's first recipient of the Dave Rimington Trophy, honoring the nation's most outstanding center.

October 3, 2009 — Stephfon Green (120) and Evan Royster (105) gain more than 100 rushing yards to lead Penn State past Illinois, becoming the first tandem of Nittany Lion running backs to crack the century mark in Big Ten play.

Nov. 21, 2009 — Quarterback Daryll Clark delivers a record-breaking performance in his final Big Ten game, throwing for 310 yards and four TDs to lead a 42-14 win at Michigan State. Clark breaks the school records for season (22 by Todd Blackledge, 1982) and career (41) touchdown passes and finishes the season with 24 and 43, respectively.

January 1, 2010 — Penn State defeats No. 13 LSU, 19-17, in the Capital One Bowl on a Collin Wagner field goal with :57 to play. The Nittany Lions (11-2) secure their first consecutive 11-win seasons since 1985-86, and finish No. 9 in the final Associated Press poll. Daryll Clark becomes Penn State's season total offense leader with 3,214 yards and the first Nittany Lion quarterback to eclipse 3,000 passing yards in a season (3,003).

September 4, 2010 — Rob Bolden becomes the first Penn State true freshman quarterback to start a season-opener in 100 years (Shorty Miller, 1910) and leads Penn State to a 44-14 win over Youngstown State. Bolden goes 20-of-29 for 239 yards, with two touchdowns and one interception to deliver the best passing performance by a Penn State true freshman quarterback in program history.

September 18, 2010 — Penn State beats Kent State, 24-0, for its 500th victory since Joe Paterno joined the coaching staff in 1950. The shutout was the Nittany Lions' 41st since Paterno became head coach.

September 25, 2010 — Collin Wagner ties the school record with five field goals to lift the Nittany Lions past Temple, 22-13.

November 6, 2010 — Penn State rallies from a 21-0 deficit late in the first half to beat Northwestern, 35-21, giving Joe Paterno his 400th career victory on the field. Paterno becomes the first Football Bowl Subdivision coach with 400 wins and just the third in NCAA history. Matt McGloin throws a career-high four touchdown passes to lead the rally. The comeback is Penn State's largest at home under Paterno and matches the biggest comeback all-time under the Hall of Fame mentor (trailed 21-0 at Illinois in 1994; won, 35-31).

October 29, 2011 — Silas Redd rushes for 100 yards or more for the fifth consecutive game and scores the game-winning touchdown with 1:08 to play to lift Penn State to a 10-7 win over Illinois. The Nittany Lions improve to 8-1 overall and become the first team in Big Ten history to win five consecutive conference games by 10 points or less. The victory is the 409th of Joe Paterno's career on the field moving him past legendary Grambling coach Eddie Robinson for the most wins in NCAA Division I history and No. 2 all-time for all NCAA divisions. Paterno's career on the field record stands at 409-136-3 over 46 years in what would be the final game for the Hall of Fame coach and icon.

November 9, 2011 — The Penn State Board of Trustees announces Penn State President Graham Spanier and head football coach Joe Paterno have been relieved of their duties, effectively immediately, in the wake of the Jerry Sandusky investigation. Long-time assistant coach and defensive coordinator Tom Bradley is named interim head coach for the remainder of the 2011 season.

November 12, 2011 — In an emotionally-charged Senior Day in Beaver Stadium, Penn State rallies from a 17-0 deficit to within 17-14 against new Big Ten rival Nebraska, but falls by three points. Prior to the game, student-athletes, coaches and team personnel from both squads joined at midfield in a moment of reflection and prayer for the victims of child abuse.

November 18, 2011 — The family of Joe Paterno announces the legendary coach is suffering from a treatable form of lung cancer.

November 19, 2011 — Penn State scores on four of its initial five possessions en route to a 20-14 win at Ohio State and a share of the inaugural Big Ten Leaders Division Championship. The Nittany Lions play their seventh consecutive conference game decided by 10 points or less (6-1 record).

January 6, 2012 — Bill O'Brien is named Penn State's 15th head football coach. O'Brien was the offensive coordinator/quarterbacks coach with the New England Patriots in 2011, helping the Patriots to their second Super Bowl in his five years on the coaching staff. Like Joe Paterno, O'Brien graduated from Brown University, where he played linebacker and defensive end from 1990-92.

January 22, 2012 — Joe Paterno dies of lung cancer at the age of 85 in State College, surrounded by his family. Three days of private and public viewings and memorial services bring tens of thousands of people to campus to pay their respects.

July 23, 2012 — The NCAA announces sanctions against Penn State after the conviction of Jerry Sandusky and the release of the Freeh Report. Included in the sanctions are a four year bowl ban and reduction in scholarships, the vacating of all 112 victories from 1998- 2011, 111 of which were under Joe Paterno, and giving current squad members the opportunity to immediately transfer to another institution until August 2013.

July 25, 2012 — Seniors Michael Mauti and Michael Zordich, flanked by their teammates, pledge their commitment to Penn State and to keeping the 2012 team together less than two weeks from the start of training camp.

September 1, 2012 — In his first game as head coach, Bill O'Brien's Nittany Lions take a 14-3 halftime lead over Ohio, but the Bobcats rally to post a 24-14 win in Beaver Stadium.

September 15, 2012 — Matt McGloin throws four touchdown passes, three to sophomore Allen Robinson, to lead the Nittany Lions to a 34-7 win over Navy in Beaver Stadium for Bill O'Brien's first career victory. September 29, 2012 — Matt McGloin runs for a pair of touchdowns and throws for another and Michael Mauti grabs two interceptions, returning one a school-record 99 yards, to lead Penn State to a 35-7 win at Illinois in the Big Ten-opener for Bill O'Brien's first conference win.

October 6, 2012 — Matt McGloin completes a school-record 35 passes and scores the go-ahead touchdown with 2:37 to play, sparking Penn State to 22 points in the fourth quarter in a 39-28 comeback Homecoming win over No. 24 Northwestern.

November 24, 2012 — Thirty-one seniors are introduced before the Wisconsin game in an emotional ceremony and then lead Penn State to a 24-21 overtime win over the eventual Big Ten champions. Sam Ficken caps a 3-for-3 day on field goal attempts with a 37-yard game-winner, giving the Nittany Lions their first home overtime win.

November 24, 2012—Beat Wisconsin in OT W 24-21) Ineligible for Bowl game because of sanctions. Season record 8-4; (6-2 Big Ten)

November 26, 2012 — Bill O'Brien sweeps Big Ten Coach-of-the-Year honors and six Nittany Lions are named first-team all-conference, led by Michael Mauti, the Butkus-

Fitzgerald Linebacker-of-the-Year, and Allen Robinson, the Richter-Howard Receiver-of-the Year. Defensive end Deion Barnes is named Big Ten Freshman-of-the-Year and is joined by tight end Kyle Carter as a first-team Freshman All-American.

January 17, 2013 — Bill O'Brien is named Bear Bryant Coach-of-the-Year, earning his third national coaching honor, joining accolades from the Maxwell Football Club and ESPN.com.

February 2, 2013 — Former Penn State All-America end Dave Robinson becomes the sixth Nittany Lion selected for enshrinement in the Pro Football Hall of Fame.

August 2013 — Before season, PSU had an open competition for QB. True Freshman Christian Hackenberg won the position; started all 12 games for the Nittany Lions. He was the headliner of the recruiting class. Other stalwarts in the class included end, Adam Breneman. John Butler was named Penn State's new defensive coordinator. Looked for similar season to 2012 (8-4) but it was not as good (7-5)

September 2013 —PSU Team coached for second year by Bill O'Brien. PSU was in the second season of a four year NCAA ban from sex scandal.

September 2013. Penn State opened the season with two non-conference wins, Syracuse & East Michigan but lost to the UCF Knights, who ultimately went on to a BCS bowl, the Fiesta,

October 12, 2013 Great victory. Defeated Michigan in a quadruple-overtime thriller. PSU alternated losses and wins for the remainder of the season, losing to Ohio State, Minnesota, and Nebraska, and defeating Illinois, Purdue, and Wisconsin.

November 30, 2013—End of season win against Wisconson W (31-24). Season record 7-5 (4-4 Big Ten)

Post Season 2013—Christian Hackenberg was named Big Ten Freshman of the Year. Backup QB Tyler Ferguson, who announced he would transfer. Soon after the season, two coaches—Ron Vanderlinden and Charlie Fisher—left Penn State for undisclosed reasons. A few weeks later, Coach O'Brien accepted the head coaching position with the Houston Texans, leaving the Nittany Lions after two seasons.

January 11, 2014—the Nittany Lions hired Vanderbilt's James Franklin to replace Bill O'Brien as head coach for the 2014 season.

September 9, 2014—With NCAA's announcement to lift Penn State's bowl ban, the Nittany Lions have an opportunity to take advantage of a weakened Big Ten.

October 11, 2014—Penn State football vs Michigan at Michigan Stadium in Ann Arbor. The Wolverines defeated the Nittany Lions 18-13. Season is not a Paterno-like season.

October 27, 2014—Joe Paterno supporters sign the 409 sign at the Student Book Store on October 24, 2014. The petition was created by PeoplesJoe.com to oppose the win take-away by the NCAA.

November 15, 2014—The Nittany Lions' win v Temple features a strong rushing performance and plenty of takeaways.

November 22, 2014—The Nittany Lions saw Akeel Lynch top 100 yards for the second straight game. But the team missed Belton for much of the game and unfortunately couldn't run out the clock on the Fighting Illini and thus suffered a loss.

December 1, 2014—Board Chairman Keith Masser wrote a letter to trustees granting them access to documents that went into Louis Freeh's report.

December 27, 2014—Penn State defeated Boston College in Pinstripe Bowl; finished season 7-6 (2-6 Big Ten). This is Coach Franklin's first season as head coach.

February 13, 2015—The Big Ten says Penn State will get its bowl revenue this upcoming season instead of keeping the ban on revenue in force.

April 17, 2015—Ten Penn State football players from 2014 prepare for the NFL Draft, which began on April 30, 2015.

July 23, 2015—Three years ago, the NCAA imposed harsh sanctions on Penn State following the aftermath of the Jerry Sandusky sex abuse case. Since then, the sanctions have been lifted following a lawsuit against the sport's governing body, but those pursuing the case say there is still more to be discovered.

October 9, 2015—Brandon Bell, Jason Cabinda and Troy Reeder continue the tradition of Linebacker U.

November 21, 2015—The Nittany Lions lost to the Michigan Wolverines 28-16 during the annual white out game and Senior Day at Beaver Stadium on Saturday, Nov. 21, 2015.

January 2, 2016—Penn State lost a close one to Georgia L (17-24) in the Pinstripe Bowl; finished season 7-6 (4-4 Big Ten). Coach Franklin has delivered two 7-6 seasons.

January 9, 2016—Penn State defensive coordinator Bob Shoop agreed to become the new defensive coordinator at Tennessee.

February 4, 2016—On National Signing Day, Penn State football adds 20 new recruits to the program. Penn State alums and fans are ready for a bright future.

Chapter 9—Penn State Football – The First Six Years

Six No Coach Years

Year	Coach	Record
1881	Unofficial	1-0
1887	No Coach	2-0
1888	No Coach	0-2-1
1889	No Coach	2-2
1890	No Coach	2-2
1891	No Coach	6-2

PSU 1887 Football Team

1887: PSU's first year of football No coach

Penn State's official football program began in 1887 with a two game season, both games against Bucknell. The first was played at Bucknell's Lewisburg campus and the second was played at the Old Main Lawn at Penn State's main campus.

Though PSU likes to have its official and unofficial football notions kept separate, the fact is the first game was played against the University of Lewisburg at Lewisburg in 1881. No, it was not official but it was played and played well by PSU. Additionally, the 1881 team in retrospect, has taken credit for the blue and white uniforms, not the pink and black worn by the 1987 team. Ivan P. McCreary made a difference

In 1881, this all got started because a determined student, Ivan P. McCreary decided to set up the game, put a team together, and manage the Penn State boys to victory. Since Walter Camp had not yet formed all of the real rules of American football, the 1881 lads played by a mixture of rules that were part rugby and what at the time was known as American football.

McCreary did not play in the game, but he did umpire (The term used at the time for football officials.) At the end of the game as the story goes, he sent a telegraph 50 miles away to Penn State friends that read "we have met the enemy and they are ours, nine to nothing."

Over time as documents were found that chronicled the day, such as the 1882 edition of the University of Lewisburg Mirror, more information was gleaned about the game. "The State College Team was well uniformed and disciplined whereas our boys ... were up to their dodges."

When the official 1887 team was formed they had a copy and so they studied the American Football Rulebook. This had been written by the great Walter Camp in 1886 and refined for the 1887 season. The official PSU team was not taught by any other team or organization and so they gained their knowledge of the game from Camp's writings. They had a lot of mettle for sure.

Camp's rule book from 1887 is still available in a reprint. Walter Camp is known as the Father of American Football. He described in this booklet, the transition of rugby to

American Football showing the rules dating to 1876 and the then the current Rules for the 1887 season.

Penn State had a great team but who would have supposed otherwise. They won both games in 1887, one at Lewisburg, 54-0, and the other on the Old Main Lawn on the State College campus, 24-0. The old main lawn was just that, a huge lawn in front of the main building. Thus from the outset Penn State fielded great teams that gave lickings rather than take them. The 1887 team was one of 13 Penn State teams over the years that were undefeated.

In 1887, football as we know it was not completely defined. Association football, rugby, and even soccer were having a major influence at the time on the college football rules and game play. For its first five years, the soon to be "Nittany Lions," football team had no coach. In fact, the whole idea of Penn State football was so tentative that there was a five-year gap from when the first unofficial season occurred until football was "resumed" in 1887. Once PSU's President made it official, the count to 130 successful seasons began.

Penn State 1888 Football Team

1888: Penn State Football No Coach

Record 0-2-1; without a coach, Penn State sported its own uniforms of blue and white. In muddy terrain, it was reasonably easy to tell the players from the ground until they were completely coated with mud. In stark contrast to the 1887 team, the 1888 team is the only winless team in Penn State history. Harry Leyden (1887–1889) played quarterback in 1888, and both he and the team would do a much better job in 1889.

The season scores are as follows: October 31, Dickinson at home -- Old Main Lawn T (6-6); November 7, Dickinson away at Carlyle PA (0-16). Late November Lehigh at home -- Old Main Lawn L (0-30.

1889: Penn State Football No Coach

With no coach working in the off-season, it was tough getting scheduled games in those first five years. Penn State played Swarthmore in its first game of the season on and got back on the winning side W (20-6) at home – Old Main Lawn. Next two games were losses at Lafayette L (0-26) and at Lehigh L (0-106).

You read that right. It was surely a record-breaker demonstrating how new the team was to real competition. As the season finale, Bucknell was back and even they were tough but Penn State prevailed W (12-0) in a game played at home on the Old Main Lawn.

1890: Penn State Football No Coach

Penn State played four different teams this year and produced a 2-2 record just as in 1889. They lost on October 10 at University of Pennsylvania L (0–20) and came back just two days later on October 12 and lost at Franklin & Marshall in Lancaster, PA L (0–10).

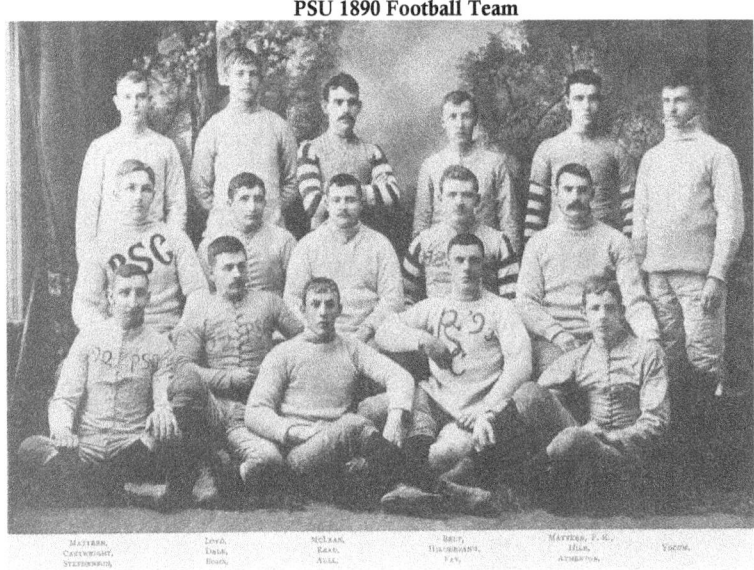

PSU 1890 Football Team

These were both football games though they were losses. On November 15, Penn State played the Altoona Athletic Association on the Old Main Lawn at State College, PA and won big W (68–0). They capped off the season at the Bellefonte Academy in Bellefonte, PA and came away with a win W (23–0)

1891: Penn State Football No Coach

1891: Still with no head coach, for its fifth season, the team was able to schedule an eight-game season starting with a win on October 2 at Lafayette W (14–4). Then the next day it was off to Lehigh on October 3 where Penn State lost in a battle of the to-be Nittany Lions against the Mountain Hawks. L (2–24). Even in defeat, PSU was playing much tougher than in their prior three seasons.

PSU traveled for a nice win at Swarthmore on October 17 and won 44–0. On October 24, it was at Franklin for a win W (26–6). Then it was off to Gettysburg on October 27 for a nice win W (18-0). Bucknell began to toughen up and got back on Penn State's schedule for 1891. Penn State lost in a close battle on November 7 L (10-12). After a trip to Dickinson on November 26, Penn State came back with a win as Dickinson forfeited. The next game was a big win at Haverford on December 5, W (58–0).

Penn State was getting so much more mature as a football team that the university thought maybe it was time for a coach. The administration hired George Hoskins at the first football coach.

Back in those days, it was often very tough to get a game so colleges would agree to play prep schools and sometimes even high schools to keep their edge.

Chapter 10 — Penn State Football First Coach -- George Hoskins

Coach # 1

Year	Coach	Record
1892	George Hoskins	5-1
1893	George Hoskins	4–1
1894	George Hoskins	6-0-1
1895	George Hoskins	2-2-3

Finally, PSU had coaches and scheduled games

Penn State 1892 Football Team with 1st Coach Hoskins in a Tie

Penn State was now established both within the institution and outside with other universities as an independent football school, ready to play a full season and ready to be successful. The University upped the ante in 1892 by reaching into its finances to hire its first football coach.

Picture shows the disorganization of the game of American football at the time

1894 American Football Game

George "Doc" Hoskins Penn State Coach #1

George Hoskins was hired in 1892 as Pennsylvania State University's first head football coach. He resigned at the end of the 1895 season to become head coach at Bucknell and served a trainer for the Cincinnati Reds Baseball organization.

George "Doc" Hoskins served as Penn State's first head coach, while also a player for the Nittany Lions. A three year letterman at center, he had been the athletic trainer at Vermont before being appointed Penn State's first director of physical training and first instructor of physical education. His duties included coaching the football team to a PSU # 1 win percentage with a record of 17-4-4.

Hoskins was a great coach for Penn State. His .760 winning percentage ranks highest in school history, surpassing notable coaches such as Joe Paterno, Hugo Bezdek, and Rip Engle

Though a student athlete himself, (he played center), Hoskins was the first head coach of PSU. Thus, Penn State's 1892 football season was its first with a formal head coach. George "Doc" Hoskins was at the helm. He did a fine job in his four years and really gave football a big boost at Penn State.

1892 Penn State Football Season Coach George "Doc" Hoskins

The 1892 team record was a very respectable 5-1 for the season. They began slowly with a first game loss at the University of Pennsylvania, a very tough opponent at the time L (0–20).

Then Penn State played a home game against Wyoming Seminary from Northeastern, PA, which is about three hours from Penn State, and just over the five miles from where I live. "Sem," as we call it was and is still a prep school. I found it interesting that they would play college teams. Many teams of the day, in order to get games would play prep schools and even high schools sometime. Prep schools of course would also play high schools just to get a game. PSU did a great job against SEM, who had traveled to the Old Main Lawn for the game. PSU won the game W (40-0).

The Pittsburgh Athletic Club did not care if you were a college team, pro-team, high school team, or a prep team as they, like every other football team at the time were happy just to get a game. They brought their athletic manliness into the Old Main Lawn on October 27, and fought a hard battle but could not score. PSU got a nice W (16-0).

The no-longer pushover Bucknell team came to the Old Main Lawn on November 12 and were beaten soundly but no pushover W (18-0). After this it was Lafayette W (18-0) and Dickinson W (16-0). Penn State had learned to win and no PSU team ever wanted to lose again after tasting both the thrill of victory and the agony of defeat. Hoskins was a fine coach while he had the reins at PSU

1992 Football Facts / Tradition

This was the first Penn State football championship team. They were crowned in 1892 having won The Pennsylvania Intercollegiate Foot-Ball Association trophy, edging out Bucknell with a 4-1 league record.

Bucknell quickly became Penn State's first "football rivalry". During this rivalry, games were often heated and hotly contested. The final game between Penn State and Bucknell was played October 2, 1948, Penn State winning 35-0 at what was called, "New Beaver Field." Penn State finished with a 28-10 record against "rival" Bucknell. World War II was tough on a lot of once successful college football programs and many schools completely dropped the sport during and some after the war was over.

Bucknell continues to compete in football in the Division 1 - Football Championship Subdivision of the NCAA. Over the years, PSU has grown to be about 25 X the size of Bucknell's student enrollment of 3600.

1893 Penn State Football Season Coach George "Doc" Hoskins

The 1893 Penn State Nittany Lions football team represented the Pennsylvania State University. The team was coached by George Hoskins in his second year as head coach. FYI, the school did not adopt the Nittany Lion as its mascot until 1907, and Penn State did not become a university until 1953. Nonetheless, we sometimes intentionally refer to the team as the Nittany Lions, and we refer to the institution as PSU. As long as we all know the facts, we will continue to do so as there are few fact checkers from the 1890's around today to get upset with either reference.

The 1893 football team would be the first to play on Beaver Field, Penn State football's first permanent home.

Penn State 1893 Football Team with 1st Coach Hoskins with a hat

Undefeated seasons were tough to come by as all teams were in their infancy but some had more money to spend on their programs. PSU began the season at Virginia and came back home with a nice W (6–0). Playing again at U of P in Philadelphia, PSU found this well-oiled machine still just a bit much and were defeated L (6-18).

Penn State had just built its 500 seat stadium named Beaver Field and Pittsburgh came to Beaver Field for the first time and the first game on the new home field. The Nittany Lions prevailed W (32–0). Then it was a game at Bucknell in a high scoring win W (36-18) followed by the Pittsburgh Athletic Club, a tough bunch of independents from the left side of Pennsylvania for a close on W (12-0) .

1894 Penn State Football Season Coach George "Doc" Hoskins

The 1894 Penn State Nittany Lions football team represented the Pennsylvania State University in the college football season. The team was coached by George Hoskins for the third year and for the second year, PSU played its home games on Beaver Field in University Park, Pennsylvania.

This was a very successful season for Hoskins and Penn State, gaining a 6-0-1. Penn State was undefeated and untied just once in a close match at Navy on November 10 at Annapolis. The team got rolling quickly on October 13 against Gettysburg at beaver Field with a really big win W (60-0). Penn State football was in graduate school for sure as they played and beat the once impregnable Lafayette at home on October 20, W (72-0).

The Navy tie came next (6-6 at Navy. Then, with a 2-0-1 record, Penn State rolled through its next four games, which were all away. The margins of victory were not big but the determination to win was well established for Penn State teams. First at Bucknell W (12-6); Then, Washington & Jefferson W (6-0), Followed by Oberlin of Ohio W (9-6), and the last game against the Pittsburgh Athletic Club at Pittsburgh on November 29, right after Thanksgiving W (14-0).

1895 Penn State Football Season Coach George "Doc" Hoskins

Considering the team played just seven games, which was a typical season in 1895, having played three ties, Penn State's record looks a lot worse than it actually was. 2-2-3. The 1895 Penn State Nittany Lions football team represented the Pennsylvania State University in college football and this year, the team tied or lost the close games compared with 1894 when in all cases, they won or tied. The team was coached for the fourth and last year by George Hoskins.

The season started well at home on September 25 with a W (26-0) v Gettysburg. Penn State then travelled to upstate NY to play Cornell at Ithaca and came away with a tie T (0-0). Off to Bucknell for a W (16-0) and it looked like a normal successful year for Coach Hoskins.

Then, on November 9, Penn State traveled to the University of Pennsylvania and played a game at Franklin Field, which had just been dedicated for the Penn Relays in April, 1895. Penn State had never beaten Penn at the time and this time, they had a really tough time in defeat L (4-35).

Being down a bit from their first loss in two years, the worst that could happen happened when the Nittany Lions traveled to Pittsburgh to play the Athletic club and for the first time were defeated L (10-11) by the slimmest of margins. Penn State came back from these two losses and scored two ties at Washington & Jefferson T (6-6) and Western Reserve at Cleveland T (8-8).

George Hoskins somehow had some eligibility left as a player. Since many colleges and universities were trying to save a buck on their football programs, many for years had no coaches, and then when they decided to pay for a professional coach, they often picked one of the more seasoned members of the team to coach or they lured another student/coach from another institution to coach at their school.

George Hoskins we might say was stolen by Pitt as many student coaches were stolen during this early time period in college football. Though a well-respected coach at Penn State, as you will read in the next chapter, when Sam Newton brought his Penn State team to Pittsburgh in 1896, there was a major brawl and coach / player Hoskins was right in the middle of it. He wore out his welcome at Penn State and Hoskins coached just one year at Pitt before he left and went to Bucknell.

Chapter 11 — Penn State Football – the Sam Newton Era

Coach #2 Sam Newton
Coach #3 Sam Boyle

Penn State faced some tough years

1896	Sam Newton	3-4
1897	Sam Newton	3-6
1898	Sam Newton	6-4
1899	Sam Boyle	4-6-1

1896 Penn State Football Season Coach Samuel Newton

The 1896 Penn State Nittany Lions football team represented the Pennsylvania State University in the 1896 college football season. The team was coached by in his first year by Samuel Newton and it played its home games on Beaver Field in University Park, Pennsylvania.

Penn State 1896 Football Team

Sam Newton's gang started off the season with a nice win against Gettysburg W (40-0). This was followed by a trip to Pittsburgh that will be forever remembered in the annals of Penn State Football.

Samuel B. Newton

Newton pictured in *La Vie 1900*, Penn State

When George Hoskins faced Penn State ion October 3, 1896 as a player / coach for Pitt at Beaver Field, he was clearly the enemy. They say from this game on, he was an enemy without any sense of fair play.

The football game became the biggest brawl ever at Beaver Field, and to those watching who covered the game as reporters for the Student Newspaper *Free Lance*, the brawl was instigated as a result of Hoskins' dirty play. Mr. Hoskins impressed none of his one-time admirers that day on Beaver Field. Despite the brawling, Penn State defeated Western PA 10-4 in what was literally a tough game.

According to Free Lance, while playing center and coaching for Western University of Pittsburgh (now Pitt) at Beaver Field where he had coached the prior four years, " he gave such an exhibition of unmanly defiance of all fair rules which degrades the game as to make it a lasting example of the "antis" who hold up to public opinion. This "did more injury to the prestige of the game of football than its promoter can repair."

The four years of great coaching and mentoring that Hoskins had done for Penn State had turned sour. It seems that forgiveness would take a while to bring his good work back into good graces.

For all of his bad points in this game he had a great record at Penn State and today teams would be trying to coach him into coaching but his behavior was a big negative. Penn State went through a chilly period trying to get its program back on track after Hoskins' tenure. Reports from that era indicate that the folks at Penn State did not think things were ok in the coaching ranks until as they say, a "Pop and a Mother" came aboard.

We will get there soon enough in this book but it was William "Pop" Golden who compiled a 16-12-1 record as the head coach from 1900 to 1902 while also serving as trainer. Pop Golden did more than coach and help condition athletes, however.

Following the 1902 season, Golden took the job as Penn State's first Athletic Director and he continued to stay with the football staff as an assistant coach until 1909. Golden presided over the "golden" years of Penn State's unprecedented growth in athletics—most notably football. He started the first training table and he helped raise additional funds by working with alumni and others to turn sports into a profit-maker for the university. He also did recruiting for Penn State.

The 1902 season was his best as a coach and it also featured the best individual performance ever by a Penn State back. Andy Smith scored five touchdowns, and kicked two extra points in a 55-0 rout of Susquehanna. Smith was then stolen by the University of Pennsylvania.

On October 10, in another home game at Beaver Field, Penn State defeated Dickinson W (8-0). SO far, nobody was missing Hoskins but that would quickly change when Penn State went on the road for the last four games of the season.

On October 24, PSU went to Princeton and were soundly defeated L (0-39). The Ivy League back then was tough. Even

Bucknell on October 31, had its way with the Newton's team L (0-10). Then, as expected, Penn played tough again at Franklin Field and beat Penn State L (0-27). Penn State had lost three in a row and had one game left against the Carlisle Indians. They were beaten again this time by a wide margin (5-48).Sam Newton's first season, which started with major promise did not end well.

1897 Penn State Football Season Coach Samuel Newton

The 1897 Penn State Nittany Lions football team r was coached by Samuel Newton and played its home games at Beaver Field in University Park, Pennsylvania.

Samuel Newton was in his second year when the 1897 Penn State Nittany Lions football team experienced its second losing season in a row.

After a win in the opening game W 32-0 against Gettysburg, the Penn State team went to sleep, losing five away games in a row to Lafayette L (0-24), Princeton, (L (0-34), Penn L (0-24), Navy L (0-4), and Cornell L (0-45). Penn State came back and won games 7 and 8 by defeating Bucknell W 27-4) and Bloomsburg Normal W (10-0. Penn State finished the season with a loss L (0-6) against Dickinson.

It was a dismal season and there was not much good in the season and so we tell the story with a minimum of words.

1898 Penn State Football Season Coach Samuel Newton

The 1898 Penn State Nittany Lions football team was coached by Samuel Newton in his third and last year as head coach. The team made a great comeback from 1897 with a ten game schedule, the most in history, and a positive win-loss record at 6-4.

Things started well on September 24 to begin the season against Gettysburg at home on Beaver Field... a rare home game. Penn State clipped a win W (47-0). Then came an early season encounter against a team that Penn State had never defeated, the University of Pennsylvania, at Franklin Field, the best of the best at the time, and though there was hope, it quickly disappeared as Penn defeated Penn State L (0-40).

Tough as they always had been Lafayette played their best against Penn State on October 8, but lost to the PS team from University Park, W (5-0).

Susquehanna marched into Beaver Field on October 20 and went down quickly W (45–6). Navy, always tough away at Annapolis defeated PSU at Worden Field in Annapolis, MD L (11–16)

PSU then lost to Princeton away L 0–5, and on October 29, the team traveled to Pittsburgh to play the Duquesne Athletic Club, but lost L (5–18) On November 5, PSU redeemed itself against Bucknell away W (16–0). Then, on November 19 at Washington & Jefferson, PSU won again W (11–6). On Nov. 25 v. Dickinson, Penn State had regained its form and won W 34–0.

The 1899 Penn State Nittany Lions football team was coached by Sam Boyle and played its home games on Beaver Field in University Park, Pennsylvania. PSU had few home games in their small field but this year, there were three.

The first game against Mansfield was played at home (38-0). This was followed by Gettysburg, which were defeated W (40-0). Then, the really tough games began such as PSU's first game against Army, which, because of the nature of the cadets, very infrequently played away. On October 7, PSU defeated Army W (6-0).

No games were easy. On October 13, Penn State played to a T (0-0) tie against Washington & Jefferson, and the first loss came at Princeton L (0-12). Navy always tough hosted the team in Annapolis and beat Penn State L (0–6). Then it was Dickinson, a more local team at home W (15–0).

1899 Penn State Football Season Coach Sam Boyle (1st Season)

1899 Penn State football team coached by Sam Boyle

It had been a reasonably good season until November with multiple losses starting on November 4 v Bucknell L (0–5). This was followed on Nov. 11 by a tough Yale team at Yale L (0–42). It seemed like PSU would never be able to beat Penn and on Nov. 17 at the continually upgraded Franklin Field in Philadelphia, PA, PSU could not dig out a win (L 0–47)
On November 25 at the Duquesne Athletic Club in Pittsburgh, PA, the non-collegians were pleased to put it to the collegians L (5–64).

Winning was very important for Penn State but as good a team as PSU could field there were a lot of other good and even better teams, even some that were not constrained by college rules that wanted to win more or had better players to win the games of the day.

Chapter 12 — PSU Football – the Pop Golden Era

Coach # 4 Pop Golden
Coach # 5 Daniel A. Reed

Penn State faced some tough years

1900	Pop Golden	4-6-1
1901	Pop Golden	5-3
1902	Pop Golden	7-3
1903	Daniel A. Reed	5-3

PSU Team Pop Golden Coach -- 1900

1900 Penn State Football Season Coach Pop Golden (1st Season)

The 1900 Penn State Nittany Lions football team was coached by Pop Golden in his first year as head coach. Penn State continued to play its home games at Beaver Field in University Park, Pennsylvania.

Pop Golden (left) won his first game with Penn State on September 23 with a win W (17-0) over Susquehanna at Beaver Field. The team then went to Pittsburgh and won W (12-0) on September 30.

The following week, October 6, at Army in West Point, NY, Penn State tied T (0-0) in a scoreless match.

Next came the Ivy League. First at Princeton; the Tigers defeated PSU handily L 0-26) and on October 17, the Penn Quakers defeated Penn State at Franklin Field L (5-17).

On October 20, PUS lost to Dickinson L (0-18). Next was Duquesne Athletic Club at Pittsburgh, L (0-29); and then Penn State came back against Bucknell at Williamsport on November 3 W (6-0). On November 10, Navy defeated Penn State at Annapolis L (0-44).

Gettysburg then played Penn State at Beaver Stadium W (44-0). On November 29, PSU wrapped up its first season under Pop Golden at Buffalo L (0-10). Season results were 4-6-1.

1901 Penn State Football Season Coach Pop Golden

The 1901 Penn State Nittany Lions football team r was coached by Pop Golden in his second year as head coach. The team played three less games but had a much better record than in 1900, finishing at 5-3.

The season began on September 22 when Susquehanna came to Beaver Field and Penn State won their season opener W (17–0). The in-state Pittsburgh rivalry was next played at Pittsburgh on September 29. Penn State won another nice game W (37-0).

Still no luck at Penn, Penn State lost to the Quakers, L (6–23) and then to Yale at New Haven L (0–22). On October 26, it was the Middies of Navy at Annapolis for a nice PSU Win W (11-6). The Homestead Athletic Club at Pittsburgh resulted in the third loss of the season L (0–39). On November 16, PSU played Lehigh at Williamsport W (38-0). The final game of the season was at home against Dickinson. PSU captured the W (12-0).

1902 Penn State Football Season Coach Pop Golden

In 1902, the Penn State Nittany Lions football team were coached for the third and final year by Pop Golden. This was Golden's finest year as the team finished the ten game season with a very nice 7-3 record.

The season began at home on September 20, against Dickinson Seminary at Beaver Field for a W (27-0). Pittsburgh came to town to play PSU at home and lost W (27-0). Still no luck with the University of PS as the Nittany Lions traveled again to Franklin Field and were defeated L (0-17).

On October 11, Villanova came to Beaver Stadium. PSU prevailed against the Wildcats (32-0). On October 18, Penn State traveled to Connecticut and were defeated by Yale L (0-11). The next week Penn State beat Susquehanna at home for a big win W (55-0). On November 1, PSU beat Navy at Annapolis W (6-0) and the following week at home beat Gettysburg W (37-0). On November 22, PSU played Dickinson in Carlyle and won W (23-0). In its first game against the Steelton YMCA at Steelton, PA, Penn State lost a really close game L (5-6).

1903 Penn State Football Season Coach Daniel A. Reed

The 1903 Penn State Nittany Lions football team was coached by Daniel A. Reed in his first and only season as varsity football head coach. The team had a winning season at (5-3)

PSU Football Team 1903 Coach Daniel A. Reed

Penn State through 1903 had good fortune in its opening day games, which almost always to this point had doubled as home openers. This was no different with Dickinson Seminary being defeated on September 19 W 60-0). Allegheny was the next home game on October 3 W 24-5).

Bad fortune was staring Penn State in the face as it made its annual trek to the University of Pennsylvania on October 10 and were defeated again L (0-39.) Yale was the next week at New Haven CT L (0-27). Penn State then went to Pittsburgh and soundly won the game W (59-0).

On October 31, PSU trekked to Annapolis to play Navy and won the game W (17-0). Dickinson gave PSU trouble on November 14 and beat Penn State L (0-6). On November 26, Daniel A Reed's team finished the season with a win W (22-0) against Washington & Jefferson in Pittsburgh, PA.

Chapter 13 — Penn State Football — Tom Fennell Era

Coach # 6

Penn State faced some tough years

1904	Tom Fennell	6-4
1905	Tom Fennell	5-3
1906	Tom Fennell	8-1-1
1904	Tom Fennell	6-4
1905	Tom Fennell	5-5

1904 Penn State Football Season Coach Tom Fennell

PSU Football Team 1904 Tom Fennell Coach -- Left

The 1904 Penn State Nittany Lions football team was coached by Tom Fennell in his first season. The team continued to play its home games on Beaver Field in University Park, Pennsylvania. Fennell was coach for five years in total. This year his record was good for a first year PSU coach at 6-4.

Tom Fennell

Fennell pictured in La Vie 1906, Penn State yearbook

Fennell began his PSU career with a baptism of fire loss against Pennsylvania September 24 at Franklin Field. Penn State to this point had never beaten a Penn team but this time Fennell's team came very close L (0-6). The team sprung right back and defeated Allegheny at home W (50-0) and then on October 8 lost at Yale L (0-24).

West Virginia came to Beaver Field on October 15 and established a rivalry. Penn State beat the Mountaineers W (34-0. PSU then beat Washington & Jefferson at Pittsburgh on October 22 W (12-0), followed by another home win—this time against the Jersey Shore Athletic Club W (30-0). November 5, PSU lost at Navy L (9-20) and came back the following week at Dickinson for a nice win W (11-0)

On November 19, Geneva played PSU at Beaver Field W (44–0), and on November 24 (Thanksgiving Day) PSU lost at Pittsburgh (5-12) to end the season at 6-4.

1905 Penn State Football Season Coach Tom Fennell

The 1905 Penn State Nittany Lions football team was coached by Tom Fennell. Soon, in 1907, we will be able to honestly refer to Penn State as the Nittany Lions. In fact, we use PSU all the time but in fact the official university status was not granted until 1953. When we say, PSU, think Penn State. For the record, PSU did not adopt the Nittany Lion as its mascot until 1907. We have two more years to wait until Fennell's fourth year.

The season began comparatively early this year on September 16 when Penn State won its home opener at Beaver Field against Lebanon Valley W (23-0). California PA next came to Beaver Stadium and PSU got a nice victory W (29-0). Penn State took a trip on October 7 to Harrisburg PA to play a national powerhouse team known as the Carlisle Indians. The Carlisle Indians defeated a tough Penn State squad in a reasonably close game L (0-11). I started to wonder if this were a gymnasium pick-up team or whether it was a bonafide school. It was the latter. Here is what I found:

The Carlisle Indians football team represented the Carlisle Indian Industrial School in intercollegiate football competition. The school had an active football program for 25 years from 1893 until 1917, when it was discontinued. The Indians were a fine team, compiling a 167–88–13 record and a 0.647 winning percentage.

With this enviable record, it makes the Carlisle Indians the most successful defunct major college football program. During their period of activity in the early 20th century, Carlisle was a national football powerhouse, and regularly competed against other major programs such as the Ivy League schools. There are several notable players and coaches that were associated with the team, whose names are immediately recognizable. These include Glenn "Pop" Warner and Jim Thorpe.

On October 14 at Beaver Field PSU defeated Gettysburg W (18-0). Penn State was then defeated at Yale L (0-12) and when Villanova came to Beaver Field on October 28, PSU defeated them W (29-0)

PSU then played Navy at Annapolis and lost a close on (5-11) Geneva came to Beaver field the following week on November 11 and were soundly defeated W (73-0) The following week PSU traveled to Dickinson and defeated them in a close on W (6-0).

West Virginia played PSU at Beaver Field on November 24, and for the second straight week, PSU won the game by a score of W (6-0). Penn State completed the season the following week on Thanksgiving Day, November 30 at Pittsburgh by the same score W (6-0). Fennell's team was 8-3 and things looked good for PSU.

1906 Penn State Football Season Coach Tom Fennell

The 1906 Penn State Nittany Lions football team was coached by Tom Fennell for the third year. The team had a great record 8-1-1, with a tie T (0-0) tie against Gettysburg and an away loss at Yale L (0-10).

The season began at Beaver Field against Lebanon Valley W (24-0) followed by another home win against Allegheny W (26-0) and a very close away win against the tough Carlisle Indians W (4-0). Then, on October 13 came the LT (0-0) v Gettysburg and the loss at Yale L (0-10).

It was a close-game year with a lot of shutouts both ways. PSU beat Navy at Annapolis on November 3 W 5-0), followed by a W (12-0) against Bellefonte Academy at home. Then another W (6-0) at Dickinson and on November 24, a home win against West Virginia W 10-0. PSU had a great defense but had a tough time scoring points. Pittsburgh was the final game on Thanksgiving November 29 W (6-0).

1907 Penn State Football Season Coach Tom Fennell

The 1907 Penn State Nittany Lions football team was coached by Tom Fennell in his fourth year. This was the first year when Penn State adopted the Nittany Lion as its official mascot. The team finished with a respectable 6-4 record.

Penn State began the season with a W (27-0) at Altoona PA v the Altoona Athletic Association. The following week Geneva came to Beaver Field and were beaten by the Nittany Lions W (34-0). PSU went to Williamsport to play Carlisle and the Nittany Lions were handed their first a defeat of 1907 L (5-18). Grove City came to Beaver Stadium and left with a defeat. W (46-0). PSU played at Cornell, another tough Ivy League competitor on October 19 and managed to squeak out a W (8-6).

Penn State welcomed Lebanon Valley the following week to a manhandling W (75-0). Then PSU defeated Dickinson away W (52-0) and on November 16, the Nittany Lions lost a real close one at Navy in Annapolis L (4-6)

On Thanksgiving November 28, PSU traveled to Pittsburgh for the rivalry game and came home with a loss L (0-6), finishing the season at 6-4. This was the fourth winning season for Coach Tom Fennell

1908 Penn State Football Season Coach Tom Fennell

The 1908 Penn State Nittany Lions football team was coached by Tom Fennell in his fifth and last season as the head coach of Penn State. Fennel resigned after this season from Penn State and from football. He had the makings of a great coach!

The 1908 season began at Beaver Field with an unprecedented loss in a home opener delivered on September 19 by Bellefonte Academy L (5–6). The win was so close to being made, it could be tasted.

On September 26, PSU defeated Grove City at Beaver Field W (31-0). On October 3, the Carlisle Indians booked a game with PSU to be played in my home town of Wilkes-Barre PA. They were too tough for the 1908 Fennell team which lost L (5-12).

Having scheduled Penn again for an October 10 game at Franklin Field, Penn State again did not have enough to take down the Quakers. Penn State lost again to Penn L (0-6). One day PSU would win but it was not today.

On October 17 PSU played Geneva at Beaver Field and won big W (51-0). The next week at Beaver Field, West Virginia came in and were defeated W (12-0). Always struggling with Ivy League teams, PSU lost a close one at Ithaca, NY to Cornell on October 31 L (4-10).

Bucknell arrived on November 7 ready to take on the Nittany Lions but were sent back home with a defeat W (33-6). Navy was next on November 14. Always a powerhouse in the early days and the war years, Penn State lost at Annapolis L (0-5). On Thanksgiving Day, PSU played Pittsburgh at Pittsburgh in the big rivalry game again and this time the Nittany Lions got to take home the gravy W (12-6)

Summary of the Fennell years

Tom Fennell was named Penn State's first full-time head coach in 1904 and compiled a 33-17-1 record in five seasons. He was hired exclusively to coach football and held no additional duties. A graduate of Cornell, where he was a standout in football, Fennell gave up the Penn State post after the 1908 season. He returned to law practice in Elmira, N.Y., and later became a judge. Somehow back then, a judge was a more lucrative position than a football coach.

Chapter 14—The Hollenback Era

Coach # 7 Bill Hollenback
Coach # 8 Jack Hollenback

1909	Bill Hollenback	5-0-2
1910	Jack Hollenback	5-2-1
1911	Bill Hollenback	8-0-1
1912	Bill Hollenback	8-0
1913	Bill Hollenback	2-6
1914	Bill Hollenback	5-3-1

1909 Penn State Football Season Coach Bill Hollenback

Though Penn State had some very fine coaches in its early years including Jim Fennell, who figured he would rather be a judge, the notion of Penn State Era coaches really began with Bill Hollenback, who was like a Knute Rockne, though never as celebrated for Penn State. William Marshall "Big Bill" Hollenback was as good as it gets.

PSU Football Team 1909 Coached by Bill Hollenback -Right

His brother Jack, who filled in one year while Bill tested the waters at Missouri was no slouch either. The Hollenback brothers coached the Penn State Nittany Lions football teams from 1909 to 1914. In Bill's five seasons, he compiled a 28–9–4 record and a .732 winning percentage. Jack Hollenback's team was 5-2-1 with an expected loss v never PSU-beaten Penn and a tough game at Thanksgiving v Pittsburgh. Jack Hollenback could have coached anywhere.

Bill Hollenback's 1911 and 1912 teams were declared national champions. The University was not a university back then and for its own reasons fails to claim these championships. I think they should.

Bill Hollenback's first team after Fennell's 5-5 season was also undefeated with two ties and no recognition but, ladies and gentlemen of the jury, he got no credit for this. He followed a 5-5 coach and went undefeated. Think about how good this guy was in 1909!

Nonetheless it was PSU's first undefeated season in some time. This was a tremendous coach and if we can add his brother as a fine extension, they were as good as it gets in football...ever!

Bill Hollenback, still a kid but a tough kid, nonetheless, trying to find out what the world had to offer, took a ride to the University of Missouri in 1910 to test his mettle and his abilities and to see if what he thought he wanted was what he really wanted. Good for him! What did he know? He intended to find out and did!

He came back to Penn State. Good for us! After making history, and after his brother made history, this great coach made big time history with two consensus national championships that are not on the PSU list. Beaver Field with a capacity of 500 fans at the time, was not big enough to ever pay the other big teams for coming to play. Penn State realized this as all other teams in the US were planning stadium expansions. Before expansions Penn State took on many road trips just to gain major capacity turnouts. With a stadium that could offer real revenue on ticket sales, it would not be long that more teams were coming to University Park and its New Beaver Field (30,000)

Bill Hollenback's teams played all of their home games at the New Beaver Field, which opened in 1909. This field could pay for the whole PSU football program at the time, and because of it, and Bill Hollenback, PSU was able to achieve much more than otherwise.

What a difference a coach makes!

If I were a songwriter after writing a few of these great moments' books, I feel I know the difference between good teams and bad teams. I would write a song to the sound of what a difference a day makes and it would be "What a difference a coach makes!" Bill Hollenback (left) was a difference maker. Joe Paterno was also a difference maker!

I played a little football in High School but was never great but I was pretty good in baseball and started in college as a pitcher and had some great games. I had a great coach. I was a great little league coach taking a team that was a non-winner and two out of three years providing championships while all kids played more than the minimum. I coached soccer teams to championships when nobody else could. I knew what to do and I know good coaches know what to do. What a difference a coach makes!

Tom Fennell was a great coach but maybe he doubted himself about coaching. Who knows! He brought glory to Penn State for sure but maybe he disappointed himself in his last year (5-5) and left the program and became successful because it was in him. He was destined for success...if it were not football, it would be something else...such as the courtroom.

Bill Hollenback was as good a coach as it gets. He was a man with a Paterno spirit. He came back from Missouri to help make Penn State great again!

The 1909 Penn State Nittany Lions football team was coached by Bill Hollenback and for the first time ever played its home games in the New Beaver Field in University Park, Pennsylvania.

The 1909 season went down as one of the most dangerous in the history of college football. The third annual survey by the Chicago Tribune at season's end showed that 10 college players had been killed and 38 seriously injured in 1909, up from six fatalities and 14 maimings in 1908. The nation was beginning to examine changes to college football to make it safer.

American football rules 1909

American football rules were continually evolving and were much different in 1909 than the sports rules a century or even fifty years later. Many of the present standard notions such as a 100 yard field; four downs to gain ten yards; and the 6-point touchdown) would not be adopted until 1912.

Field goals were drop kicks and they were worth four points until 1909, when their value was reduced by one point to 3 points each. Touchdowns stayed at 5 points until 1912. The rules changes about field goals came about because players and spectators felt that two field kick goals should not be of greater value than a touchdown (five points) from which a goal is scored.

Since 1912, a touchdown has been worth six points which accommodates the latter thinking. Until 1909, anybody on the team could receive a forward pass. This changed by declaring various line positions as ineligible. Wikipedia offers a nice summary of the 1909 rules of consequence. The rules in 1909 were:

- Field 110 yards in length
- Kickoff made from midfield
- Three downs to gain ten yards
- Touchdown worth 5 points
- Field goal worth 3 points
- Game time based on agreement of the teams, not to exceed two 45 minute halves
- Forward pass legal, but subject to various penalties

The game of American football was evolving as were the institutions that chose to participate.

The 1909 Games

Bill Hollenback was a stickler for the importance of conditioning and winning. In the first game at Penn State's New Beaver Field against Grove City, Hollenback's newly invigorated Nittany Lions, playing with a new coach and in a new stadium gained a nice victory W (31-0).

Penn State then tied the Carlisle Indians on October 9 in Wilkes-Barre, PA T (8-8). On October 16, the Nittany Lions defeated Geneva at home W (46-0). The next week, Bill Hollenback's team made history against the University of Pennsylvania with a tie T (3-3). This was the first time playing the Quakers at Franklin Field that the Nittany Lions escaped defeat.

The Ivy League was beginning to lose its edge. Previously the "Big Four" (Harvard, Yale, Princeton and Penn) had dominated college football. Just about every year one of these teams was on the Nittany Lions' schedule.

On November 6, The Nittany Lions shut-out Bucknell at Lewisburg W (33-0). On November 12, West Virginia came to New Beaver Field and were defeated soundly W (40-0) Finally, to wrap up the season on what had become a regular Thanksgiving Day game, PSU played Pittsburgh at Forbes Field and defeated their western rivals handily W (37-0). At 5-0-2, Bill Hollenback had brought another undefeated season to Penn State fans but then, he decided to leave for an offer at Missouri. His older brother jack would take the team in 1910.

1910 Penn State Football Season Coach Jack Hollenback

The 1910 Penn State Nittany Lions football team was coached by Jack Hollenback, (picture below) Bill's older brother. Bill had taken a year to test the water outside Pennsylvania.

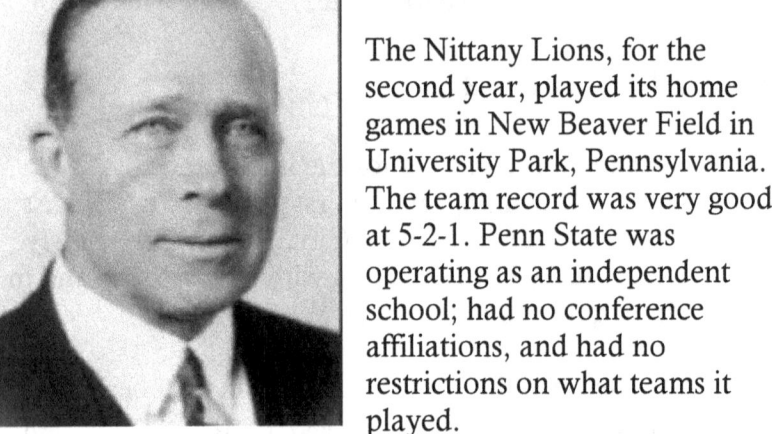

The Nittany Lions, for the second year, played its home games in New Beaver Field in University Park, Pennsylvania. The team record was very good at 5-2-1. Penn State was operating as an independent school; had no conference affiliations, and had no restrictions on what teams it played.

The season started a bit late on October 1 at New Beaver Field as Penn State shut-out the Harrisburg Athletic Club by a whopping W (58-0). Carnegie Teach played at New Beaver Stadium the following week on Oct. 8 and were defeated by an even greater margin W (61-0). A rare third home game in a row found the Nittany lions overpowering the Sterling Athletic club W (45-0).

On October 22, it was off to the Ivy League in Franklin Field against Penn. The game as usual was tough with Penn State on the small side of the score L (0-10). Villanova came into New Beaver Field the following week and tied the Nittany Lions T (0-0) St. Bonaventure tested our mettle the following week, November 5, and lost to the Nittany Lions W (34-0).

Bucknell was next at home for another overpowering PSU win W (45-3). The final game of the season was the Thanksgiving rivalry v Pittsburgh. The Nittany Lions suffered their second away-game loss of the season in a close match L (0-11). Jack Hollenback had done a fine job for Penn State with a 5-2-1 record.

Though he coached Penn State for just one year, Jack Hollenback was a fine coach just like his younger brother Bill. Bill had taken the head position at Missouri and for those of us on the sidelines, it wee as if Jack stepped up to help his little brother go after what might have been a life's dream. When it did not work out for Bill, though he surely had a claim to the job, Jack stepped aside and brother Bill came back and took up the task just as he had left it. Long before the PSU greats like Engle and Paterno, the Hollenback brothers were surely impressive.

The Nittany Lions were 5-2-1 in a season which saw admission charged for the first time when Penn State met Bucknell on Nov. 12 at Beaver Field. A Pennsylvania graduate in dentistry, Hollenback also coached at Franklin & Marshall (1908-09) and at the Pennsylvania Military College (Widener) in 1911 before opening a dental practice in Philipsburg, Pa. Brother Bill also had a dentistry degree but opted for football over dentistry. Jack later joined his brother briefly in the coal brokerage business in Philadelphia.

1911 Penn State Football Season Coach Bill Hollenback

The 1911 Penn State Nittany Lions football team was coached by Bill Hollenback, who had succeeded his brother Jack who had succeeded his brother Bill a year earlier. Jack stepped down so his brother could come back to Penn State as its coach after a one-year trek to Missouri. In 1909, Hollenback had an undefeated season with two ties (5-0-2). This year his team produced another undefeated record with just one tie. The team was recognized retroactively as a co-national champion by the National Championship Foundation.

Since there were no national championships per se awarded back in 1911 or 2012; they were awarded post-facto by much respected groups / committees such as the NCF to make life fair, though after the fact. Though nothing really official existed from 1911 and 1912, Penn State does not appear to refute the claim that this acknowledgment by the NCF is official as do most scribes, pundits and officials. PSU thus has four consensus national championships—1911, 1912 (Bill Hollenback), and 1982 and 1986 (Joe Paterno).

These and other titles, whether shared or solo, which in fact, the NCAA does recognize, one day may be considered official by Penn State University. All things considered, Penn State is more than already halfway to recognizing those titles as the 1911, 1912, 1969, 1982 1986, and 1994 seasons are already showcased on the suites at Beaver Stadium.

The Repeating Brothers Hollenback

More than likely, this was the only time ever in college football that a brother team coached the same team as one coach. It was like sandlot football rules: "Hey, I can't coach next year so my brother has the team. See ya in two." You gotta be impressed with the Hollenback brothers.

Though I never read this in any chronicle about them, I think they loved each other as brothers and would do anything for each other including taking over a huge varsity football program at Penn State while still having a head coaching job. That is impressive for sure. The Hollenback brothers are the type of coaches that you wish, like Joe Paterno, would have stayed around twenty or thirty or forty or fifty years. What a duo!

The boys were born in Blue Bell, PA Born in Blue Bell, Pennsylvania, Hollenback attended Phillipsburg High School. Both Hollenback's got their dental degrees from Penn Dental and instead of dentistry, the field of endeavor they worked together in happened to be football.

As an undergraduate at the University of Pennsylvania from 1904 to 1908, Bill Hollenback became one of the school's most renowned football players. He played end in 1904. During the 1904 season, Bill was unable to play because of a broken leg. Jack had already graduated so he could not fill in.

After returning from the injury, Hollenback was moved to the fullback, a position he played from 1906 to 1908. He was known as Big Bill Hollenback for a reason. He was big and tough. He was selected as an All-American fullback in each of his three years as fullback for Penn.

When a senior in 1908, Bill Hollenback was the captain of the undefeated Penn team that was named national champion. When the world famous Jim Thorpe gives you a compliment, it is not without deserving. In Wilkes-Barre, PA, my home town, we would call that as good as "praise from Caesar himself."

Thorpe's Carlisle Indians team played Penn to a 6–6 tie in 1908. The legendary Jim Thorpe called Hollenback his "greatest and toughest opponent." Hollenback had gotten praise from Caesar himself.

In 1921, after his PSU years and on to other ventures, he still had the bug to play. So, Bill Hollenback played professional football for the Union Quakers of Philadelphia alongside future Philadelphia Eagles founder, co-owner and coach, Bert Bell.

In 1925, when he had stopped playing, Bill Hollenback still made some history. He served as the referee for the Pottsville Maroons' 9–7 victory over the Notre Dame All-Stars, featuring the legendary Four Horsemen, at Shibe Park. There is not much information about the game but it was very controversial and it resulted in a tussle that stripped the Maroons of their 1925 NFL championship.

The 1911 Games

Another late season start at New Beaver Field saw Geneva rolling into town on for the season opener on September 30, and then being carried out shortly after the trouncing win W (57-0) suffered at the hands of the Nittany Lions. Gettysburg came home to PSU on Oct.7 and lost W (31-0). PSU was ready to take on the Ivy League again and this time it was Cornell at Ithaca, NY. The Lions gained a big win in a close match W (5-0) before touchdowns were worth six points. Villanova was next at New Beaver Stadium W (18-0)

Because they had the premiere team in the East at the time, Penn somehow was able to negotiate a deal with Penn State that they would not be required to play on New Beaver Field or Beaver Field or the Old main Lawn or any field at home in which Penn State Played its games. That's a pretty good deal if you can get it.

On October, 28 Penn State visited Franklin Field again to play a team they had never beaten—the Penn Quakers. Coach Bill Hollenback had been an All-American three times at Penn as a player and he knew something about the team, having just graduated from Penn in 1908. For the first time since Penn State payed its first unofficial game in 1881 and its first official game in 1887, after the many years of traveling to Penn and getting beaten, Penn State pulled off a grand victory W (22-6) At the time, Penn was regarded as just about the best there was. Well, not exactly. In the game, Penn State's "Shorty" Miller shocked the crowd of 15,000 at

Franklin Field by running back the opening kickoff 95 yards for a touchdown.

Penn State students met the wagons returning the football team from the Lemont train station after Penn State beat powerhouse Pennsylvania for the first time, 22-6, on October 28, 1911 in Philadelphia.

Something happened to Penn in 1911though they were still a tough team. Penn had a one loss-season in 1910 but had a tough time with a lot of teams, including Penn State. Nonetheless, it was a great victory defeating the elusive Penn after well over twenty-years of attempts. PSU was having a wonderful year with Bill Hollenback as coach.

On November 4, St Bonaventure was defeated at New Beaver Field W (46–0). Now that PSU had a bigger field and a better reputation, more teams were willing to come by for a share of the larger pot. On November 11, Colgate went home from New Beaver Field with a loss but a moral victory in a close one W (17–9). Navy was the only blemish—a tie T (0-0) at Annapolis. Then, like clockwork as the Thanksgiving Turkeys were waiting for all the happy Panther supporters, the Nittany Lions came in to Forbes Field and gobbled them all up, though the match was very close W (3-0).

1912 Penn State Football Season Coach Bill Hollenback

The 1912 Penn State Nittany Lions football team was coached for the third time in total by Bill Hollenback in his second consecutive year. He had a knack in building a great team and coaching the team to victories. He was the reason for such bug success again for the Nittany Lions for the 1912 college football season.

Bill Hollenback brought to State College, the second of Penn State's retrospective national championships. Like the Bill Hollenback teams of 1909 and 1911, this team was also undefeated but they were also untied, In fact, this group of players were so good that they were scored upon once (6 points by Cornell). Just the year before the touchdown was worth just five points.

Penn state was led by players Shorty Miller and Pete Mantle. With so many players with M in the last name, that team was knows as the "M" Squad and they hammered out a perfect 8-0 season. At just five feet five inches tall, Shorty Miller was one heck of a football player and a great running back. He was quick and fast and because he had those "little legs," he could stop on a dime, cut and go the other way. He was tough to tackle.

Though short even for the roaring tens, he was also the team's QB and the safety on defense. Miller was a leader. He even returned punts for the Nittany Lions. With his left hand as a unique attribute, Miller threw for a school record nine touchdowns in 1912, a record that stood for over 50 years.

Pete Mantle was the other guy in the backfield and he was big and tough and even tougher to stop. Miller credits him with being the best passer on the team as he could really throw a ball. Mantle was the first PSU player to be indicted into the College hall of Fame. He ran for over 700 yards in this championship season.

Though reasonably close in geography, PSU and OSU had not played each other. The Big Bill Hollenback team of 1912 is known for playing the first of a series of games against eventual rival Ohio State. There is some irony here as Ohio State has always been considered a tough team. Yet, in this Bill Hollenback game, the vaunted Ohioans walked off the field with seven minutes left because Penn State was getting away with unnecessary roughness. The Buckeyes forfeited because of the brutal play of the Nittany Lions once the real score was 37–0. The official score because of the forfeit is 1–0, but the game ball lists the score as 37–0. How about those apples?

Not really trying to be unfair here but facts are facts. The game play of the 1912 team was legendary and tough. Other teams of the era were opting not to play Penn State because of things like shoestring tackles that would put players out of football for a long time, and literally smash-mouth football. PSU gave no team a break during this period but it did hurt their scheduling of subsequent game.s

This extremely successful consensus NCF National Championship season began with a win, in the middle there were wins, and at the end, there were more wins. That's all there was—Penn State wins, and plenty of them!

October 5, home, Carnegie Tech, W (41-0); Oct. 12 home New Beaver Field, Washington Jefferson, W (30-0); Oct 19, Percy Field in Ithaca, Cornell, W (29-6); Oct 16, home, Gettysburg, W (25-0); November 2, Franklin Field, Penn, 2nd victory in a row W (14-0); November 9, a slugfest trouncing shutout at home v Villanova W (71-0).

The next two games should have been tough but were not. Bill Hollenback had some magic about destroying the resistance in the opposition. He was quite a coach. On Nov. 16, at OSU, PSU soundly defeated the Buckeyes W (37-0); Then came Thanksgiving on November 28, 1912 at Pittsburgh's Forbes Field. Pitt wished it had played as well as

Ohio State but it had not and lost by one additional point W (38-0).

The PSU record was 8-0. It was that simple.

1913 Penn State Football Season Coach Bill Hollenback

The 1913 Penn State Nittany Lions football team was coached by the previously undefeated coach Bill Hollenback. The team was coached by "Big Bill" Hollenback. Following a 26 game unbeaten streak for coach Hollenback (not the program, which had losses in 1910), the Nittany Lions closed out the 1913 season with six straight losses. Hollenback was 26-0-3 going into this season. How could this be? All the losses were close but something was in the wind. Something seemed to happen to the moxie of Bill Hollenback, though, once again, the losses were mostly close. In 1914, he was 5-3-1, a big improvement but, something seemed to be wrong.

PSU started with two wins at home against Carnegie Tech W (49-0) and Gettysburg w (16-0). All of a sudden the sunlight left the team. Three straight road games brought no victories. Washington & Jefferson L (0-17); Harvard L (0-29) and U of Penn L (0-17). It was as if everybody was waiting for Bill Hollenback for a big payback.

PSU played a new team—Notre Dame at home in a close one (7-14), Navy at Annapolis L (0-10), and of course the season ender at Forbes Field L (6-7). Overall, there were few cheers at PSU in 2013 for the Nittany Lions first losing season with a Hollenback as coach.

A little bit about the Notre Dame game

On November 8, 1913, the Chicago Tribune wrote: "The game was the hardest fought and the most brilliantly played or ever seen at Penn State. With the exception of five minutes each at the close of the first half and the opening of the second half, Penn State outplayed the visitors."

That is how a sportswriter saw the first ever Penn State-Notre Dame game in 1913. In that first game, a stocky, rugged captain by the name of Knute Rockne scored one touchdown to lead the Notre Dame Fighting Irish to a 14-7 win over Penn State in State College. No matter how many times PSU and ND have played over the years, it has been a respectable rivalry.

1914 Penn State Football Season Coach Bill Hollenback

The 1914 Penn State Nittany Lions football team was coached by Bill Hollenback in his fifth and last season with Penn State. Hollenback played a tough season. The games he was supposed to win, he won and the games that were suppose d to be tough, his PSU team lost. I

This season was a lot better than the prior one but perphaps because the home games were more like almost definite wins and the away games were battles. No team expected to get let off the hook easy by a Bill Hollenback coached team. Perhaps the aura of getting whooped by a Hollenback team did not set well with the better teams and when they played Penn State they were better prepared. Let's take a closer look at this last season of Bill Hollenback.

Early on from Sept. 26 on when PSU played Westminster at home, it looked like the Nittany Lions had regained the idea of how to win. Westminster came to Beaver Stadium and upset nothing W (13-0) but the game was close. Muhlenberg appeared at the gate and played in New Beaver Stadium and were defeated but it was still a close game W (22-0).

Gettysburg lined up for Beaver Field next on October 10 and were beaten W (13-0). Ursinas, a new opponent played at beaver stadium and were soundly defeated on October 17, PSU looked like it had gotten its offense back W (30-0). Harvard was next at Allston MA and the results were a tie T (13-13).

Lafayette and Lehigh, two mid-eastern PA tough teams were next on the away schedule and PSU did not fare well, losing on October 31 to Lafayette L (17–0) and on November 7 at Lehigh L (7–20).

On November 13, Michigan State came to New Beaver Field to play the Nittany Lions and they won the very close game L (3–6). The season ended again against a tough Panther team at Pittsburgh's Forbes Field. Penn State lost L (3–13). Though not as disappointing, once you taste undefeated seasons, all losses become somewhat intolerable, though no team can meet that high a bar. The record was 5-3-1, which in any man's league, especially considering the rest of Hollenback's record, it was very respectable.

Chapter 15—The Dick Harlow Era

Coach # 9

1915   Dick Harlow   7-2
1916   Dick Harlow   8-2
1917   Dick Harlow   5-4

The World War I Years

1915 Penn State Football Season Coach Dick Harlow

The 1915 Penn State Nittany Lions football team was coached by first year coach Dick Harlow who took over for the retired Bill Hollenback.

Dicke Harlow was a tackle on the great PSU teams of 1910 and 1911. The Nittany Lions continued to play home games in New Beaver Field in University Park, PA. Stadium capacity was 30,000, which was nice sized at the time.

Dick Harlow was one heck of a coach and he left way too soon. His forte was in pioneering modern defensive schemes.

Because of choice or chance, he would often field undersized teams, and his uniquely coordinated stunts would focus on getting around or between blockers rather than trying to overpower them.

Dick Harlow

Harlow as Penn State boxing coach in 1920

His offenses were based on doing the opposite of what was expected. He used deception and timing rather than power and bulldozing. He used shifts, reverses, and lateral passes. Harlow was one of the great ones. He was honored with an induction into the College Football Hall of Fame as a coach in 1954.

The season began September 15 at home v Westminster. The Lions started the season with a win W (26-0). On October 20, PSU hosted Lebanon Valley W (13-0). Games against Penn were no longer destined to be losses and so this time a PSU played the Quakers in Franklin Field it was a different game W (13-3).

After this road game, Gettysburg came to town W (27-12) followed on October 23 by West Virginia Wesleyan W (28-0). Harvard had become in many ways the nemesis that Penn had been and in a game in Allston MA, the Crimson defeated the Nittany Lions L (0-13). Lehigh was hosted by PSU the following week on Nov. 3, for a nice, hard fought win W (7-0). PSU then traveled to Lafayette in Easton to soundly defeat the Leopards W (33-3). On November 25, the Thanksgiving rivalry was continued at Forbes Field against Pittsburgh. The Panthers prevailed L (0-20).

1916 Penn State Football Season Coach Dick Harlow

The 1916 Penn State Nittany Lions football team was coached by Dick Harlow.

On September 23, the Nittany Lions began their season at New Beaver Field against Susquehanna with a nice win (27-0). Westminster came to PSU on September 30, were shutout big-time by the Nittany Lions W (55-0). Bucknell came in and scored the first points in 1916 against PSU at home and PSU defeated them in a rout W (50-7). West Virginia Wesleyan came to town on October 14 and left after losing to PSU W (39-0).

Always a tough game, Penn State played Penn at Franklin Field on October 21 in Philadelphia and went home disappointed L (0-15). PSU had its share of home games. This time it was Gettysburg and the Nittany Lions prevailed W (48-2). Geneva came to New Beaver Stadium next on November 4 and hit a revved up Nittany Lions machine in a huge blowout W (79-0).

Lehigh and Lafayette were next. The Lehigh game was played away at Taylor Stadium in Bethlehem and PSU came away with a close win W (10-7). Next was Lafayette at new Beaver Stadium. Lafayette was upset big-time by Penn State W (40-0). Thanksgiving was late this year and so, almost two weeks later Penn State traveled to Forbes Field for the Turkey game rivalry and left disappointed by a big score L 0-31).

Not a bad season for second year coach Dick Harlow, 8-2.

1917 Penn State Football Season Coach Dick Harlow

The 1917 Penn State Nittany Lions football team r was coached by Dick Harlow in his third and last season. After two 2-loss seasons, this season was also on the winning side but there were two more losses and one less w less games played. The Nittany Lions finished at 5-4. Dick Harlow, a fine coach left Penn State after the 1917 season.

September 29 PSU played the Army Ambulance Corps in Allentown, PA in a close match. It was the second-last year of World War I. The Nittany Lions won W (10-0. It was the first time in many years that Penn State opened its season away. Gettysburg came to PSU the following week for a real trouncing W (80-0) followed by St. Bonaventure for an even more lopsided game W (99-0).

It was an eight day period with a lot of scoring records. First PSU beat Gettysburg 80-0 and then Penn State broke its one-week old team scoring record with a 99-0 win over St. Bonaventure at Beaver Field. Nine players scored touchdowns, in the game, including three by Harry Robb.

Later in the season more records were set as Harry Robb tied "Bull" McCleary's season record for touchdowns with 13 by scoring three TDs as Penn State played Maryland for first time and won 57-0, at Beaver Field.

At 3-0. The Nittany Lions traveled to Washington, PA on October 20 to play Washington and Jefferson and were defeated L (0-7). On to Gettysburg. A week later on October 27 at home, PSU defeated West Virginia Wesleyan in a very close match W (8-7).

Penn State had a habit of playing the finest football teams in the country at this time by engaging with teams from the Ivy League. This time the Nittany Lions traveled to Memorial Field in Hanover, NH on November 3, to play the Big Green of Dartmouth University. It was a close, tough game but Penn State could not gain the win L (7-10).

Lehigh came to New Beaver Field on November 10 and beat Penn State L (0-9). Maryland came the next week and the Nittany Lions were more than ready, soundly defeating the Terrapins W (57-0). As usual, the season ending Thanksgiving football game was at Pittsburgh and the Nittany Lions lost (6-28).

Chapter 16—The Hugo Bezdek Era

Coach # 10

1918   Hugo Bezdek   1-2-1
1919   Hugo Bezdek   7-1
1920   Hugo Bezdek   7-0-2
1921   Hugo Bezdek   8-0-2
1922   Hugo Bezdek   6-4-1
1923   Hugo Bezdek   6-2-1
1924   Hugo Bezdek   6-3-1
1925   Hugo Bezdek   4-4-1
1926   Hugo Bezdek   5-4-1
1927   Hugo Bezdek   6-2-1
1928   Hugo Bezdek   3-5-1
1929   Hugo Bezdek   6-3

1918 Penn State Football Season Coach Hugo Bezdek

The 1918 Penn State Nittany Lions football team was coached by Hugo Bezdek in his first year. The high quality picture above is from his second year coaching. Looking back, for sure Bezdek's first season was a strange season right in the heated battles of the war, with just four games and a losing season 1-2-1. It was the worst season in ten years, and one of the worst all-time. Penn State had a tough time getting its season started and when started, it did not do well. World War I was coming to an end.

1918 was a disruptive season for many college programs as the final battles of World War I were being fought. Things were tough across the country. In July 1918, Dick Harlow, a fine coach asked to be relieved of his contract as head coach to enter the military service. He said he would return but everybody knew what the priority was at the time.

There was bad news for the team and the university and the family of Levi Lamb, a lineman on the 1912-1914 teams. On July 18, 1918 Lamb was killed near Soissons, France, while leading his army platoon against a German stronghold. He is one of two former players to die in World War I as 1912 teammate Red Bebout was killed on a French battlefield on Sept. 29, 1918. No matter what players suffer today, sometimes working so hard for no gain during the season, it is nothing like the war period.

Without a coach to schedule and manage games, on August 25, 1918, Penn State announced that Hugo Bezdek, manager of the Pittsburgh Pirates Baseball Club, had been hired as head football coach and director of physical education.

Bezdek had supervision over intercollegiate sports. November 27, 1918.

Penn State finished a strange season in November—we will discuss the sparse details—because of World War I by losing, 28-6, at Pitt and finishing with a 1-2-1 record. In the fall of 1919, a year later, Dick Harlow kept his word and returned to Penn State after war cleanup operations to serve as assistant coach to Hugo Bezdek. Bezdek and Harlow had a symbiotic relationship and were good friends.

There is some irony here as Bezdek was a great coach (picture below) who got a poor start. He would coach at Penn State until 1930, the same exact coaching years and tenure as Knute Rockne of Notre Dame Fame with just one time difference. Bezdek did not coach in 1930, Rockne's last year at Notre Dame.

The games of 1918

Hugo Bezdek - Penn State Football coach from 1918-1929

PSU began its season very late on November 2 at home against the Wissahickon Barracks and played to a tie T (6-6) Rutgers was next at New Beaver Stadium L (3-26). PSU recovered somewhat in a close game at Lehigh W (7-6_ on November 16 just five days after the end of World War I on November 11 (Veterans Day).

The annual Pittsburgh rivalry game was played again on Thanksgiving, November 28, Penn State lost the game; its second of the season L (6-28). Though it was a loss, with the end of the war, everybody had a lot for which to be thankful.

1919 Penn State Football Season Coach Hugo Bezdek

The 1919 Penn State Nittany Lions football team was coached by Hugo Bezdek. Hugo had really gotten situated as coach and now that the war was over, he was able to build a fine team and they had a great record at 7-1. It was just the one close loss L (13-19) at Dartmouth in New Hampshire that kept the team from a perfect season. Nonetheless Coach Bezdek had fine team and he put together a fine season.

Gettysburg was the first to come to Beaver Stadium for a PSU win W (33-0). The home and season opener was played on October 4. Bucknell was next at New Beaver Stadium for a close match W (9-0). Then came the loss at Dartmouth on October 18.

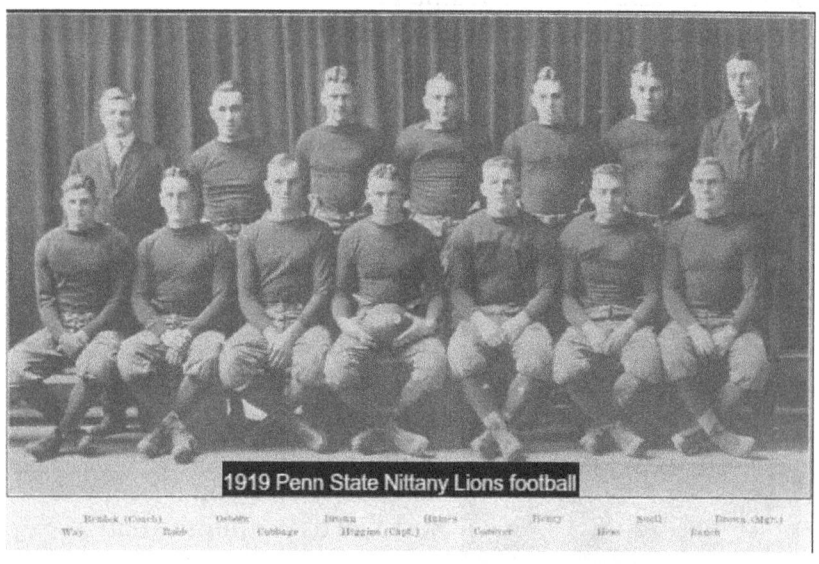
1919 Penn State Nittany Lions football

From here, Ursinas came to visit and were beaten by a toughened Penn State team W (48-7). The always tough University of Pennsylvania hosted the Nittany Lions and were defeated on November 1 W (10-0). Then on November 8, PSU defeated Lehigh at home W (20-7). PSU took on its third Ivy League school on November 15 at Cornell. The Nittany Lions defeated the Big Red at Schoellkopf Field in Ithaca W (20-0). The annual Thanksgiving trek to Forbes

Field to play Pittsburgh was on November 27. PSU prevailed W (20-0).

1920 Penn State Football Season Coach Hugo Bezdek

The 1920 Penn State Nittany Lions football team was coached by Hugo Bezdek. This year the team got seven wins just like 1919, but there were no losses. Penn State was undefeated in 1920 but the season was not perfect. After winning their first seven games to start the season, on November 13, the Nittany Lions played at Lehigh to a tie T (7-7) and the following week on November 25 (Thanksgiving), they tied Pittsburgh T (0-0) at Forbes Field. All the other games were wins.

The First five wins were at New Beaver Field: September 25 Muhlenberg W (27-7); then October 2, Gettysburg W (13-0), then October 9, Dartmouth W (14-7). The following week on October 16, North Carolina State traveled to Beaver Stadium and were beaten W 41-0). Lebanon Valley did not know what hit them in PSU game 5 when the Nittany Lions scored their highest number of points ever W (109-0).

The last two wins were at Penn W (28-7, and Nebraska at home W (20-0). It was on November 6, 1920 that Penn State won its fourth major intersectional game at Beaver Field in its first game against Nebraska, 20-0, on Pennsylvania Day. Glenn Killinger and Charlie Way combine to lead the victory as each scores a touchdown and Killinger passes for another.

Following these two wins came the two ties T (7-7) at Lehigh, and T (0-0) at Pitt.

1921 Penn State Football Season Coach Hugo Bezdek

The 1921 Penn State Nittany Lions football team was coached by Hugo Bezdek in his fourth year. Penn State and Coach Bezdek had another great undefeated season with two ties again. This time, the team garnered eight wins and the first tie was against Harvard on October 20 T (20-20). The second tie was against Pitt on Thanksgiving. Two seasons in a row, neither Penn State nor Pitt scored a point on Thanksgiving Day T (0-0). The first four wins before the Harvard tie were all at home in New Beaver Field.

On September 24, Lebanon Valley came to town and played twice better on defense than the prior year W (53-0. PSU shut out Gettysburg on October 1, W (24-0) Gettysburg scored 24. PSU also shut out North Carolina State one week later W (35-0). The fourth win came from Lehigh on October 28 (28-7). This was followed by the tie T (20-20) at Harvard.

On October 29, The Nittany Lions traveled to the Polo Grounds where the NY Baseball Giants played to take on Georgia Tech W (28-7). Carnegie tech was next at home and the score was the same W (28-7). PSU traveled to Franklin Field to play Navy and won W (13-7) against the Middies. November 24 was Thanksgiving and the annual Pittsburgh excursion to Forbes Field was another tie. In a late season game on December 3, he Nittany Lions traveled to the West Coast to play the Washington Huskies and won the game W (21-7)

1922 Penn State Football Season Coach Hugo Bezdek

The 1922 Penn State Nittany Lions football team was coached by Hugo Bezdek. At 6-4-1, PSU opponents got to rejoice this year because, after two unbeaten seasons in a row, and five straight wins in 1922, it appeared nobody was ever going to be able to defeat Hugo Bezdek again.

The season began a little early this year and after five straight wins at New Beaver Field, nobody had beaten the Nittany Lions. The five wins began on September 23, St. Bonaventure W (54-0); then Sept. 30, William and Mary W (27-7). Next came Gettysburg W (20-0), then on October 14, Lebanon Valley W (32-6). On October 21, Middlebury was the next PSU victim W (33-0). Then came Syracuse and still the Nittany Lions were unbeaten after playing the October 28 game at the Polo Grounds to a tie T (0-0) against Syracuse.

Then, the magic ended for 1922 on November 3, Navy neat Penn State in Washington DC L (0-14). PSU rebounded the next week against Carnegie Tech at home (W 10-0). In a really tough match against Penn on November 18, PSU missed out by one point L (6-7) and then in the November 30 game against Pittsburgh in Forbes Field, the Nittany Lions lost a close on L (0-14).

With a 6-3-1 record going into the Bowl season, Penn State was selected to play in the January 1 Rose Bowl against USC. The Trojans prevailed against a tough Nittany Lions team in a close game, giving PSU its first Bowl Game Loss (3-14)

1923 Penn State Football Season Coach Hugo Bezdek

The 1923 Penn State Nittany Lions football team was coached by Hugo Bezdek for the sixth year. The team looked better than its last year as it posted a 6-2-1 record for the season. Penn State won as many games, tied as many games, played two less games and lost two less games than the prior year. There was no Rose Bowl invitation this year, though the overall record was better.

On September 29, a scrappy team from Lebanon Valley came to New Beaver Field and brave as they were facing the Nittany Lions, the left in defeat! (58-0). North Carolina State visited earlier this year on October 6 and played a nice game but PSU won the close game W (16-0). Gettysburg was next at home and they played well but lost W (20-0). Navy came to New Beaver Field in a rare appearance and lost to the Nittany Lions W (21-3).

PSU got an October 27 ticket to Yankee Stadium to play West Virginia and the game ended in a tie T (13-13).

Penn State and West Virginia tied, 13-13, on October 27, 1923 at Yankee Stadium in New York.

PSU traveled north on November 3, to Syracuse against the Orangemen and the Lions were sent home with a defeat L (0-10). Georgia tech traveled over 1000 miles to play the Nittany Lions at New Beaver Field and just about pulled off a win but were shut-out W (7-0).

The always tough University of Pennsylvania were next on the schedule and these games were always played at Franklin Field in Philadelphia. The Nittany Lions did quite well and shut out the Quakers, W (21-0). November 29—posing as Thanksgiving Day was late again and it was Pittsburgh that got to rejoice and be glad and they had the most to thank for as PSU was defeated by an always tough Pitt team L (3-20)

1924 Penn State Football Season Coach Hugo Bezdek

The 1924 Penn State Nittany Lions football team r was coached by Hugo Bezdek in his seventh season. He and the team performed very well again with just one more loss and one extra game from the 1923 season. 6-3-1.

On September 27, Lebanon Valley had matured enough as a football team that they actually scored against the Nittany Lions W (47-3). It was their first score against Penn State.

North Carolina State, usually tough managed six points in a W (51-6) drubbing at New Beaver Field on October 4, my historical wedding anniversary date. My lovely bride and I of course had about 51 more years to tie the knot and about 25 years for the stork to make either of our deliveries. Thank God nobody who reads this who knows us will have a calculator available.

Gettysburg kept getting tougher as Penn State was scheduling tougher teams. This year's Gettysburg team came to New Beaver Field on October 11 and lost respectably W (26-0). Georgia Tech was never a team to just say OK, we lost and so when Penn State traveled the 1000 miles to play at Bobby Dodd Stadium, the team knew there was going to be a real football game. It was so close, the mathematicians were trying to define an asymptote. Nonetheless PSU were handed a defeat from a tough Yellowjackets team L (13-15) by a scintilla.

On October 25, Syracuse, a really tough team came into New Beaver Field not ready to come out a loser. They did not. PSU lost L (6-10). This broke Penn State's 29-game winning streak at New Beaver Field. It came to an end as Syracuse wins the PSU Homecoming game, 10-6. The win streak had begun after a loss to Rutgers during World War I in 1918.

The Nittany Lions went off to Annapolis on November 1 to play the Middies of Navy and squeaked out a win against the always-tough Naval Academy W (6-0). On November 8, Carnegie Tech fought hard at New Beaver Field but lost W (22-7) nonetheless.

Tougher than nails as always, at Franklin Field, PSU played Penn to a tie T (0-0). Marietta then came to New Beaver Field for an inaugural game and lost W (28-0). Perhaps it was the train ride but PSU was really having a tough time with Pitt in their Thanksgiving game extravaganza. This was another year that Forbes Field saw Pitt defeating the Nittany Lions L (3-24).

1925 Penn State Football Season Coach Hugo Bezdek

The 1925 Penn State Nittany Lions football team was coached by Hugo Bezdek in his eighth season. Though the roaring twenties were at the height of their roaring, the Nittany Lions with a 4-4-1 record clearly had not out-roared as many teams as it had in the recent past.

Starting with two home games, first against Lebanon Valley on September 26, the Nittany Lions found an aggressive and tough team to beat W (14-0). On October 3 in another home encounter. Franklin and Marshall played tough but were defeated W (13-0). Georgia Tech had booked Yankee Stadium again and when the Nittany Lions came to play, the game was as usual, tight, but this time the Yellowjackets turned in a victory L (7-16).

The next two games were at New Beaver Field, first v Marietta W (13-0) and then v Michigan State W (13–0). PSU traveled to Syracuse and were beaten ever so slightly by the Orangemen L (0-7). Then, Notre Dame, coached by Knute Rockne on November 7, came to New Beaver Field and encountered a steadfast and tough PSU team who played to a tie T (0-0).

The history of the PSU-ND series includes some of the best teams and players in college football history. In this game in 1925, nobody would budge. The Lions battled Coach Knute Rockne's Irish squad to a 0-0 tie in State College. The Irish went into the game as heavy favorites, but a determined Penn State squad stopped the Irish. After the game, a writer for the Tribune wrote "the greatest factor today was the old-time fighting spirit displayed by the 11 blue-clad warriors of Penn State."

PSU then traveled to West Virginia at Mountaineer Field and lost L (0-14). The final scourge of the year in a not-so good season came from Pittsburgh in the Thanksgiving Holiday Classic on November 26 in Pitt's new stadium L (7-23). This was the first time the annual Thanksgiving Day game was held at the new Pitt Stadium.

Mike Michalske, one of the "Great Ones."

"Mike" Michalske's illustrious career as a football player began at Penn State, where he was an All-American. All that I could find on his suggests he was a great football player and he is on the list of the 11 best players in PSU history.

After graduating in 1926, he joined the New York Yankees of the American Football League (yes, there was once a Yankees football team!). The Football Yankees joined the National Football League in 1927. In 1929 Michalske joined the Green Bay Packers, who were then coached by "Curly" Lambeau, where he played at guard position during the Packers' championship seasons of 1929 - 1931. At the end of the 1937 season, Mike retired from professional play. As an aside, now you know the origin of the name Lambeau Field.

Mike went on to coach at St. Norbert College, The Lafayette School for Boys, Iowa State University, Baylor University, Texas A&M University, and The University of Texas.

In 1963, Mike was inducted into the Green Bay Packers' Hall of Fame. In 1964, its second year, he was the first guard inducted into the NFL Hall of Fame. He was also inducted into the Wisconsin Athletic Hall of Fame, and was honored with the Red Smith Award. Not too shabby for an offensive lineman.

1926 Penn State Football Season Coach Hugo Bezdek

The 1926 Penn State Nittany Lions football team was coached by Hugo Bezdek. No coach delivers great seasons every year but this season at 5-4 was just a bit better than the last one 4-4-1 for Penn State. PSU settled for no ties in 1926.

For the first three games, PSU nestled at home and played a bunch of teams that often opened seasons for the Nittany Lions. On September 25, Susquehanna offered little resistance and PSU got a huge victory W (82-0). Lebanon Valley, coming into its own played tough but were shut out on October 2 at home W (35-0). Marietta came in next at New Beaver Field W (48-6). The Marietta game made history as it was Penn State's 200th win. Cy Lungren ran back a kickoff 95 yards for a touchdown to spark the win.

On October 16, Higo Bezdek's PSU team traveled to South Bend Indiana to play the Fighting Irish of Notre Dame. The prior year at New Beaver field, the game was tied. This time, Notre Dame enjoyed their home field advantage and defeated the Nittany Lions L (0-28). This game also made history as Penn State lost its 100th football game with the Notre Dame win in the Nittany Lions' first visit to South Bend, Ind.

Syracuse was next at home on October 23, but the Nittany Lions came up short L (0-10).On October 30, George Washington came to State College on October 30 and were defeated W (20-12). The next week, on November 6, PSU traveled to Franklin Field to play Penn and again were defeated by this Ivy League team by a field goal L (0-3).

On November 13, a tough Bucknell team played PSU at New Beaver Field in a close match and the Nittany Lions won the game W (9-0). In the Thanksgiving season-ender for PSU, the annual Pittsburgh game was played at the new Pitt Stadium for the second year and the Nittany Lions could not make it happen again and lost L (6-24).

1927 Penn State Football Season Coach Hugo Bezdek

The 1927 Penn State Nittany Lions football team was coached by Hugo Bezdek to a 6-2-1 record which surely made it seem that PSU was moving again from the prior year's 5-4.

On September 24, PSU opened its season with Lebanon Valley W (27-0) and had two more home games before traveling to Franklin Field in Philadelphia on October 15 for a nice win against Penn W (20-0). On October 1, Gettysburg W (34-13) and on October 8, for the first time in a long time, Penn State was beaten by a recharged Bucknell L (7-13).

PSU then traveled on October 22 to Syracuse and won a close one W (9-6). Lafayette then came to New Beaver Field and were handled easily by the Nittany Lions W (40-6). George Washington was next on November 5 at home W (13-0). New York University came to New Beaver Field on November 12 and played a tough match to a tie T (13-13). Wrapping up the season on Thanksgiving, Penn State could not contain a tough Pitt Panthers team and were defeated L (0-30)

1928 Penn State Football Season Coach Hugo Bezdek

The 1928 Penn State Nittany Lions football team was coached by Hugo Bezdek in his eleventh year with the team. It was a tough year with tough games and PSU did not measure well under the circumstances of the season. The University more or less had had it with football and sports and felt it needed to concentrate on academics instead of sports.

At the time, Penn State had decided and in fact was in the process of downgrading its entire athletic program. There had been nationwide criticism of colleges because some who cared little about sports believed that they had emphasized sports to the detriment of academics. In this year of 1928, Penn State made a bad situation even worse.

The school eliminated all new athletic scholarships, and football went into an immediate decline. Not to jump the gun ahead of Hugo Bezdek's tenure but what had been one of the best teams in the country in the early and mid-1920s became one of the worst of the 1930s. Except for 1929, Penn State did not have another winning season until 1937, and the 1931 team was the worst of them all with a 2-8 record. The 1932 record wasn't much better at 2-5.

Hugo Bezdek was a great coach, regardless but he was not a magician. Looks like our next eight years won't have much good news other than that the program survived. Amen!

On Sept. 29, Lebanon Valley, getting tougher each year played in New Beaver Field and the Nittany Lions prevailed W (25-0). Other home games included October 6 v Gettysburg W (12-0). After this, the good times were over as Bucknell bet the Nittany Lions at home on Oct 13, L (0-6). PSU must have had a different scholarship roster than Penn at Franklin Field on Oct. 20 L (0-14).

On October 27, Syracuse tied PSU at home T (6-6) and then the vaunted ND Irish coached by Knute Rockne came to Franklin Field, a neutral site and they barely beat the Nittany Lions L (0-9).

On November 10, the last home game for PSU was against George Washington W (50–0). Then, PSU went to Fisher Field in Easton, PA to play a tough Lafayette team and lost L (0-7). It was not a great year and Thanksgiving would provide no additional reason for thanks on November 29 at Pitt Stadium, PSU lost to Pitt L (0-26).

1929 Penn State Football Season Coach Hugo Bezdek

The 1929 Penn State Nittany Lions football team was coached by Hugo Bezdek in his 12th season. His career paralleled Knute Rockne's but he got another position ad Penn State as Director of Athletics in 1930 and did not put in a 13th year as Rockne had.

Moreover, neither Bezdek nor his successor Bob Higgins had the *schmooze factor* as Rockne had to help his players get free rides to PSU. This would be Bezdek's finest season since the slide and it would be the best that PSU could muster for the next nine years. The PSU scholarship plan for athletes had kicked in and it was surprising to many that this year's 6-3 season was as positive as it was for the Nittany Lions.

The first three games of the season were all played at New Beaver Field: Niagara W (16-0): Lebanon Valley; W (15-0), and Marshall W (26-7)

PSU went on the road for three games beginning October 19 at New York University L (0-7). Then it was Lafayette at home with a nice but close win W (6-3).

Not having had a lot of luck with Syracuse, on November 2, at Archbald Stadium, PSU squeaked out a thriller game W (6-4). PSU never took Penn for granted and so the game on November 9 v Penn at Franklin Flied was no exception. This game looked at time that it could go either way but Penn State defeated Penn in a big win W (19-7).

Bucknell had beefed up and had clearly not gotten the message that colleges were supposed to lay down at their opponent's feet so that the world would believe that academics were superior to athletics. Bucknell cared about Football as did PSU, but Bucknell chose to finance their team and they literally whooped Penn State on November 16, L (6-27).

Penn State would have loved to have its Thanksgiving trip to Pitt Stadium be a Nittany Lions success. But, it was not! On November 28, in this yearly rivalry, Pitt defeated Penn State in much the same way that Penn had done for many years. Final score L (7–20)

Hugo Bezdek got a better offer from PSU as Athletic Director for the whole University. This is a tribute to the PSU culture. Ata time when athletic competition was being minimized across the country, Hugo Bezdak was still a hero at Penn State. The University offered a better job and he accepted.

Chapter 17—The Bob Higgins Era

Coach # 11 Bob Higgins
Coach # 12 Joe Bedenk

Year	Coach	Record	
1930	Bob Higgins	3-4-2	Coach # 11
1931	Bob Higgins	2-8	
1932	Bob Higgins	2-5	
1933	Bob Higgins	3-3-1	
1934	Bob Higgins	4-4	
1935	Bob Higgins	4-4	
1936	Bob Higgins	3-5	
1937	Bob Higgins	5-3	
1938	Bob Higgins	3-4-1	
1939	Bob Higgins	5-1-2	
1940	Bob Higgins	6-1-1	
1941	Bob Higgins	7-2	
1942	Bob Higgins	6-1-1	
1943	Bob Higgins	5-3-1	
1944	Bob Higgins	6-3	
1945	Bob Higgins	5-3	
1946	Bob Higgins	6-2	
1947	Bob Higgins	9-0-1	
1948	Bob Higgins	7-1-1	
1949	Joe Bedenk	5-4	Coach # 12

1930 Penn State Football Season Coach Bob Higgins

The 1930 Penn State Nittany Lions football team was coached by Bob Higgins in his first year as Penn State's head coach.

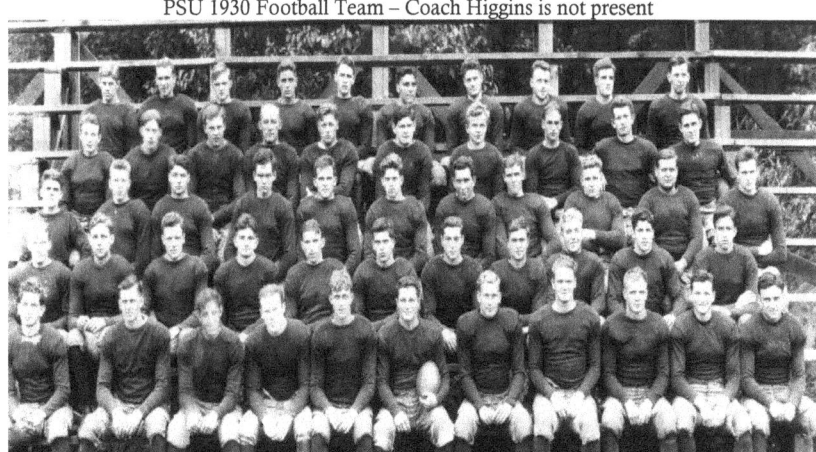

PSU 1930 Football Team – Coach Higgins is not present

Bob Higgins was born Nov. 24, 1893. He was a native of Corning, N.Y. He came to Penn State as a student in 1914 and soon became one of the best players of all time. He was an All-American Selection in 1915 and 1919 and his talents helped him get selected into the College Football Hall of Fame in 1954.

Bob Higgins

Higgins was one of only five players in the history of Nittany Lion football to earn five letters. He served as captain of the team as a senior when he was named to the 1919 Walter Camp All-American team.

Higgins was a multi-faceted athlete who also lettered in baseball, boxing and wrestling. After College, he played two years of professional football with the Canton Bulldogs.

His coaching career before Penn State included stays at West Virginia Wesleyan and Washington University in St. Louis, before he returned to Penn State in 1928 as an assistant.

Bob Higgins was appointed the Lions' head coach in 1930. Eventually, he got through the scholarship reduction period that lasted until 1938-1940, and he compiled a very respectable 91-57-11 record in 19 seasons—the most ever seasons for any PSU coach at the time.

We'll cover his great 1947 team in this chapter. It was unbeaten in the regular-season and tied Southern Methodist, 13-13, in the 1948 Cotton Bowl. Higgins, who died in 1969, received many honors as a player and as a coach. For example, he is a college hall-of-famer and he was selected by the International News Service (precursor to UPI) in 1915 and Walter Camp in 1919. His 85-yard touchdown reception against Pittsburgh was immortalized in Knute Rockne's "Great Football Plays."

1930 Games

Niagara came to Happy Valley on September 27 in the season and home opener and were beaten W (31-14). At home, Lebanon Valley played the Nittany Lions on October 4 and PSU shut them out W (27-0). PSU manhandled Marshall in a high scoring shutout the following week at home on October 11. The Nittany Lions traveled to Easton, PA to play a stubborn and stingy Lafayette team, and settled for a tie T (0-0).

Colgate came to New Beaver Field on October 30 and beat the Nittany Lions L (0-40). Bucknell did the same thing a week later at Lewisburg L (7-19). This was followed by a tie on November 8 at home against Syracuse T (0-0).

On November 15, Penn State traveled to play the Iowa Hawkeyes at Kinnick Stadium in Iowa City, IA and for the third week in a row, the Nittany Lions were beaten. This time it was L (0-19). For the Season ender on Thanksgiving Day at Pitt Stadium, PSU fell to rival Pittsburgh L (12-19).

1931 Penn State Football Season Coach Bob Higgins

The 1931 Penn State Nittany Lions football team was coached by Bob Higgins in his second year at the helm. Penn State was in year two of its eight game slump due to scholarship restrictions. Bob Higgins team struggled for just two wins in ten games this year. With good players at a premium, the Nittany Lions had a tough time beating anybody.

The home and season opener was September 26 against Waynesburg, and as would happen eight times this particular season, the Lions were defeated L (0-7). PUS came back at home on October 3 to beat Lebanon Valley in a rare 1931 win W (19-6). The Nittany lions then lost at Temple L (0-12) and On October 17, lost to Dickinson at home L (6-10).

The Nittany Lions traveled to Syracuse on October 24 and were defeated by the Orangemen L (0-7). For the first time in history, Pitt traveled to New Beaver Field and prevailed against the Nittany Lions L (6-41). Colgate came back to New Beaver Field and beat the Nittany Lions L (7-32)

Penn State wet to Lafayette and lost in a shutout to the Leopards L (0-33). The West Virginia Mountaineers were next on November 21 at Mountaineer Field L (0-19). After losing seven straight games, Bob Higgins Nittany Lions said: "enough already," and put one away at Franklin Field against Lehigh on November 28 W (31-0).

A closer look at the Temple Game

This year (1931) was the first meeting between the Temple Owls and the Nittany Lions. Penn State Historian Lou Prato calls the ten year period of which this was year 2, the "purity period." The University had decided not to offer scholarships and did not scout players. For that reason, the Lions looked for new opponents. In essence to be competitive in the games, they needed to downgrade the schedule. Along the way, they picked up Temple and began a long-standing series that continues to this day.

In a book about great moments in football, we do need something for comparison. Prato calls 1931 the worst season in Penn State history. Because of that purity period. It showed again in 1932 when the Lions lost to the Owls 13-12. The series with Temple was then resumed in 1940, when Penn State had found a way around the purity period.

Prato said by giving players jobs and putting them in fraternities, Penn State managed to provide some financial aid to the athletes. The Lions won the 1941 matchup 18-0, then lost to the Owls 14-0 in 1941, the last Penn State loss in the series until 2015 when the Owls scored 27 unanswered points to notch a 27-10 victory over the Nittany Lions -- their first since 1941 so far.

1932 Penn State Football Season Coach Bob Higgins

The 1932 Penn State Nittany Lions football team was coached by Bob Higgins in his third year. For whatever reasons after the dismal 1931 season, Penn State scheduled only seven games and recorded a 2-5 season for 1932.

Though they had a poor record, the pundits suggest that the 1932 team was not a bad team. Considering that with the scholarship ban, it had to depend on what today are known as walk-ons. They say that with a little luck-and better kicking-it would have won more games. Four of the opponents on the schedule were still giving scholarships, but only Harvard and Colgate were considered superior foes by sportswriters, and they won easily. Harvard had also reduced its schedule with no explanation.

The games against the other scholarship teams, Syracuse and Temple, came down to the last minute, while the Lions did beat overmatched Lebanon Valley and Sewanee.

Waynesburg should not have been such a surprise to the Nittany Lions as the year before this smaller school had already pulled off an upset at Beaver Field, winning 7-0 in the first meeting between the teams. After that upset, Ted Hoyt, reporter for the Philadelphia Evening Ledger wrote, "And who ever heard of Waynesburg in football? Offhand, it's an even bet no local (Philadelphia) rooter knows whether Waynesburg is a school, a small college or a semipro eleven."

For those paying attention, they would have noticed that Frank Wolf, the Waynesburg coach was the difference makers in the successive upsets over the Lions. Wolf was a former Penn State football player, who played quarterback in the war-shortened 1917 season.

Pundits respected Wolf and suggested that he was an "innovative" coach and that if any opposing coach knew how to beat Penn State, it was Wolf. He had one of the smartest offenses around. He used a double wing and every running back was running around in the backfield every play. Of course football rules were not as tight then but they say it was fun to watch the Waynesburg team in action. It surely was not fun for Penn State players.

The Seven games of 1932

On October 1 at New Beaver Field, the Nittany Lions began the season at home beating Lebanon Valley W (27-0). Waynesburg, a new team that had upset the Lions in the previous year came to New Beaver Field on October 8 and pulled another upset L (6-7). On October 15 at Harvard Stadium in Allston, MA, Penn State was beaten big-time L 13–46.
Though a very close match, nonetheless Penn State fell to Syracuse at home on October 22 L (6-12).

On October 29, Penn State traveled to Hamilton, NY, home of the Major League Baseball Hall of Fame, and lost against a tough Colgate team L (0-31). On November 5, Swanee made its appearance for the first time at New Beaver Field and were beaten by the Nittany Lions W (18-6) for the second and last win of the season for Penn State. On November 12, Penn State lost in a very close match to Temple L (12-13) at Temple Stadium in Philadelphia. PSU finished at 2-5 for a year in which more good things could have occurred but did not. For the first time in a long time, there was no Pitt game.

1933 Penn State Football Season Coach Bob Higgins

The 1933 Penn State Nittany Lions football team was coached by Bob Higgins. The team improved somewhat to a .500 record at 3-3 with a tie. For some reason, more teams seemed to be paring down their schedules to seven games and focusing on intramural sports for all students.

October 7, Lebanon Valley came to New Beaver Field W (32-6_. October 14, Muhlenberg defeated the Nittany Lions at New Beaver Field in a very close match L (0-3) Lehigh was next on October 21 at home and the Nittany Lions won W (33-0). Against Columbia at New York on October 28, PSU fell short L (0-33).

PSU played Syracuse at Archbold Stadium on October 28 and lost in another close game L (6-12). Johns Hopkins came for the first time to New Beaver Field and were beaten by the Lions W (40-6). Penn State then traveled to Franklin Field and played Penn to a tie T (6-6). The season record was 3-3-1.

1934 Penn State Football Season Coach Bob Higgins

The 1934 Penn State Nittany Lions football team was coached by Bob Higgins. In 1934, Higgins' PSU team had a so so year at 4-4. The team played one more game than in the last two years. The country seemed to be getting over (not 100%) its predisposition at the time in these depression years that playing sports at the collegiate level was bad.

Since not all teams shut down their athletic scholarships, typical powerhouses such as Penn State were overwhelmed by alumni and friends who were bugging the administration to make life better for the team.
Eventually the coach right after Bob Higgins, Joe Bedenk, would benefit as Penn State adapted to the needs of athletics and academics. Somehow it was forgotten that the lucky sports people who received scholarships for their athleticism

also got an opportunity to compete in the real world with a college degree from a great institution, Penn State,

Seasons had begun to start later and this year, 1934, the date was October 6 at home and the opponent was Lebanon Valley who had muscled up and had become a real football team. Penn State beat them in a tough game W (13-0). Gettysburg, an annual opponent came to New Beaver Field and could not withstand the determination of the Nittany Lions W (32-6). It helps to understand that Penn State was playing with walk-ons and other schools were still offering scholarships.

Penn State then took on Lehigh on October 20, at Taylor Stadium in Bethlehem, PA W 31–0. Next was October 27 at Columbia in New York, NY L (7–14) Syracuse traveled the distance to play PSU at New Beaver Stadium and they defeated the Nittany Lions L (0–16). Syracuse was becoming a favorite PSU rivalry.

On November 10 at Pennsylvania, PSU played the Quakers at Franklin Field in Philadelphia, PA to a disappointing loss L (0–3). Playing another Pennsylvania school on November 17 at home, Lafayette, always tough at the time, lost to the Nittany Lions at New Beaver Field W (25–6). On November 24, the difference between a winning season and a .500 season was the stakes of the game for PSU when it traveled to Memorial Stadium in Lewisburg PA to play perennial rival Bucknell. This time, Bucknell had just a little bit more moxie than the Lions in a close game won by Bucknell.

PSU was not turning around the program that had been in the doldrums and was expected to stay there for another few years. It is amazing that Bob Higgins did so well during this period. Then when PSU permitted its teams to win with a few scholarships, Higgins knew how to deliver. Higgins was a great coach, and he really bolstered the PSU reputation, and even more than that—he never gave up... no matter whether the deck was stacked against him or not!

1935 Penn State Football Season Coach Bob Higgins

The 1935 Penn State Nittany Lions football team was coached by Bob Higgins in his sixth year at Penn State. His 1935 record was 4-4, which was a theoretical mirror image of the final record of 1934. Higgins worked with what he had and a *give-up* coach might not have done so well with all walk-ons. Bob Higgins taught a lot of great kids how to play great football because he had to and because he wanted to. Nobody with God's best talent was knocking on the door of Penn State at the time because it was an institution that made them pay tuition to play for the university.

On October 5, they typical first game opponent, a tougher and tougher Lebanon Valley team came to New Beaver Stadium and gave the Nittany Lions a tough time though not enough to win. PSU prevailed W (12-6) If it were not for a safety, the results of the Western Maryland encounter on October 12 at New Beaver Field would have been a tie but PSU got the safety and won the game W (2-0).

Lehigh played PSU at New Beaver Stadium and the Nittany Lions shut them out W (26-0). PSU reengaged with Pitt on October 26 at Pitt Stadium and lost a close game L (0-9). On November 2, it was an away game at Syracuse in which the Orangemen cut it close but won against PSU L (3-7).

Villanova a great Philadelphia school came to play football against Penn State on November 9 and were on the losing side of a fine game W (27-13). Always loving those wins against Penn, PSU would be denied again this year at Franklin Field L 6-33). Just as PSU won by a safety earlier this season, Bucknell beat the Nittany Lions the same way on November 23 at Bucknell (L (0-2).

1936 Penn State Football Season Coach Bob Higgins

The 1936 Penn State Nittany Lions football team was coached by Bob Higgins in his seventh year. Times were tough for PSU as the walk-ons were not about to bring the University national championships or even braggable seasons. The 3-5 1936 season was another of the lollygaggers that only PSU lovers at the time cared about. Academicians were quite pleased as athletics had been minimized so well by the administration that PSU had taken itself out of the national picture for the seventh year.

A lot of brave hearts came forth and got to play football at a great university. However, with PSU saying no and choosing not to offer degrees to all of the exceptional athletes in America who were graduating as great football athletes, the university and the team suffered, There were few of America's exceptional teammates who had the tuition in their pocket when great universities were offering them a free ride, who came to Penn State. Thus, there were very few if any recognized great athletes from whom these great and powerful scrappy PSU walk-ons could learn the full knack of the game. Just a few scholarship athletes would have helped in many ways.

On October 3, Muhlenberg, at New Beaver Field W (45-0); October 10—Villanova at home L (0-13), October 17—Lehigh away L (6-7), October 24—Cornell away L (7-13).

Finally a rival such as Syracuse came into New Beaver Field ready to win and who were defeated and in fact shut-out W (18-0). Pittsburgh, ranked # 5 on the country hosted PSU on November 7, and beat the Nittany Lions L (7-34). U of P then hosted PSU to a loss L (12-19). The newly recharged Bucknell played PSU in a tough game on November 21 but lost to our Lions despite their fine efforts W (14-0). The Bucknell game ended the season and there were no more Thanksgiving games.

1937 Penn State Football Season Coach Bob Higgins

The 1937 Penn State Nittany Lions football team coached by Bob Higgins in his eighth season. Many college programs would have dumped Higgins as an inadequate coach because of his record to this point. Give PSU credit for keeping one of its greatest coaches of all time on the sidelines with his team as the university was sorting out whether it wanted to win football games or not.

Without a great coach such as Bob Higgins, who knows how ell all-walk-on teams would have performed against the talented teams AD Hugo Bezdek had scheduled for them to play. In a nutshell, the word is "Bravo" to coach Higgins for keeping PSU football respectable while it was wondering if it needed to survive at all.

This season Higgins team broke out of the funk from the last eight years and posted a winning record (5-3). This would not be the last PSU winning record as all college teams began to offer scholarships to deserving athletes again and the academician's seemed OK with the university having a winning record in college sports.

On September 25, PSU raveled to Cornell for a season opener and were defeated in a very tough match L (19–26). Three home games awaited the Nittany Lions upon their return from Cornell. These three games were wins and then after the great victories, PSU went to Syracuse on October 30 and were defeated in a very close match (13-19) The home games were on October 2 Gettysburg W (32–6), October 9 Bucknell W 20–14, and a tough Lehigh team W (14–7).

Penn was back on the schedule on November 6 at Franklin Field and PSU showed its moxie W (7–0). Back at home, Maryland came by on November 13, and played a close match W (21–14). With this game Penn State clinched its first winning season since 1929 and the first in Bob Higgins' coaching regime by beating Maryland in the last minute at Beaver Field.

The Thanksgiving day rivalry had been nipped by not playing each other for a few years at Thanksgiving time. A pre-Thanksgiving game on November 20 was played against a very strong #1 ranked Pittsburgh team at Pitt Stadium in Pittsburgh, PA, a long-time rivalry and PSU played tough but lost the game L (7–28). PSU finished with a 5-3 record as Pitt went on to be National Champions. There is suspicion from this scribe that Penn State was playing with both hands tied as other schools paid athlete with scholarships to matriculate at their universities.

Bob Higgins' Nittany Lions finished their first winning season in seven years 5-3, and nobody was complaining.

1938 Penn State Football Season Coach Bob Higgins

The 1938 Penn State Nittany Lions football team was coached by Bob Higgins in his ninth year. Though the Scholarship ban was mitigated, the teams were not ready to be formed based on a poor track record. So, Higgins had a tough 1938 season. Think about with all the losses he sustained in PSU's dark seasons how bright it will be as we move forward through the rest of Bob Higgins's seasons as he captured the hearts and mind so Americans what loved PSU football.

In 1938, the season began at home for two games. The first v Maryland on October 1, a rivalry, was won in a shutout W (33-0). Bucknell, a team that had gotten tougher and tougher came into Beaver stadium and won a shutout L (0-14). PSU went to Lehigh on October 15, and defeated the Mountain Hawks in an embarrassment W (59-0).

At Cornell, PSU did well but not well enough as Cornell prevailed L (6-21). On October 29 Syracuse at New Beaver Field, PSU won W (33-6). Then at home on November 5, Lafayette defeated PSU L (0-7).

PSU played a big tough Penn team at Franklin Field on Nov. 12 and tied in a tough contest T (7-7). The Pitt rivalry was next and it looks like nobody wanted to play on Turkey Day as the November 19 game against the #5 in the nation Panthers was put in the PSU loss column L (0-26). PSU's season of 3-4-1 was not so good but not so bad, either.

1939 Penn State Football Season Coach Bob Higgins

The 1939 Penn State Nittany Lions football team rebounded this year to 5-1-2 after some poor years. The team was coached by Bob Higgins in his tenth year. The apparent doom and gloom of the *walk-on era* had finally faded and the Penn State administration had finally permitted Coach Higgins to invite scholarship athletes to the campus as many other Division I type teams had been doing for since 1928, when PSU imposed its own ban.

Penn State played eight games and had just one loss, which was a shutout blowout against Cornell in the third game of the season on October 14 in Ithaca, NY. L (0-47). The ties were in the middle of the season and near the end of the season. The first was at Syracuse T (6-6) on October 28, and the second was at Army T (14-14) in Michie Stadium, West Point, NY.

The Nittany Lions opened the season with two wins at New Beaver Field. The first game on October 7, was against Bucknell which had been playing tough football over the past several years W (13-3). The next home game was against Lehigh on October 4 and the Lions came through with a big win W (49-7). The next week was the loss at Cornell followed by the Syracuse tie and then another home game on November 4 v Maryland W (12-0).

Penn State knew that it had recovered when on November 11, it beat Penn at Penn W (10-0). The Army tie was next followed by what in years past would have been a

Thanksgiving Day game against Pitt. New Beaver Field was the site of the game on November 25, and PSU had gotten so good that the once hard to ever beat Pitt Panthers lost W (10-0)

In this game, future All-American Leon Gajecki led Penn State to its first victory over Pitt in 20 years in this 10-0 upset before a record-tying crowd of 20,000 at Beaver Field. Penn State finishes the year with its best record since 1921 at 5-1-2. It's amazing what a little funding for football will do.

1939 Thanksgiving Story

Here is a little known fact: In 1939, President Franklin Delano Roosevelt declared November 23rd, the next-to-last Thursday of the month, to be Thanksgiving Day. This break with tradition was prompted by requests from the National Retail Dry Goods Association to extend the Christmas shopping season by one week.

I was wondering as I wrote about so many PSU v Pitt games prior to this year, as to why Thanksgiving always seemed to be on the last Thursday during this period. The above answers that question for me but then again, why not Friday?

I know this is not a football story but it is a neat story anyway and it did affect the annual PSU Pitt game so we include it here simply because it is quite interesting.

In 1929, F.B. Haviland asked president Hoover to move Thanksgiving to Friday? Obviously Hoover said: "No!" Haviland hoped that American workers could get a nice three day weekend. It did not happen. But, why not?

Did you ever wonder why we carve our succulent gobblers on the fourth Thursday of November? It clearly is not because Thanksgiving Thursday sounds better than Thanksgiving Friday.

The Thanksgiving idea as we all know happened with the Pilgrims. In 1789, President Washington declared that Thursday, Nov. 26, would be a "Day of Public Thanksgiving," according to the National Archives. It became more or less, a holiday to celebrate. But subsequent to 1789, the date for the holiday was announced by a yearly presidential proclamation.

It was thus celebrated on various days and months. None of us were living then and American football had yet to be invented, so even our grandparents do not remember the notion of a floating Thanksgiving holiday.

When President Lincoln made his Thanksgiving proclamation in 1863, the last Thursday of November became the standard.

In 1939, there was a big dispute over the date. Two Thanksgiving holidays were observed as the dispute was so large. People were outraged that the holiday was changed by the President just so the people would spend more money.

According to the Franklin D. Roosevelt Presidential Library and Museum, a five-Thursday November fell in 1933 and some retailers asked President Roosevelt to move the holiday up a week so there would be an extra week of shopping and it would help the retail trade. The president denied the request and Americans ate their turkey on the last Thursday as always in 1933.

But, as we know, Roosevelt was president for a long time, and it was plenty long enough for a change of heart when he got another request from merchants. The dispute lasted two years. A few governors decided their states would have Thanksgiving on the last Thursday of the month as usual and that's how some people ended up celebrating it a week earlier or later than others.

1940 Penn State Football Season Coach Bob Higgins

The 1940 Penn State Nittany Lions football team was coached by Bob Higgins. The team played eight games again and had a nice 6-1-1 record. As usual, home games were played in New Beaver Field in University Park, Pennsylvania.

The season began at home v Bucknell on October 5 W (9-0). West Virginia was next on October 12 at home W (17-13). The Nittany Lions then were off to Lehigh on October 19 w (34-0). Then Temple away on October 25 W (18-0)

South Carolina, ranked # 18 at the time came to University Park on November 2, and PSU defeated them W (18-0). PSU traveled to Syracuse on November 9 and tied the Orangemen T (13-13). Juniors Bill Smaltz and Lenny Krouse teamed up for the greatest passing day to date as Smaltz completed 14-of-21 passes (including 12 in succession that remained a record until 1994) for 193 yards and two touchdowns and Krouse caught 10 passes for two touchdowns and 155 yards (yardage is still the most in game by a junior)

On November 16, New York University played the Lions at New Beaver Field W (25-0). Chuck Peters set the all-time kickoff return record with a 101-yard touchdown return on the opening kickoff of this impressive win over NYU. It was his second touchdown runback of the season (96 yards against Temple to open the second half) and it set the season record for kickoff touchdown returns that for years was shared with Curt Warner (1980).

The only loss of the season was the last game on November 23, against an always tough Pittsburgh Panther team at Pitt Stadium L (7-20).

1941 Penn State Football Season Coach Bob Higgins

The 1941 Penn State Nittany Lions football team was coached by Bob Higgins in his twelfth year as head coach. PSU were on a comeback roll and this year, they were also increasing the game son the schedule to 9 from 8. This 7-2 season is a great season for Bob Higgins and the Penn State Nittany Lions.

In researching all about Bob Higgins, I was so glad to hear about the scholarship problem being in Higgins early years because his overall record is so good, these years, such as 1941 are the make-up years that are part of getting that great record of Higgins, great! Unlike fiction, in this book we've got some great reading ahead as Higgins is coach for eight more years and he has a lot of wins to amass.

This year, thought here were nine games the season began in October, on the 4th, my wedding anniversary. It was not a good season opener as the Nittany Lions had traveled to Civic Stadium in Buffalo NY, lots of miles from Colgate's Hamilton campus, and were defeated in a clawing match by the Red Raiders L (0-7).

On October 11, Bucknell, a recent tough team came to New Beaver Field and gave it up to Penn State W (27-13) in a tough match. Temple, a great academic institution had become a tough team in the 1930's and had a lot of moxie when the Nittany Lions came to their stadium on October 18 and were beaten in a close battle L (0-14).

In 1941, that was the end of the losses. Lehigh visited New Beaver Field and were defeated on October 25 W (40-6). Penn State then traveled to the Polo Grounds on a rare Friday game on October 31. At the same exact date, Mount Rushmore was completed. The opponent for PSU was New York University and the Lions disposed of this team in a shut-out W (42-0).

An always tough # 18 ranked Syracuse team came to Penn State on November 8, to play a game of football at New Beaver Field in what had become a rivalry match. Penn State took all the marbles this day against the Orangemen in a great win W (34-19). West Virginia's defense held PSU to 7 points on November 15 while PSU shut-out the Mountaineers at home W (7-0).

Always expecting a tough game, PSU traveled to Pitt Stadium to take on the Panthers and beat them good in this long time rivalry W (31-7). Finishing up the season just a little later than normal, PSU played South Carolina at Carolina Stadium W (19–12) for fine 7-2 season for Higgins. Soon Coach Higgins would be getting national recognition for the Penn State Nittany Lions.

1942 Penn State Football Season Coach Bob Higgins

The 1942 Penn State Nittany Lions football team was coached by Bob Higgins in his thirteenth season. There was no bad luck, PSU played eight games and somehow kept missing undefeated by one game 6-1-1. After doing well consistently for the last several years before 1942, PSU had gained respect again as a national powerhouse for football. Penn was the only ranked team that Penn State played this year.

This year, 1942, the team was ranked at # 19 by the AP. Better years would surely come but this meant that PSU had gone full circle from the beginning of Higgins tenure to this year. Again, thanks to Bob Higgins, Penn State was again a respected national contender.

On October 3 Bucknell played PSU at New Beaver Field in State College, PA. PSU had a nice win against a recently toughened Bucknell team W (14–7). October 10 found a scrappy Lehigh team challenging the Nittany Lions at Taylor Stadium in Bethlehem. PSU won but it was not so easy W (19-3).

Traveling to Cornell on October 17, to Schoellkopf Field in Ithaca, NY, PSU and the Big Red Bear tied T (0-0). Nobody could score but there was a lot of game in the game. On October 24, PSU hosted Colgate, and beat the Red Raiders at New Beaver Field W (13-0).

The lions traveled to West Virginia on October 31 to play the Mountaineers in a rivalry game at Morgantown Field and were defeated L (0-24). On November 7, Syracuse came to New Beaver Field, State College, PA in a rivalry match W 18-13. PSU had become tough as nails under Higgins with great athletes playing for the Blue and White, and a great coach.

On November 14, at Franklin Field, PSU played its only ranked opponent of the year Pennsylvania at Franklin Field, and the Nittany Lions claimed its share of national respect with a win W (13-7). This was one of the biggest upsets of the Higgins era, Penn State literally shocked Penn, 13-7, before 50,000 at Franklin Field behind the punting of Joe Colone and the running and defensive play of Larry Joe, who was carried off the field at the end of the game.

Always sweating out what was most often the last game of every season. Penn State played rival Pitt on November 21 at New Beaver Field. The new toughened Penn State team under Bob Higgins brought home a big win W (14-6). At 6-1-1, PSU was ranked #19 in the nation by the AP.

1943 Penn State Football Season Coach Bob Higgins

The 1943 Penn State Nittany Lions football team was coached by Bob Higgins in his fourteenth year. All college football teams with good coaches or great coaches need great players to be great. Good and great coaches such as Bob Higgins do the best they can with what they get and every now and then, things happen on the field that make the season better or worse than it should have been.

After a 6-1-1 season in 1943 and a # 19 finish in the AP poll, PSU had one less win and two more losses than in 1942. So, there was no ranking and no bowl games but the team did fine. Pundits might suggest that this year, Higgins team suffered a 5-3-1 season but in such a successful season there was little suffering. It is always nice to win every game but sometimes this cannot be done because of many different circumstances.

The 1943 season began early at home on September 25, with Bucknell playing tough again but losing to PSU W (14-0). On October 2, the Nittany Lions played North Carolina at Kenan Stadium in Chapel Hill, NC. The Tarheels overwhelmed the Lions L (0–19).

Colgate was always tough and this game at home was no different as the Red Raiders tied PSU in a scoreless battle T (0-0). A tough Navy team was next at Annapolis on October 16 L (6–14). On October 23, at Maryland PSU got a shutout W (45-0) and then on October 30 at home v West Virginia, PSU played great and won W (32-7.

On November 6 PUS played away at Cornell and were beaten L (0–13). Then, on November 13, Temple played at PSU and were defeated in a close match W (13-0). The Pitt rivalry, though no longer on Thanksgiving Day was still important for the cross-state competitors. PSU had a great team and were ready to win and did at Pitt Stadium W (14-0)

1944 Penn State Football Season Coach Bob Higgins

The 1944 Penn State Nittany Lions football team was coached by Bob Higgins in his fifteenth season. Higgins was a great coach and played this year to a 6-3, nine game season.

The Penn State schedule was like all college teams, made up by athletic departments and not by coaches in the 1940's. Football had again become respectable.

On September 30, a fine PA team, Muhlenberg, played PSU at New Beaver Field; but lost the game W (58–13). PSU took the opportunity to play Navy in the middle of the war years on October 7. Navy won at Navy in Thompson Stadium • Annapolis, MD L (14–55). So many great athletes took turns at Navy to play the best teams in America, with Penn State being one of them.

Few teams beat Army or Navy during the war years. Having a great football team helped in recruiting for a particular service academy to help the war effort. Even the service academies competed against one another to get the best football players available.

The season began on October 14 v Bucknell at home W (20-6). Then, on October 21, PSU traveled to Hamilton NY and beat Colgate W (6-0).

On October 28, PSU hosted West Virginia and the Mountaineers were just a scoch better as the game ended with WV winning L (27–28). On November 4, PSU traveled to Syracuse and defeated the Orangemen, W (41–0).

Temple, always a tough team hosted PSU on November 11 at Temple Stadium • Philadelphia, PA, and almost got a win but PSU squeaked out a thriller W (7–6). Back at home on November 18, Maryland was defeated W (34–19). Then came the season crescendo as in many prior years—Pitt at Pitt on November 25. Almost but not exactly Pitt claimed victory in a close one L (0-14).

1945 Penn State Football Season Coach Bob Higgins

The 1945 Penn State Nittany Lions football team was coached by Bob Higgins in his sixteenth season with the team. The team played just eight games and had a very respectable record of 5-3.

On September 29, Muhlenberg was defeated in the home opener / season opener at New Beaver Field W (47–7). On October 6, Colgate played PSU at home W (27-7). Near the end of the war, Navy was still playing great football and ranked # 2, the Middies shut out PSU L (0-28) at Thompson Stadium in Annapolis, MD.

On October 20, PSU played at Bucknell and managed nice win W (46–7). Then a tough and often victorious Syracuse team played at New Beaver Field and lost to PSU W (26–0).

Moving through the 1945 season, on Nov. 10, PSU played Temple at home W (27–0). Next came a game on Nov. 17, against the #12 ranked Spartans of Michigan State at Spartan Stadium in East Lansing, MI, a team that would soon become a PSU rivalry. PSU lost L (0–33).

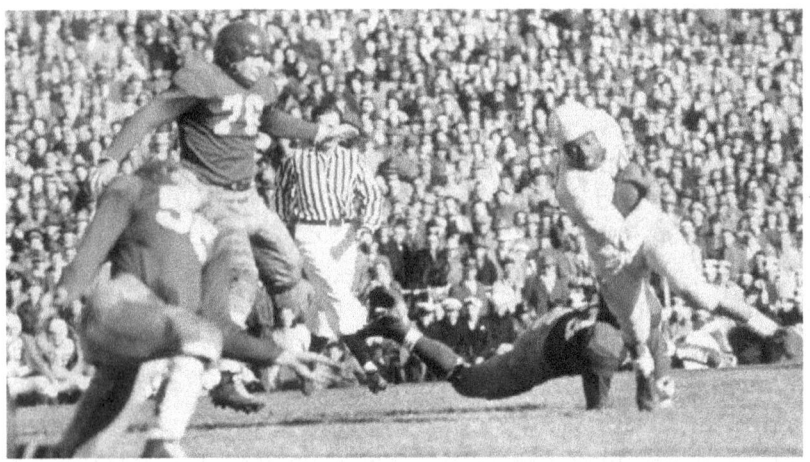

Freshman tailback Wally Triplett was Penn State's first African-American player to start a game (Michigan State, 1945) and was instrumental in the Nittany Lions compiling a 23-3-2 record from 1946-48.

On November 24 at Pittsburgh in Pitt Stadium • the Panthers rivalry was in full bloom a Pitt mustered all it could to defeat a steadfast PSU team that was not ready to budge but lost anyway, L (0–7).

1946 Penn State Football Season Coach Bob Higgins

The 1946 Penn State Nittany Lions football team was coached by Bob Higgins in his seventeenth season as coach. There still was no Beaver Stadium and so Higgins and the great PSU teams of his ear played their games at the New Beaver Field in University Park, Pennsylvania. As time went on, New Beaver Field would not be enough to hold the crowds but that day had yet to come.

On October 5, PSU played Bucknell at the New Beaver Field in State College, PAW (48–6). Syracuse was next on the road W (9–0). Then at home v Michigan State in a cliff-hanger L (16-19).

Colgate was next on Oct. 26 at Colgate W (6-2). Then Fordham at home on November 2, W (68-0) and in another home game the next week Nov. 9, PSU defeated Temple W (26-0).

A tough Navy team invited PSU in for a loss but the Nittany Lions won the game at Annapolis W (12-7). The season ended at Pittsburgh in the rivalry game on November 23. PSU tried its best but Pitt won in a very close match L (7-14).

Game scheduled for November 29. Penn State canceled its final game of season on November 9. The game was to be played on Nov. 29. University of Miami (Fla.) officials requested that Penn State not bring its two African-American players, Wally Triplett and Dennie Hoggard, on the trip.

Guard Steve Suhey was very vocal when he said "We are Penn State there will be no meetings." Suhey earned first-team All-America honors in 1947 and was a member of arguably the most prominent family in Penn State football history. Suhey married a daughter, Ginger, of Penn State All American and head coach, Bob Higgins, and three of their sons — Paul, Larry and Matt Suhey — played for Penn State in the 1970s. Kevin and Joe Suhey became fourth-generation members of the Higgins-Suhey family to play for the Nittany Lions during the 2000s.

1947 Penn State Football Season Coach Bob Higgins

The 1947 Penn State Nittany Lions football team was coached by Bob Higgins in his eighteenth season. The team was 9-0 in the regular season, which might have been good enough for national championship but in the bowl game, the best they could do was tie. PSU had its best season under Higgins, undefeated in regular season with a tie in the bowl game. Bravo PSU and Bravo Bob Higgins for a # 4 consensus finish in 1947.

Guard Steve Suhey earned first-team All-America honors in 1947 and was a member of arguably the most prominent family in Penn State football history. Suhey married a daughter, Ginger, of Penn State All-American and future head coach, Bob Higgins, and three of their sons — Paul, Larry and Matt Suhey — played for Penn State in the 1970s. Kevin and Joe Suhey became fourth-generation members of the Higgins-Suhey family to play for the Nittany Lions during the 2000s.

Nobody beat Penn State throughout the whole season so let me just repeat the scores. They are all wins for PSU. We all knew Higgins had it in him from watching him from 1928 and finally in 1947, he produced a superior team. This time, however, his boys made national news.

On September 20, in a game played at Hershey Park Stadium in Hershey, PA PSU defeated Washington State W (27-40> Then, on Oct. 4, at home, PSU played Bucknell W (54-0).

In a runaway game at Fordham on Cot. 12, in New York, PSU won in a blow0ut W (75-0). The Lions were ripping this year and they played tough Syracuse at home and creamed them W (40–0).

A tough West Virginia team played PSU at home on Oct. 25 W (21-14. Then, on November 1, Colgate came in W (46-0). PSU then traveled to Temple on Nov. 8 for a close but sure W (7-0). Post war Navy was not as tough as usual on November 15 at Municipal Stadium in Baltimore Md. W (20-7).

Still undefeated and having to face season spoiler Pittsburgh on November 22, the PSU Lions ranked # 5 at the time whipped Pitt at their home stadium W (29-0).

PSU won a Cotton Bowl Berth in 1947 because they were one of the top teams in the nation.

On January 1, 1948, just a few days from my birthday (I mean my birth-date when I first began to breathe) PSU and SMU battled hard to come up with the best they could, a tie T (13-13). The Cotton Bowl Classic, before the days of the tie breakers, ended in 1947 in a tie game. Bravo to both teams. Higgins coached PSU finished # 4 in the final season rankings.

Wallace Triplett, Maurice Hoogard Cotton Bowl

The January 1, 1948 was the last bowl game Penn State played before Joe Paterno was on its coaching staff. It was a historic moment in college football for another reason. It was amid the backdrop of segregation in Texas that two Nittany Lions became the first black players to compete in the Cotton Bowl at Dallas Stadium.

Wallace Triplett and Dennie Hoggard helped Penn State gain a comeback 13-13 tie against Southern Methodist that marked the first time a team with African-American players competed in Texas against a team from a segregated university.

The story of Mr. Triplett for sure is truly inspiring. For Triplett, now 90, (April 21) the 1948 Cotton Bowl was among the first benchmarks of his historic career. He became the first African-American to start a football game for Penn State. He also became the first black player to be drafted by, and play for, a National Football League team in 1949.

Wallace Triplett played four seasons in the NFL, two with the Detroit Lions. There he was a teammate of Doak Walker, SMU's all-America tailback against whom Triplett competed in Dallas. The 1948 Cotton Bowl ended in a tie after the late Hoggard nearly caught the game-winning pass on the final play.

"Doak used to tell me, 'Wally, the best thing about that game was that there was no winner,'" Triplett said. "And I agreed with him." The 1947 # 4 team was one of Penn State's best, finishing the regular season 9-0, and outscoring opponents 319-27. The high-scoring offense featured Triplett at wingback and Pen Argyl's Elwood Petchel at tailback.

1948: Penn State, with running back Wally Triplett (pictured, right) and end Dennie Hoggard, plays SMU in the Cotton

Penn State's postseason plans stalled, however, because head coach Bob Higgins would not accept an invitation from a bowl that wouldn't allow Triplett and Hoggard to attend. In 1946, Penn State players voted not to play a scheduled game at the University of Miami, which had the same policy. A year later the players decided there would be no vote.

"[All-America lineman] Steve Suhey said, 'We're Penn State, there will be no meetings,'" Triplett said. "And that was it."

(Suhey's comment is said to have precipitated the "We are Penn State" chant, but Penn State football historian Lou Prato has traced the cheer's origin to the 1970s).

Southern Methodist, meanwhile, was 9-0-1 and ranked No. 3 after winning the Southwest Conference and wanted to face the best opponent possible in the Cotton Bowl. To coach Matty Bell, that was No. 4 Penn State.

Penn State's appearance in the 1948 Cotton Bowl was significant on several fronts. Wally Triplett and end Dennie Hoggard became the first African-Americans to play in the Cotton Bowl game and helped Penn State to a 9-0-1 record in 1947, with the only blemish a 13-13 tie with Southern Methodist in the Cotton Bowl. Behind a defense that posted six shutouts, Penn State won its first Lambert Trophy and its No. 4 final ranking was its highest in program history to date.

The game itself was a classic in Cotton Bowl history. Petchel rallied Penn State from a 13-0 deficit by throwing two touchdown passes, one to Triplett in the third quarter.

On the final play, Petchel threw a pass in the end zone intended for Hoggard, though Triplett was nearby as well. An SMU player deflected the pass, which floated toward Hoggard

1948 Penn State Football Season Coach Bob Higgins

The 1948 Penn State Nittany Lions football team was coached by Bob Higgins in his 19th and last season. After an undefeated regular season in 1947, it was tough to equal such a performance but Higgins came close with a 7-1-1 record. He was a great coach and in many ways put PSU back on the map. He never had the benefit of a scholarship team.

PSU began at home at New Beaver Field with Bucknell on October 2, W (35-0). Then, away at Syracuse PSU beat the Orangemen W (34-14). Back home with West Virginia on Oct, 16. PSU won W 37-7.

Michigan was always a great football power, having taught some teams in the 1800s how to play the new game of American football. What a great accomplishment for Michigan to come into State College and play PSU to a tie (14-14).

Then annual foe Colgate played PSU at their home field and lost W (32-13). Off to University of Pennsylvania and ready to play, the Nittany Lions won in a close match against a great Penn team at Franklin Field W (13-0) This PSU game was played before the largest crowd to date — 71,180 — and the Nittany Lions defeated Penn at Franklin Field,. The game was sparked by a razzle-dazzle touchdown run-and-pass play of Fran Rogel-to-Chuck Drazenovich-to-Elwood Petchel-to-Rogel.

Temple played tough for a while but got exhausted and PSU prevailed on Nov. 13, W (47–0). On Nov. 20, Pittsburgh, a team that was the season spoiler for many years played the role again against the Lions L (0–7). In a late season finale, PSU traveled to Washington State on November 27 at Rogers Field in Tacoma, WA and beat the Cougars in a close one W (7–0).

1949 Penn State Football Season Coach Joe Bedenk

The 1949 Penn State Nittany Lions football team was coached by Joe Bedenk. Bob Higgins had coached at Penn State for nineteen years and had an enviable record of 91–57–11 after having gone through the walk-on years.

Bedenk was named head coach after he had coached the offensive line for several years. After a single 5–4 season, Coach Bedenk requested a return to coaching the offensive line, and Penn State brought in Rip Engle as head coach in 1950

In September, the first class of scholarship players since 1927 entered Penn State but were sent to California State Teachers College to reside because of crowded housing conditions on the main campus. Among the freshmen are future starters Joe Yukica, Don Barney, Jim Dooley and Joe Gratson. The drought was over.

September 24 PSU kicked off its season with a kick in the pants on a L (6-27) to Villanova at home, Things did not get better as a tough Army team beat PSU by a wide margin L (7-42) at Michie Stadium in West Point, NY. The Nittany

Lions took on Boston College, new to the schedule on October 8 and picked up their first win of the season and first win for Coach Joe Bedenk W (32-14). Nebraska came to New Beaver Field on October 15 and PSU won that encounter W (22-7).

A tough Michigan State team hosted the Nittany Lions on October 22 and beat PSU in a shutout at Spartan Stadium L (0-24. Penn State would win its next three games under Joe Bedenk until Pittsburgh delivered a loss to the Nittany Lions on November 19 in the season closer L (0-19) . On October 29, Syracuse traveled to New Beaver Field to take on the Nittany Lions and PSU won the game W (33-21).

On November 5, the Lions traveled to West Virginia and beat the Mountaineers at Mountaineer Field in Morgantown W (34-14). PSU traveled on November 14 to defeat Temple at Temple Stadium W (28-7). Coach Bedenk finished the season at 5-4.

Chapter 18 — The Rip Engle Era

Coach # 13

1950	Rip Engle	5-3-1
1951	Rip Engle	5-4
1952	Rip Engle	7-2-1
1953	Rip Engle	6-3
1954	Rip Engle	7-2-
1955	Rip Engle	5-4
1956	Rip Engle	6-2-1
1957	Rip Engle	6-3
1958	Rip Engle	6-3-1
1959	Rip Engle	9-2
1960	Rip Engle	7-3
1961	Rip Engle	8-3
1962	Rip Engle	9-2
1963	Rip Engle	7-3
1964	Rip Engle	6-4
1965	Rip Engle	5-5

Top row, left to right: Dan Radakovich, Joe McMullen, George Welsh, Joe Paterno, J.T. White Bottom row, left to right: Frank Patrick, Earl Bruce, Rip Engle, Jim O'Hora taken during the football Field Day in 1963

On April 22, 1950 Charles A. "Rip" Engle, who had been head coach at Brown University was named the new Penn State head football coach to replace Joe Bedenk.

Engle was the innovator of the famous Wing-T formation. His teams experienced tremendous success leading Engle to a career PSU record of 104-48-4.

In May of 1950 Engle named former Brown University quarterback Joseph V. Paterno to his Penn State staff. He promptly assigned Paterno to coach quarterbacks. Rip Engle coached his last game in 1965 with a win over Maryland, 19-7 ending a 16 year stint as Penn State head football coach.

During his tenure Penn State did not endure a losing season. Engle officially retired February 18, 1966. A day later Joseph V. Paterno was hired head football coach of Pennsylvania State University. The rest, as they say, is history.

1950 Penn State Football Season Coach Rip Engle

The 1950 Penn State Nittany Lions football team was coached by Rip Engle in his first year. Coach Engle compiled a 5-3-1 record in his first year with the Nittany Lions.

The regular season and the home season began on September 30 at New Beaver Field against Georgetown with a nice win for Coach Engle in his first game as PSU head coach W (34-14)

On October 7, #4 ranked Army hosted PSU at Michie Stadium in West Point, NY L (7–41). Engle's team lost its second game in a row at Syracuse on October 14 L (7-27). The third loss in a row came v a shutout v the Nebraska Cornhuskers the following week, October 21 at Memorial Stadium in Lincoln NE L (0-19). The next and last blemish on Engle's first year record came the next week at home against Temple as the teams played to a tie T (7-7). PSU would win its remaining four games to finish a good season.

The first win was no pushover on November 4 against Boston College at Alumni Field in Chestnut Hill MA W (20-13). The next win was on November 11 at home against West Virginia W (27-0). Home again the following week v Rutgers in a close match W (18-14). Engle capped off his first season with a win at Pittsburgh W (21-20). Pittsburgh had been a spoiler for many years and it was a good start to the Engle years to have achieved this fine victory on December 2.

1951 Penn State Football Season Coach Rip Engle

The 1951 Penn State Nittany Lions football team was coached by Rip Engle. The team had a 5-4 record for 1951.

The season began at home on September 29 v Boston University W (40-34). On October 6 PSU traveled to Allentown v Villanova L (14-20). Nebraska was next on October 13 at Lincoln W (15-7).

On October 20, PSU came home to play Michigan State L (21-32). West Virginia was next on October 27 W (13-7). On November 3, the Nittany Lions traveled to Ross-Ade Stadium in West Lafayette, Indiana to play Purdue. The Lions were shut out L (0-28).

Syracuse played PSU at home on November 10 W (32-13). On November 17, PSU traveled to Rutgers Stadium and beat Rutgers W (13-7). Again the season finale was a close loss against a tough Pitt team at Pittsburgh L (7-13).

1952 Penn State Football Season Coach Rip Engle

The 1952 Penn State Nittany Lions football team was coached by Rip Engle and played a fine season with a record of 7-2-1. PSU was back to ten games per season. The season began earlier on September 20 at home against Temple W

(20-13). Purdue came to New Beaver Field on September 27 and played the Nittany Lions to a tie T (20-20). On October 4, William and Mary lost to the Nittany Lions at New Beaver Field W (35-23).

On October 11, PSU played at West Virginia W (35-21). On October 18, Nebraska came to State College and were defeated W (10-0).Then, on October 25, Penn State traveled to Spartan Stadium and were beaten by Michigan State L (7-34). PSU played Penn at Franklin Field on November 1 and beat the Quakers W (10-0).

On November 8 at Syracuse PSU lost to the Orangemen L (7-25). Rutgers played hard and tough on November 17 and were beaten by the Nittany Lions in a close match W (7-6). Pittsburgh hosted Penn State again at Pitt Stadium and the Nittany Lions won the game W (17-0)

1953 Penn State Football Season Coach Rip Engle

The 1953 Penn State Nittany Lions football team was coached by Rip Engle. They played home games in New Beaver Field in University Park, Pennsylvania. The Field had room for 30,000 fans. This season's record was 6-3 and the team played nine games.

Wisconsin was the opener on September 26 at Camp Randall Stadium in Madison. Penn State suffered its first loss on the season (0-20). It was not a good beginning as PSU lost again on October 3 in Franklin Field against Penn L (7-13). On October 10, PSU traveled to play Boston University at Nickerson Field and prevailed W (35-13).

On October 17, Syracuse traveled to New Beaver Field and lost to the Nittany Lions W 20-14). PSU played TCU at home on October 24 W 27-21). The following week, October 31, it was West Virginia at home. PSU suffered a close loss L (19-20).

With a 3-3 record, PSU put it in gear and won the next three games. The first at home on Nov. 7 v Fordham W (28-21); the next on November 14 at Rutgers W (54-26) and the final game at Pittsburgh on November 21 W (17-0).

1954 Penn State Football Season Coach Rip Engle

The 1954 Penn State Nittany Lions football team was coached by Rip Engle in his fifth year. The team finished with a 7-2 record and achieved a #16 ranking in the coaches poll and a #20 in the AP.

September 25th kicked off the season at Champagne Illinois as PSU beat Illinois in a very close match W (14-12). Another way game on October 2 at Syracuse found the Nittany Lions defeating the Orangemen W (13-0). The Home Opener on October 9 was against Virginia W (34-7). After the game the Nittany Lions were ranked # 9 but not for long. On October 16, West Virginia came into New Beaver Field ready for victory and they got it in a close match L (14-19).

PSU was ranked # 20 when the Nittany Lions lost to TCU at the Amon G. Carter Stadium in Fort Worth Texas L (7-20). Penn was next on October 30 at Franklin Field W (35-13) On November 6, Holy Cross played the Lions at New Beaver Field and were beaten W (39-7). Rutgers came the following week and were beaten W 37-14). Pitt played tough as usual at Pitt Stadium but nonetheless the Nittany Lions triumphed W (13-0)

1955 Penn State Football Season Coach Rip Engle

The 1955 Penn State Nittany Lions football team was coached by Rip Engle. The team talent pendulum swings and changes from year to year as one team is better than another and vice versa. This year's team made it above .500 with a 5-4 record but otherwise, it was not a stellar year. Rip Engle had better years as you will see. He coached the Lions until 1965.

On September 24, Boston University visited New Beaver Field and the Nittany Lions won W 35-0). PSU traveled to play # 6 Army on October 1 and lost the game L (6-35). On October 8 PSU played in City Stadium (the Tobacco Bowl) against Virginia W (26-7)

On October 15, a tough Navy Squad came into Beaver Stadium and defeated the Lions L (14-34). Penn State played at Mountaineer Field on October 22, and were defeated by West Virginia L (7-21). On October 29, PSU got its fight back to play Penn at Franklin Field and came home with a victory W (20-0).

On November 5, #18 Syracuse played the Nittany Lions at home and in a nailbiter, PSU won the game W (21-20). On November 12 PSU defeated Rutgers at Rutgers Stadium W (34-13). Finishing up this season at 5-3 going into the Pitt game at New Beaver Field home, the Nittany Lions put another L in the right column L (0-2) and finished the season at 5-4.

Player Highlights Lenny Moore 1955

Leonard Edward Moore was born November 25, 1933. He played halfback at PSU and he played pro for the NFL Baltimore Colts from 1956 to 1967.

Moore was simply great. He was NFL Rookie of the Year in 1956 and was a Pro-Bowler seven times. He was inducted into the Pro Football Hall of Fame in 1975.

Moore could to it all and Joe Paterno had him do it all just as Moore did for his great college and pro football career. He was both a great runner and receiver. He would line up both in the backfield as a halfback and split wide as a flanker, and the talented Moore was equally dangerous at both positions

Lenny Moore was among the greatest players to wear the blue and white. In 1954, he became the first Nittany Lion to rush for more than 1,000 yards in a season, gaining 1,082 with 11 touchdowns. Moore was a dynamic runner, receiver and kick returner, accumulating 3,543 all-purpose yards from 1953-55. Moore was selected by the Baltimore Colts in the first round of the 1956 NFL Draft and had a brilliant 12-year career with the Colts, playing in seven Pro Bowls and gaining induction into the Pro Football Hall of Fame in 1975.

His QB at Baltimore was the great Johnny Unitas. To play so many years in the NFL you have got to be pretty darned good and pretty darned tough.

Moore averaged at least 7.0 yards a carry in several seasons. He pulled in 40 receptions for 687 yards and seven touchdowns in 1957, the first of five straight years in which he would have 40 or more catches. In 1958, he caught a career-high of 50 passes for 938 yards and seven touchdowns. This year, he helped the Colts win the NFL championship. Then in 1959, Moore had 47 receptions for 846 yards and six TDs as the Colts repeated as champions.

Leonard Edward Moore is a football player that I have been hearing about forever or so it seems from when I was a little tyke. I remember Lenny playing with Johnny Unitas and the Baltimore Colts but I do not remember well if at all at Penn State and that surely may be my fault. In my defense, I was just seven years old and we did not have a TV until I was 8. . Upon making the transition from PSU to the Colts, Moore was immediately great as a pro and had a fantastically productive first pro season.

As noted above, he was named the NFL Rookie of the Year. Here is a pic from 2009 with JoePa at the Syracuse game. Joe Paterno was Assistant Coach when Lenny played in 1955. You can see just by looking at this picture that the two had great admiration for each other.

Pro football Hall of Famer and former Penn State running back Lenny Moore embraces coach Joe Paterno before the start of the Syracuse game at Beaver Statdium. Moore served as honorary captain for the Lions.

Joe Hermitt (jhermitt@pennlive.com) captured the essence of JoePa and Lanny Moore and their relationship in the above picture. This is from the Syracuse game September 15, 2009. Thank you to Pennlive for the use of the picture and the article to make this book and even more outstanding read for Penn Staters.

Here is Hermitt's article about Lenny Moore and their chance meeting:

"Ever have one of those moments when you just wish you could crawl under a rock and hide? You know, you do or say something so stupid that you would give your right arm to be able to take it back?

"Welcome to my world.

"It was about a half an hour before game time this past Saturday. Several recruits headed to their seats, both teams were leaving the field after pre-game warm-ups and Penn State coach Joe Paterno had just finished screaming at a cameraman who made the mistake of going onto the field to film him during stretches. In other words, it was business as usual at Beaver Stadium.

"I was following Paterno, shooting photos as he headed toward the tunnel. An older man approached the coach, reached out and grabbed him from behind. Paterno, at first surprised, immediately broke into a huge smile, as if seeing an old friend for the first time in a long while.

"The two embraced, not something you see Joe do very often, shared a few words and parted, as the coach needed to join his team in the locker room. Figuring the man must be someone special to Paterno, I headed over to find out who he was. I introduced myself, told him I had snapped his photo with Paterno and asked his name.

"The man smiled broadly and responded, "Sure, my name is Lenny Moore".

"After what seemed an eternity, I managed to coherently apologize. Profusely. To add to my trauma, his escort from Penn State burst out laughing, saying, "That was priceless, you should see your face."

"But a funny thing happened. Moore, wearing a perplexed look, asked why I was apologizing. In fact, he went on to say that he used to read the Patriot and would love to get a copy of the photo I had just taken. Would I possibly be able to send him one? I offered to email it to him but, much like Paterno, he doesn't have email. So he pulled out a business card and handed it to me.

"Simple and to the point, the card read, Lenny Moore, his address and telephone number and in the top right corner, "Christ is Lord". No mention of Pro Football Hall of Fame membership or of being one of the greatest players to ever play at Penn State.

Moore played for the Nittany Lions from 1953-55 and as the Altoona Mirror's Neil Rudel writes, "In an era where the players went both ways, playing offense and defense, Moore averaged a ridiculous 8.0 yards per carry, a record that still stands among the season leaders - 55 years later. He also led the team in interceptions twice and punt return average three times, including a blurry 17.5 per in '54."

Moore played for the Baltimore Colts from 1956-67, was selected to the Pro Bowl seven times, had his number, 24, retired and was elected to the Pro Football Hall of Fame.

In his post-game news conference Joe Paterno said, "Lenny Moore was probably the best football player I've ever coached, all-around."

Wow.

So as the legendary Moore stood on the sideline preparing to serve as honorary captain at the mid-field coin toss, he could not have been more gracious to a well-meaning, but foolish photographer who didn't even know his name.

Baltimore Colts running back Lenny Moore in action.

God, I still feel like climbing under a rock. Thanks Mr. Moore, your photo is on the way."

1956 Penn State Football Season Coach Rip Engle

The 1956 Penn State Nittany Lions football team was coached by Rip Engle in his seventh year as head coach.

The team opened up the season against Penn on September 29 at Franklin Field and came away with a nice, convincing win, W (34–0). On October 8, at West Point, PSU lost to Army L (7-14). On October 13, Holy Cross played at New Beaver Field and PSU outmanned them W (43-0).
On October 20, PSU traveled to Columbus to play Ohio State and beat the Buckeyes W (7-6). On October 27 at home, PSU beat West Virginia W (16-6). November 3, at Syracuse Penn State lost to the Orangemen in a close game L (9-13). Boston University played the Nittany Lions at New Beaver Field on November 10, and were defeated W (40-3).

On November 17 at Home, PSU beat North Carolina State W (14-7) in the season ending rivalry, the Nittany Lions and Pittsburgh Panthers played to tie T (7-7)

1957 Penn State Football Season Coach Rip Engle

The 1957 Penn State Nittany Lions football team was coached by Rip Engle in his eighth season. Engle directed the team to a nice 6-3.

The season opener was against Penn at Franklin Field. Penn State played tough and won the close match W (19-14).

Army was still invincible from the War years when PSU played the Cadets on October 5 at New Beaver Field. Army was a little too much for the Nittany Lions but each time the games are closer. This one was for Army L (13-27). William and Mary played a tough game on October 12 but the Nittany Lions beat them W (21-13). Vanderbilt, where current PSU mentor James Franklin coached before PSU beat the Lions at New Beaver Stadium L (2-32).

PSU played an always tough Syracuse team in Archbold Stadium on October 26 and beat the Orangemen W (20-12). West Virginia played PSU at home on November 2, and the Lions pleased the crowd at New Beaver Field with a W (27-6). The Nittany Lions traveled to play against Marquette on November 9, and won at Marquette Stadium in Milwaukee W 20-7).

On November 16 in a game at Holy Cross in Fitton Field, Worcester, MA, PSA squeaked out a close on W (14–10). November 23 was rival Pittsburgh and this time the Lions were inches away from winning at Pitt Stadium but Pitt prevailed L (13-14). The 6-3 season was a good one for Rip Engle and the Nittany Lions.

1958 Penn State Football Season Coach Rip Engle

The 1958 Penn State Nittany Lions football team was coached by Rip Engle in his ninth year. Penn State played a tenth game in 1958 and without that game the season would have been 6-3, but with the tie at West Virginia on November 8 T (14-14) the record was 6-3-1.

The season began early on September 20 at Nebraska and PSU could not muster enough to win the game L (7-14). Still not coming home, PSU played Penn at Franklin Field and really handed the once formidable Quakers a whooping W (43-0). Army was still tough as nails and beat PSU at West Point on October 4 L (0-26).

On October 11, Marquette was the team to play in the home opener at New Beaver Field. PSU dominated W (40-8). PSU went to Nickerson Field in Boston on October 28 to play Boston University W (34-0). Back home again on October 25, Syracuse came to play and defeated the Nittany Lions L 6-14). Furman came on November 1 and the Lions put them away W (36-0).

PSU traveled to Morgantown to play West Virginia on November 8 and as noted above, tied the game T (14-14). Holy Cross played the Lions at New Beaver Field on November 15 W (32-0). In the see-saw battel for dominance in the end of season intra state-rivalry, it was Penn States turn to win at Pitt Stadium W (25-21).

1959 Penn State Football Season Coach Rip Engle

The 1959 Penn State Nittany Lions football team was coached by Rip Engle in his tenth season of sixteen with PSU. This was the first eight-win year for an Engle team and it brought them a shot at the Liberty Bowl which they won on December 31, 1959 v Alabama W (7-0). The Lions finished at 9-2.

Penn State was winning very game all year until it ran into some old rivals. By now, by reading this book's review of all the games by coach, you know who they are. PSU was 7-0 when it ran into an always stubborn Syracuse team at home. Syracuse was ranked #4 when they played at New Beaver Field. In a brawl, they barely beat Penn State L (18-20) to put the first blemish on Engle's 1959 team. Think about what would have happened if PSU won that game. Syracuse went on to win their first and only National Championship with the help of future Heisman trophy winner Ernie Davis.

In the See-Saw end of season match, looking for every opportunity to have a one-loss season, Pittsburgh spoiled it for the Nittany Lions in a well-fought game L (7-22)

The Season began like any other but winning became a habit for the Nittany Lions. First, On September 19, PSU beat Missouri at Missouri W (19-8), then, at home PSU beat VMI W (21-0). Home again v Colgate W (58-20). Finally, PSU beat Army away at West Point W (17-11). The 1959 season was looking very good.

PSU was ranked # 10 when it played Boston University on October 17 at home W (21–12). A trip to Cleveland Municipal Stadium to play Illinois brought the Lions another victory W (20-9). Then, on October 31, a road trip to West Virginia was a success W (28-10)

When PSU lost to Syracuse on November 7 L (18-20), the Lions were 8-0 and ranked # 7 in the nation. On November 14, the # 10 Nittany Lions got their breath with a home win against Holy Cross W (46-0)., Next was Pittsburgh at Pitt Stadium, an always-tough game to win. On November 21, Pittsburgh was energized and beat the Lions L (7-22)

After waiting a month for a chance for national exposure in the Independence Bowl, # 14 ranked Penn State knocked off # 11 Alabama in a real battle of the trenches W (7-0) PSU had a great season 9-2, finishing # 10 in the coach's poll and

12 in the AP. 1959 was a fine year for Rip Engle and company.

1960 Penn State Football Season Coach Rip Engle

The 1960 Penn State Nittany Lions football team was coached by Rip Engle in his eleventh year. This year the Nittany Lions played their games in the newly opened Beaver Stadium in University Park, Pennsylvania. The team played ten games and finished their first season in their big, brand new stadium with a fine 7-3 record. PSU finished # 16 for the season and if the number of bowl games were as today, PSU would have assured itself of a bowl game match.

The 500-seat Beaver Field, then the 30,000 seat New Beaver Field, and in 1960, the new Beaver stadium were all named for James Beaver, President of the Board of Trustees. The Nittany Lions played at the original Beaver Field and New Beaver Field from when they moved off the lawn until 1959.

The university decided to disassemble the stadium and move it to its current location after the 1959 season. PSU played its first game in the rebuilt stadium on September 17, 1960 against Boston University. Beaver Stadium's horseshoe configuration enabled it to have a seating capacity of 46,284, but as we all know it fits well over 100,000 today after many expansions.

As noted, the Season began in triumph against Boston University on September 17 in a brand new stadium. There was a nice piece of history (30,000 original seats) packaged up as a starter kit for Beaver Stadium, and it sure helped for the first game at Beaver Stadium to be a triumph for the Nittany Lions W (20-10) over Boston University It had to be a great day.

Of course the moment has faded since it first occurred but the first game in Beaver Stadium certainly deserves to be on the list of the best games at Beaver Stadium. Surviving members of the first team to play in the first game at New Beaver Field in 1909 were on hand to celebrate the event. Unfortunately, with university classes not yet scheduled and students arriving just in time to begin their classes, there was in fact a disappointing crowd of 22,559--less than half the 46,000 capacity. Yet, they did turn out in the rain for what the pundits referred to as a lackluster Penn State win.

Unlike new parents who have had a boy often want the next one to be a girl, Penn State would have been pleased to keep the one-game Beaver Stadium streak going but Missouri had other plans and beat the Nittany Lions in game 2 of the inaugural season L (8-21) Shaking the dust of the home defeat, on October 8, PSU traveled to West Point to play Army and for the second time in two years, they beat the Black Knights W (27-16).

PSU traveled northeast on October 15 to play an always tough Syracuse team, ranked # 4 at the time. Syracuse was the defending National Champions from 1959 and Ernie Davis, a future Heisman was making teams pay for scheduling Syracuse on their season games list. In another close game PSU paid the price for having Syracuse on its schedule L (15-21). But the Nittany Lions played quite well.

On October 22, it was off to Memorial Stadium in Champagne IL to play the Fighting Illini In another close match, PSU was on the lesser side L (8-10). West Virginia pulled into Beaver Stadium iteration # 1 on October 29 and went home defeated by PSU W (34-13)

Maryland came in next on November 5, and met the same fate W (28-9). PSU had to leave its new Digs for Fitton Field in Worcester Mass on November 12 to beat Holy Cross W (33-8). PSU then paid Pitt back for a few losses over the years on November 19 at Pitt Stadium W (14-3).

The Nittany Lions had competed so well with its 6-3 record that it got a shot at Oregon in the Liberty Bowl on December

17 at JFK Stadium in Philadelphia, winning the game W (41-12). Bravo Nittany Lions!

1961 Penn State Football Season Coach Rip Engle

The 1961 Penn State Nittany Lions football team was coached by Rip Engle in his twelfth season. The lions pounded out a #19 finish and a #17 in the AP with an overall season ending 8-3 record including a Gator Bowl win v Georgia Tech.

On September 23, Navy came into town and played tough but left with an L (20-10). PSU picked up Miami on its schedule at Miami and played a tough game in the Orange Bowl but Miami won nonetheless L (8-25). Boston University hosted PSU on October 6 and lost to the Nittany Lions W (32-0). An always tough Army squad came to Beaver Stadium and beat PSU in a very close match by L (6-10).

With Ernie Davis still chugging out the yardage and on track for a Heisman in 1961, Syracuse lost to PSU on Oct. 21 at Beaver Stadium W (14-0). The new Stadium helped PSU beat California of PA in Beaver Stadium the following week on October 28 W 33-16). PSU then left home and went south to Maryland and were beaten by the Terrapins in a very close match L (17-21).

On November 11 at West Virginia, PSU scratched out a W (20-6). On November 18, at home, PSU defeated Holy Cross W 934-14). Pitt came into Pitt Stadium looking strong as usual but lost on November 25 at Pitt Stadium W (34-14)

With a 7-3 record against good teams, PSU was invited to the Gator Bowl on December 30, 1961 against Georgia Tech in Gator Bowl Stadium, Jacksonville, FL. PSU won the Gator Bowl W (30–15) for a fine 8-3 season.

1962 Penn State Football Season Coach Rip Engle

The 1962 Penn State Nittany Lions football team was coached by Rip Engle in his thirteenth of sixteen seasons. The team played its second set of home games in the brand new Beaver Stadium in University Park, Pennsylvania.

Navy was first on the Beaver Stadium list on September 21 for the season opener / home opener combo game. Penn State came in ranked #9 and beat Navy W (41-7). Ranked # 4 when Airforce Came in to Beaver Stadium for the first time and the Nittany Lions managed a victory against the tough Air Force Falcons W (20-6) Still ranked #4, PSU played at Rice Stadium in Houston Texas against Rice University and beat then W (18-7).

Things had been going too well when PSU traveled to West Point and Army beat them in a real close one L (6-9).

After Army, PSU was unranked and hosted Syracuse at Beaver Stadium. The Nittany Lions barely beat the Orangemen in a close match W (20-19).

The Nittany Lions like to plan perfection but sometimes execution does not match the plan. In this game Penn State blew a 14-point first quarter lead before a record Homecoming crowd of 48,356, but they put their mettle together and decided to win.

The men from Penn State University came from behind with five minutes left in the game on an 8-play, 65-yard drive to take a 20-19 lead. They needed to hold the Orangemen or all would have been for naught. The game was still in doubt until Hatch Rosdahl blocked a 44-yard field goal attempt with 28 seconds remaining.

When we think of football being exciting, we do not often think of any negatives to the excitement. However, in this phenomenally exciting nail-biter, two (not just one) spectators died of heart attacks. To this day it is not known whether they were Orangemen or Nittany Lions fans.

It was not long before the Lions were back in the hunt in the top 20. PSU then played the California team at California Memorial Stadium in Berkeley and managed a close win W (23-21).

On November 3, Maryland was next on the schedule at Beaver Stadium W (23-7). On November 10, it was West Virginia at home W (34-6). Then the Lions took a trip to Fitton Field in Worcester, MA on November 17 to play Holy Cross and won W 48-20). Big rival Pittsburgh always seemed to hang around until the end of the season and plop a bad one on the Nittany Lions. This time PSU did the damage and while in a # 9 ranking, won at Pitt Stadium W (16-0).

At 9-1 with a fine year with just one blemish v Army, the Nittany Lions were invited to play on December 29 vs. Florida at Gator Bowl Stadium in Jacksonville, FL. Florida won the close match L (7–17). PSU finished at 9-2 for a fine season.

1963 Penn State Football Season Coach Rip Engle

The 1963 Penn State Nittany Lions football team was coached by Rip Engle in his fourteenth of sixteen seasons. The team played its third set of home games in its brand new Beaver Stadium in University Park, Pennsylvania. The regular season finale with Pittsburgh was postponed from Nov. 23 to Dec. 7 following the assassination of President John F. Kennedy on Nov. 22 in Dallas, Texas. Even football history cannot undue history, though we wish it could.

PSU traveled to the West coast to Hayward Field in Eugene Oregon on September 21, to play the Webfoots of Oregon University. PSU won W (17-7). Another first time game was at Beaver Stadium First on September 28 v UCLA, W (17-14). On Oct. 5 Rice came to Beaver Stadium and lost to the

Lions W (28-7). Army, which always takes everything seriously beat PSU on October 12 at Beaver Stadium in a nailbiter L (7-10).

The eternally tough Orangemen hosted PSU on October 19 at Archbold Stadium and won the rivalry in a close game L (0-9). West Virginia came to State College on October 26 and lost to PSU W (20-9). PSU traveled south to Maryland's Byrd Stadium on November 2, and barely beat the Terrapins in a close match W (17-15).

On November 9 at #10 Ohio State in Ohio Stadium, PSU dug in and managed a close victory W (10–7). In a late season home game against Holy Cross, PSU won W (28-14).

Pittsburgh had some great players in 1963 and finished ranked #3. On December 7, PSU had a great team also and lost this entanglement to a fine Pitt Team at Pitt in a game that could have gone either way L (21-20). PSU finished # 16 with a fine 7-3 record.

1964 Penn State Football Season Coach Rip Engle

The 1964 Penn State Nittany Lions football team was coached by Rip Engle in his fifteenth year. Even though the team was just 6-4, its strength of schedule prompted the coach's poll to rank PSU # 14 in 1964.

September 19 PSU opened up its season at home with a loss to #10 ranked Navy L (8-21). September 26, PSU traveled to California to play UCLA at the LA Coliseum L (14-21). My wife often says where there is two, there is three. In a very miserable start PSU lost to Oregon L 14-22) at Beaver Stadium on October 3. A tough Army team invited PSU to play at West Point on October 10, and in a very close game PSU beat Army W (6-2) making the team record 3-1 going into the fifth game.

The last loss of the season was on October 17 in another close battel at home against Syracuse L (14-21). West Virginia gave the Nittany Lions a nice breather when the teams played in Morgantown, WV for a PSU win W (37-8). On October 31, Maryland came to play at Beaver Stadium but were defeated anyway by the Nittany Lions in a tough match W (17-9). Ohio State hosted the Nittany Lions the following week on November 7. The Buckeyes were shut-out by PSU W (27-0). On November 14, Penn State then traveled to Houston Texas to play the Cougars and left town with a nice win W (24-7).

Pittsburgh, an old-time rivalry was doing poorly at 3-5-2 after a 9-1 season in 1962, marched into Penn State's Beaver Stadium on November 21. The Panthers marched back out after being shut down by PSU W 28-0)

There have been a lot of cold games in the history of Beaver Field, New beaver Field, and Beaver Stadium. In one of the two coldest games in the history of Beaver Stadium, Penn State dominated its bitterest rival before what was a record crowd of 50,144 before the big Stadium expansions.

They were forced to brave the wind, snow flurries, and wind chill temperatures of zero. It was just the eighth time since the Pitt series began in 1893 that the annual year-end game was played at Penn State and the first time since 1955. Penn State warmed the hearts and minds of their fans with this fine W (28-0) victory.

1965 Penn State Football Season Coach Rip Engle

The 1965 Penn State Nittany Lions football team was coached by Rip Engle's in his last season as head coach of Penn State. Penn State ironically had one of its worst records this year (5-5) as it proves the ups and downs of college football results. Rip Engle was a fine coach. With sixteen seasons of coaching PSU behind him Engle had had enough. He never had a losing season.

On September 25, Michigan State shut out PSU in the Beaver Stadium home and season opener L (0-23))-pits home. On October 2, UCLA traveled from California to make the Nittany Lions record 0-2 with a close game L (22-14). Penn State traveled to Boston College's Alumni Stadium on October 9 to defeat the Eagles W (17-0) for the first win of the season. On October 16, trying its luck on the road a second week in a row, PSU lost at Syracuse L (21-28).

On October 23, Penn State beat West Virginia in a runaway at Beaver Stadium W 44–6. The Lions traveled to California to play California on October 30, and were defeated L (17-21). Next was Kent State at home on November 6 with a nice PSU win W (21-6). Navy came to State College on November 13 and played a close game but the Nittany Lions prevailed W (14-6). On November 20, Pitt was having a recovery year and at Pitt Stadium they had recovered enough to defeat PSU in a very close game L (27-30). PSU played a tenth game later than usual on December 4 at Maryland's Byrd Stadium and defeated the Terrapins in a close match W (19-7).

This 5-5 season was Rip Engle's last. Penn State appointed Joe Paterno as Head Coach of the Nittany Lions.

Chapter 19 — The Joe Paterno Era from 1966 to 1980

Coach # 14

1966	Joe Paterno	5-5
1967	Joe Paterno	8-2-1
1968	Joe Paterno	11-0
1969	Joe Paterno	11-0
1970	Joe Paterno	7-3
1971	Joe Paterno	11-1
1972	Joe Paterno	10-2
1973	Joe Paterno	12-0
1974	Joe Paterno	10-2
1975	Joe Paterno	9-3
1976	Joe Paterno	7-5
1977	Joe Paterno	11-1
1978	Joe Paterno	11-1
1979	Joe Paterno	8-4
1980	Joe Paterno	10-2

Coached 45 great seasons 1966 to 2010 and part of 2011.

With 409 victories, Joe Paterno is the winningest coach in NCAA FBS history.

He put together bowl victories, two consensus National Championships—1982, 1986, and five undefeated and untied seasons – 1968, 1969, 1973, 1986, and 1994. Four of Penn State's unbeaten teams (1968, 1969, 1973, and 1994) won major bowl games and yet were not awarded a national championship. You make the call on that one, please! At the end of the 2011 season, he was the winningest coach ever in Division I with a 409-136-3 record. He was the best coach ever!

1966 Penn State Football Season Coach Joe Paterno

The 1966 Penn State Nittany Lions football team was coached by Joe Paterno in his first season as head coach of Penn State. Paterno helped the team achieve a 5-5 record, which coincidentally was the record for PSU in Rip Engle's last season.

September 17 was the First Paterno-led game at home (Beaver Stadium). PSU beat Maryland in a lose match W (15-7).

It is always a good feeling and often a harbinger of good things to come when a new coach wins his first game, especially a home game. Paterno brought in the big one when he was still more or less a kid at 40 years old. Tons of victories later, and Paterno teams would bring in over 400 victories for the good of Penn State University, a great school, and a great football program. September 17th was simply the first. The attendance was almost at max to see this game with 40,911 excited Penn State Fans ready to see the Nittany Lions play ball.

The first come-uppance for the team came soon after the first victory when PSU traveled to Army on October 1, and lost L (0-11). The next week on October 8, PSU was back at home and the Lions beat Boston College W (30-21) bringing the record to 2-1. The JoePa team went to the Los Angeles Memorial Coliseum on October 15 and were overwhelmed by UCLA L (11-49) Joe Paterno was getting a baptism of fire.

But, this tough coach, a one-time quarterback would endure and succeed.

On October 22, The Nittany Lions played at West Virginia for a nice win W (38-6). The California University played PSU at Beaver Stadium on October 29, and PSU did quite well W (33-15_ before 33,332 fans. On November 5, at Beaver Stadium in what was termed an ABC Regional, PSU played Syracuse in a nail biter won by Syracuse L (10-12) before with 45, 126 in attendance—a veritable packed house at the new Beaver Stadium.

On November 12, PSU played at #5 ranked Georgia Tech and were shot-out L (0-21). Pittsburgh had been playing sporadic since its great years and in 1966, Joe Paterno's first team were ready in their annual venture, played this time at Pitt Stadium. Penn State was please to deliver a shellacking to Pitt W (48-24).

1967 Penn State Football Season Coach Joe Paterno

The 1967 Penn State Nittany Lions football team was coached by Joe Paterno and played its home games in the recently built Beaver Stadium in University Park, Pennsylvania. It did not take Joe Paterno long to break out of the regular pack of American coaches. Rip Engle and many PSU coaches were very good coaches.

Joe Paterno at 45 years was a remarkable, unquestionably great coach. In his getting to know you first year, he was 5-5 but those days for the most part were gone. In 1967 Paterno showed his mettle and delivered a great 8-2-1 season to PSU fans. Penn State had been a National power. Joe Paterno made Penn State a "you better notice us" national phenomenon.

Nobody likes to begin a season with a loss and when PSU traveled to Navy at Annapolis on September 23, the Nittany Lions planned to win. But a scrappy and tough US Navy team beat them by one point L (22-23). Miami Florida plays its home games at the orange Bowl, and in game 2 on September 29, PSU played Miami at this famous venue and beat the Hurricanes W (17-8).

UCLA, still very tough, and remembering their win the prior year came to Beaver Stadium on October 7, expecting an easy game like 1966 but it did not happen. UCLA beat the Nittany Lions but they worked for every point and the difference was just two points L (15-17). This PSU team hated to lose more than most teams. They would not suffer another loss for the rest of this season.

On October 14, PSU played Boston College at Alumni Stadium in Chestnut Hill, MA, and swamped the Eagles W (50–28). On October 21, West Virginia played the Lions at home W (21–14). On October 28, an always-tough Syracuse team coached by Ben Schwartzwalder played a tough game at Archbold Stadium but the Lions prevailed W (29–20) before 41,750. On November 4 at Maryland, Penn State took away a convincing win (38–3).

Back at home on November 11, the #3 ranked NC State team came into Beaver Stadium and the Nittany Lions won again W 13-8) in a very historical game. The Nittany Lions stopped a fourth-and-goal at their one-yard line with 44 seconds left to upset No. 3 North Carolina State and give Coach Joe Paterno his first signature victory. Paterno has called the tackle by Mike McBath, Dennis Onkotz, and Jim Kates: "one of the greatest plays in Penn State history." Joe ought to know.

Ohio was next on November 18 at Beaver Stadium in University Park, PA. PSU exploded for a W (35–14). In the last regular game of the season, with a record of 7-2, PSU played its nemesis Pitt at Beaver Stadium on November 25, and beat their cross-state rivals in a blowout W (42-6). PSU finished the regular season in Joe Paterno's second season at 8-2, a great record with most wins on the back-end.

For this great record, the Nittany Lions were invited to the Gator Bowl which was on ABC TV played in Jacksonville Florida against Florida State University on December 30, 1967. It was a really tough game and no team got the edge. This is one bowl game that ended in a tie (T 17-17) before 68,019—all of whom were disappointed.

1968 Penn State Football Season Coach Joe Paterno

The 1968 Penn State Nittany Lions football team was coached by Joe Paterno in his third season. The 1968 team was Paterno's first perfect season. He had gone from 5-5 to 8-2-1, to 11-0, and still could not get the pundits, the scribes or the coaches to give Penn State the championship it deserved. No matter what you think of the BCS, this is the scenario that it was created to avoid.

Was it fair the Penn State was denied the National Championship with a perfect record and eleven games played? How about going 11–0? Regardless of the fairness factor, the voters ruled. The Nittany Lions finished behind 9–0 Ohio State and 9–0–1 USC in both polls. Not fair for sure. PSU should claim a piece of this championship as many other schools have done when fairness was not achieved. Just a thought. Every game was a win in 1968. Every game, including the big Orange Bowl game on January 11, 1969

On September 21, a # 10 ranked Navy team lost at Beaver Stadium to Penn State in a convincing match W (31-6). After the game, PSU was ranked # 4. Kansas State then played at Beaver Stadium on September 28, and were beaten handily W (25-9). West Virginia then played a #3 ranked PSU at Mountaineer Field and lost the game to a powerful PSU team W (31-20).

PSU then played UCLA in California on October 12 and beat the Bruins for the fourth win of the season W (21-6). Somehow after this victory, Penn State had slipped down one notch to # 4 in the polls. Who knows why? After a week bye, PSU played at Boston College's Alumni Stadium in Chestnut Hill, MA, and won a shutout W (29-0) against the Eagles.

Army, always tough, were not tough enough in a really tough game to beat Penn State. The Lions won this close match W (28-24) before 49,653, a virtual sellout of the original Beaver Stadium. After these two wins, PSU was still in 4th place.

Regardless of the polls, Penn State could not have won this game against Army without a little intervention. Surely many were praying as it came down to an onside kick.

All-America tight end Ted Kwalick swooped up the football coming out of a pile of players on an onside kick attempt in this game with 2:29 left. Kwalick was not an All-American by acclamation. He had earned it. In this game, the tight end took the ball in addition to all hopes for an Army victory across the goal line 53-yards after he had snagged the kick in the air. This was a very important touchdown for the 1968 season as it avoided an upset that would have ruined Penn State's first undefeated season under Paterno.

Player Highlights Ted Kwalick

Ted Kwalick was indicted into the Polish American Hall of Fame on June 9, 2005. Having three children of Polish descent and living in a Polish / Irish family, I can say that I believe that Ted Kwalick enjoyed this honor as much as his College Hall of Fame induction.

Kwalick was born in Pittsburgh, on the other side of the state from where I live, but he came to mid Pennsylvania to play football. He became a star at Penn State University for his outstanding play. He put in a three year highly successful tenure with the Nittany Lions as a tight end, catching 86 passes for 1,343 yards and 10 touchdowns—all Penn State records.

Kwalick was the school's first two-time All-American (1968, 1969). He helped lead the Nittany Lions to a perfect 11-0 record and a victory in the Orange Bowl in 1969 (the season being reported).

Kwalick was selected seventh overall in the NFL draft by the San Francisco 49ers, and he quickly made an impact the way great players most often do. He made the NFC Pro Bowl three straight seasons (1971-73) playing in three NFL West Championship games.

Kwalick after the Maryland Game

In 1972, Kwalick scored nine touchdowns and averaged an amazing 18.8 yards per catch. After six seasons with the 49ers he played his last three years with the Oakland Raiders. In 1977 the Raiders beat the Vikings in Super Bowl XI giving Kwalick his Super Bowl ring. Kwalick was inducted into the College Football Hall of Fame in 1989.

As an aside, the all-time great lefty quarterback Kenny Stabler was steering the Raiders ship at that time. Ted

Kwalick was the guy on the end of the defensive line getting the ball back for him to play another set off downs. Guys like "Snake" Stabler at QB made pro football at the time almost as interesting as college ball.

Remaining 1999 Games

Always tough national power Miami played PSU at Beaver Stadium on November 9 and lost W (22-7). The crowd was more than capacity at 50,132. On November 16 at Maryland, a then-ranked #3 PSU won big W (57–13). Still not able to budge the pundits or the coaches who had something else on their mind, PSU smothered a tough Pitt Panther team on November 23 at Pittsburgh W (65-9). Even big scores against college powerhouses could not move the Lions up in the rankings.

The Nittany Lions were still ranked at # 3, though undefeated and untied when a tough Syracuse team came to Beaver Stadium on December 7. It was a respectable game W (30-12) but clearly PSU dominated against the national power Syracuse squad. Played before 41,393 at Beaver Stadium. Penn State, a team accustomed to cold Pennsylvania winters beat a cold-weather team that had yet to gain the comforts of the Carrier Dome. December 7 was a cold day and if I may after the game with the rankings, it appeared that it would have to be an even colder day in Hell for Penn State to get a break, and if not a break, some fairness.

Yes, the PSU Syracuse encounter was a tough cold game. Somebody, someplace, however was warm enough to be pleading the case for some other teams to advance in the standings while PSU was neutralized. PSU did not move up a nickel in the polls all season long. Everybody knew the PSU schedule when shortly after the season began PSU was ranked # 3.

Moreover, though the PSU record was about as good as it could get in football, at 10-0, PSU's opponent for the Orange Bowl was not either of the # 1 or # 2 ranked teams in America and neither had as good a record as the Nittany Lions.

As an independent, perhaps the conferences dominated the post-season voting for opportunities. Playing # 6 Kansas, a fine team in 1967, would in no way nudge the PSU record up a notch so PSU could play for the championship. Even if the battle between the # 1 and # 2 at the time found both teams losing, the obvious bias of the press and the coaches, I regret to say would still have denied PSU its due.

The university does not complain but perhaps it should. Nothing is over until it is over. The deck was stacked against PSU by a set of biased coaches and biased pundits. Who knows? Maybe they simply did not like Pennsylvania or perhaps it was third year coach Joe Paterno, who nobody knew because he was so new and thus did not deserve a championship. You tell me? Maybe somebody had an issue with Rip Engle or Bib Higgins or perhaps the Hollenback brothers that needed to be atoned. My only excuse is that it sure seems that some set of coaches and pundits with a relationship with a past Penn State coach or team believed they had experienced some animus that now had its chance to be righted. Again, who knows?

Nonetheless, Kansas and Penn State entered the Orange Bowl for this NBC televised game on January 1, 1969, both wanting to win this prestigious game and both hoping for the best. Both were great teams and nobody could deny that. Before 77,719 fans, Penn State played one of its best games ever against a very, very tough and respectable Kansas squad. PSU won the line battle and the scoring battle but just about won the game by one point W (15-14)

Quarterback Chuck Burkhart directed Penn State to its first two undefeated seasons under Joe Paterno in 1968 and '69. In the 1969 Orange Bowl against Kansas (above), Burkhart ran for a three-yard touchdown with eight seconds left and Bob Campbell's two-point run gave Penn State one of its most thrilling victories in program history, 15-14, to cap an 11-0 season and No. 2 finish in the Associated Press poll.

1969 Penn State Football Season Coach Joe Paterno

The 1969 Penn State Nittany Lions football team was coached by Joe Paterno in his fourth season. The 1968 team was Paterno's second perfect season in a row. He had gone from 5-5 to 8-2-1, to 11-0, and now again in 1969, 11-0, and yet the coaches and the pundits denied Penn State a National Championship for the second time in ten years. As I have said before, no matter what you may think of the BCS, this is the scenario of which it was created.

Despite posting its second consecutive undefeated, untied season, the Nittany Lions did not have a fair shot at the national championship. Somehow President Richard Nixon was polled about his thinking on the matter. He said that he would consider the winner of the December 6 matchup between the Texas Longhorns and the Arkansas Razorbacks, then ranked at the top of the polls.

The coaches and the pundits mysteriously agreed with the President and they set up a scenario from which Penn State could again not compete in a championship game on New Year's Day. Sometimes even though a university does not whine, it should. PSU should have received a share of two national titles that it had earned.

Though there are no real excuses for this travesty against fair play, national champions were selected before the bowl games were played in January. Joe Paterno, who was a great speaker and a great teller of great stories—at the 1973 PSU Commencement ceremonies four years later, was quoted: "I've wondered how President Nixon could know so little about Watergate in 1973 and so much about college football in 1969." This was a national sham.

When Nixon named Texas the national champion over Penn State

President Nixon's decision to name Texas the 1969 national champion over Penn State is explored in ESPN Film.

Pennsylvania Governor Raymond Shafer got into the act and quickly got the White House's attention with Penn State's 2 season undefeated streak. Shafer quickly declared that Pennsylvania State University was the # 1 team in the nation.

A White House assistant called Paterno to invite him and the team to the White House to receive a trophy for their accomplishment. Paterno has stated many times that he responded with, "You can tell the president to take that trophy and shove it." Penn State and the entire state of Pennsylvania declined an invitation to play the Texas/Arkansas winner in the Cotton Bowl.

As we review the 1969 season, it helps to remember that now, many years later, there will be no drama reading the season's games as each and every game was won by Penn State. Not all games were blow-outs but there were many, but Penn State won all the games –the shutouts, the blow-outs, and the close-calls, one after another. Every game below that you read about was a victory for Penn State though these wins were not enough for the coach's and pundits who perhaps wanted a different team or coach to win the national prize. It sure was not right. Then again, that's why today we have the BCS

The first win came on September 20 at Navy at the Navy-Marine Corps Memorial Stadium • Annapolis, MD. PSU was rated # 3 to start. The Nittany Lions won the game handily W (45–22) before 28,796. On September 27, Colorado came to play a now # 2 ranked PSU at Beaver Stadium and lost the game W (7–3) with 51,402 in attendance. On October 4, Kansas State hosted PSU at KSU Stadium for a close Lions win W (17–14). By Beating Kansas somehow PSU went down 3 notches in the polls to # 5. On October 11, #17 West Virginia tried to move up in the polls by beating now #5 ranked PSU at Beaver Stadium but the Nittany Lions shut out the Mountaineers W (20-0).

On October 18, Ben Schwartzwalder's tough Syracuse team hosted #5 ranked, unbeaten and untied Penn State and gave the Lions quite a tussle but PSU prevailed W (15-14) After Syracuse, ranked # 8, yet still unbeaten and still untied, PSU played Ohio on October 25, at Beaver Stadium and beat the Buckeyes by a pile W (42-3), bringing back the reward of a return to #5 in the polls. At Boston College on week 7, November 1, PSU defeated the Eagles W (38-16) at Beaver Stadium before 46,652.

On November 15, after a bye week, PSU smothered Maryland at home W 4(8-0). Now #4 ranked PSU played Pitt and beat the Panthers at Pitt Stadium W (27-7). On November 29, Carter Stadium was the home for a match-up of North Carolina State v # 3 ranked PSU, still unbeaten and untied with a 9-0 record going into game 10 of the season. Penn State convincingly beat the Wolfpack W (33-8).

It looked like Ohio State would automatically be the National Championship as they were ranked # 1 and were precluded from a Bowl game so no matter what when the Bowl decision had to be made, PSU only had a chance if Ohio State lost its last game. The decision had to be made before the last game, however.

Joe Paterno admitted that he liked the way the team was treated the previous year in Miami for the Orange Bowl, but he always thought you should play the best team you could.

That means that at the time the highest ranked team in the Bowl game which when the game was played would have been either Texas or Arkansas in the Cotton Bowl. Yet, the players decided to go to Miami. When Ohio lost, it made the Cotton Bowl the battle for the National Championship or so it seemed to the coaches and pundits. Penn State and the people of Pennsylvania and Governor Schaeffer felt otherwise.

Ranked #6 Missouri put up a fight but were defeated by the #2 ranked Penn State Nittany Lions in the Cotton Bowl. Texas beat Arkansas and were crowned National Champions. Penn State finished the balloting at # 2.

1970 Penn State Football Season Coach Joe Paterno

The 1970 Penn State Nittany Lions football team was coached by Joe Paterno in his fifth season, and continued to play its home games in Beaver Stadium in University Park, Pennsylvania. After two undefeated and untied seasons, 1970 was a rebuilding season but well played nonetheless. Paterno's Lions finished with a 7-3 record, ranked #19 in the coaches polls and #18 in the AP pundits poll.

Jack Ham—a standout at Linebacker U.

Ham, Jack Raphael (nickname Dobre Shunka)
Born: December 23, 1948, in Johnstown, Pennsylvania
Vocations: Athlete, Radio Personality, Sports Analyst

Short Bio: Jack Raphael Ham, Jr. was born in Johnstown, Pennsylvania, on December 23, 1948. He attended The Pennsylvania State University where he became one of the school's all-time great football players. He then went on to a wildly successful career in the National Football League with the Pittsburgh Steelers. After retiring, he entered broadcasting and headed a drug-testing company. He currently resides in Pittsburgh with his wife, Joanne.

Here is the rest of the full "skinny" on Jack Ham. This biography was prepared by Wesley Kendle, fall 2007.

Jack Ham, a man who would leave his mark on the world of American Football, was born in Johnstown, Pennsylvania, on December 23, 1948. The undersized and underrated linebacker graduated Bishop McCort High School in 1967 and found that he had no place to go. Ham, worried that his football career might be finished, then went to Massanutten Military Academy in Woodstock, Virginia, with hopes of toughening up and honing his skills in order to work his way onto a college football team.

Just when Ham had thought his only option was to enroll as a student at The Pennsylvania State University and attempt to walk on to the football team, his high school friend Steve Smear convinced recruiter George Welsh to offer Ham a newly opened scholarship. The rest is history. Jack Ham would go on to an astounding career in football, both with The Pennsylvania State University and the NFL's Pittsburgh Steelers. He is now considered to be one of American football's greatest linebackers to ever play the position.

[My wife comes from a half Polish / half Irish family and so I know a lot more Polish than your average Harp. When I saw Ham's nickname I knew that I already knew what half of it meant. Dobre Piwo in Polish means good beer and before I was eighteen and before I had met my wife, I was well acquainted with the best of the Piwos. Considering my dad worked for Stegmaier Brewery in Wilkes-Barre, PA, all members of the family one way or another learned all the names for beer before too long.]

Jack Ham's nickname, "Dobre Shunka," means "good ham" in Polish. His nickname was not just a childhood nickname, but it stayed with him throughout his playing days. In fact, it was the name of a fan club devoted to Ham when he sported the black and gold of the Pittsburgh Steelers. Much like his nickname states, Ham became quite good at playing outside linebacker.

A turning point that he himself points to as somewhat of a springboard for his career is the spring of his freshman year of college. After a rough freshman year in a time when freshmen did not see the varsity playing field, Ham found himself on the first string going into spring practice. The confidence that the coaching staff showed throughout the spring off season had a huge impact on Ham, and it began to show the following season.

As summed up in Ken Rappoport's book The Pennsylvania State University Nittany Lions, Where Have You Gone?, Jack Ham would go on to letter in football at The Pennsylvania State University from 1968 to 1970. He was a key player in a Nittany Lion squad that would go on a 31-game unbeaten winning streak. In 1970, he was a consensus All-American. However, even throughout his outstanding successes at The Pennsylvania State University, he was still seen by many as an undersized player.

Scouting reports in the National Football League said that he was too small to make it in the pros when the Steelers drafted him in the second round of the 1970 NFL draft. Many scouts were saying that Ham's 6'1", 225-pound frame was not big enough to handle the physicality of the professional football league. For a linebacker, his height was nothing to brag about. Even when he was finally drafted and signed by an NFL team, Ham had trouble making people believe he was qualified for the job.

Art Rooney, Jr. almost ran him out of his rookie physical for the Steelers when he "thought [Ham] was the delivery boy." He was even barred from the players' entrance at Three Rivers Stadium before his debut game because the security guard at the door did not believe that he played in the NFL.

In Ray Didinger's Pittsburgh Steelers, the guard was quoted as saying, "You expect me to believe you're one of the Steelers?" However, when Ham finally reached the gridiron, there was no mistaking that he belonged there. In his 12 year pro career, spanning from 1971-1982, Ham won four Super Bowls with the Steelers' organization. He was on the All-Pro team nine consecutive years and was a unanimous selection on the NFL's Team of the Decade for the 1970s. In 1975, Ham was named the NFL Defensive Player of the Year.

Then, in 1988, Ham's former football coach, Joe Paterno, inducted him into the National Football League Hall of Fame. No more than two years later, Ham was inducted into the College Football Hall of Fame where he became the only The Pennsylvania State University player to be inducted into both halls.

There is also a life after football for Jack Ham. Immediately following his retirement from professional football, Ham decided that it was time to put to use his Business degree that he had earned from The Pennsylvania State University after graduating in 1970.

He began selling coal for a company in his native city of Johnstown. He sold the coal to other industries, such as power plants, utilities, and steel companies. Ham also headed Nationwide Drug Testing in Pittsburgh. When being interviewed for the book Penn State Nittany Lions, Where Have You Gone? by Ken Rappaport, Ham had this to say about his endeavors after football:

"I still do some of that, but I also have a drug-testing company as well here in Pittsburgh. We implement drug-free workplace programs for companies, from background checks to drug testing to writing policy for companies, so that's my main job out here."

Along with his job at Nationwide Drug Testing, Ham is also involved in broadcasting. For years he could be heard on NFL's Games of the Week on Westwood One Radio Network.

Ham also won the Penn State Distinguished Alumni Award.

No one will forget his accomplishments on the playing field. His former coach, mentor, and hall of fame inductor Joe Paterno used these words to sum up Jack Ham: "Jack Ham's career is a monument to the work ethic. He was not a highly recruited athlete, but his exceptional intelligence and capacity for hard work made him an extraordinary football player. I don't think any of us knew then what an enormous talent we were getting. Jack Ham will always be the consummate The Pennsylvania State University player."

The native of Johnstown, who has also called State College and Western Pennsylvania his home, now resides in the suburbs of Pittsburgh with his wife, Joanne. He still runs a drug testing company. Ham currently works as radio and sports analyst for the Penn State Sports Network.

1970 games

On September 19, the season began well at home against Navy with an overwhelming victory W (55-7). It looked like the old stuff was back where it was. Colorado came to Beaver Stadium on September 26, and spoiled the party with a solid game v the Nittany Lions for the first loss of the season and the first loss in three years of play, L (13-41). It was back to back losses as PSU traveled to Camp Randall Stadium on October 3 to be beaten by Wisconsin in Madison L (16-29) PSU got a win back against Boston College at Alumni Stadium W (28-3.

At 2-2, with a win in the prior week, Ben Schwartzwalder's Syracuse Orangemen came to Beaver Stadium on October 17, and won the game handily L (7-24). On October 24, Army was next game at Michie Stadium in West Point W (38-14). Now, at 3-3, the win engine went into full gear as PSU defeated West Virginia at home W (42-8), followed on November 7 at Maryland W (34-0).

On November 14, Ohio was next at Beaver Stadium W (32-22). Penn State capped off its season against Pittsburgh at home W (35–15).

1971 Penn State Football Season Coach Joe Paterno

The 1971 Penn State Nittany Lions football team was coached by Joe Paterno in his sixth season. If the man, who would soon be known and loved as JoePa knew anything at all, he knew how to win. With just one loss in an 11-1 season, I was a justified whiner in 1971 when for this stellar record, PSU was ranked at just #11 in the coach's poll and # 5 in the AP. A lot of coaches seemed to be unwilling to reward Penn State in the mid twentieth century for its valid accomplishments.

Joe Paterno's worst season so far was his first at 5-5. When any coach could follow this with 8-2-1; 11-0; 11-0; 7-3; and 11-1 records, that is one heck of a Division I coach. It is not coincidental that Joe Paterno is currently the winningest coach in the history of major league Division I football. Can you believe this fantastic start to a fantastic coaching career?

On September 18, PSU played at Navy and defeated the Middies in a blow-out 56-3. PSU then played Iowa in Iowa City and won big again W (44-14). Air Force, a very scrappy team that has habit of beating big teams—a tem which played in the Sugar Bowl in 1971, always played to win. On October 2, the Falcons were just about beaten by Penn State W (16-14). PSU played all three major service academies in 1971 with Army losing to the Nittany Lions at Beaver Stadium W 42-0) before a packed house.

With a 4-0 record, still ranked just # 9 in the nation, PSU traveled to Syracuse on October 16 and shut out a tough Orange team (31-0). PSU was hitting on all cylinders at Beaver Stadium on October 23 in scobbing TCU by a whopping W (66-14). On October 30, PSU at # 6 was off to Morgantown WV to defeat West Virginia W (35-7).

Maryland was next on November 6 at Beaver Stadium in a shootout dominated by Penn State W (63-27) before an oversold attendance of 50,144.

NC State played at Beaver Stadium the next week on November 13, and were beaten by the Nittany Lions W 35-3). On November 20, Penn State pounded Pittsburgh at Pitt Stadium W (55-18). At 10-0, a #5 ranked PSU let its guard down on December 4 at Neyland Stadium in Knoxville v the Tennessee Volunteers and lost the game L (11-31).

With a 10-1 record, ranked # 10 in the nation, Penn State won a shot at Texas in the Cotton Bowl on January 1, 1972. The game was televised on CBS so that 70,000 in attendance along with millions of fans on TV saw #10 PSU defeat #12 Texas W (30-6) in a well-played game for the Nittany Lions.

PSU Player Highlights: Franco Harris and Lydell Mitchell

What a blessing for any team to have Franco Harris and Lydell Mitchell playing in your backfield. One might ask if linemen would be necessary at all. Just kidding—honest! I can't complain because in my short high school football career I played guard and linebacker. Sure wish I had gone to Linebacker U at Penn State. Let's at look teammates (FB) Franco Harris and (RB) Lydell Mitchell.

Running backs and fullbacks did well at Penn State. We'll look at both running superstars from 1971. Let's look at the guy called on to get the 1st downs first and then the guy called on to win the games—Franco Harris then Lydell Mitchell

Franco Harris

Franco Harris

Franco Harris continues his loyalty to his college coach Joe Paterno. Surely, no matter how well you and a and several other million Penn State football fans think we knew Joe Paterno, the coach, nobody knew him like Penn State players and a lot of good guys like Franco Harris. Harris was a three year starter and standout player for the Nittany Lions. Harris is a gentle yet very tough man. He still does not let anybody, including the press push his Alma Mater or his coach around. He hits back and stings and then continues to fight back

When you are talking about the all-time best players in the NFL from Penn State, you have to start with Franco Harris. Harris was named to nine Pro Bowls and seven all-pro teams, and won four Super Bowls with the Pittsburgh Steelers. Yet, his PSU years do not get him the same level of acclaim…but they should. He started for the Lions for three years and averaged over five yards per carry each year. I am convinced that because Franco's pro career was so stellar, that the write-ups of the day focused on who he was and not who he had once been.

Nonetheless, he was one heck of a PSU football player even though I cannot find him on anybody's top ten PSU player list. He is on mine for sure.

When you dig down into Harris's great career at Penn State there was a player on the team who cast a big shadow. Fellow running back Lydell Mitchell became an All-American. Despite Mitchell's great stats the Steelers scouts still saw enough in Harris's play to draft him with their 13th overall selection of the 1972 NFL draft.

Yet, he gained more yards as a pro in his first season than in any of his Penn State Seasons, in which of course, he averaged between 5 and 6 yards per carry. He rushed for 1,055 yards and scored 10 touchdowns in his first year in the NFL and he was named Offensive Rookie of the Year and chosen for his first of nine consecutive Pro Bowls. Franko Harris was one heck of a football player. Not taking anything from All-American Lydell Mitchell, it is ironic that he had to become a pro to gain his proper recognition.

Harris was named the MVP of Super Bowl IX, 1972 NFL Offensive Rookie of the Year and AFL-AFC Rookie of the Year by UPI, and was the 1976 Walter Payton Man of the Year.

Harris is most famous for The Immaculate Reception in the AFC playoffs against the Oakland Raiders and was voted to the NFL 1970s All-Decade Team. Harris finished his Hall of Fame career with 100 touchdowns and 12,120 rushing yards. Rather than depend on the reader being omniscient about things like the Immaculate Reception, let's talk a bit about it since this is a book about the great moments in Penn State History. Undoubtedly this reception is one of the greatest moments and the most talked about moments in football history. Unfortunately for Franco Harris it did not affect his college stats as he achieved this career milestone as a pro.

It is the nickname given to what is what most living pundits today would agree is the most famous play in the history of American football. The Immaculate reception has a great ring to it. It was a divisional playoff game so it had much more than the normal coverage.

The game opponents were the Oakland Raiders vs the Pittsburgh Steelers with help from Franco Harris, and some say, help from the Lord himself. Even three Rivers Stadium could not prevent the miracle that was to occur on this Merry Christmas day December 23, 1972. Then, again if God is a Pittsburgh fan who had to worry?

Despite all of the spirits and the entire Franco Harris family and perhaps even a few Bradshaw's rooting for the right outcome, Pittsburgh was losing. So, with 30 seconds left in the game, Pittsburgh quarterback Terry Bradshaw, who still has lots of sputter during NFL game days, threw a pass attempt to John Fuqua. I cannot name one person today who knows who John Fuqua is but the ball did not reach him anyway.

It bounced off the hands of Raiders safety Jack Tatum; though it might have been Fuqua and with this more than likely the last play of the game, the world went into slow-mo. as everybody in the stadium and watching from TV sets across the land, saw the ball falling toward the ground like a rocket. Like a gift from the most high, out of nowhere, Steelers fullback Franco Harris, who had purchased a discount halo helmet attachment the night before the game at K-Mart, was there to scoop it up, right into his arms before ground-touch, and then as a schooled running back, the young Harris had enough sense and wherewithal to tuck it in and he ran for the game-winning touchdown. And, that was that. Everybody accepted the outcome. Well, not exactly.

No play that starts off so needy goes so far south without a miracle intervention from above. Even the agnostics did not know what had hit them. This play remains a source of unresolved controversy and speculation ever since, as many people have contended that the ball touched either Fuqua or the ground before Harris caught it, either of which would have resulted in an incomplete pass by the rules at the time.

Kevin Cook's *The Last Headbangers* cites the play as the beginning of a bitter rivalry between Pittsburgh and Oakland that fueled a historically brutal Raiders team during the NFL's most controversially physical era. Either way,

Pittsburgh won and Harris got another TD...one of many in his outstanding career.

Looking for some suckers who do not really want to know what really happened, the NFL happened upon their filming crew, NFL Films to make a few after bucks on the game. This group of professionals, unrelated of course to the NFL chose this play as the greatest play of all time, as well as the most controversial play of all time. The Steelers looked upon it as a calling and decided never to be chumps again. It was the first and so far the last Immaculate Reception and Franco Harris's hands had the calling.

This play was thus a turning point for the Steelers, who reversed four decades of futility with their first playoff win ever, and they mustered up enough mustard to go on and win four Super Bowls by the end of the decade. The play's name is a pun derived from the Immaculate Conception, a dogma in the Roman Catholic Church. The phrase was first used on air by Myron Cope, a Pittsburgh sportscaster who was reporting on the Steelers' victory. A Pittsburgh woman, Sharon Levosky, called Cope before his 11 PM sports broadcast on the 23rd and suggested the name, which was coined by her friend Michael Ord. Cope used the term on television and the phrase stuck.

Player Highlights Lydell Mitchell

Though he played football and graduated in 1972, Lydell Mitchell was elected into the SBC Cotton Bowl Hall of Fame on December 20, 2004 with the major tribute being his 146 yard running total in the 1972 Cotton Bowl win over Texas.

Former Penn State standout Lydell Mitchell earned on this day what some call his second hall of fame recognition of 2004. He was elected to the SBC Cotton Bowl Hall of Fame, less than two weeks after his induction into the College Football Hall of Fame. The All-America running back was be inducted with seven others on Wednesday, April 20, 2005 at Cotton Bowl Plaza in Dallas.

Lydell Mitchell was an outstanding PSU football player. He was a 1971 All-American. As a dangerous running back, he led the Nittany Lions to a resounding 30-6 victory over Southwest Conference champion Texas in the Cotton Bowl on January 1, 1972. He pulled it in for 146 yards on 27 carries and scored the go-ahead touchdown, as Penn State rallied from a 6-3 halftime deficit to score 27 unanswered points in the second half. It was nothing less than the Lydell Mitchell Show with fullback Franco Harris picking up the slack as needed.

Mitchell was the overwhelming choice as the game's Outstanding Offensive Player, as he led Penn State to its first Cotton Bowl victory. The Lions became 1-0-1 and as of 2015, are 2-0-1 all-time in the contest.

The win over the Longhorns was one of the landmark victories in the early years of the Joe Paterno era. Two years prior, an undefeated Penn State team had been overlooked, as President Richard Nixon spoke before he thought and declared Texas the 1969 national champions after a 15-14 win over unbeaten Arkansas, and the pollsters followed his lead. The 1969 undefeated, untied Nittany Lions finished No. 2 in the final AP rankings for the second consecutive year.

Lydell Mitchell was so good that the pundits did not fully notice Franco Harris but the Pittsburgh Steelers did. Mitchell led the nation in touchdowns (29) and points scored (174) in 1971. He also set three NCAA season records during his superlative 1971 campaign - most touchdowns (29), most rushing touchdowns (26) and points scored (174) - and finished fifth in the Heisman Trophy balloting. Franco Harris, one of the best football players in PSU history was kept in the shadows as the high-scoring Mitchell scored and scored and scored.

Mitchell still holds Penn State records for touchdowns in a season (29 in 1971), touchdowns in a career (41) and rushing touchdowns in a career (38) and his 246 career points scored rank fourth, the most among players other than kickers. His 1,567 yards rushing in 1971 stood as the Penn State season record for more than 30 years until Larry Johnson's 2,087-yard season in 2002.

During his phenomenal Penn State career, Mitchell won three varsity letters from 1969-71 and helped lead Penn State to a 29-4 record over that span. The Nittany Lions went 11-1 during his senior campaign to finish No. 5 in the final AP poll. In case you are not scoring at home folks, it helps to recall these fine teams were all coached by Joe Paterno, the master.

Mitchell is the first Penn Stater elected to the SBC Cotton Bowl Hall of Fame. He will join the following individuals in the SBC Cotton Bowl Hall of Fame: UCLA quarterback Troy Aikman, Arkansas halfback Lance Alworth, former CBAA executive director Jim "Hoss" Brock, Texas offensive guard Mike Dean, Tennessee fullback Andy Kozar, Tennessee tailback Hank Lauricella, and former collegiate head coach Gene Stallings.

A 35-member judging committee comprised of media representatives and athletic administrators voted from a list of 52 original nominees that included players, coaches, bowl

administrators and others who have made special contributions to the Cotton Bowl Classic.
On Dec. 7, Mitchell became the 19th Penn Stater to be inducted into the National Football Foundation's College Hall of Fame.

Think about how great Lydell Mitchell was and think about how great Franco Harris was. Consider that Joe Paterno was their coach and he got the most out of them and they loved him for it.

1972 Penn State Football Season Coach Joe Paterno

The 1972 Penn State Nittany Lions football team was coached by Joe Paterno in his seventh season. Penn State had another enviable regular season at 10-1 and with a #5 ranking in the national poll, they were invited to the Sugar Bowl in New Orleans against # 2 Oklahoma, and were defeated in a close match L (14-0), finishing the season at 10-2.

On September 16, though PSU played better than in 1971 against the Volunteers, #7 ranked Tennessee beat #6 PSU at Neyland Stadium in Knoxville L 21-28). It was the only loss of the regular season for Joe Paterno's squad. Navy played much better than the prior year at Beaver Stadium as the Lions prevailed W (21-10). On September 30, #13 PSU defeated IOWA at home in a close match W (14-10) After the win, PSU dropped to #16 in the polls and on October 7, at Illinois PSU triumphed W (35-17) over the Fighting Illini before 60,349.

On October 14, Penn State shut-out Army at West Point W (45-0). On October 21, Syracuse played the Nittany Lions but lost in a shutout W (17-0). PSU played at West Virginia the following week in a close call W (28-19). Maryland came to Beaver Stadium to defeat the #10 Nittany Lions but left with a big loss W (46-16).

On November 11, North Carolina State played # 10 PSU at Beaver Stadium. The Lions won W (37-22). On November 18, PSU was ranked # 6 and played Boston College at Alumni Stadium W (45-26). Still ranked #6, on November 25, PSU defeated the Pitt Panthers at home W (49-27).

The Sugar Bowl was played on December 31. PSU was ranked #5 with a 10-1 record when it met second ranked Oklahoma at Tulane Stadium in New Orleans before 80,123 and before million more on ABC TV. In one of its closest matches all season, Oklahoma defeated PSU L (14-0). This gave the Lions a nice 10-2 season, which for a number of reasons, could have been better.

Oklahoma had its second great year in a row under head coach Chuck Fairbanks. Offensive coordinator Barry Switzer had perfected the wishbone offense and Oklahoma could not be stopped. In 1971, the Sooners led the nation in both scoring (45 points average) and total yards (563 total yards average).

Oklahoma set an NCAA record that year by averaging over 472.4 (5196 in 11 games) rushing yards in a season. The Sooners had another like year in 1972. They were phenomenal, and ran through every team they played.

There was a big discrepancy regarding the Sooners' record and the wins for which they got credit. It turns out that the NCAA never officially forced Oklahoma to forfeit games, but they were penalized on future scholarships. TV appearances, bowl appearances, etc. By rights, their team may not have been as good if their academic record keeping on their players was kept accurately.

The beef was that Oklahoma had used players (including Kerry Jackson, the team's first black quarterback) with falsified transcripts. It was such a big deal and such an embarrassment that at one point, Oklahoma University volunteered to forfeit all its games for the 1972 season.

Eventually, the Big Eight conference asked them to forfeit just three victories despite the fact that the NCAA still recognized them after time passed. Oklahoma in looking back, now recognizes all of its wins and it claims the 1972 conference title. Penn State was involved in the controversy as a team that had played an Oklahoma that had benefitted from using ineligible players.

At the time, as a result of using ineligible players, the Oklahoma Sooners were apparently ordered (though it was softened to a suggestion over time) to forfeit seven wins from their 1972 season, including their on-field win over the Nittany Lions in the Sugar Bowl. Joe Paterno's Nittany Lions were shut-out L (14-0) as noted but they had played a tough game against the Sooners.

Despite the prevailing thought on the legitimacy of the Sooners' season, Joe Paterno and the Penn State Administration refused to accept the forfeit, and the bowl game is officially recorded as a loss. There is some irony compared with how Coach Paterno was treated when it was his turn in the penalty box in 2011. Paterno, just about forty years earlier opted not to mess with Oklahoma's wins and losses.

Who knows if the QB and some other players made a difference? PSU had a shot at being 12-1 instead of 11-2. Who knows what that would have meant? Penn State was not interested in being handed any gifts that it had not earned on the field. As it turned out, officially PSU is listed as # 8 in the coach's poll and #10 in the AP poll.

1973 Penn State Football Season Coach Joe Paterno

The 1973 Penn State Nittany Lions football team was coached by Joe Paterno in his eight season. Penn State had another undefeated and untied season just four years after having two undefeated and untied seasons in a row. Despite having a perfect 12-0 season, PSU for the third time in six years was denied a proper ranking by the Coaches and by the AP. They slotted Penn State at # 5 after its third perfect season in six years. No wonder many felt that the system was rigged.

When like me, one walks slowly through the Paterno record—in my case because I am forming words and scribing it; in your case, as you are reading my words, you get the full sense of what an awesome achievement it was for the University, the players involved, and this awesome coach. Looking at the results season by season, nobody was as good as Joe Paterno in his eight seasons. You'd have to look outside of Penn State in 1973 to find a Rockne or a Leahy to match the outstanding record of Joe Paterno.

Penn State's third undefeated season under Joe Paterno was led by John Cappelletti who would become the first Penn State player to win the Heisman Trophy.

In an early season start on September 15, at Stanford #7 PSU defeated the Cardinal W (20-6). At Navy on September 22, PSU shut out the Middies W (39-0. At # 6 on September 29, the Nittany Lions played its home opener and scored a win against Iowa W (27-8). At Falcon Stadium on October 6, PSU beat the Falcons W (19-9).

Ironically after the win, PSU lost a point in the standings. The #7 Lions battered a game Army squad on October 13 at Beaver Stadium on October 20 W (54-3) Off to Archbold Stadium in Syracuse, #5 PSU beat the Orangemen W(49-6) After winning game after game, the 6-0 Nittany Lions would never get above # 5 in the polls for the rest of the season. It was as if other teams had a lock on the top 4 slots.

On October 27 West Virginia was roughed up by a tough Lions team W 62-14 before an over-crowd of 59,138, an expansion built in in 1972 had brought capacity to 57,538. On November 3 #6 PSU defeated Maryland at Byrd Stadium W (42-22).

This was followed by a close win on November 10 at home against NC State W (35-9).

In this best of Beaver Stadium game, John Cappelletti, #22, solidified his credentials for the Heisman Trophy with his best running day ever in this wild shootout in freezing cold and snow. Cappelletti set a school record of 41 carries that is still unbroken in rushing for 231 yards and three touchdowns.

Ohio University was next at Beaver Stadium on November 17 W (49-10) At 10-0, ranked # 6, PSU played Pittsburgh at home and defeated the Panthers W (35-13).

The powers-that-be saw something that few at Penn State saw. These mysterious powers felt it appropriate to match the powerful 11-0, #5 ranked Nittany Lions against a twice beaten 9-2, #13 LSU in the Orange Bowl on January 1. PSU defeated LSU W (16-9). PSU ended its perfect season 12-0 and LSU finished with three defeats 9-3. It may not have been the Nittany Lions finest game but one thing is for sure. Joe Paterno knew how to win football game.

Orange Bowl Game Highlights

The Undefeated Penn State Nittany Lions moved its record to 12-0 on the season as it took advantage of consistently poor LSU field position to win 16-9.

LSU had a good game as it out-gained the Nittany Lions 274 yards to 185 and held Heisman Trophy winner John Cappelletti to 50 yards. Cappelletti nonetheless was the difference maker as he scored the Nittany Lions' final touchdown on a one-yard plunge in the second quarter. The game's big play was a spectacular 72-yard touchdown catch by Chuck Herd off a pass from Tom Shuman early in the second quarter.

LSU got a lot of yardage but not of lot scores. The Tigers scored first on a three-yard run by Steve Rogers, and Penn State retaliated with a 44-yard field goal by Chris Bahr to make it 7-3 at the end of the first quarter. Herd's catch and Cappelletti's plunge put PSU ahead 16-7 at the half. That was the game.

Although Penn State finished undefeated, the polls still had the Nittany Lions ranked at #5.

1974 Penn State Football Season Coach Joe Paterno

The 1974 Penn State Nittany Lions football team was coached by Joe Paterno and played its home games in Beaver Stadium in University Park, Pennsylvania. At # 7 in both polls and with a 10-2 record, and a fine Cotton Bowl win, Penn State had a remarkably great year after so many previous great years. It's like the flow of great athletes would never stop.

On September 14, #20 Stanford lost to #8 Penn State (24-20) at Beaver Stadium before a capacity overflow crowd of 58,200. On September 21, a tough and always crafty Navy team came to Beaver Stadium meaning business and they smacked PSU with a close loss L (6-7). On September 28, PSU traveled to Iowa and shut out the Hawkeyes W (27-0). It was a tough year playing the service academies as PSU barely beat Army at West Point W (21-14). After a week bye, on October 12, Wake Forest suffered an overwhelming defeat, a shutout, at the hands of Penn State W (55-0). On October 19, PSU defeated Syracuse at home W (30-14). On October 26 in Morgantown, West Virginia, PSU defeated the Mountaineers W (21-12).

A #15 ranked Maryland made its way to Beaver Stadium to play #10 ranked Penn State on November 2. The Terrapins were defeated in a close match W (24-17). Then ranked # 7 PSU traveled to North Carolina State at Carter Stadium in Raleigh, NC on November 9, and were beaten in a lose match L (7-12). Ohio University next came to Beaver Stadium on November 16 and lost to #11PSU W (35-16).

On November 28, #10 PSU, at 9-2, challenged #18 Pittsburgh at Three Rivers Stadium in Pittsburgh, PA before 48,895 and the national ABC audience and succeeded in victory W (31–10).

The Cotton Bowl

With a 9-2 record, ranked # 7 ranked PSU won a berth to the Cotton Bowl and on New Year's Day, beat #12 Baylor in Dallas Texas before 67,500 onlookers as well as the entire CBS TV audience W (41–20).

1975 Penn State Football Season Coach Joe Paterno

The 1975 Penn State Nittany Lions football team was coached by Joe Paterno in his tenth year. With a 9-2 regular season record and a berth in the Sugar Bowl at the New Orleans, Louisiana SuperDome on December 31, 1975, PSU, with Joe Paterno, an unbelievably successful coach at the helm, had a great season.

Seasons started to begin earlier and earlier form October twenty years earlier to September with games close to Labor Day weekend such as the September 6 nail-biter at Temple in Franklin Field, Philadelphia in which # 6 PSU won W (26-25). On September 13, Stanford played at Beaver Stadium and the #10 Nittany Lions winning the encounter W (34-14). #3 ranked Ohio State, coached by the master, Woody Hayes, hosted #7 Penn State on September 20 and defeated the Nittany Lions in Columbus L (9-17). Iowa played a #12 ranked PSU squad on September 27 at Kinnick Stadium and PSU triumphed W (30-0).

Next on the season agenda was Kentucky on October 4, playing at Beaver Stadium, the #12 Nittany Lions pulled of a close one W (10-3) bringing the season record to 4-1, A tough #10 ranked West Virginia team played # 9 ranked PSU on October 11 at Beaver Stadium and were shut out in a blow-out W (39-0). On October 18, the #9 ranked Lions played at unranked Syracuse and defeated the Orangemen W (19-7). The next week at Beaver Stadium (October 25), PSU shut-out Army W (31-0).

Ninth ranked PSU next played #14 ranked Maryland on November 1 and in a tough game beat the Terrapins W (15-13). In almost a reverse mirror image of the Maryland game a # 8 ranked PSU was beaten by NC State L (14-15) at home. The regular season ended after a one week bye with PSU barely beating Pitt at Three Rivers Stadium W (7-6).

PSU had a lot of close matches this year but as usual, in most of them at least Joe Paterno knew how to lead his team to victory. With a 9-2 record, an 8th ranked Penn State squad was invited to the Sugar Bowl to play a tough # 4 ranked Bear Bryant Alabama team on New Year's Eve, 1975. In a very close and tough match. Alabama defeated Penn State to win the Sugar Bowl L (6-13) before a nationwide TV audience in addition to 75,212 in the New Orleans Superdome. Penn State finished with a 9-3 record, ranked # 10 in both polls. It was another very good season for PSU and Joe Paterno.

1976 Penn State Football Season Coach Joe Paterno

The 1976 Penn State Nittany Lions football team was coached by Joe Paterno in his eleventh year and played its home games in a just expanded Beaver Stadium in University Park, Pennsylvania. In 1969, PSU found another 2000 seats for Beaver Stadium. In 1974, over 9000 seats, extended the capacity to 57,536. In 1976: South end zone bleachers expanded, adding 2,667, extending capacity to 60,203. Coming up in 1978, another big expansion of 16000 seats was coming and the growing still would not be done.

For any other program in any other year, Penn State's 7-5 record in 1976 would have been chalked up as well above .500 and very acceptable. Looking at the season, you will find an awful lot of close games that in other years went the Lions' way. Just one in the other direction and the team is 8-4, which sounds a lot better. Nonetheless, this was still a darn good year when you consider the problems that other teams with coaching instabilities have. Nice job again JoePa.

On September 11 Penn State ranked at # 10 played Stanford at home W (15-12). On September 18, Ohio State played the Nittany Lions in Beaver Stadium to a crowd of 62,503, and defeated Penn State in a tight slugfest L (7-12). Iowa came to Beaver Stadium on September 25, and for the second week in a row, PSU lost a nailbiter L (6-7). Three makes a charm and Kentucky on October 2, defeated the Nittany Lions, then ranked at # 20, at Commonwealth Stadium L (6-22).

PSU defeated Army on October 9 at home W (38-16), followed by Syracuse at home on October 16 W (27-3). On October 23, it was off to Morgantown and a win against West Virginia W (33-0). No longer a ranked team, PSU pulled off a win in a very close game against Temple on October 30 at Veterans Stadium before 42,005 W (31-30).

Unranked North Carolina State, another tough team was ready when they came to Beaver Stadium on November 6 to play unranked PSU. The Nittany Lions won handily W (41-

20). Then on November 13 came Miami, always tough, especially at home playing in the Orange Bowl stadium. PSU won W (21-7). Pittsburgh had become a player again after going to sleep for a few years. Ranked # 1 in the nation at the time, Pitt defeated #16 PSU at Three Reivers Stadium on November 26 L (7-24).

With 7 wins, ranked #20, PSU was eligible for a Bowl game. They played in the Gator Bowl in Jacksonville Florida on Monday, December 27, 1976 against the University of Notre Dame. Notre Dame won a tough battel v PSU L (9-20) before 67,827 and an ABC television audience.

1977 Penn State Football Season Coach Joe Paterno

The 1977 Penn State Nittany Lions football team was coached by Joe Paterno in his twelfth season. PSU recovered from a tough 7-5 season and experienced one loss to Kentucky at home on October 1, the fourth game of the season by just four points L (20-24).

Four points doth make a season as the Kentucky game is all that separated Paterno's tough Penn State squad from another perfect, undefeated and untied, season. The one loss made all the difference in the world as the Nittany Lions finished #4 in the Coach's poll and #5 in the AP poll. It was another great year for Penn State on the field.

In a rare Friday night game, on September 2, #13 ranked PSU began its season away at Giants stadium against Rutgers and won decisively W (45-7) before 64,790. It already looked like a great season. On September 17, after a bye week, Houston came to Beaver Stadium and were beaten by #10 PSU W (31-14). Maryland was the next home game on September 24 W (27-9). Operating at 3-0, and ranked #4 before the Kentucky game Penn State lost its only game of the season on October 1 L (20-24).

On October 8 Utah State were beaten by the #10 ranked Nittany Lions in a close match W (16-7). Then, on October 15 in the ongoing rivalry with Syracuse, #10 PSU beat the Orangemen in Archbold Stadium W (31-24). West Virginia was next on October 22 at Beaver Stadium W (49-28). An always tough Lou Saban coached Miami squad rolled into Beaver Stadium on October 29 to play a # 9 ranked Nittany Lions team. Miami was not having a good year and won just three games in 1977. They were pounded by PSU W (49-7). PSU then traveled to Carter Finley Stadium to play North Carolina on November 5 W (21-17.

Penn State coach Joe Paterno and his quarterback Chuck Fusina discussed things late in the fourth quarter in Pittsburgh, Saturday, Nov. 26, 1977.

Ranked #9, PSU played Temple at Beaver Stadium on November 12 and defeated the OWLs W (44-7). The intrastate rivalry game between #10 Pitt and #9 Penn State was next on November 26, the Saturday after Thanksgiving. The Nittany Lions scored a victory in a nailbiter W (15-13) in front of 53,000 at Pitt Stadium.

With a 10-1 record, ranked # 9, PSU played Arizona State on Christmas day in the Fiesta Bowl at Sun Devil Stadium, Tempe Arizona and won decidedly W (42-30).

1978 Penn State Football Season Coach Joe Paterno

The 1978 Penn State Nittany Lions football team was coached by Joe Paterno in his thirteenth year. This Chuck Fusina led-team was phenomenal. In 1977, four points to Kentucky in the fourth game separated PSU from a perfect season. This year, PSU did not lose a game until the Sugar Bowl when it was a seven point difference against a Bear Bryant coached Alabama team that kept PSU from the National Championships.

PSU was 11-0 and ranked # 2 going into the game. Alabama was 11-0 and ranked #1. Alabama won the game and the National Championship. PSU finished 11-1 and were ranked # 4 in both polls. Joe Paterno was a phenomenon. SO was Bear Bryant. My buddy George Mohanco, a former Pennsylvanian has a saying, whether he invented it, I do not know but it applies to 1978. "Sometimes you eat the bear and sometimes the bear eats you." This time Bear Bryant had the better dinner.

Penn State started the season at # 3 with a game on September 3 at Veterans Stadium at Temple. Temple played extremely tough but the Lions got the W (10-7). This was a strange game. It was dominated by a typically unsung hero, punter Casey Murphy. Former Navy coach and relatively new Temple coach Wayne Hardin had Murphy punt "unexpectedly," on nearly every third down. Murphy averaged more than 48 yards on 11 punts. He backed up the surprised Penn State team inside its 6-yard line three times. PSU was fighting up-hill all day because of the Owls' punter

The Nittany Lions put together what it took to win W (10-7), but it was not easy. It was a late field goal. Joe Paterno honored Coach Hardin's cunning after the game: "That's the best coaching job anybody's done against us ever."

Rutgers was next at the newly enlarged (by 16,000 seats) Beaver Stadium on September 9 v #3 PSU. The Nittany

Lions won W (26-10) in front of a newly enabled attendance of 77,154. Woody Hayes' # 6 ranked Ohio State Buckeyes expecting a win were turned back by # 5 ranked PSU at Ohio Stadium on September 16 W (19-0). SMU was defeated on September 23 at Beaver Stadium W (26-21)...

TCU was blown away W (58-0) by #5 PSU on September 30. Kentucky, the team that spoiled the 1977 season with a four point win were shown how it's done by # 4 PSU in an October 7 shutout in Lexington, KY W (30-0). After a bye week, Syracuse came into Beaver Stadium on October 21, and #2 PSU beat the Orangemen W (45-15). On October 28, the West Virginia Mountaineers were defeated by #2 PSU in a blowout at Morgantown, WV, W (49-21).

On November 4, 1978 in a home match at Beaver Stadium before 78,019, #2 ranked Penn State beat #5 ranked Maryland W (27-3). This was a nationally televised "Battle of the Unbeatens." It was the Nittany Lions' biggest--and most hyped--home game since the stadium was built in 1960. With 16,000 seats added since 1977, a record crowd of 78,019 watched No. 2 Lions overwhelm No. 5 Maryland, finally becoming a media darling in the race for the national championship.

Let's take a closer look at this game as it is one of the most memorable in PSU history. Maryland had a great team in 1978 and so did Penn State. Before they came to Beaver Stadium, the first Saturday in November, the Terrapins were rolling over their opposition.

They were ranked # 5 with eight straight wins behind them. They had already pummeled NC State 31-7. NC State would finish ranked # 18. Maryland had the ACC title in the bag if they beat Penn State.

PSU for its part was doing so well at #2. Maryland might be looking at a national title with a win. PSU however was on a 16-game winning streak and as expected, the welcome for

Maryland would not be warm, and the Lions were prepared to play tough.

Maryland got the ball first, and then they got a feel for Penn State's defense on a 3rd and 8. Bruce Clark and Matt Millen pounded Terrapin QB Tim O'Hare for a 1-yard loss and a punt. The Nittany Lions began to drive down a short field immediately with nice runs by backs Booker Moore and Matt Suhey. This ended with a Matt Bahr 33-yard field goal.

Booker Moore then fumbled but it did not hurt Penn State as the "D" got the ball right back. From there, Mike Guman caught a 14-yarder and a nice 34-yard run set up a Chuck Fusina 1-yard TD drive as the second quarter began. Maryland seemed to get some adrenalin going and quickly converted a 39-yard field goal.

With PSU now ahead by 7, they held the Terrapins on a tough 3-and-out, and then after the punt when it was PSU's turn, Bob Bassett's snagged a 22-yard one-handed grab which put PSU again in field goal position. Matt Bahr was an automatic and he claimed the three points for PSU. Although the powerful defense held Maryland to just 12 rushing yards, the Nittany Lions still led by just 13-3 at the half.

In the 3rd quarter Pete Harris got an interception and the Terrapins benched their QB and put in reserve Mike Tice. It seemed like a good move as Maryland took the ball deep into PSU territory, but the drive was thwarted by Karl McCoy's interception. Fusina finished off this drive by pin-pointing a 63-yard pass to Tom Donovan making the score Penn State 20, Maryland 3.

McCoy grabbed another interception late in the third, and before long Booker Moore gobbled up 34-yards on a scamper to the Maryland 16. Four plays later, Moore scored on a 4-yard run for the touchdown.

As the game was closing, Maryland's kept in their starters and came to a fourth and goal from the 3 but were denied the score by Penn State's backup unit. The underclassmen got a standing ovation from the Nittany Lions fans.

Penn State's defense had been dominant all season long and this day would be no different as they brought forth their best performance in the 27-3 victory over #5 Maryland in Beaver Stadium. It was the Lions 17th straight victory.

For his role in the game, QB Chuck Fusina made the cover of Sports Illustrated. As noted in this 1978 season record, PSU just got by North Carolina State and #15 Pittsburgh to become # 1 in the polls. Even after undefeated seasons, this was the first #1 ranking in Joe Paterno's already legendary career. As an independent, PSU could go just about anywhere for their bowl, so they picked the SEC for a match-up with #2 Alabama in the Sugar Bowl – discussed at the end of 1978 highlights below.

A tough North Carolina team played #2 ranked PSU at Beaver Stadium on November 11 and were beaten by the Lions in a close call W (19-10).

This 1978 game was a typical nailbiter. No. 2 Penn State was holding on to a 12-10 lead with 4:40 left and with the crowd of 59,424 growing restless, Penn State's Matt Suhey (shown on the left) returned a punt 43 yards for a touchdown to clinch the victory.

As soon as Suhey scored, it was announced that #1 Oklahoma had lost three days later, and so Penn State was ranked #1 for the first time ever.

Operating with a 10-0 record, ranked #1 in the nation, for the first time ever, playing nemesis cross-state rival Pittsburgh, anything could have happened on November 24.

PSU was steady and steadfast in its resolve to win and the Nittany Lions shut-out Pitt W (17-0) at Beaver Stadium and had just enough offense to keep Pittsburgh from thinking it had a chance. For its 11-0 season PSU was ranked #1 but there was another team with an 11-0 record, looking up at PSU from the # 2 slot.

The Sugar Bowl 1978

Alabama, coached by the inimitable great, Bear Bryant, a man with the great coaching stature of Joe Paterno, with a great team, was ranked #2. The Sugar Bowl eventually got the #1 and # 2 teams to play each other even though Coach

Paterno would have preferred the Orange Bowl, the last game played on New Year's Day. That did not happen. Destiny was in the hands of both of these teams.

With its 11-1 1977 season behind them coming in with just four points separating PSU from a National Championship bid, PSU had high expectations for the 1978 season. Before game time. Nobody could say that the 1978 Penn State squad had disappointed anybody. PSU had a great season after barely escaping Temple in game 1.

While some games were relatively close, the Nittany Lions generally won each game with ease. Its defense was #1 in the nation. This was a Paterno hallmark at Linebacker U. It held teams to ten points or less. #1 ranked PSU had made it to the gates of the national championship. The great 1978 Penn State football team was ready for a win.

Alabama also had great expectations coming into the 1978 season. In 1977, they too were 11-1 11–1, losing only to Nebraska. They had devastated Ohio State in the 1978 Sugar Bowl much to Woody Hayes' chagrin. They were third in the country coming into their bowl game. The two top teams lost and Alabama naturally believed that it rightfully had earned the honor of being national champions. Notre Dame had rolled over #1 Texas in the 1978 Cotton Bowl Classic, and the Irish jumped from 5th to 1st to become national champions. The Crimson Tide felt robbed and it was their big motivation for 1978. There they were again with just PSU to get by. Alabama was also ready for a win.

And, so, this year's edition of the New Year's Day Sugar Bowl capped off the 1978 season and was the 45th edition of the Sugar Bowl, it was played in New Orleans, Louisiana on January 1, 1979 at the Louisiana Superdome. A close score of L (7-14) gave Alabama head coach Bear Bryant his fifth National Championship. After such a fine season, Joe Paterno was still looking for his first.

1979 Penn State Football Season Coach Joe Paterno

The 1979 Penn State Nittany Lions football team was coached by Joe Paterno. No team can have a championship every year. After back to back 11-1 seasons, PSU kept working hard. The University football program did not take the night off. Joe Paterno's squad compiled a 7-4 regular season record and won the Liberty Bowl, making the record 8-4. PSU was top-twenty ranked in both polls—#18 in the Coach's poll and #20 in the AP.

Ranked # 7, PSU defeated Rutgers W 45-10) on September 22 to begin the season at home September 15. On September 22, Texas A&M beat the Nittany Lions at Beaver Stadium L (14-27). #6 Nebraska played host to Penn State on September 29 and defeated the #18 Lions too easily L (17-42) Seems like a little bit of rebuilding was going on. Maryland was next on October 6 at Byrd Stadium. Penn State triumphed over the Terrapins W (27-7).

On October 13, Penn State beat Army at Beaver Stadium W 24–3 before an attendance of 77,157. Syracuse moved its October 20 game to Giants Stadium from Archbold Stadium and were shut-out by the Nittany Lions W (35-7). On October 27, the Mountaineers of West Virginia were beaten by PSU at Beaver Stadium W (31-6). PSU was coming back but there was another few tough ones on the schedule. The first loss was Miami on November 3. The Hurricanes played the #19 Nittany Lions at Beaver Stadium and prevailed L (10-26). The next loss was v #11 Pittsburgh at Beaver Stadium on December 1 L (14-29).

In between, PSU traveled to NC State and beat the Cougars in a defensive battle W (9-7). Temple was next to play #18 PSU at Beaver Stadium W (22-7). At 7-4, Penn State accepted an invitation to the Liberty Bowl

On December 22, the unranked Nittany Lions beat # 15 ranked Tulane in the Liberty Bowl W (9-6). The game was played in Memorial Stadium in Memphis Tennessee before a crowd of 50,021 and a nationwide TV audience on ABC. After the Liberty Bowl victory, PSU moved back into the top twenty—#18 in the Coach's poll and #20 in the AP.

1980 Penn State Football Season Coach Joe Paterno

The 1980 Penn State Nittany Lions football team was coached by Joe Paterno in his fifteenth season with Penn State. The team had a great season, winning two more games than in 1979, and finishing with a 10-2 record, ranked #8 in both polls. I am in awe about how consistent a winner, coach Paterno was with his PSU teams. Bravo!

Penn State began the season on September 6 ranked at #18 and playing Colgate at home. PSU had added about another 6500 seats to Beaver Stadium bringing its official 1980 capacity to 83,77. On September 10, after a bye week, PSU defeated Texas PSU walloped Colgate W (54-10). A & M at Kyle Field in College Station Texas W (25-9). #3 Nebraska, having another great year, beat the Nittany Lions at Beaver Stadium on September 27 L (7-21). Then it was Missouri on October 4 at Faurot Field in Columbia MO in a close match W 29-21).

On October 11, PSU traveled to Byrd Stadium in College Park MD to play Maryland and beat the Terrapins W (24-10). Syracuse played its annual game against Penn State, this year at Beaver Stadium before a capacity crowd of 84,000. The Lions came out on top W (24-7). On October 25, it was West Virginia at Mountaineer Field in a close win for PSU (20-15). Miami of Florida played at Beaver Stadium on November 1, and were beaten by the Nittany Lions W 27-12). North Carolina came to State College the following week on November8 and were beaten by Penn State W 21-13).

Temple opted to play its November 8 home game v PSU at Veterans Stadium before 49, 313. The Nittany Lions thumped the Owls pretty good W (50-7). On November 28, Dan Marino led the # 4 ranked Pittsburgh Panthers in their win against #5 Penn State at Beaver Stadium L (9-14). Penn State was invited to the Fiesta Bowl with a 9-2 record.

Ohio State was coached by Woody Hayes who, like Joe Paterno knew how to coach young men to play football at its best. Paterno's Nittany Lions defeated the Hayes Buckeyes W (31-19) before 66,738 and an NBC national audience. The game was held won December 26 with Ohio State ranked #11 and Penn State ranked #10. It was a nice night at Sun Devil Stadium in the Tempe Arizona desert. Penn State was ranked # 8 in both polls after this victory. JoePa and a great team had brought another fine season to Penn State University.

Player Highlights Matt Millen

Matt Millen was an All-American Selection in 1978. The Hokendauqua, Pa. native played Defensive tackle of the Nittany Lions. He was also selected by Walter Camp and United Press International. Millen was a terror on Defense with 54 tackles, including nine quarterback sacks. He even blocked a punt and caused two fumbles as a junior.

He had an unfortunate senior year or he would have killed it in the stats and honors categories. He was a great football player. He missed most of his playing time during senior year with an injury. After graduation, he played with the Oakland/Los Angeles Raiders (1980-88), San Francisco (1989-90), and Washington (1991) of the National Football League.

Former player Matt Millen

In Millen's 12-year NFL playing career, he played on four teams that won the Super Bowl. Millen won a Super Bowl ring with each of the three teams for which he played; moreover, he won a Super Bowl ring in each of the four cities in which he played (the Raiders won championships in both Oakland and Los Angeles during his tenure).

Millen was president and CEO of the NFL Detroit Lions until 2008.

Chapter 20 — The Joe Paterno Era from 1981 to 1995

Coach # 14

Year	Coach	Record	Notes
1981	Joe Paterno	10-2	
1982	Joe Paterno	11-1	National Champions
1983	Joe Paterno	8-4-1	
1984	Joe Paterno	6-5	
1985	Joe Paterno	11-1	
1986	Joe Paterno	12-0	National Champions
1987	Joe Paterno	8-4	
1988	Joe Paterno	5-6	
1989	Joe Paterno	8-3-1	
1990	Joe Paterno	9-3	
1991	Joe Paterno	11-2	
1992	Joe Paterno	7-5	
1993	Joe Paterno	10-2	(6-2 Big 10)
1994	Joe Paterno	12-0	(8-0 Big 10)
1995	Joe Paterno	9-3	(5-3 Big 10)

Coached 45 great seasons 1966 to 2010 and part of 2011.

1981 Penn State Football Season Coach Joe Paterno

The 1981 Penn State Nittany Lions football team was coached by Joe Paterno in his sixteenth season. Coach Joe Paterno did it again—a 9-2 excellent regular season and a victory over USC in the Fiesta Bowl giving a 10-2 combined record and a #3 position in both polls.

Cincinnati played #9 PSU on September 12 and were pummeled by the Nittany Lions in a home season opening shutout W (52-0). PSU went to Osborne. Ranked at #3, PSU traveled to Lincoln, Nebraska and beat Nebraska in a close match W (30-24). At home on October 3, PSU shut-out Temple W (30-0). PSU then took on Boston College at home and beat the Eagles W (38-7) on October 10.

On October 17, #2 ranked PSU traveled to the Carrier Dome to beat Syracuse W (41-26). West Virginia was next on October 24 to play # 1 ranked PSU at Beaver Stadium W (30-7). #1 ranked Penn State traveled to unranked Miami to play the Hurricanes and were beaten in a heartbreaker L (14-17). The next week after the major disappointment in Miami, #6 ranked PSU took on North Carolina State in Raleigh NC and scored a victory W (22-15).

#5 Penn State got another shot at #6 Alabama, the team that had messed up its shot at a championship in 1978. Though it was an important game PSU was outplayed and lost to the Crimson Tide L (16-31). Unranked Notre Dame came to Beaver Stadium the following week on November 21, and were beaten by the Nittany Lions in a very close game W (24-21). After two losses, PSU was out of first place and down to # 11 in the polls.

The Nittany Lions delivered one of their most satisfying wins when quarterback Todd Blackledge (above) and the defense sparked a turnaround from a 14-0 deficit to a 48-14 win at No. 1 Pitt on November 28, 1981. Penn State beat Southern California in the 1982 Fiesta Bowl to finish 10-2 and ranked No. 3, setting the table for the Nittany Lions' 1982 National Championship.

On November 28, Penn State said enough is enough and shellacked #1 ranked Pittsburgh at Pitt Stadium W (48-14) in Dan Marino's last year. Incidentally, with Pitt's 11-1 record, PSU had put the only blemish on its season. The Pitt Team came back from the PSU loss, played and beat the # 2 team in the country Georgia 24-20 in the Sugar Bowl.

On this day in 1981 Penn State pulled off one of its finest come from behind victories, snapping back from a 14-0 second-quarter deficit to rout No. 1 Pitt, 48-14, and end the national title chances of the Sugar Bowl-bound Panthers before a national television audience and 60,260 at Pitt Stadium. The victory was sparked by interceptions of Dan Marino passes by Roger Jackson and Mark Robinson and the passing combination of Todd Blackledge to Kenny Jackson.

Player Highlights Todd Blackledge

When I first saw Todd Blackledge play at the Carrier Dome v Syracuse years ago, I was amazed at the passing after having seen so many games in which Penn State would run the ball almost all the time even if the situation clearly called for a pass. Before Blackledge, it seemed Paterno was always squeamish about passing.

Penn State Football, Todd Blackledge

On this day v Pittsburgh facing the consummate passer of all time, Dan Marino, JoePa had to let Blackledge throw—but would he? He sure did. Not only did Coach OK a vaunted passing attack, it was as if PSU had been a passing team forever. Blackledge could not do anything wrong. He played one heck of a game

He was so good that Todd Blackledge upstaged the best passer in football Dan Marino at quarterback. Penn State got its biggest upset since Joe Paterno became the head coach in 1966, a huge 48-14 victory over top-ranked Pittsburgh that ended the Panthers' 17-game winning streak, and ended their day in the championship sun. .

Marino was a junior at the time, and as the QB, so far in the game he had put Pitt out ahead so quickly that it looked like the crying towels would be needed. Marino had already thrown for two touchdowns to put the Panthers ahead by 14-0 in the first 10 minutes.

Blackledge, Penn State's sophomore quarterback got some breaks and took advantage of them. There were a series of Panther mistakes that in a flash turned the game around.

Before the Panthers knew it, the game was tied and then they were losing.

Blackledge threw two touchdown passes to Kenny Jackson, ran for one touchdown and wound up with 12 completions in 23 attempts for 262 yards before a crowd of 60,260 in Pitt Stadium.

Blackledge was elated. "This was the best game of my life," he said. Marino was not his usual pinpoint self with 22 completions in 45 attempts for 267 yards. His big problem was that he got only 80 yards in the second half. He was intercepted four times and his team lost three fumbles. The seven turnovers killed the Panthers.

"We can't cry," said Marino, who had taken Pitt to be the #1 team in the nation with 34 touchdown passes before this day in this season. "They did a good job and beat us outright today. We just made too many mistakes, and you can't win with so many fumbles, penalties and interceptions."

Going back into the archives, the Nittany Lions had a tough time finding another such significant victory. They had to go back to 1964 when PSU shocked OSU, 27-0, and toppled the Buckeyes from the No. 1 rank in midseason.

Clemson had been ranked No. 2 before this day became the only undefeated and untied major team in the nation. If Clemson moved up to No. 1 the following week in the two wire service polls, the Tigers would become the seventh team to hold the top spot this season. Pitt was the sixth team and Penn State was one of the others, along with Michigan, Notre Dame, Southern California and Texas. All were beaten and had dropped from the top spot.

Penn State, which finished the regular season at (9-2), was ranked 11th by The Associated Press and ninth by United Press International going into the game. The Nittany Lions, scheduled for the Fiesta Bowl would be preparing to play

Southern California on Jan. 1, the same day Pitt (10-1) would be play Georgia (9-1) in the Sugar Bowl.

The outcome of this upset was unclear. It made it possible for Georgia, last year's final No. 1 team, to gain the No. 1 ranking again, barring an upset the next Saturday against Georgia Tech. The Bulldogs, ranked No. 3 before all the games on this day, were expected to move up to No. 2 behind Clemson, which would be playing Nebraska in the Orange Bowl Jan. 1. If Nebraska won and Pitt lost in bowl action, Georgia could be No. 1.

Pitt was a one-touchdown favorite over PSU going into today's game. Coming out, the Panthers' had suffered their first loss since, and a big one, since they were beaten by Florida State in the fifth game of the 1980 season. The triumph was Paterno's 150th as Penn State head coach against 33 losses and one tie. His two losses this particular season came against Miami and Alabama. Not an Upset, Says Paterno.

Paterno, an assistant coach at Penn State when the Lions beat Ohio State 17 years prior, said: "I didn't think this was an upset. Who says so?"

One of his former players, Irv Pankey, an offensive tackle on Penn State's 1978 team, added, "This without a doubt is the best victory ever." Pankey, then a member of the Los Angeles Rams, was at the game because the Rams were to meet the Steelers at Three Rivers Stadium Sunday.

Pitt began stumbling after its early two-touchdown lead. Marino gave Penn State its first chance just when it appeared Pitt was moving in for a possible third touchdown. When he passed from the Penn State 31 on the first play of the second period, the ball was intercepted by Roger Jackson deep in the end zone. This put the Lions on their 20 and Blackledge went to work immediately.

Helped by a face-mask penalty of 15 yards, Penn State got to the Pitt 31 in five plays. Blackledge then hit Mike McCloskey at the Pitt 2. Chuck Meade, the fullback, went over on the next play and the conversion made the score 14-7.

Penn State stopped Pitt with an interception and a fumble recovery the next two times the Panthers had the ball and the Lions took over on their 20 late in the second period. Blackledge completed three successive passes to get to the 7. The third of these was a 53-yard toss to Jackson.

Blackledge went in from there on a quarterback draw that caught Pitt with a huge defensive hole right in the middle.

Fumbles Plague Panthers

Pitt fumbled the ball away again on its final chance to score in the first half at the Penn State 22, then continued its series of mistakes when Bill Beach, a fullback, fumbled and lost the ball to Penn State at the Lions' 43 early in the third period. In the next three minutes, Blackledge won the game with his two touchdown passes to Jackson.

The first, for 42 yards, found Jackson at the 10, where he made a beautiful pirouette around Tim Lewis, the right cornerback, and left Lewis grasping out of bounds. The next, for 45 yards, was easier as Jackson get 15 yards behind the defenses and alone.

They were Jackson's fifth and sixth touchdown receptions of the season, tying a Penn State record. "Kenny Jackson really came through for me," Blackledge said. Jackie Sherrill, Pitt's coach, said, "Oh, the turnovers. Penn State did a fine job throwing the ball deep and Kenny Jackson is a great ballplayer."

After those two touchdowns by Jackson, Penn State scored again on two field goals by Brian Franco and two touchdowns. The first of these late touchdowns came when Curt Warner, the tailback, went 9 yards toward the end zone, fumbled and Sean Farrell, the Penn State strong side guard, fell on the ball in the end zone. Then Mark Robinson made the second of his two interceptions of Marino passes and ran the ball back 91 yards for a score.

Warner Pressed Into Duty

Curt Warner, Penn State's best tailback, did not start the game because of recent leg injuries. But when Jon Williams also got hurt early in the game, Warner came in and ran for 104 yards to finish his junior season with 1,044 yards rushing. He had missed two full games and most of two others this season.

The triumph was Penn State's 40th in the series, against 38 defeats and three ties. Paterno would not compare this victory with any previous ones in his 31 years as an assistant and head coach at Penn State but said, "I've never been around a squad with more tough luck. People are disappointed we didn't win every game, but I'm glad for the squad. We played a lot of difficult defenses, and injuries to so many like Warner have been tough luck."

Sherrill said, "They outplayed us simply and we made too many mistakes. Next one is against Georgia."

When it was all over, PSU was # 3 in both post season polls whereas Pitt was # 2 in the Coach's poll and #4 in the AP poll. Texas, which had a loss and a tie played Clemson and lost but yet was given the #4 slot in the Coach's Poll and were ranked above Pitt at # 2 in the AP poll. The Clemson

Tigers, who were unbeaten and untied, claimed the national championship with #1 ranking in both polls after their victory over Nebraska in the Orange Bowl. No wonder we have the BCS today.

As the standout quarterback at Penn State, Blackledge started for the Nittany Lions from 1981 to 1983, going 31-5 through three seasons. After leading Penn State to the national championship in 1982, Blackledge won the Davey O'Brien Award as the nation's most outstanding quarterback, and he finished sixth in the Heisman Trophy voting. His passer rating was 10th among the nation's quarterbacks that season. In the 1983 NFL Draft, Kansas City selected Blackledge seventh overall. He played for the Chiefs for five seasons before joining the Pittsburgh Steelers in 1988. He retired in 1989.

Blackledge was one of seven former NCAA student-athletes selected to receive the 2008 Silver Anniversary Award, which recognizes former student-athletes who completed successful collegiate careers and have gone on to excel in their chosen professions.

That same year, along with seven other former NFL players, Blackledge visited U.S. troops in the Middle East, where he coached in the USO's flag football tournament, Operation Gridiron: Huddle with the Troops.

In 2009, he was awarded Penn State's Distinguished Alumni Award. He is a member of Penn State's Board of Visitors for Penn State's Center for Sports Journalism.

Blackledge lives in Canton, Ohio. In the offseason he coaches high school basketball.

Blackledge received a Bachelor of Arts degree in speech communication from Penn State in 1983, graduating Phi Beta Kappa. A first-team Academic All-American, he also earned the Eric Walker Award that year from Penn State, given annually to the senior believed to have most "enhanced the esteem and recognition of the University."

Player Highlights—Mike Munchak

Mike Munchak was born about eighteen miles north of my home town. He was ready to play offensive lineman (Guard) for Penn State from 1978-1981 but he was injured in 1980 and he missed the season as his knee was recovering. Nobody has lots to say about offensive Tackles or Guards so just being honored is a big deal as everything is a team effort. Munchak came back and was fully healed in 1981. He was a talented starter in both 1979 and 1981. During his senior year, he was named a second team All-American and was subsequently drafted 8th overall by the Houston Oilers.

He had a great but short professional career. During the 1982 NFL Draft, Munchak was chosen as the Houston Oilers first round draft pick (8th overall), making him the first offensive lineman drafted that year. In his rookie season, he quickly earned a starting position at the left guard position. He remained in that position for 12 seasons. During that time he garnered nine Pro Bowl nominations, four All-Pro, nine Second Team All-Pro, seven All-AFC, and four second team All-Pro selections. He was a great player. In addition, he was selected for the 1980s All-Decade Team. Munchak's 12-year tenure tied for second most seasons played with the Houston Oilers.

Mike Munchak has been in the hunt for the PSU coaching job since 2011. As much was Munchak would be welcome, most PSU football fans want James Franklin to kill it this year and break out of the 2011 funk.

1982 Penn State Football Season Coach Joe Paterno

The 1982 Penn State Nittany Lions football team was coached by Joe Paterno in his seventeenth season. After a disappointing loss at Birmingham to #4 Alabama in game 5 L (21-42), a resilient and very tough Penn State squad came back and brought home all the marbles. The Nittany Lions won every game for the rest of the regular season, and defeated the #1 Georgia Bulldogs 27–23 in the Sugar Bowl. Added to their 11-1 record Penn State's fine play gave Joe Paterno his first consensus national championship.

Watching the season records grow over the years, I still cannot get over how many games Paterno won and we are only in his seventeenth season. In 1982, JoePa was just in his mid-50. He surely knew how to get the most out of his players. That is the job of a great coach. Another great coach, Frank Leahy, at Notre Dame, a bit before Paterno's time, had a saying that I think was the same type of saying JoePa would use to get the most out of his lads. Leahy said: "Lads, you're not to miss practice unless your parents died or you died." That about says it all!

On September 11, # 7 ranked PSU defeated Maryland at Beaver Stadium in a very close game W (39-31). On September 18 Rutgers played a # 8 ranked Penn State and lost by a mile W (49-14).

2 Nebraska, coached by the Great Tom Osborne, with his own share of national championships, always a tough team played #8 PSU at Beaver Stadium on September 25. Osborne's team got its only loss (W (27-24)) of the season in a very close game.

There are those that have this game characterized as the greatest game ever at Beaver Stadium. See write-up under picture on next page.

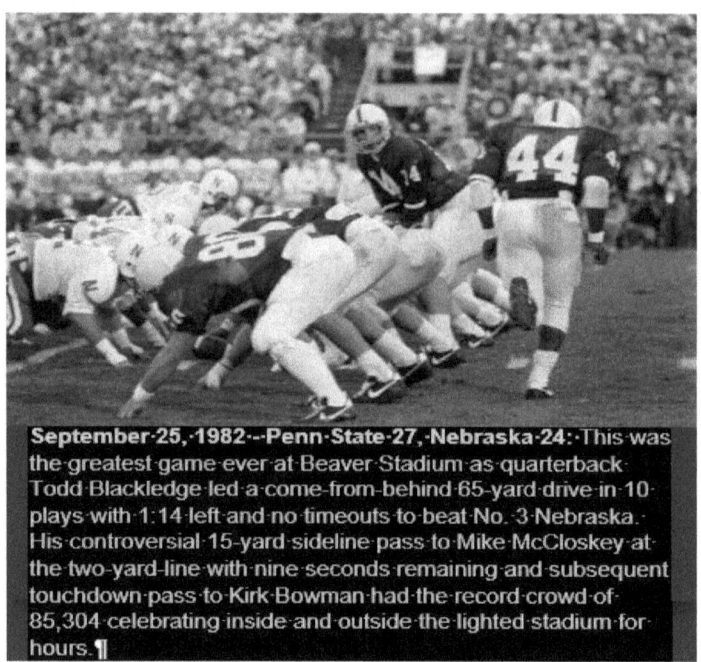

September 25, 1982 -- Penn State 27, Nebraska 24: This was the greatest game ever at Beaver Stadium as quarterback Todd Blackledge led a come-from-behind 65-yard drive in 10 plays with 1:14 left and no timeouts to beat No. 3 Nebraska. His controversial 15-yard sideline pass to Mike McCloskey at the two-yard-line with nine seconds remaining and subsequent touchdown pass to Kirk Bowman had the record crowd of 85,304 celebrating inside and outside the lighted stadium for hours. ¶

On October 9, came the loss at Alabama L (21-42). Alabama lost four of its next seven games which took them way out of the hunt for the championship.

Always ready to create havoc with a great PSU season, Syracuse played the #8 Nittany Lions at Beaver Stadium and lost W (28-7). West Virginia played #9 PSU in Mountaineer Stadium and gave up a loss W (24-0). Alumni Stadium in Chestnut Hill (Boston) was the scene for #8 PSU to shellack the unranked Eagles W (52-17). On November 7, #7 PSU then shut out and literally pounded NC State at Beaver Stadium W (54-0). #13 Notre Dame hosted # 5 PSU on November 13, as Penn State needed every win to have a shot at a championship. In a close match, #5 PSU (8-1) outplayed Notre Dame and got the W (24-14)

PSU v ND 1982

Yogi Berra may not have been a football player but his saying that it ain't over 'til it's over rand true in the 1982 matchup between Notre Dame and Penn State. In 1982, the Irish were coming off a 31-16 upset over then-No. 1 Pittsburgh when the No. 5 Lions came to South Bend.

Historical Nick Gancitano (Penn State) Field Goal against Notre Dame 1982

Notre Dame scored first, but a one-yard run by quarterback Todd Blackledge and two field goals by Nick Gancitano put the Lions up 13-7. Freshman sensation Pinkett, who would go on to have his best games of his career against the Lions, took a kickoff 93 yards for a touchdown and a 14-13 ND lead.

Blackledge, however, responded with a 48-yard-scoring strike to Curt Warner and Penn State went on to a 24-14 victory en route to its first national championship.

At 10-1, on November 26 # 2 Penn State played a tough #5 Pittsburgh at Beaver Stadium. The Nittany Lions controlled the game and won W (19-10). Penn State was the #2 team in the nation and they got a chance in the Sugar Bowl to play the #1 ranked team.

This year's Sugar Bowl was the type of game from which they make movies. The game would determine the 1982 national champions unless both teams played like pikers, which was highly unlikely for the recognized two best teams in the nation.

Georgia had a tough schedule and the Bulldogs had not lost a game. At 11-0, they thought they were pretty good. Penn State at 10-1, with a non-sequitur loss to Alabama felt pretty good about themselves. The game itself, for the first time in many trips to the great field for Penn State and Joe Paterno, would determine the national champion. Win, you're in; Lose, you're out and probably not even #2!

The game was played in the Louisiana Superdome in New Orleans, LA. It was called the Sugar Bowl but neither team had decided to sweeten anything for their opponent. Penn State at # 2, Georgia at #1—it was a game scheduled by the gods. And so it happened on January 1, 1983 that the Pennsylvania State Nittany Lions defeated the great Georgia Bulldogs in a phenomenally tough football game W (19-10). 85,522 attendees plus a national ABC TV football audience enjoyed the game. Only half, my half, thankfully, enjoyed the score.

Curt Warner PSU great, Elected to College Football Hall of Fame

When elected into the hall of fame, the PSU career rushing leader became the 17th Nittany Lion Player to Gain this honor. Think about all the greats in PSU history in which a running game was preferred over a passing game. PSU simply bulled over its opponents. Well in that scenario, former Penn State All-America tailback Curt Warner, the Nittany Lions' man who holds the career rushing yardage leadership for all of PSU football's 100+ years of varsity football, was noted as worthy to become elected to the College Football Hall of Fame.

Warner is the now the 17th Penn State player to receive college football's ultimate honor. Not too shabby

Warner was inducted with other members of the Class of 2009 at the National Football Foundation's 52nd annual awards dinner on December 8 at the Waldorf-Astoria Hotel in New York City. He became the 22nd member of the Penn State program inducted, joining Joe Paterno, 16 other former players and four Nittany Lion coaches. The most recent Penn State player so honored was offensive lineman Keith Dorney in 2005. This is a great honor. Warner expressed his humble appreciation:

"I am deeply honored to have been elected to the College Football Hall of Fame," said Warner, who lives in Camas, Wash., near Portland, Ore. "It's always a good day when you receive news like this. I am honored and privileged to join such a distinguished group of players and coaches."

Hailing from the small town of Pineville, W. Va., Warner was a standout at Pineville High School, graduating in class of 90 students. He went on to lead the Nittany Lions in rushing in 1980, '81 and `82, helping Penn State capture its first National Championship in 1982. Warner was instrumental in Penn State's 31-5 record during his final three seasons, which included two Fiesta Bowl wins (Ohio State and USC) and a 27-23 win over Georgia in the 1983 Sugar Bowl in the National Championship game.

When Warner's brilliant career ended, he owned 42 school records. His 3,398 career rushing yards and 18 100-yard rushing games remain Penn State records more than 25 years later. The Nittany Lions were 18-0 when he eclipsed the century mark. Warner is the only Penn State running back to be selected a two-time first team All-American and is one of just 14 Nittany Lions all-time to earn first team All-America honors twice.

"Curt Warner was an outstanding running back," said head coach Joe Paterno, who was inducted into the Hall of Fame in 2007. "In all my years at Penn State, we have had a lot of exceptional backs, and he is one of the very best of that distinguished group. Curt was a leader for the great teams we had in the early 1980's and played a big part in helping us win our first national championship. Curt was a very good student, has been very loyal to Penn State and has made a positive impact on his community in Washington.

"Curt is most deserving of induction into the College Football Hall of Fame, and we are very pleased that he will be joining its prestigious membership," Paterno added.

"We are thrilled Curt Warner's outstanding career will be recognized with his enshrinement in the College Football Hall of Fame," said Tim Curley, Penn State Director of Athletics.

"Curt was a fantastic representative of the University and was a great leader on our 1982 National Championship team. Curt has earned numerous professional accomplishments in football and business and has made many contributions to the community. We are very pleased with his well-deserved election and earning college football's ultimate honor."

Curt Warner 17th Nittany Lion player to gain induction

As a freshman in 1979, Warner gained 391 yards on 84 carries (4.7) and scored two touchdowns in a reserve role to leading rusher Matt Suhey. In 1980, Warner gained 922 yards on 196 carries (4.7) and scored six touchdowns, helping Penn State to a 10-2 mark and No. 8 final ranking. He ran for a then-Penn State bowl record 155 yards on 18 carries, including a 64-yard touchdown run, to earn Offensive player of the Game honors as the Nittany Lions beat Ohio State in the 1980 Fiesta Bowl.

In 1981, the Walter Camp Football Foundation and United Press International selected Warner a first team All-American. He ran for 1,044 yards on 171 attempts (6.1) and scored eight touchdowns. The Nittany Lions were 10-2, ranked No. 1 for two weeks at mid-season, ending the season with a 48-14 win at No. 1 Pitt and a 26-10 win over USC in the Fiesta Bowl to finish No. 3 in the polls.

Warner gained 145 yards and scored twice vs. the Trojans, out-rushing Heisman Trophy winner Marcus Allen by 60 yards, en route to winning Outstanding Offensive Player accolades in Tempe for the second consecutive year.

As a senior in 1982, Warner gained 1,041 yards on 198 carries (5.3) and scored eight times, again earning first team All-America honors. He also gained 335 receiving yards with five touchdowns. He was awarded the Hall Foundation Award as Penn State's Senior MVP. Warner eclipsed the 100-yard mark in each of the final five games of 1982, including a season-high 183 yards and three touchdowns in a win at Boston College.

After losing at Alabama in the fifth game of the 1982 campaign, the Nittany Lions reeled off six consecutive wins to climb back to 10-1 and No. 2 in the polls and earn a berth in the Sugar Bowl against unbeaten and No. 1 Georgia for the national title. For the second consecutive year, Warner out-gained the Heisman Trophy winner, rushing for 117 yards and two touchdowns in the Nittany Lions' monumental 27-23 win.

He scored from two yards out in the first quarter to open the scoring and added a nine-yard run in the second frame for a 17-3 lead. Warner fought through leg cramps to gain 63 yards in the second half. Georgia's Herschel Walker gained 103 yards on 28 carries vs. the Penn State defense.

Warner said identifying the top highlight of his Penn State career was difficult. "It would probably be the (1983) Sugar Bowl. We had to battle the entire game to beat Georgia. That game epitomized what we were about and culminated all of the hard work we had put in during our careers."

In addition to his Penn State career rushing and 100-yard rushing game records, Warner also holds the school record for all-purpose yards in a game, with 341 yards at Syracuse in 1981. He ran for a career-best 256 yards vs. the Orange that day.

His 280 all-purpose yards vs. Rutgers in 1979 remain a school freshman record. The only Nittany Lion to post more than 1,000 all-purpose yards in all four of his years, Warner is No. 2 in Penn State career all-purpose yards (4,982) and career rushing attempts (649).

The Nittany Lions' all-purpose yardage leader from 1980-82, Warner scored 33 career touchdowns - 24 carrying the ball, six as a receiver and three on kickoff returns. He had 992 career return yards and 662 receiving yards in addition to his 3,398 rushing yards.

Warner earned his Penn State degree in speech communications in May, 1983.

Penn State career rushing leader Curt Warner

After playing in the 1983 Hula Bowl, Warner was the third overall selection in the 1983 NFL Draft by the Seattle Seahawks. He led the AFC in rushing his rookie season with 1,449 yards on 335 carries (4.3), scoring 13 touchdowns to help the Seahawks reach their first AFC Championship game. He suffered a torn ACL in the 1984 opener and missed the rest of the season. Warner gained a career-best 1,481 yards in 1986 and added 41 receptions.

Warner earned Pro Bowl selections in 1983, '86 and '87 and was named All-Pro in 1983, '85, '86 and `87. He gained 6,844 career yards and scored 56 touchdowns, while playing with Seattle (1983-89) and the Los Angeles Rams (1990). Warner also gained 1,467 career receiving yards. He was inducted into the Seattle Seahawks Ring of Honor in 1994 and is one of only eight Seahawks players to be so honored.

Warner was very appreciative of the opportunity to play for Paterno. "I really don't think his players fully appreciate Joe Paterno until they leave," he said. "After you have left Penn State and are out in the world, then you begin to understand the things he talked about and taught us. It was a privilege to play for Joe Paterno.

He is a great person and a great coach. He prepares you for life and he has my utmost respect."

A four-year letterman, Warner was coached by Fran Ganter, who was a member of the Penn State coaching staff from 1971-2003 and is now the Nittany Lions' Associate Athletic Director for Football Administration. "Franny was an outstanding coach and teacher," Warner commented. "We still talk on a regular basis and have an outstanding relationship."

Warner has owned a Chevrolet dealership in Vancouver, Wash. since 1994. Warner and his dealership annually sponsor several safety events in the community. He is the founder and president of the Curt Warner Autism Foundation and is a member of a local Rotary chapter.

Warner serves as the running backs coach for the Camas High School football team. He also has contributed $1,500 the past three years for a scholarship presented by the Clark County Chapter of the National Football Foundation and College Hall of Fame.

Curt and his wife, Ana, have three teenage sons -- Jonathan, and twins, Austin and Christian (14) -- and a baby daughter, Isabella.

Paterno was inducted into the College Football Hall of Fame in 2007, becoming one of the first three active coaches to gain induction.

Other members of the Penn State program enshrined in the College Football Hall of Fame, located in South Bend, Ind., include ex-coaches Hugo Bezdek, Rip Engle, Dick Harlow and Bob Higgins along with former players John Cappelletti, Keith Dorney, Jack Ham, Glenn Killinger, Ted Kwalick, Rich Lucas, Pete Mauthe, Shorty Miller, Lydell Mitchell, Dennis Onkotz, Mike Reid,

Additional information on the College Football Hall of Fame Class of 2009 can be found at www.footballfoundation.com.

1983 Penn State Football Season Coach Joe Paterno

The 1983 Penn State Nittany Lions football team was coached by Joe Paterno in his eighteenth year. The team achieved an 8-4-1 record with an Aloha Bowl game victory over Washington. Even with four regular season losses, the Lions were ranked at #17 in the Coach's poll. Clearly after a national championship it is safe to call 1983 a rebuilding year for Penn State. New players equal a new team.

Nobody can win every game every season. Even Alabama, after doubling the score against PSU in their 1982 match could not sustain its good fortune and lost its last four games...of course this helped PSU in achieving the championship in 1982. So, unless students and coaches were all ironmen in football, the conclusion is that nobody can will all the games all the time. Yet great coaches such as Joe Paterno always try.

In its earliest season start since the inception of the program in the 1880's, on August 29, #4 Penn State lost to Tom

Osborne's #1 ranked Nebraska team in the Kickoff Classic L (6-44). Teams do not forget the teams that have messed them up as PSU did the prior year to Nebraska. Cincinnati was next on September 10 at Beaver Stadium, and a Lions team that was not accustomed to losing lost again to the Bearcats. Iowa on September 17 kept throwing the bad sludge at Penn State. Not having won a game in this short season so far, PSU lost again to the Hawkeyes L (34-42)

Temple chose the Vet to play an unranked PSU on September 24 and came close to an upset over the Nittany Lions W (23-18) PSU had its first win of the season. On October 1, Rutgers asked PSU to play in Giants Stadium and the Nittany Lions defeated the Scarlet Knight. Not forgetting the Alabama loss a year previous, Penn State took on Alabama's Crimson Tide on October 8 at Beaver Stadium and won a nice game W (34-8). On October 15, PSU then played Syracuse at the Carrier Dome and defeated the Orangemen W (17-6).

At the time, it was just as impossible to get a full bus trip to Beaver Stadium for a game but Syracuse was just two and a half hours from the IBM Scranton Branch Office. The tickets were affordable and available and so every other year, my IBM cohorts and I ran a bus trip to see PSU play Syracuse in the Carrier Dome.

I saw this game and many others until the series was canceled. I can remember how disappointed we all were when the games ended, but we kept going to Syracuse for a little while afterwards. One time an IBM football game flier read that *this year's Penn State Football game will be Syracuse v Army*.

The kids loved seeing the Army Cadets next to our bus, but it was not the same as all of us seeing PSU taking on the bad guys with JoePa at the Carrier Dome in 69 degree indoor weather. I do recall one game in which Todd Blackledge threw a pass on first down and before the clock had reached 14:50 in the first quarter, Penn State was up 7-0.

On October 22, #4 ranked PSU beat West Virginia at Beaver Stadium in University Park, PA W (41-23). On October 29, Boston College had its way with Penn State in a rare win at Foxborough MA. L (17-27). On November5, at home, PSU beat Brown University W (38-21).

PSU was doing pretty well against Notre Dame at the time and in 1983, on November 12, things were no different. PSU beat the Fighting Irish in Beaver Stadium in a close match W (34-30) before 85,899.

The summarized scoop on this see-saw game between these rivals is that the two teams met on a frigid November afternoon at Beaver Stadium. Doug Strang had his best day as a Lion, completing 24 passes for 274 yards and three touchdowns. But his performance was overshadowed by ND's Pinkett, who would have his best game of his career (at least up until then) with 217 yards rushing and four touchdowns. In a see-saw battle, Notre Dame took a 30-27 lead late in the fourth quarter, but Strang's roll-out keeper with less than a minute to play enabled Penn State to win 34-30.

Cross-state rival #17 Pittsburgh hosted Penn State on November 19, and the teams tied T (24-24).

On December 26, PSU played Washington at Aloha Stadium in Honolulu, Hawaii in the Aloha Bowl. 37,212 watched the game on the field while millions of others watched it on ESPN. Penn State won the game W (13-10).

Player Highlights Kenny Jackson

Kenny Jackson, from Mount Holly, NJ, who played Flanker for the Lions, was an All-American Selection in 1982 and 1983.

Kenny Jackson

He was selected by the Associated Press in 1982 and by NEA in 1983. Jackson was Penn State's first All-American wide receiver, catching 41 passes for 697 yards and seven TDs in 1982. He owned 27 school records after his senior year. Jackson was a #1 draft pick, played with Philadelphia (1984-88, 90-91) and Houston (1989) in the National Football League.

He served on the Penn State football coaching staff from 1993 to 2000 and was an assistant coach with the Pittsburgh Steelers from 2001-03.

1984 Penn State Football Season Coach Joe Paterno

The 1984 Penn State Nittany Lions football team was coached by Joe Paterno in his nineteenth year at age 56. With a 6-5 record this can be called a rebuilding year to a rebuilding year. Lots of losses.

The pundits ranked PSU at #11 as this could have been the comeback year but it was not. On September 8, Rutgers was defeated just barely by the #11   Lions at Beaver Stadium W (15-12). Still winning some close games, #12 ranked PSU beat #5 Iowa W (20-172) on September 15 at Kinnick Stadium • Iowa City, IA. On September 22, #7 PSU then beat William & Mary at Beaver Stadium W (56-18). Then #2 Texas came in to Giants Stadium to ruin the winning party. They played PSU before 76,833 and the Longhorns beat the Lions L (3–28.

Maryland played next on October 6 v a PSU team that had not yet begun to roll. In a very close game the Nittany Lions eventually prevailed at Beaver Stadium W 25–24. At Bryant-Denny Stadium, on October 13, Alabama squeaked out a victory against the Lions L (0–6). Syracuse then played at Beaver Stadium against #19 PSU but lost W (21-3). With a better team in 1984, on October 27, #18 West Virginia was ready for a win and they got it on their home field in a close game against a floundering #19 PSU team L (14-17)

PSU beat Boston College at home on November 3 W 37-30). Notre Dame had been beaten and roughed up a few times in the early 1980's and it wasn't forgetting the notion of payback. On November 17, in the old Notre Dame Stadium. PSU did not have what it takes and ND beat PSU with a big score L (7-44).

In a weak year, Pittsburgh was not about to get beaten by PSU so it played like the dickens and defeated the Nittany Lions L (11-31) at Beaver Stadium, with many PSU fans in attendance. It is much easier writing about Penn States big winning seasons than a slow-down season.

1985 Penn State Football Season Coach Joe Paterno

The 1985 Penn State Nittany Lions football team was coached by Joe Paterno for the twentieth year and played its home games in Beaver Stadium in University Park, Pennsylvania. You may recall in the 1983 summary, I suggested that the season was 8-4-1 because of rebuilding, and then with a 6-5 season in 1984 I admitted that the rebuilding needed rebuilding. Along the way, noticing that an Alabama team lost four games after beating Penn State, I realized that nothing is certain in college football. But, Joe

Paterno knew how to win. That was certain and in 1985, he showed it again on his way to 1986.

On September 7, Maryland was ranked at #7 when #19 Penn State went to Robert Byrd Stadium to play the Terrapins. As season openers often are as the sluggishness is removed from the routine, this game was very close and a fine Maryland team lost by just two points to Penn State W (20-18). Close was the order of the season as a tough Temple team came to Beaver Stadium ton September 14, to play ball, and play hard they did as PSU escaped with a two-point victory W (27-25).

East Carolina, not a frequent visitor to Beaver Stadium came to play the #10 Nittany Lions and they played a nice game but lost W (17-10). On September 28, Rutgers duplicated the East Carolina score W (17-10) in Giants Stadium before 54,560.

I am conditioned that when I see Alabama, I think tough and I think potential loss. I am sure Bear Bryant and subsequent coaches preach that message. Not in 1985. #8 ranked PSU beat #10 Alabama on October 12 W (19-17) in a nailbiter for sure. PSU was #6 when the Orangemen hosted the Nittany Lions at the Carrier Dome in 69 degree weather in Syracuse. PSU won another close game with a great defense W (24-20). PSU at #3 then played West Virginia on October 26 and triumphed with a shutout W (27-0). On November 2, BC came to Beaver stadium and were beaten in another close match by #3 ranked PSU W (16-12). On November 9, Penn State traveled to Riverfront Stadium in Cincinnati and won W (31-0).

On November 16, a new regular, Notre Dame, then an unranked opponent, played the #1 ranked Penn State at Beaver Stadium W (36-6).

In the Beaver Stadium historical annals, no game ever had been played in such drenching, cold rain. The heavy rain started Friday night and did not let up until the game was long over. Despite regional TV able to take the fans out of the inclement weather, over 84,000 fans showed up. They expected to see a close game but watched as the top ranked Nittany Lions annihilated Notre Dame en route to an 11-0 regular season and berth in the national championship game vs. Oklahoma in the Orange Bowl.

On November 16, an undefeated PSU team beat Pitt at Pitt W (31-0). PSU was ranked #1 at 11-0 undefeated and were invited to play Oklahoma in the Orange Bowl.

Bowl Game Destroys Undefeated Season

The game was about five or six weeks after the team was in shape and had their last taste of a real football game. Miami had the same circumstances so there are no excuses but PSU had obviously lost its edge. On January 1, 1986, # 1 PSU played #3 Oklahoma in the Miami Orange Bowl and lost the game to a Miami team that played better than Penn State L (10–25). 74,148 saw the game on the field and NBC showed the game to the willing in the rest of the country. It was a great season, 11-1 with a #3 finish in both the Coach's and the AP polls.

1986 Penn State Football Season Coach Joe Paterno

The 1986 Penn State Nittany Lions football team was coached by Joe Paterno for the twenty-first year. Penn State defeated the Miami Hurricanes 14–10 in the 1987 Fiesta Bowl to win Paterno's second consensus national championship. Joe Paterno knew how to win football games.

On September 6, Penn State opened up this successful season at home against Temple. Temple had been having problems winning against PSU for some years and in fact it still does and this year was no different. #6 ranked Penn State won its home opener W (45-15). Boston College moved its September 20 game from Alumni Stadium to Foxborough to play a tough #5 ranked PSU team. The Eagles played a close game but lost to the Nittany Lions W (26-14). East Carolina lost at Beaver Stadium on September 27 against a #7 ranked PSU squad W (42-7). PSU had a knack of scheduling its easier games in the beginning to get the team accustomed to the routine before engaging tough game. PSU defeated Rutgers at Beaver Stadium next on October 4, W (31-6).

Cincinnati brought its football team to play #5 ranked PSU at Beaver Stadium on October 11. It was a close game but the Nittany Lions won W (23-17). On October 18, Syracuse played PSU at Beaver Stadium and were defeated easily by the #6 Nittany Lions W (42-3). A tough Alabama team waited for game seven when PSU was 100% ready for the Crimson Tide. The PSU squad made quick work of the vaunted Alabama team at Tuscaloosa W (23-3). At 7-0, with the Alabama game behind them PSU moved up in the rankings to #2 in the country. On November 1, PSU traveled to Mountaineer Stadium to play a fine West Virginia team and beat the Mountaineers W (19-0)

On November 8, #2 ranked Penn State played Maryland at Beaver Stadium and won a very, very close match W (17-15). A loss would have virtually ended PSU's championship dreams. Playing the unranked Fighting Irish at Notre Dame Stadium on November 15, it was expected to be close and it was but the #3 ranked 9-0 Nittany Lions prevailed W (24-19).

At 10-0, ranked # 2 on November 22, PSU needed just one more win v Pittsburgh at home to have a perfect regular season. The Nittany Lions got that win W (34-14) before 85,722, and also got a shot at winning the national title in the Fiesta Bowl v #1 ranked Miami.

PSU clinched a spot in the national championship game by beating arch rival Pitt. That it was Pitt made this an extremely gratifying moment. The bitterness of the long-time rivalry emerged with five fist fights, a number of late hits and four offsetting penalties for unsportsmanlike conduct. Many who watched every moment of the game, still enjoy the image of Joe Paterno running across the field late in the game to help break up a scuffle in front of the Pitt bench. They say that was a lifetime priceless moment.

A game marred by fighting!

Rob Biertempfel of the PSU Collegian Student Newspaper wrote about a "game marred by fighting. Here is how he saw the contest:

The Collegian Nov 24, 1986

Game marred by fighting

A funny thing happened Saturday afternoon in Beaver Stadium. They started playing football and a hockey game broke out.

The 86th gridiron clash between the Penn State Nittany Lions and Pitt Panthers was at times more like a boxing match than a football contest, as proved by five fights, three ejections, seven personal fouls and 77 yards in penalties. At one point, late in the fourth quarter, Lion Head Coach Joe Paterno sprinted across the field to help break up a scuffle near the Pitt bench.

The image of Paterno running into a fight may have brought comparisons with Maryland Head Coach Bobby Ross' incident with a referee a few weeks ago, but this situation was different.

The scoreboard showed 4:26 remaining and Penn State ahead 34-14 when Pitt's Teryl Austin returned a punt to the Panthers' 18-yard line. After he was run out of bounds, he flipped the ball into the facemask of Penn State's Brian Chizmar. Five Lions came to Chizmar's defense and the melee was on.

"The next thing I knew I was surrounded," Austin explained afterwards. "Everyone got into it."

The Pitt bench emptied, Penn State players rushed onto the grass and Paterno angrily ran into the fight. Television microphones picked up the coach calling the fighting players a disgrace to the game as he tried to separate them. When the mud had settled, the Lions were assessed a 15-yard personal foul penalty.

Paterno was livid at the referees all day for doing what he thought was an inadequate job. After the game, he explained his anger.

"I thought the officials started wrong when they started with a personal foul here and a personal foul there," he said. "That means nothing and I think the game got a little out of hand. I'm going to sit down and tell my kids not to talk about it because I don't think it's good for football when you play in games like that.

"I've never been in a football game with Pitt when we had so much of that kind of stuff."

Pitt Head Coach Mike Gottfried, who got his first taste of the Penn State-Pitt rivalry Saturday, was much more direct in his comments.

"I'm not going to let an hour go by the rest of next year without remembering what they (Penn State) did," he grumbled after the game in a voice deadened by yelling. "I'm never going to forget what their coach did to me on that sideline, and how their fans embarrassed us."

The game's first confrontation came after Penn State's D.J. Dozier had sliced through the Panther defense for a 26-yard touchdown and a 17-7 Lion lead. As Dozier slowed down in the end zone, Panther cornerback Quinton Jones gave the senior tailback some assistance off the field with a slap and shove. Center Keith Radecic stood up to Jones and was joined by quarterback John Shaffer. The fight that ensued resulted in offsetting personal fouls which enraged the partisan crowd and Paterno, who responded by screaming at the officials.

Penn State cornerback Duffy Cobbs said that Paterno's vocal reaction surprised the team.

"Usually he's the one who tries to calm us down," he said. "When I saw him, I said, 'Anything goes now.'"

Radecic agreed, but noted that the afternoon saw more than its share of intensity.

"He did some things today that were a little uncharacteristic, but I think we all did," he said. "I think we all lost our poise a little bit. There were definitely too many personal fouls and unsportsmanlike contact calls. In the heat of the game you never know what will happen."

The rest of the game had its share of scuffles, taunts and shoves, and at least three players were ejected from the game. Pitt lost linebacker Jerry Wall and wide receiver Bill Osborn. Wall identified linebacker Don Graham as the Penn State player thrown out.

The players themselves seemed to take the fierce play in stride, saying that the nature of the rivalry caused spirited play to turn into violence.

Pitt's Steve Apke, who scuffled with former high school teammate Shaffer in the second quarter after Dozier's touchdown, said the game was out of the referees' hands.

"The refs tried to keep it under control, but things like that are going to happen," the senior linebacker said. "It's a big rivalry; that's just playing hard. When the score starts getting out of hand, people start getting frustrated."

Penn State's Bob White also tried to shrug off the scuffles.

"I think that in a lot of ways that's kind of expected," the senior defensive lineman said. "That's the nature of the game over the years. Things did get out of hand out there for a while. But when you've got a bunch of guys that are going at each other the way we were going at each other, those things are going to happen."

1986 Fiesta Bowl Game

Taking advantage of the long New Year's weekend, this January 2, 1987 encounter was scheduled for Friday. It was another game of the century with #1 Miami coached by Jimmy Johnson, the coach everybody loved to hate, and Joe Paterno, a great winning coach at the helm for the #2 ranked Penn State. The Fiesta Bowl game was played in Sun Devil

Stadium in Tempe, AZ (Fiesta Bowl). It was televised by NBC and watched on the field by 74,098. PSU won the game W 14–10 and the national championship.

Shane Conlan inducted into College Football Hall of Fame

By Dustin Hockensmith | dhockensmith@pennlive.com
on May 22, 2014 at 1:58 PM, updated May 22, 2014 at 2:45 PM

Former Penn State linebacker Shane Conlan was one of 16 inductees into the 2014 College Football Hall of Fame. One of three Nittany Lions on the ballot, Conlan made the cut as a two-time All-American who helped lead Penn State to an undefeated record and the 1986 national championship. Running back D.J. Dozier and offensive lineman Steve Wisniewski also made the final vote.

Conlan thanked late legendary coach Joe Paterno and former defensive coordinator Tom Bradley in his acceptance speech. He added that the Nittany Lions were the only program to offer him a scholarship as a three-sport athlete from Frewsburg High School in upstate New York.

"It's been a tough time last few years at Penn State," Conlan said, beginning to choke up. "So, most of all I want to thank two people that are most important to me in my life, one being the late, great Joe Paterno. Thank you so much for all you've done. We miss you, Coach. And my defensive coordinator Tom Bradley, who found me at a very small school. I had no offers except for one, Penn State, and he went to bat for me."

Conlan played a pivotal part in one of the most memorable games in Penn State history, recording eight tackles and two interceptions in a 14-10 win over No. 1 Miami in the 1987 Fiesta Bowl. Conlan and the Nittany Lions also reached the 1985 national championship game, where they lost to Oklahoma.

Penn State linebackers Trey Bauer (35) and Shane Conlan (31) pat each other on the back as Miami's Aoatoa Polamalu watches following Conlan's fourth quarter interception in the Fiesta Bowl, Friday, Jan. 3, 1987, Tempe, Ariz. Penn State defeated Miami 14-10. (AP Photo/Jim Gerberich)

"Shane was one of the greatest linebackers in our long and outstanding Linebacker U heritage and we are thrilled for him," athletic director Dave Joyner said. "His intense, physical play and leadership were exciting to watch. Most importantly, though, is how he has conducted himself on or off the field; always with humility and class. His demeanor, drive and success after football serve as another example for all our student-athletes -- past, present and future. We are very proud of Shane and elated he has earned college football's most prestigious honor."

Conlan was a four-year letter winner who twice led the team in tackles, finishing his career with 274 career stops, seventh-most in school history. He was the No. 8 pick in the 1987 NFL draft and went on to play nine seasons in the NFL, winning NFL Rookie of the Year honors and being named to three Pro Bowls.

Conlan is now the Vice President of Corporate Sponsorships for the Pittsburgh Power of the Arena Football League.

"The Penn State football family is ecstatic that Shane Conlan has been selected for induction into the College Football Hall of Fame," Penn State coach James Franklin said. "Shane is one of the primary reasons why so many people know about the unrivaled tradition of Linebacker U. Shane was a fierce, tough competitor and leader and we are excited that he is being appropriately recognized for his outstanding career with his enshrinement in the Hall of Fame."

Conlan was part of a class that combined inductees from all levels of college football in one class, the National Football Foundation said in a press release. He was one of three linebackers inducted, along with late Alabama star Derrick Thomas and Maine's John Huard.

1987 Penn State Football Season Coach Joe Paterno

The 1987 Penn State Nittany Lions football team was coached by Joe Paterno in his 22nd year as head coach. The team's aggregate record including its Citrus Bowl major loss to Clemson L (10-35) Bowl was 8-4 and after a #1 finish in 1986, PSU finished out of the top 20 at #22. It was

Paying homage to the national championship team and recognizing the loss of senior athletes, PSU was ranked #11 to start the season on September 5 v Bowling Green at Beaver Stadium. PSU looked good v Bowling Green W (45-19). Alabama as a first test came early in Beaver Stadium and the Crimson Tide gave PSU their first loss since the Orange Bowl game after the 1985 season L (13-24). Overall, it was not a bad game. #20 PSU then shutout Cincinnati on September 19 at home (W (41-0). On September 26, the Nittany Lions played at Boston College W (27-17).

On October 3 v Temple at Beaver Stadium, the #14 Nittany Lions beat Temple W (27-13). The following week Rutgers came to town and PSU defeated the Scarlet Knight W (35-21). #13 Syracuse had picked itself up and dusted itself off while #10 PSU had been winning national championships.

The Orangemen were waiting on October 17 at the Carrier Dome and they soundly defeated PSU L (21-48). On October 31, at home, PSU barely beat West Virginia played (25-21).

On November 7 at Maryland #16 PSU beat the Terrapins W (21-16) in another close battel. Pittsburgh had been getting shellacked in recent years by Penn State but this time, in a tough game on November 14, the Panthers beat the Nittany Lions at Pitt Stadium L (0-10). Notre Dame came to Beaver Stadium on November 21. In a nailbiter PSU beat the Fighting Irish by one point W (21-20).

This game may have been the coldest ever at Beaver Stadium with 30 mile an hour winds, snow flurries and wind chills of zero to 18 degrees the numbing 84,00 shivering fans. Notre Dame scored with 30 seconds remaining and went for the win but quarterback Tony Rice was tackled short of the goal by linebacker Pete Curkendall. "It was a moment that will always be frozen in the history of Penn State football," Paterno said.

PSU v ND

PSU was invited to the Citrus Bowl in which they played a tough Clemson Tigers team on January 1, 1988 in Orlando. Clemson won decisively L (10-35.

1988 Penn State Football Season Coach Joe Paterno

The 1988 Penn State Nittany Lions football team was coached by Joe Paterno in his 23rd season. With a 5-6 record, this is the first losing season in Joe Paterno's first 23 years. A double rebuilding process was underway. PSU was unranked and the team did not qualify for a bowl bid.

Penn State began its season fine with a nice win on September 10 at Virginia W (42-14). The wins continued the next week, September 17, at home v Boston College W (23-20). Rutgers came to Beaver Stadium on September 24 and gave a signal that this would be a tough year by beating PSU L (16-21). Temple played PSU at the Vet and were defeated on October 1 by a wide margin W (45-9).

Cincinnati made the short trip to Beaver Stadium on October 8 and were rebuffed W (35-9). A Syracuse still feeling its oats from the prior year's major victory came to Beaver Stadium on October 15 and handed PSU another defeat L (10-14). By this time, PSU was ready for tough teams for sure. The Lions handled Alabama well on October 22 but not well enough to win L(3-8). West Virginia was ranked #7 when PSU played the Mountaineers in Morgantown. It was all about WV's offense L (30-51).

On November 5, PSU beat Maryland in a close home game W (17-10). Pittsburgh then came to PSU on November 12 and beat the Lions L (7-14). The next game was PSU's chance at a bowl win as Notre Dame was ranked #1 when it hosted the Nittany Lions on November 19. PSU could not match the Irish and lost L (3-21). Overall, this was PSU's worst season under Joe Paterno at 5-6 with no post season honors. Stay tune for our summary of 1989 to see how well the JoePa team recovered.

1989 Penn State Football Season Coach Joe Paterno

The 1989 Penn State Nittany Lions football team was coached by Joe Paterno in his 24th season. At 8-3-1, the team made a great comeback from the 5-6 record of 1988. Additionally the Lions were #14 in the Coach's poll and #15 in the AP poll. Moreover, they played and beat BYU in the Holiday Bowl W (50-39).

PSU started the season ranked #12 on September 9 at home with a loss to the Virginia Wahoos L (6-14) before 85,956 at Beaver Stadium. Games at Beaver stadium attract even more fans than bowl games. Temple was next at Beaver Stadium on September 16 (W (42-3). On September 23, Boston College came to State College and were beaten by the Nittany Lions in a very close, low-scoring game, W (7-3). On September 30, Penn State traveled to Austin Texas and beat the Longhorns W (16-12).

On PSU shut out Rutgers at Giants Stadium in East Rutherford, NJ W (17–0). On October 14, PSU beat Syracuse at the Carrier Dome W (34-12). Then, in a nailbiter at Beaver Stadium, the #14 Nittany Lions barely lost to #6 Alabama L (16-17). On November 4, at Beaver Stadium, #16 Penn State played #13 West Virginia W (19-9). On November 11, at Maryland PSU tied the Terrapins T (13-13).

On November 18, at Beaver Stadium, #1 Notre Dame defeated #17 Penn State W (23-34). A week later at Pittsburgh, PSU came back to beat the Panthers W (16-13).

Penn State was invited to the Holiday Bowl with a 7-3-1 record and the #18 Nittany Lions defeated the #19 Cougars at Jack Murphy Stadium in San Diego, California. The attendance was 61,113 plus a nationwide ESPN TV audience.

1990 Penn State Football Season Coach Joe Paterno

The 1990 Penn State Nittany Lions football team was coached by Joe Paterno in his twenty-fifth season. The team had a great 9-2 record.

Without the early almost-wins in the first two games of the season, Penn State would have been playing for another national championship. The first was a home opening loss on September 8 to Texas in a nailbiter to open the home season L (13-17) and the next was in game #2 in another nailbiter at # 6 USC in the Coliseum in Los Angeles California Southern California on September 15 (L (14-19). Both were close but as the smoke shop manager would say, but "no cigar!" Until the Blockbuster Bowl loss to Florida State L (17-24), the Nittany Lions from game 3 on, had a perfect season. The final record was 9-3 and the team was ranked # 10 in the Coach's poll and # 11 in the AP poll.

On September 22, PSU beat Rutgers W (28-0) at Beaver Stadium to start a nine-game win streak. Temple was next in line at Beaver Stadium on October 6 W (48-10). Syracuse played very tough at Beaver Stadium on October 13 W (27-21). PSU then traveled to Boston College's Alumni Stadium W (40-21). Then came a great win in the Alabama rivalry game on October 27 in Tuscaloosa W (9-0)

#24 PSU played the next week, November 3 in Morgantown and beat the Mountaineers W (31-19). At #21 PSU played at home on November 10 and beat Syracuse W (24-10). A tough #1 ranked Notre Dame squad hosted Penn State at Notre Dame Stadium on November 17 and JoePa's team, ranked #18 at the time pulled off its magic and destroyed the Fighting Irish's championship hopes W (24-10). #11 Penn State then played rival Pittsburgh at home on November 24 and beat the Panthers in a close game W (22-17).

PSU was then ranked #7 and they played Bobby Bowden's #11 Florida State team in the Blockbuster Bowl on December 28 at Joe Robbie Stadium in Miami Gardens, FL and were beaten in a heartbreaker of a game L (17-24.) The Nittany Lions' final record was 9-3 and the team was ranked # 10 in the Coach's poll and # 11 in the AP poll.

1991 Penn State Football Season Coach Joe Paterno

The 1991 Penn State Nittany Lions football team was coached by Joe Paterno in his 26th season. They won 11 games including the Fiesta Bowl W (42-17 v Tennessee.) Their two losses were at unranked USC on September 14 L (10-21) and against #2 ranked Miami in Florida L (20-26) on October 12.

#7 PSU was invited and accepted play in the Kickoff Classic on August 29 v #8 ranked Georgia Tech at Giants Stadium. PSU triumphed W (34-22). On September 7 at home, PSU shellacked Cincinnati in a humunga-scoring game W (81-0) before an attendance of 94,000. Beaver Stadium was enhanced this year. An upper deck was added to north end zone along with an additional 10000 seats added Then on September 14 came the loss to USC, followed the next week by a nice win against BYU in Beaver Stadium before 96,304 W (33-7). After the BYU game PSU was ranked # 10.

After a bye week, on September 28, Boston College were defeated by the #10 Nittany Lions at Beaver Stadium W (28–21). On October 5, PSU beat Temple at Veterans Stadium W (24-7). #9 ranked PSU then were beaten by #2 ranked Miami in Florida L (20-26). On October 19, Rutgers played the Nittany Lions at Beaver Stadium W (37-17).

On October 26, West Virginia played #8 Penn State at Beaver Stadium and lost big W (51-6). On November 9, PSU clobbered Maryland in Baltimore W (47-7). PSU was tough and they had one heck of an offense led by QB Tony Sacca. On November 16, PSU beat a Lou Holtz coached Notre Dame team at Beaver Stadium in University Park, PA) W 35–13 with 96,672 in attendance. On November 28 at Pittsburgh, #6 ranked Penn State beat the panthers W (32-20)

#6 PSU played in the Fiesta Bowl on January 1 1002 v #10 Tennessee in Sun Devil Stadium before 71,133 onlookers and a National NBC TV audience. The Nittany Lions played a great game W (42-17). PSU finished 11-2 and were ranked # 3 in both polls.

1992 Penn State Football Season Coach Joe Paterno

The 1992 Penn State Nittany Lions football team was coached by Joe Paterno in his 27th season. After three great years, 8-3-1, 9-3, and 11-2, one could almost expect a rebuilding year. This year's 7-5 record was a winning season but it was not a contender season as the past three.

The season opened at Nippert Stadium in Ohip against Cincinatti on September 5 as the #8 Nittany Lions beat a determined Bearcats team in a close match W (24-20). The home opener was on September 12 v Temple in a slugout. # 10 PSU prevailed W (49-8). Eastern Michigan played at Beaver Stadium before 94, 892 on September 19. #10 ranked PSU shellacked the Eagles W (52–7).

PSU played Maryland at home on September 26 and beat the Terrapins W 49-13). At 4-0, ranked # 8 PSU played Rutgers at Giants stadium and won a nice game W (38-24). PSU had five wins in a row. Having escaped anything bad this season the Penn State Nittany Lions unfortunately would soon notice that the losses were about ready to come home to roost.

October 10, it was another battle of the titans at Beaver Stadium in University Park, PA as #2 Miami (FL) had their sights on defeating PSU. The Hurricanes won the game but it was a nail-biter L (14-17). Boston College knew had to create nailbiting in the PSU stands also and just about beat the Nittany Lions on October 17, L (32-35).

Two games that could have gone either way went the wrong way. On October 24, West Virginia hosted PSU in a tough contest and the #14 Lions beat the Mountaineers W (40-26). A tough BYU invited the Nittany Lions to play at Cougar Stadium on October 29 and beat PSU L (17-30) in the biggest loss so far in the season.

PSU was now 6-2 with a trip to Notre Dame coming on November 14. The #8 Fighting Irish squeaked out a thriller one point win v #22 PSU L (16-17). Pittsburgh came to Beaver Stadium on November 21 and the Lions beat them handily W (57-13).

PSU accepted an invitation to the Blockbuster bowl with a 7-4 season. The game was played January 1, 1993 at Joe Robbie Stadium in Miami Gardens, Florida. #13 Stanford was hoping to make quick work of #21 Penn State. It was not quick and the game was tough but PSU was beat fairly that day by a Stanford team that had come ready to play ball L (3-24).

1993 Penn State Football Season Coach Joe Paterno

The 1993 Penn State Nittany Lions football team was coached by Joe Paterno in his twenty-eighth year. Joe Paterno figured it was time to stop his run as an independent and begin playing Big Ten teams more regularly. So, PSU joined the Big Ten Conference in 1990 and began play in 1993.

Penn State then won its first Big Ten championship in 1994, and the Nittany Lions won two more in 2005 and 2008. As a deep Penn State fan all my life, after reviewing his life in his football record, I cannot believe what a great coach Joe Paterno was. The mold from which he was cut created the greatest football coaches of all time.

At the end of the 1993 season, PSU was ranked #7 in the Coach's poll and # 8 in the AP with a 10–2 record (6–2 in Big Ten play). The complexion of the PSU schedule would change forever as a result of its playing in the Big Ten

Conference. The same-ole same-oles were no longer on the schedule but the schedule was always exciting.

Until we all get comfortable in recognizing all the Big Ten teams that PSU would now play, for the two years left in this chapter, we will put a BT in front of all Big Ten Teams on the playing schedule.

On September 4, BTMinnesota played #17 Penn State in a home game at Beaver Stadium. PSU won W (38-20) I think it was a nice gesture that PSU's first Big Ten encounter was at home. The Nittany Lions had gotten rid of that "rebuilding year," and were now moving on to their normal modus operandi of regular winning. On September 11, in a non-Big-Ten game, USC played #15 PSU before 95,992 and the Nittany Lions won the game by a sliver W (21-20). A win is a win. On September 18, #14 PSU traveled to BTIowa and shot out the Hawkeyes W (31-0). Longtime foe Rutgers played on September 25 v the Nittany Lions and lost W (31-7).

On October 2 #9 PSU played at Maryland and ran roughshod over the Terrapins W (70-7). An always powerful BTMichigan team visited PSU on October 16 and beat the Nittany Lions in a close game W (13-21). Another tough opponent BTOhio State, took command of the game at Columbus and defeated PSU L (6-24). Few teams ever beat Penn State by a large score. On November 6, BTIndiana played the Nittany Lions at Beaver Stadium and the Lions won W (38-31).

On November 13, #16 PSU defeated BTIllinois in Beaver Stadium W (28–14). The next week on November 20, at BTNorthwestern, PSU gained another victory W (43-21). Still on the road a week later on November 27, #14 PSU beat #25 BTMichigan State at Spartan Stadium in East Lansing MI W (38-37). This was as close a game as it gets.

Let's talk about this game a bit more as from my perspective it is one of the best games and great moments in PSU football history. This game set the stage for the 1994 undefeated season and put out a fair warning that Penn State was for real. Some in the good ole boys crowd did not care as they seemed to like establishment football. We'll get to that after sone great front work introducing ths game, this one point victory, which demonstrates the mettle and the resilience of the Penn State football program. Go Lions!

The Season ends with a great game v Michigan State

As we have been touting in this book from way back when PSU won its first game in 1881, the Nittany Lions dominated college football as an independent for over 110 years before the university joined the Big Ten in 1993.

Fast forwarding to recent history as few of us remember the 1890's, the Nittany Lions had won six bowl games from 1980-89, including three Fiesta Bowls and one Sugar Bowl. Penn State had finished in the AP Top Ten five times just in the 1980's, and twice in the 1980's the team brought in national championships. This was a team that transcended graduating classes. Through its great coaches and players, PSU always knew how to win and when Joe Paterno began his legacy after Rip Engle gave him the keys, Penn State further upped the ante. Just try to beat the Nittany Lions!

PSU won the National Championship again as everybody knows in 1994. But, because we are kind to our opponents, we just whisper about this triumph.

You see, the vaunted 1994 team was not awarded the big prize after a 12-0, undefeated, untied season. It was because the coach chose not to embarrass Indiana and the Hoosiers made the score closer than the game ever was. It was as if the football establishment was waiting to deny Penn State's possible best team ever, the national championship.

Paterno's teams had recorded great seasons before 1994 with a 37-12 record leading up to the great 1994 season in which nothing went wrong in games but the afterthoughts were mostly sour.

1993, the year in which we now find ourselves examining, was also a great effort and a great result though often overshadowed by the undefeated 1994 team. The pundits say that the final game of that season against Michigan State, the game we have been discussing, set the tone for the run to the top in '94. Penn State showed its mettle and the future looked bright. Nobody could deny a great Penn State Team the Championship in 1994. All PSU had to do was win, win, and win again, and our great University did exactly that. But, we spend enough time on that when we cover 1994 so let's continue with the 1993 season.

In 1993, Penn State was the new guy on the block in the Big Ten. The well talented but less experienced than talented Lions opened a great season with five back-to-back wins. Eventually, the team met Michigan and Ohio State consecutively and these opponents were a measurable cut above the five prior teams. Penn State was not intimidated at all.

The Lions competed with Michigan well for the first three quarters, but the Wolverines kept Ki-Jana Carter from the goal line in the opening play of the fourth quarter. It was hard to take, I regret to say that it sure seemed to take the oomph out of the PSU attack. Officially, the game ended when Kerry Collins threw a rare interception within the last minute of the game, but it seemed to end with Carter's almost TD.

Ohio State gave the Nittany Lions their second loss at Ohio Stadium just two weeks later. PSU had been 6-2 against Ohio State before this encounter but the last time was when they played the Buckeyes in the 1980 Fiesta Bowl. The Nittany Lions back then crushed OSU but the Buckeyes had improved for sure and they were ready for vindication against the Lions.

They got their day. The Buckeyes held Penn State to just two field goals and Kerry Collins was intercepted multiple times. The cylinders were not firing right on O or D. Ohio State finished the '93 season with just one loss. Tough players in 1993 were ready to play but with one year under their belts, they knew better how to get the job done. Fans such as me often forget that most players are between 17 and 23 years old. Some of us have kids that are way older than that!

Despite these two consecutive losses, in 1993 Penn State came back strongly and won-out the rest of their season. It was not a cake-walk. The season topping game was their close win in East Lansing, where they squeaked out the win against a stubborn Michigan State to take home the legendary Land Grant Trophy.

The Big Ten was really on to something when they designated Penn State and Michigan State as rivals, meaning they would duel it out annually to prove which land-grant school was bigger and tougher and of course, badder than the other.

This great game is worth discussing. Michigan State was ranked #25, and Penn State was sitting at the number #14 spot. Neither team was a contender. However, as we know, the honor is everything in college football.

On game day, the field of play was a disaster, and the team play on both sides of the colors reflected that. Michigan State nonetheless broke out of the pack with a 13-0 lead early on. Soon, Joe Paterno would send Mike Archie right up the middle (in true Paterno form) to put some points on the board.

Michigan State wasted no time to respond with another seven points, and this is pretty much how this game went for the rest of the second quarter. By halftime Penn State had slimmed that difference to a one-score deficit, 23-17. The Nittany Lions were just down by 6, and they seemed confident in their stride.

The Spartans turned to their strong passing game in the third quarter, and they increased their lead to 37-17. Some were asking, "Is the Nittany Lions' recent winning streak over?."

All of a sudden, or so it seemed, the Lions were alive and roaring again: Collins completed a 40 yard pass to Bobby Engram, and Penn State was ready to control the game. They got even more when the reliable Linebacker U defense recovered a fumble on Michigan State's 38. Collins drove the Nittany Lions down the field again, and with a Brian O'Neal touchdown, he made it a one score game.

The defense took over and forced a three and out, and gave the ball back to the PSU offense on its own 48. Collins faked a handoff and lofted a beautiful 52 yard pass to Engram (that's three touchdowns in about four minutes, if like me, you are keeping track).

The Spartan offense was inert for the remaining ten minutes and the PSU D helped the team big time to take that Land-Grant Trophy back to Happy Valley. It was a good year for Happy Valley as The Nittany Lions finished their first Big Ten season at the number three spot in the conference.

After the win in East Lansing in 1993, Penn State didn't lose a game until late September, 1995. Yes, folks, that means there were no losses in 1994—not a one. You'll read about it next.

The Nittany Lions put a beating on more than a few of the teams they faced in '94. They pounded #21 Ohio State when the Buckeyes traveled to Happy Valley. After they took a 35-

0 lead at halftime, Paterno played guys from all over the depth chart, and still managed to put 63 points on the board. On average, the Nittany Lions' scoring drives lasted less than two minutes each.

This offense was arguably one of the best in the history of college football. With a final score of 63-14 v the vaunted Ohio State Buckeyes, it was a game to treasure and a game future Ohio State teams would not forget.

Joe Paterno had been a hapless coach in convincing the NCAA and other powers that PSU was for real. His 1994 team was Paterno's fifth to go undefeated. Joe Pa had a bit less than half of his career left.

As Penn Staters it is OK that we toot our own horns while the rest of college football tries to turn off our lights. Penn State completed its 1994 season 12-0, number one in the Big Ten, and number two in the nation. But, again, this is not good enough for most who do not understand why 12-0 would not at least bring about a tie for the national championship.

When the university decides to claim some of these championships as other teams in the NCAA choose to do, I would expect that there will be a lot of writing after the asterisk.

Number two? Another all too familiar story for Penn Staters who can remember '94 (or have heard about it for as long as they can remember). As history would have it, Penn State was crushing Indiana when Paterno pulled his starters. The Hoosiers scored a couple late touchdowns to make the score look a whole lot closer than it actually was.

And then something happened that never ever happens: the voters dropped the ball Sunday morning. Based on the box score, Penn State appeared to have struggled with Indiana (there was no struggle involved). Nebraska, who beat #2

Colorado, was voted up to number one, and Penn State dropped to number two.

I guess we're more than twenty years too late for a college playoff that could bring about the respect and the glory with which the Penn State 1994 team should be acclaimed. So, if not in public, we surely can know it privately.

1994 Citrus Bowl

Penn State had a great 9-2 record going into the Bowl Season. The Lions were invited to the Citrus Bowl in Orlando Florida on January 1, 1994 at 1:00 PM (prime time New Year's Day) to play #6 Tennessee.

Penn State would not be denied the victory over this substantially higher ranked opponent W (31-13) before 72,456 plus the nationwide ABC TV audience. Nobody was more thrilled than I. Despite the outcome, it did not look good at first as the game began.

Tennessee got off to a great start at were ahead 10-0 after a quick 46 yard field goal and a 19-yard TD pass from Shuler to Cory Fleming. There were 72,000 singing Rocky Top and that was not the Nittany Lions favorite tune. At 10-0 but very early, it appeared the Vols might take it to the Lions with a big rout.

But with Kerry Collins calling the signals and Bobby Engram catching the pigskin when thrown to him, the Nittany Lions were about to roar. On second down from their own 36 yard line, Collins hit Engram on a wide receiver screen over the middle. Engram picked up a block and outran the defenders down to the Tennessee 29-yard line.

After the game, Engram had no problem noting: "That play set the tone...They saw we had some speed after all, and you could just see it in their eyes they weren't sure they could stop us." It was not long before PSU scored on a 3 yard TD run by Carter, who had been sitting out with a knee injury since the Illinois game. Carter was ready.

Tennessee came right back with an impressive drive down to the PSU 28-yard line where linebacker Tyoka Jackson got a tip on the ball in the air, and safety Lee Rubin intercepted it for the Lions at the 13-yard line. This was as close as Tennessee would come to the goal line for the rest of the day. The rout was on but it was not as originally thought. Penn State got hot and The Volunteers were cold.

Before the break-away, Craig Fayak hit a field goal to tie the game and UT responded with a 50-yarder of their own to take a 13-10 lead. With 1:08 to go in the half, Collins moved the ball down the field with a 12 yard draw play to Mike Archi. He then tossed an eighteen yarder to Engram. With 10 seconds to go at the UT 14 yard line, Penn State called their final timeout. Everyone expected Joe Paterno to elect for the field goal, but to their amazement the offense went back out on the field.

Tennessee sat back in pass defense expecting the Lions to take a shot at the end zone, but Paterno called a draw play to Carter instead. Carter broke a tackle at the line and sprinted into the end zone to give the Nittany Lions a 17-13 lead at halftime. The pundits felt that PSU had sent this message to the Volunteers with this play: "We can do anything we want to do, and there is nothing you can do to stop it."

Joe Paterno let it out at half time in the locker room: "Who do they think they are, telling us they need a better opponent,"

Paterno yelled out to a fully-tuned in team of Nittany Lions: "I'm tired of this Orange team! I'm tired of this Orange Stadium! I'm tired of seeing Orange! Let's go out there and kick the Orange out of them!" Coaches inspire teams.

Penn State did exactly that. The Lions took the second half kickoff and marched 60 yards, with Collins hitting Brady wide open in the end zone to make it 24-13. Engram later added a 15-yard TD catch, and the defense shut out the Vols. The tough PSU D sacked Shuler four times. The final score was Penn State 31, Tennessee 13.

This was one game that even the players felt the negative hype and it had irritated them. Perhaps it had even inspired them. When it was all over, Kerry Collins let it be known that the Penn State team was irritated by the lack of respect for Penn State in the pregame media coverage.

"We heard all week about Heath Shuler and everybody was underestimating us, "Collins said. "We thought all along that we were the better team. All we had to do was come out and prove it." Paterno himself felt obliged to add: "We never thought Tennessee was better than us."

1994 Penn State Football Season Coach Joe Paterno

The 1994 Penn State Nittany Lions football team was coached by Joe Paterno in his 29th year. Hard as it is to believe Penn State had another perfect record at 12-0. But, again, they were not national champions. Instead, they were bequeathed a # 2 ranking, and thus were denied another national championship. Life sometimes is not fair. Some say the reason PSU did not win the championship is that the Big Ten was not a respectable conference.

I don't buy that. I think there are dominating love-fests by the coaches and the AP and they feel a successful program such as Penn State does not need the benefit of the doubt. They were right to a degree but how about fairness? This is not the first time being cheated for Paterno nor for Penn State.

During the season, just two days after beating Ohio State, 63-14, -- yes, 64-13, Penn State University received 28 first-place votes in the Associated Press media poll and 32 first-place votes in the CNN/USA Today coaches' poll. They should have and did and they played flawless perfect ball the rest of the way.

Yet, somehow, two months later, after winning its final five games, Penn State got just 10 1/2 first-place votes in the AP poll and just eight first-place votes from the coaches. Meanwhile Nebraska got 51 1/2 first-place votes from the writers and 54 firsts from the coaches. What happened? Nebraska was declared #1 and Penn State got the runner up spot at #2. Nobody could tell Joe Paterno his team wasn't the 1994 national champions.

"Who said we didn't win a championship?" Paterno mused. "(A portion of) the media (and the coaches' panel) said we didn't win a championship. We think we won a championship. We did everything we could and we're going to assume we're champions. And that's not to take anything away from Nebraska.

"But I think this team did everything it could, and it's certainly a national-championship-caliber football team. We're going to assume that, that's all. We're going to treat ourselves as champions. I'm going to treat them as champions. And I know Penn State will treat them as champions."

Whatever Penn State Fans or Nebraska fans or anybody who watches a lot of football thought about the ranking situation, it did not matter. What was clear, however, was that the coaches and media members were too lazy to analyze all of the top teams in depth to help them form a proper conclusion. This surely was a reason to get rid of such a system. It had become a popularity contest.

Reality often does not matter when perception is the deciding factor in any difficulty. The perception at this time in 1994 for those with a sentimental affinity for Nebraska was that Nebraska had beaten Miami by one touchdown in the January 1995 Orange Bowl and that made them automatic national champions. It was as if Richard Nixon had made the proclamation again against Penn State.

This time, rather than president Nixon's exuberance with his buddies at a football game, it was a media-driven perception that negated anything Penn State might have done in the Rose Bowl or anything the Nittany Lions accomplished in their record-setting season.

Find me another team that played the likes of Penn State in a year other than 1994 and I will show you a national champion. It did not matter that Miami, ranked # 3 when they played Nebraska had lost to Washington, a team that had four losses.

Miami in 1994 was not what Miami once was. They were ranked #3. Oregon, Penn State's Rose Bowl foe was not what it once was either. But Miami is perceived as a football giant, while Oregon is looked on as a joke. However, Oregon defeated Washington, a team that had defeated Miami 21-7 but none of the pundits cared that Miami was no longer Miami!

There was no way Penn State could overcome that dichotomy of impressions. Facts were not permitted on the table. To this day, I wish the University put 1994 on the table as a national championship. The players and the coach earned it but the university went with the establishment.

Neither Penn State nor Nebraska played much of a non-conference schedule. Their conferences were supposed to be tough enough. Their best wins were over Southern California and UCLA, respectively. Who wants to make a bid on the better team USC or UCLA? Was the Big ten a tougher conference in which to excel or was the Big 8?

Which conference, the Big Ten or Big Eight, tasked a team more to excel in order to win? Did any of the coaches or the pundits in the AP after the season ended perform a real look-see? Or, perhaps they merely wanted to write their stories or share their opinions without doing real checking? Any rational analysis would suggest that, top to bottom, the Big Ten was much tougher than the Big 8 – hands down. Yet, it did not matter in the voting, but on mattered in the overall notion of a fair system.

Other than Colorado, which got to pound a beleaguered Notre Dame team in the Fiesta Bowl, the Big Eight was comprised of six stiffs. There was no excellence there.

The Conference's only other bowl teams, Kansas State and Oklahoma, lost their postseason games to Boston College and Brigham Young, respectively, by the combined score of 43-13. So, how good was the Big 8 in 1994 and why were they given so much preference over the Big Ten? Why did the Big Ten conference not fight harder to claim a win for PSU, a new member of their prestigious organization?

Conversely, the other Big Ten bowl teams - Michigan, Illinois, Wisconsin and Ohio State - were 3-1 in their bowls. Ohio State lost to Alabama, 24-17, in the final minute. The other three won their games by the combined score of 88-34. So, how could PSU, the Big Ten Champion, be shut out in 1994 in their finest season by a bunch of blowhards that seemed to like a great coach such as Tom Osborne more than a clear championship team coached by Joe Paterno? Say it ain't so, Joe!

1994 Games of the Season

All-Americans Bobby Engram (left) and Kerry Collins celebrate Penn State's thrilling 31-24 win at Michigan on October 15, 1994 in Penn State's first game in Ann Arbor. Engram and Collins were among five first-team All-Americans that led the Nittany Lions to Big Ten and Rose Bowl titles, becoming the first Big Ten team to finish 12-0.

On September 3 to open the season, #9 PSU played BTMinnesota at 8:00 PM at the Hubert H. Humphrey Metrodome, Minneapolis. It was not scheduled to be a blowout but it was nonetheless W (56–3).

On September 10 at 3:30 PM, a #8 ranked PSU beat #14 USC, a tough team always, at Beaver Stadium in University Park, PA. USC was never in the game. On September 17, BTIowa played #6 PSU at Beaver Stadium W (61–21). Then on September 24, at home, #5 ranked PSU shellacked Rutgers W (55–27) before 95,379.

On October 1, #4 PSU traveled to Franklin Field v Temple W (48–21). On October 15, playing #5 Michigan, a #3 ranked Nittany Lions team had its way with the Wolverines in a tough battle against a powerful Big Ten opponent at

Michigan Stadium, Ann Arbor, MI. W (31–24). The attendance was 106,382 in the Big House!

On October 29 at 3:30 PM. Penn State played a powerhouse of a team ranked at #21. Ohio State played the #1 ranked Nittany Lions at Beaver Stadium and in the biggest upset of a BTOhio State team ever, Penn State could not hold back in its leathering the Buckeyes on National TV W (63–14). OSU was not a bad team at all but PSU was that good.

PSU V OSU Oct 29 Right after Game Started

It is a sweet enough victory to repeat what happened. Penn State handed Ohio State its worst defeat in 48 years in what remains one of the most satisfying victories ever for Lion fans. The lopsided win by the No. 1 Nittany Lions over the No. 21 Buckeyes was impressive enough to write home about. However, it was not impressive enough to keep Penn State on top of the next AP poll. Penn State went on to win its first Big Ten Championship, becoming the conference's first 12-0 team, but as noted finished No. 2 in the final polls.

On November 5, somehow PSU was now # 2 in the game v BTIndiana at Memorial Stadium at Bloomington, IN. It was close but all Penn State W (35–29). Big Ten teams were tough to beat as PSU found out. On November 12 at Memorial Stadium in Champaign, IL, PSU beat the Fighting Illini W (35–31). On November 19, PSU defeated without a doubt the BTNorthwestern Wildcats at home W (45–17)

On November 26, Michigan State came to win at Beaver Stadium v #2 PSU at Beaver Stadium in University Park, PA. The Nittany Lions won decidedly W (59–31) in a high scoring game.

With an 11-0 record, Penn State was ready to win the Rose Bowl on January 2, 1995 to assure itself of a National Championship. The Nittany Lions had beaten every team that it had played and it had one game left, the Rose Bowl

Having won the Big Ten Championship in just its second year and nationally ranked for some reason at # 2 instead of # 1, already declared the Big Ten champion, PSU accepted the Rose Bowl offer to play Pac 10 leader #12 Oregon. Oregon was no worse or no better than Miami at the time but Oregon had three tough losses heading into the Bowl game. When the Rose Bowl was over in Pasadena California, shown on ABC and seen before 102,247 in attendance, Penn State had its way with Oregon W (38-20). Yet, the pundits were not swayed even a little.

This was such a great season, let's talk about it just a little bit more:

1994 Season Recap

On October 23, 2004, Derek Levarse writing for the PSU Collegian Student Newspaper asked us all to remember a great Paterno season from the past—1994. Penn State went undefeated yet this phenomenal season is not chalked up on any permanent record books as a national championship. In my research for this book, I have found the work of student journalists to be energetic, insightful, and darned interesting. I include this piece here. It would have been even more controversial if we had all read it after the bowl games in January 1995. It is so well written, I wish I had written it myself. Enjoy:

Title: "Remembering the glory days 10 years after Penn State's undefeated 1994 campaign"

The dream was already over, they said. Destiny, taken out of their hands the night before by an undefeated Nebraska team. NBC's Bob Costas had declared the Cornhuskers national champs and the bloom was off the Rose Bowl.

None of it mattered. Jan. 2, 1995, was to be a celebration for Penn State and no one -- not the 'Huskers, the pollsters, nor the Oregon Ducks standing across the line of scrimmage -- was going to stop it.

It's the first offensive play of the game for the Nittany Lions. First-and-10 from the Penn State 17 and Ki-Jana Carter is getting the ball. He has to.

Close your eyes and just listen. You're at home, in the crowd, on the sideline -- it's all the same. The Heisman Trophy runner-up has done this so many times this season that you don't need your eyes to tell you what's happening.

There's still a buzz in the Rose Bowl as Kerry Collins delivers the ball to his tailback. It slows to a murmur as Carter hits a hole that is quickly filled at the line of scrimmage by Ducks cornerback Herman O'Berry.

Then, an explosion.

The murmur becomes a full-fledged shout and you know, somehow, he's done it again. O'Berry is suddenly in the distance as the 5-foot-11 Carter has shed his tackle.

The receivers, Bobby Engram and Freddie Scott, seal off their men and the rest is involuntary. The shout is deafening now. Carter has hit the open field and the blue-and-white partisanship in Pasadena rises to its collective feet.

Oregon's vaunted Gang-Green defense can only watch as he streaks down the field without laying another hand on him.

This was 83 yards, 13 seconds, six points and one undefeated season that a group of guys wouldn't trade for anything in the world.

"I just wanted to get down that field as fast I could to celebrate with him," Engram said, still beaming about the play nearly 10 years later. "That was just an amazing play, coming in the Rose Bowl—that was the game we all grow up watching."

Two years before for Engram and the Lions, the Rose Bowl was the furthest thing from their minds. In 1992, Penn State's final season as an independent, the Lions finished what was then considered a mediocre season at 7-5.

Things would improve considerably for the '93 Lions who capped off a 10-2 season with a 31-13 thrashing of Tennessee in the Citrus Bowl.

But none, save perhaps the guys with no names on their jerseys themselves, could have foreseen the offense that the Lions would unleash upon the nation the following season.

It was Carter at tailback. Engram and Scott as the formidable duo at receiver. Kyle Brady, a 6-foot-6 All-American at tight end who could catch as well as he could block. An offensive line that featured two future long-term NFLers in guards Jeff Hartings and Marco Rivera.

And then there was Collins, the quarterback at the center of it all. This was not the prototypical Joe Paterno quarterback. Todd Blackledge and John Shaffer, whom the Penn State coach had under center for his two national championships, did not have the physical gifts of Collins.

Penn State's Kerry Collins—:"Lots more than just a quarterback."

"Obviously the quarterback is the leader, the focal point," Engram said. "Kerry, he's just a guy who made everything click. He made all of the good, tough throws, he was tough in the pocket and he was pretty much the leader."

It was a wealth of talent that came from two of the top-rated draft classes in the country at the time, and it all culminated in a 12-0 season that will forever be known as one of the greatest in school history.

It was a wholly unique experience, even for some of the most talented of the bunch who had never enjoyed the success this team would breed.

"No, not to that extent," Brady said. "It was brewing around there for years, though. The recruiting class behind mine was No. 1 in the country. And you know, sometimes that stuff doesn't always pan out. But that class turned out to be everything it was advertised as."

But why was it that this skilled group was able to come together? How much of it was pure talent and how much were the Penn State program and the coaching responsible for it?

The '94 team might have been fueled mainly by pure talent, but Brady doesn't think that things are so much different still.

"Like any team, it's all about consistency," Brady said. "There are talented guys on those teams, but it's just a matter of playing consistently, when they have the opportunity, they have to score. And I think that consistency is what's been missing for a few years now."

It's hard now, in the days when 7-5 would be a remarkable finish to the current season, to not wonder how large a gap in talent there is from 10 years ago. It's easy to lay blame on the coaching staff, but it certainly made the tough decisions in the past.

Like navigating around Paterno's self-proclaimed troika of starting running backs -- Carter, Mike Archie and Stephen Pitts.

Paterno stuck with Carter, who answered everyone's questions with a 181-yard, three-touchdown performance in the Lions' opening game rout of Minnesota, 56-3 at the Metrodome.

And the numbers only mounted as the Lions won their next four games by a total of 119 points. All of them were decided by the half, ensuring the starters wouldn't take on the typical wear and tear of Big Ten football as the Lions entered the meat of conference play.

"I got spoiled so bad by that team, we averaged 30-40 points a game," Brady said. "Then I got drafted and played for the Jets and I was like, 'What's going on?' In college, I was out of the game that year by the third quarter every game because we were beating the other team so badly."

Five dustings of inferior teams and a No. 3 ranking meant little, though. Still looking to prove themselves to the Big Ten, the Lions will tell you that there are three games that will forever stick in their minds as the most memorable, all for vastly different reasons.

A date in Ann Arbor with undefeated Michigan, a bizarre afternoon in Illinois and, of course, a trip to Pasadena and a controversy that would help change the face of college football forever.

Time froze and Engram's eyes went wide.

Here it was, right in front of him, coming at an unreasonable speed. Collins had thrown a bullet and it was aimed squarely for him. What took only a few seconds was a moment built up from a year before.

It was the middle of a bye week and 5-0 never felt so precarious. Historically, the Wolverines have had that effect on Penn State.

After all, it was Michigan that spoiled Penn State's Big Ten coming out party in '93 with an infamous goal line stand that helped the Wolverines steal a 21-13 victory in Beaver Stadium, ultimately keeping them from the conference title and the Rose Bowl.

Michigan was ranked No. 7 with a blemish on its record courtesy of a Kordell Stewart 65-yard Hail Mary to Michael Westbrook at the Big House earlier in the season.

This was not a squad to be taken lightly.

Paterno, fully aware of the offensive talent assembled on his squad, would frequently try to get into his players' heads before the season even started in preparation for a game like this. Anything to ready his squad for the rigors of the Big Ten and national gauntlets.

"He really put the hammer down on us as an offense," Brady said. "We as an offense were a lot of older guys, more mature, and we understood what he was doing. We developed a hand signal, where we'd make a circle with our fingers and we'd say, 'Nothing penetrates this circle. Nothing fazes us.' He was trying to put pressure on us like we'd face in a game."

Curiously though, there would be no head games this week. No rigorous practices, no screaming, just a quiet and confident Joe.

And if that didn't make all the difference on the Lions' final sustained drive, when Collins found himself staring down Engram.

Engram had cut inside of Michigan cornerback Chuck Winters, finding himself in single coverage after Archie pulled Winters' deep help by going in motion before the play.

Collins saw it, Engram hauled it in, and the Lions took a 31-24 lead on the Wolverines in the fourth quarter.

"Oh, it was a huge catch," Engram said. "I had a good day but it was an up and down day and we were able to come through and win it. That one's up there pretty high because of the simple fact it was in the last minute and it won the game for us."

History might show that Engram's touchdown grab was the one that silenced the Big House and its then-third highest crowd in college football history of 106,832. But it wasn't the nail in the coffin.

Engram's catch may have been the deciding points, but his memory is perhaps a little off. The score came with 2:53 remaining on the clock and a powerful maize and blue offensive machine needing 80 yards for the tying score.

Wolverine's running back Tyrone Wheatley quickly put the lump back in the throats of Lions fans after the kickoff as he rumbled through several tacklers and reached the 50-yard line.

And then there it was. One of Michigan's two star wideouts, Amani Toomer streaking open past safety Kim Herring as Todd Collins floated the pass to him. Toomer and his counterpart, the speedy Mercury Hayes, had been giving the Lions fits all game long. The future New York Giant Toomer had a knack for big plays and had already torched the Lions seven times for 157 yards and here came what was to be the biggest of them all.

But by some twist of fate, some cosmic force that seemingly watch over Nittany Nation this season, the ball fell just beyond the outstretched hands of Toomer. The would-be score hit the ground with a thud as morose as the groans in Michigan Stadium.

A sigh of relief for most on the visitors' sideline. For most.

"Relieved," Paterno would say after the game, "wouldn't be a word I would use."

Though the defense may have disappointed Paterno on the previous two plays, it came up huge afterwards. Tim Biakabutuka ran just short of the sticks on second down and was then dropped for a loss by linebacker Phil Yeboah-Kodie on third-and-short.

On fourth down just across midfield, Michigan coach Gary Moeller called for a pass. The Lions put pressure on Collins, however, and the pass went toward Hayes.

There was Lions cornerback Brian Miller. Arms outstretched as the ball seemingly fell in between both men.

Somehow, it was Miller who emerged with the football. The Penn State sideline and an entire town in central Pennsylvania erupted.

"Seeing him with the ball and knowing it was finally over," Engram said, his voice trailing as he put his memories and emotions into words. "Knowing it was all done, that all the hard work paid off ... it was better than I could have imagined."

The win earned the Lions a No. 1 ranking and an exorcising of demons from the previous year, but not a rest.

Despite a 63-14 homecoming annihilation of Ohio State the following week, a 35-29 win at unranked Indiana that was not as close as the score would indicate, dropped the Lions down to No. 2.

The stage was set for a Saturday that years later, players would simply call, "The Game," culminating (with apologies to John Elway) with "The Drive."

To think it all started with a guarantee.

Not from the undefeated Lions, but from Illinois coach Lou Tepper. The Fighting Illini were boasting one of the top defenses in the country heading into their matchup with Penn State, allowing just 11.3 points a game.

Tepper declared that if his offense could score 28 points against the Lions, his stingy defense would take care of the rest. Loudmouth Illini linebacker Dana Howard had been in this situation before, guaranteeing an upset over Ohio State earlier in the season.

"We haven't let anyone put up those kinds of points and yards and I don't think we will Saturday," Howard said in the week leading up to the game. "If they try to run, we'll smack them in the mouth."

The smack in the mouth came first, not on the field at Memorial Stadium, but the night before the game at the hotel. The one conveniently located next to Illinois' fraternity row. Noise was one thing. Staying on the sixth floor of the hotel, things weren't so bad for the Lions.

Prank calls in the middle of the night were another, especially to Collins' room. Coincidence? Several players at the time wondered aloud, A) how people got the number in the first place and B) how the hotel front desk let the calls go through.

Still, this was nothing entirely bizarre. As far as distracting the opposing team goes in the annals of collegiate pranks, just the calls could be written off for what it was.

But on game day, Saturday morning, the Area 51-esque conspiracy theories were out in full force.

The Lions woke up that day only to discover that the power in the hotel had gone out. What was at first a minor inconvenience -- no television, no lights -- quickly became a disaster that would have been funny, had it not been so tragic.

No electricity means no elevators. Some of the coaches and trainers happened to be placed several floors above the players, making it a long voyage just to get taped up. No electricity means no pregame meal. The large prepared banquet couldn't be cooked.

The end result of things was another hike down to the ground level and a meal that wasn't quite up to the Paterno standard.

"It was crazy," Engram said. "The power went out and the next thing you knew we had to move all of our stuff down and we had to order pizza, subs and chips and stuff. Next thing you know, we're in the game."

Not just in the game, but down 21-0 after a series of mishaps and turnovers on par with the events at the hotel. But the Lions pulled close with a Collins to Scott touchdown off of a fake reverse and would find themselves going into the half down 28-14.

Tepper had his 28 points. Would it be enough?

"The way we felt at halftime ... you know, we just said to the defense, 'Hold those guys and we'll win this game. You hold the score and we'll win this game,' Brady said: "We had so much confidence at half, as opposed to panic, there wasn't any of that. Just a confident assurance."

Confident enough that when they took the field late in the fourth quarter, trailing 31-28 and at their own 4-yard line, there still wasn't any question what the result would be.

"Ninety-six yards, guys," Collins told Engram and Brady in the huddle. "We're gonna go 96 yards."

Ki-Jana Carter breaks away v Illinois in crucial win to undefeated season

Inspired efforts from Collins, Engram, Brady and Carter on a crucial third-and-short at midfield led to this -- an Illini defense with no fight left in it and a handoff to fullback Brian Milne.

For the second time that day, Milne capped off a 95-plus-yard drive with a touchdown plunge. And a 35-31 victory that punched the Lions' ticket to the Rose Bowl.

But as impressive as the 18-point victory over the Ducks would be, it would be equally bittersweet. The dream matchup with Nebraska would never come to pass.

Oh, what could have been?

The postseason is improved these days, though perhaps not enough to the tastes of some on the '94 team. Ten years later and Penn State and Nebraska would have surely played each other for the national title thanks to the BCS system currently in place.

Instead, the Rose Bowl's conference affiliations mandated that the Big Ten champion Lions squared off against the Pac-10 champion Ducks. Meanwhile, the Cornhuskers drew No. 3 Miami in the Orange Bowl and won in dramatic fashion, 24-17. That pedigree was enough to give Tom Osborne's squad the title from both the writers and the coaches.

"Oh man, if only we could have found out," Brady said. "I've joked around with guys on that [Nebraska] team like Zach Wiegert and he's sure they would have knocked our blocks off and I'm sure we would've knocked their blocks off. It's a shame it didn't get to happen. We'd always say we'd meet them in a cornfield in Kansas somewhere just to play them."

Engram agreed.

"We tried everything we could," he said. "We didn't even need it to be televised, we just wanted to play and settle it all. Unfortunately, that wasn't in the plans."

That's pretty much the sentiment of the entire team. The fact that if the '94 season would have occurred 10 years later under the current BCS system doesn't ease the sting much.

Despite changes to the postseason since his collegiate days, Brady is still disgusted with the state of college football in general.

"The whole system is bringing shame upon college football," Brady said. "And I know that sounds like a strong statement, but that's how I feel."

Brady cited the 2000 season, when both Miami and Florida State were 10-1 at the end of the regular season -- the Seminoles' lone loss coming against the Hurricanes -- but Florida State was placed in the title game against undefeated Oklahoma by the BCS system.

"Where's the justice in that?" Brady said. "It's an ugly, ugly fact that it's all about the money and the university and bowl people filling their pockets. And it's so obvious that's what's happening that it discourages me from watching college football games sometimes.

"For the guys that played, pouring their hearts out and it might not happen, their dreams might not happen, just because some white-haired guys in an office are sitting around with smiles on their faces and filling their pockets. And it's at the expense of kids and their dreams."

Despite the still harsh realities of the system, the '94 season did as much to bring about change to college football as anything. It furthered an ageless controversy and ultimately would help bring about change.

Few undefeated teams in history -- whether they won a title or not -- can make that claim.

It's a testament to the team that Penn State isn't able to hold a 10th anniversary celebration for Homecoming against Iowa this weekend. Too many of the guys are still in the NFL.

There are plans for the spring though, a reunion of sorts to be held at April's Blue-White game. For most of the team, especially those still playing, keeping in touch has proven difficult, exchanging pleasantries on the field before games in the pros.

But 12-0 is 12-0.

"I still consider them all my friends, even if we don't stay in touch," Brady said. "This team has a special bond because of that season."

And no amount of time will take that away.

On behalf of myself and all PSU fans, I say PSU was & is # 1.

1995 Penn State Football Season Coach Joe Paterno

The 1995 Penn State Nittany Lions football team was coached by Joe Paterno in his thirtieth year as head coach. His PSU Nittany Lions had a great season at 9-3, and their record on the Big Ten was 5-3.

On September 9 v Texas Tech at Beaver Stadium, PSU beat the Red Raiders W 24–23. On September 16 at home PSU ranked # 7 at the time beat Temple in a mismatch W (66–14). Then, on September 23 @ 7:30 PM at Rutgers, played at Giants Stadium in East Rutherford, NJ # 6 PSU beat the Scarlet Knights W 59–34. Then, at the end of September (30), BTWisconsin tried to beat # 6 PSU at Beaver Stadium and succeeded in a close match L (9–1).

On October 7, #5 BTOhio State remembered how bad they were beaten in the prior year and the Buckeyes would have no more as they beat # 12 PSU at Beaver Stadium in a very close match L (25–28). On October 14, #20 PSU played BTPurdue in Ross–Ade Stadium • West Lafayette, IN, and squeaked out a win W (26-23). #18 Iowa was ready to take on # 19 PSU at Kinnick Stadium in Iowa City, IA but PSU won the game W (41–27) before 70,397. On October 28, Indiana played #16 PSU at Beaver Stadium and could not keep up, W (45–21)

On November 4, a good winning #6 BTNorthwestern team took on #12 PSU at Ryan Field in Evanston, IL, and PSU lost to the Wildcats on ABC L (10–21).

On November 18 at 12:00 PM, #12 Michigan planned to beat #19 PSU at Beaver Stadium in University Park, PA on ABC TV, yet PSU prevailed before 96,677 W (27–17).

The Snow Bowl v Michigan Pre-Cleanup

To many football historians who love Beaver Stadium games, this match is simply remembered as "The Snow Bowl." Three days before the game, a surprise 18-inch snowfall made it necessary to use hundreds of paid volunteers to clear the field. But with snow piles all around them, 80,000 freezing fans watched holder Joe Nastasi score a two-yard touchdown off a fake field goal with 2:40 left to secure the Lions' second of three consecutive victories over the tough Michigan Wolverines.

Michigan State came so quickly afterwards at Spartan Stadium, after a long ride that the Lions were ready and PSU beat the Spartans W (24-20).

Having such a good year, 8-3, #15 PSU got to play in the Outback Bowl on January 1, 1996 at 11:00 AM v #16 Auburn in Tampa Stadium •at Tampa, FL. Penn State was up for the match and won handily W (43–14(before 65,313. The Nittany Lions finished 9-3, #12 in the Coach's poll and #12 in the AP. Everybody was looking for 1996

Player Highlights Bobby Engram

We cannot discount in the same year of receivers, there was an Engram, Glenn, and Johnson who led their teams' potent offenses

Many of the facts from the article below are from David Comer, PSU Collegian Oct 28, 1995 (with poetic modifications)

Who is best, Bobby Engram, Keyshawn Johnson, or Terry Glenn?

Most of us, including yours truly would simply say Bobby Engram because he is from Penn State. But, for this one time in our lives, we would be 100% right for a lot of wrong reasons. It just had not been proven yet! This question was being asked continually in the football 1995 season.

Bobby Engram

One of these guys is from a small town in South Carolina. Another guy called the gang-infested South Central section of Los Angeles his home. And the third is a native of a college town in Ohio. So, who are they?

Bobby Engram, Keyshawn Johnson and Terry Glenn are from contrasting backgrounds and played college football in different regions of the country. But the trio is linked by the extraordinary abilities each one brought to the athletic table and then to the gridiron.

They make the spectacular catches look routine and after they have the ball, make defenders look foolish. They have been the best receivers in college football, and ironically, play at schools rich in tailback tradition -- Engram at Penn State, Johnson at Southern Cal and Glenn at Ohio State.

The pieces of this article for this pro—Penn State Book are regarding Bobby Engram, a PSU Great And so despite the greatness of Keyshawn, and Terry, Bobby is our focus guy right here, right now.

It's simple. When the Penn State offense needed a big play, Engram made it. He beat defensive backs deep with his speed or he would turn a simple five-yard catch into a 50-yard gain by using his strength to break tackles and elusiveness to make defenders miss. He was a team player who always had somebody else of the other side of the thrown ball.

In the season under the microscope, Engram had44 receptions for 814 yards and seven touchdowns (six receiving, another on a fumble recovery). Many of his catches seem to come while the No. 16 Penn State offense is struggling or needs a spark. He is just ready to come through and more importantly, does come through.

Bobby Engram has been mentioned in other areas of this book because you can't get away from the things he has done to make Penn State great. This area is for Bobby Engram, a guy who deserves a big thank you from the PSU fans like me. Thank you Bobby!

Engram also contributes to the Lion running attack. His downfield blocks help Lion tailbacks turn a routine carry into a big play, and with a successful running game, Engram knows he may see more man-to-man coverage from opposing secondaries.

"I like to block," said Engram. "I have no choice being at Penn State. It's part of the position. We have to go downfield and mix it up. It helps the running game, and I really enjoy it." But Engram is at his best when he has the ball. Bobby Engram made 52 grabs for 1,029 yards and seven touchdowns last season. He became the first Penn State receiver to eclipse 1,000 receiving yards in a year and he won the initial Biletnikoff Award as the nation's top receiver, because of course, he was the nation's top receiver.

"He is so intelligent, understands the game so much and is such a great competitor to go along with his wonderful instincts and wonderful athletic ability that it sets him off," Nittany Lions Coach Joe Paterno said. "He is willing to do anything it takes to get the job done. He will block, run the football and be a decoy. There is no ego involved with him. He wants to be in clutch situations." He loves the team and wants the team to win.

Engram thrives under pressure. He enjoyed a superb senior season and before it was over already held eight Penn State records, including most career receptions (148) and touchdown catches (27).

In the Lions' season-opening 24-23 win against Texas Tech, Bobby Engram, just a bloke on the line, made all seven of his catches in the second half for 106 yards, atoning for two fumbled punts earlier in the contest. During the Lions' 26-23 victory at Purdue Oct. 14, Engram set career highs with nine catches and 203 yards.

"Any time he gets his hands on the ball, he can make big plays happen," Lion quarterback Wally Richardson said. "He brings big-play capability to our offense."

Engram also gives the Nittany Lions offense a clutch receiver and a player who wants the ball in his hands in the fourth quarter of a close game. He has been the go-to-guy in the Penn State passing attack since he dazzled the Beaver Stadium crowd by catching a school record of four touchdown passes to lead Penn State to a 38-20 win to start the 1993 season. It was a successful return to the Penn State football program for Engram, who sat out the 1992 season for disciplinary reasons. JoePa said no to Bobby when Bobby was bad! Bobby won't be bad any more!

A positive person at all times try on this comment: "I looked at that game as my coming out party," Engram said. "I just wanted to get on that football field. I played my freshman year, but I didn't really play because I had so many things on my mind."

Engram had another important matter on his mind after his last season. Would he forgo his final year of eligibility and declare himself eligible for the 1995 NFL Draft or would he return to Penn State for an encore performance? The Camden, S.C., native decided the NFL could wait.

"Was I surprised he came back? No. We sat down and I tried to get the best information I could as to what would happen to him if he went into the draft," Paterno said. "A lot of them felt that if he stayed, he would be better off as far as how high he would be drafted and what his future would be in pro football.

"I told him exactly what I had heard and I said, 'It is up to you Bobby.' Bobby decided to stay. I think he made the right decision." Joe Paterno faced a lot of life decisions which he could not make but he made the right calls.
Opposing defenses wouldn't be happy and would not agree. They wished Engram were playing on Sunday afternoons instead of on Saturdays. Engram was that good!

Bobby Engram might not be picked as player on a sandlot team some would say. I am 5 foot 10 myself and I know how hard it was to play with guys who think they can control everything. I was not in Bobby Engram's league for sure but nobody controlled me either. Engram's lack of size, 5-foot-10, 187-pounds -- small by NFL standards – became the only question surrounding his professional football future. But Jim

Schwartz, a scout with the Cleveland Browns, thought in many ways it would benefit Engram.

"Some guys [he said] like (Eric) Metcalf use their lack of size to their advantage," Schwartz said. "They make people miss and use their agility. Engram is more in the mold of the old Dolphin receivers Mark Duper and Mark Clayton. He's shorter. He's a big-play guy. He runs after the catch. He's an exciting player."

Some for Johnson and Glenn said that "If they say Bobby Engram is the best college football receiver in America, then bring him on. We'll show him up."

But what he does best is catch the ball deep. It's what distinguishes him from Engram, Johnson and the other receivers in the country.

Only five receivers had won the Heisman Trophy since the award was first awarded in 1935, but Engram, Johnson and Glenn were all more than worthy of recognition.

Johnson came into the season surrounded by the most hype and has lived up to his billing since Sports Illustrated put him on the cover of its college football preview.

Engram was already considered the nation's best receiver and had a great reputation coming into the season, but has not been heavily considered for the award since the Lions lost two games in a row earlier this year.

As for Glenn, he is only the third most prominent player on Ohio State's offense, behind Hoying and George.

No college football highlights show is complete without a catch from Engram, Johnson or Glenn. At schools from coast to coast, the three receivers have been quietly spectacular, but not unheard. At Penn State, however, Bobby Engram rules!

Chapter 21 — The Joe Paterno Era From 1996 to 2011

Coach # 14

Year	Coach	Record	Conference
1996	Joe Paterno	11-2	(6-2 Big 10)
1997	Joe Paterno	9-3	(6-2 Big 10)
1998	Joe Paterno	9-3	(5-3 Big 10)
1999	Joe Paterno	10-3	(5-3 Big 10)
2000	Joe Paterno	5-7	(4-4 Big 10)
2001	Joe Paterno	5-6	(4-4 Big 10)
2002	Joe Paterno	9-4	(5-3 Big 10)
2003	Joe Paterno	3-9	(1-7 Big 10)
2004	Joe Paterno	4-7	(2-6 Big 10)
2005	Joe Paterno	11-1	(7-1 Big 10)
2006	Joe Paterno	9-4	(5-3 Big 10)
2007	Joe Paterno	9-4	(4-4 Big 10)
2008	Joe Paterno	11-2	(7-1 Big 10)
2009	Joe Paterno	11-2	(6-2 Big 10)
2010	Joe Paterno	7-5	(4-3 Big 10)
2011	Joe Paterno	8-1	(5-0 Big 10)
2011	Tom Bradley	1-3	(1-2 Big 10)

JoePa Coached 45 great seasons 1966 to 2010 & part of 2011. This 15-year period, we find some of JoePa's Worst but mostly his best. Nobody could mke the tean be a contender as well as Joe Paterno!

The overall record was 11-2, (6-2 in the Big Ten). Their record included a nice win against Texas in the Fiesta Bowl

W (38-15). Penn State finished in the top ten in both polls at # 7.

1996 Penn State Football Season Coach Joe Paterno

The 1996 Penn State Nittany Lions football team was coached by Joe Paterno in his thirty-first year. Penn STtae had another great winning season with just a few disappointing games.

The 1996 season was also notable as it marked the end of ties in college football, as an overtime system was put into place across all of Division I-A. Penn State's first OT game came in 2000 v Iowa. The 1995 season had overtime rules, but only for postseason games.

The Bowl Alliance was formed to make post-season championships fairer but it did not really work well and over time the current BCS plan was adopted. For example, in 1996, there was a large controversy when #5 BYU was robbed of a spot in a Bowl Alliance game, as they were snubbed in favor of lower ranked teams from Bowl Alliance conferences. Believe it or not Congress got involved.

The Nittany Lions faced off against USC in the Kickoff Classic on August 25 before 77,716 at Giants Stadium in East Rutherford, NJ. PSU won the match W 24-7).

Player Highlights Curtis Enis

They called it Curtis Enis' coming-out party came when, in East Rutherford, NJ, the powerful sophomore tailback racked up 241 yards and three touchdowns on 27 carries in his first career start. The Trojans didn't score until pouncing on a fumble in the end zone in the final 30 seconds of the game. On November. 4: 1996, in his first try, Curtis Enis lifted #11 PSU over #7 Southern Cal by a score of 24-7. It was just his start of his college career.

As PSU's main running back while he played for the Lions from '95 to '97, Curtis Enis chalked up two 1,000+ yard seasons, including 1,369 yards and 19 TDs in 1997. He was 6th in Heisman Trophy voting in 1997. He was the 5th overall pick of the 1998 NFL Draft, though he played just 3 years in the NFL, retiring after the 2000 season because of knee problems. His best NFL season was 1999. He was a star. He rushed for 916 yards and 3 TDs.

Enis chose to Penn State after a standout career at Mississinawa Valley High School in Ohio. He had made Parade All-American and Ohio's Mr. Football (state's best player). Going to college was not easy for Curtis had a lot of good times in HS being so naturally talented. He would have to work in college to do so well with Joe Paterno.

Enis was not attentive to high school requirements. Coach Paterno made him attend The Kiski School in rural Pennsylvania for a year before enrolling at Penn State. At The Kiski School, Enis was able to work with Enis to get his grades and SAT score he needed to qualify.

Ironically, many Ohio State fans were upset that he chose to leave the state to attend college. There is some humor in how Ohio recruited Enis. The OSU recruiting computer had a few typos for example, and when they sent him a letter it was addressed to "Curtis Phenis." When they fixed the last name, they changed his first name to Chris. It has been reported that when Enis took a visit to Ohio State's campus, no one seemed to know who he was.

Enis was a standout player at Penn State for sure. With 3 seasons and two 1000 yarders, he was more than special. He was 6'0" and weighed a muscular 235 lbs. They say he was quite a load at running back. He earned All-American honors his junior year at Penn State and finished 6th in voting for the 1997 Heisman Trophy. He decided to leave school after that season and enter the 1998 NFL Draft, where he was selected 5th overall by the Bears. He was that impressive.

He gained 1,497 yards in his career and scoring only 4 touchdowns. The Bears released him after the 2000 season and he chose to retire, citing knee problems stemming from a 1998 ACL injury.

After the Kickoff Classic it was back to every day games. On September 7, in the home opener, a # 7 ranked PSU defeated Louisville at Beaver Stadium W (24-7). In another home game on September 14, Northern Illinois came to Beaver Stadium for the first time and were shut out in a blowout by the Nittany Lions W (49-0). On September 21, PSU beat Temple at Giants Stadium W (41-0) in a shutout.

On September 28, #3 PSU defeated Wisconsin in a close Big Ten match at Camp Randall Stadium in Madison, WI W(23-20). On October 5, #4 PSU lost to a very tough #3 Ohio State Team coached by John Cooper at Ohio Stadium in Columbus, OH before 94,241 L (7-38). This was followed on October 12 with a win against Purdue at Beaver Stadium W (31-14). An unranked Iowa team beat Penn State the following week on October 19 in a nailbiter match at Beaver Stadium L (20-21)

On October 26, The #17 Nittany Lions traveled to Memorial Stadium in Bloomington IN, to beat Indiana   W (48–26). The next week, November 2, at home, #15 PSU beat #11 Northwestern W34–9) before 96,596. On November 16, the #11 Nittany Lions traveled beat #16 Michigan at the Big House, Michigan Stadium in Ann Arbor, MI W (29-17). This victory followed the very next week at home by another against another Michigan team, Michigan State in a close call win W (32-29).

At 10-2, #7 ranked PSU had a great year and were invited to play on January 1, 1997 at 8:00 PM   vs. #20 Texas in Sun Devil Stadium, Tempe, AZ, in the Fiesta Bowl. The attendance of 65,106 saw the Nittany Lions beat the Longhorns W (38–15).

1997 Penn State Football Season Coach Joe Paterno

The 1997 Penn State Nittany Lions football team was coached by Joe Paterno in his 32nd year. Penn State had a respectable season overall at 9-3 (6-2 in the Big Ten). The Nittany Lions were ranked #17 by the Coaches and #16 by the AP. Their season was capped off by being invited to the Citrus Bowl in Orlando but on January 1, 1998, the #11 Lions were beaten in this game by #6 ranked Florida L (6-21).

The home season began on September 6 as #1 ranked PSU defeated Pittsburgh W (34–17) before 97,115. On September 13, PSU beat Temple at home W (52-10). On September 20, still ranked at #1, the Nittany Lions beat Louisville at Cardinal Stadium in Louisville, KYW 57–21. After this convincing win, PSU fell to #2 in the rankings as they prepared to face Illinois in Champagne on October 4. The #2 Nittany Lions beat the Fighting Illini W (41-6) to hold second place.

The real big test of the season was next as a tough Ohio State team came to Beaver Stadium on October 11, and were beaten back by the Lions W (31-27). Now, back at #1, Penn State barely beat Minnesota on October 18 W (16-15). The closeness of this game put PSU in 2nd place as the Nittany Lions played at Northwestern and beat the Wildcats in a tug of war W (30-27).

Still ranked #2 with a 7-0 record, PSU faced #4 Michigan on November 8, and were beaten by the Wolverines L (8-34). Then at #6, on November 15, PSU played #19 Purdue at Ross-Ade Stadium and beat the Boilermakers W (42-7). The Nittany Lions followed this win with another on November 22 at home against #24 Wisconsin W (35-10). Then, it was off to East Lansing, Michigan on November 29 to lose to the unranked Spartans of Michigan State in a blow-out L (14-49).

Not having recovered from the two late season crippling losses, #11 Penn State lost the Citrus Bowl to # 6 ranked Florida L (6-21).

1998 Penn State Football Season Coach Joe Paterno

The 1998 Penn State Nittany Lions football team was coached by Joe Paterno in his 33rd year. Penn State had another very respectable season overall at 9-3 (5-3 in the Big Ten). The Nittany Lions were ranked #15 by the Coaches and #17 by the AP. Their season was capped off by being invited to the Outback Bowl on January 1, 1999 in Raymond James Stadium in Tampa Florida where they beat #22 Kentucky W (26-14).

On September 5, #13 ranked Penn State played #21 Southern Miss at home and defeated the Golden Eagles W (34-6). On September 12 at home, the #9 Nittany Lions ran roughshod over Bowling Green W (48-3). On September 19, #8 PSU beat Pittsburgh next at Pitt Stadium W (20-13). After Pittsburgh the Big Ten Games began in force with #7 Ohio State first in waiting to play in Columbus. The Buckeyes played at their peak game and beat a 3-0 PSU L (9-28) before 93,479. Only Penn State and Ohio and Michigan had such huge stadiums.

On October 10 The # 13 ranked Lions flew out to the Hubert H. Humphrey Metrodome to beat a tough Minneapolis team W (27-17). Back at home the next week On October 17, PSU beat Purdie W (31-13).

On October 31, at Beaver Stadium, the Nittany Lions pitched a shutout against Illinois W (27-0). This game is known for Lavar's leap. If there is one single, memorable but isolated moment frozen in time it was LaVar Arrington's leap over the Illinois offensive line the instant the ball was snapped, tackling the runner in the backfield the millisecond the quarterback gave him the ball. That moment early in the third quarter when the score was already 21-0, had absolutely no impact on the game or the season but it will be forever known as "LaVar's Leap."

Lavar Arrington's Leap was more substance than faith

Always tough at home or away, Michigan was next on November 7 and they beat the Lions in a shutout L (0-27) at the Big House in Ann Arbor Michigan before a massive crowd of 111,019.

On November 14, an always scrappy Northwestern team were beaten by #19 Penn State at Beaver Stadium before an overflow crowd of 96,382. Then a week later on November 21 at #13 Wisconsin, the #15 Nittany Lions avoided a shutout but lost L (3-24). In a late season game v Michigan State at home, #23 ranked PSU dominated the shootout W (51-28). Overall, the #22 ranked PSU team was 8-3 and qualified to play unranked Kentucky in the Outback Bowl, winning the contest W (26-14)

1999 Penn State Football Season Coach Joe Paterno

The 1999 Penn State Nittany Lions football team was coached by Joe Paterno in his thirty-fourth year. This year the Nittany Lions had a nice 10-3 record (5-3 in the Big Ten), ranked # 11 in both polls. Their record was fine enough for a bowl game and they beat Texas A&M on December 28 in the Alamo Bowl in Texas W (24-0).

Lavar Arrington a Great PSU Linebacker

Penn State Collegian, the Student Newspaper says all that needs to be said about the great football work of LaVar Arrington, one of The Lions best linebackers of all time. There is surely lots more that can be said as Arrington is one of the greatest Linebackers from PSU. In his write-up in the Collegian author Anthony Picardi got a great perspective on Arrington's football playing days with Penn State University: Enjoy!

Being a great linebacker was a big deal at Penn State but the University sure had its share.

LaVar Arrington was born in Pittsburgh, Pennsylvania. He played linebacker and running back at North Hills Senior High School in Pittsburgh. He was always a standout. After his senior year, he was awarded the 1996 Parade National Player of the Year, the Bobby Dodd National Offensive Player of the Year, the Gatorade Player of the Year and USA Today Pennsylvania Player of the Year.

He became the second player in Pennsylvania Class 4-A history to rush for more than 4,000 career yards. Yes, he was a running back. Before Arrington, PSU was breeding linebackers so it is not a phenomenon that the coaches picked Arrington out of the crowd to make him an outside linebacker. They bred another great player. Here is the Collegian article by Anthony Picardi in italics below:

As the 1980s approached, Penn State had passed the torch to seven All-American linebackers.

In 1982, the torch fell to Shane Conlan, and he carried it to multiple national championships. When the 1980s title teams aired on

television and radio, a future All-American linebacker watched, listened and prepared to make the leap.
Seeing gold

Striding down field while holding the football firmly against his heart and shielding defensive attackers with his right arm, the bronze statuette elevates collegiate players into an elite club.

The Heisman Trophy winner was outstanding in 1982-83, rushing for 1,752 yards, breaking the goal line 17 times and carrying Georgia to a Sugar Bowl showdown against Penn State.

When Herschel Walker stepped onto the turf at the Louisiana Superdome, he used stiff arms to fend off Nittany Lions' defenders for 103 yards and a touchdown. But as the clock flashed 0:00, the scoreboard read "Penn State 27, Georgia 23."

Celebrating the Sugar Bowl victory and national championship on the Penn State sideline was a part-time starter at linebacker, who would become the first two-time All-American at the position since Dennis Onkotz.

During Conlan's collegiate career, the football program underwent a growing period. Beaver Stadium's capacity rose by almost 30,000, and lights illuminated the field for the Penn State faithful.

As Conlan progressed, so did the Penn State defense. And in his senior campaign, Conlan and the Lions were on the verge of another national championship.

Miami marched into the 1987 Fiesta Bowl sporting military fatigues, and Heisman-winning quarterback Vinny Testaverde highlighted the Hurricanes' offense.

As the "Duel in the Desert" heated up, Penn State shut down the Hurricanes. Mirroring the 1970 Orange Bowl when it intercepted seven passes, the Lions' defense dictated the 1987 Fiesta Bowl. And like Onkotz did in 1970, Conlan snagged two interceptions.

With 18 seconds remaining in the game, the Hurricanes had their final chance to overcome a 14-10 deficit. On fourth-and-goal, Testaverde dropped back to pass and had his eyes glued on the end zone. After he released the football toward the goal line, it landed in the hands of inside linebacker Pete Giftopoulos.

Testaverde threw 26 touchdown passes during the 1986-87 season, but he failed to find the end zone once at Sun Devil Stadium, and the Lions intercepted the future first-overall NFL draft pick five times.

As Conlan and Penn State celebrated their second national championship, the Keystone State rejoiced. And the blue and white caught the attention of a Pittsburgh-area football player.

Over the line

On Halloween day of 1998, LaVar Arrington leapt his way onto the highlight reel. Trailing Penn State and stringing together its best drive of the game, Illinois faced fourth-and-inches in Penn State territory. The Fighting Illini kept their offense on the field and rushed to the line.

"Based off the film reviews we had on them, I figured if they ran up to the ball, they were going on a quick count," Arrington said. "In my mind I said 'I'm going through the [center of the offensive line], and I'm going to hit the quarterback before he has a chance to get the first down.'"

Penn State linebacker LaVar Arrington takes a flying leap at Illinois quarterback Kirk Johnson. Collegian File Photo

Anticipating the snap count, Arrington bolted toward the line. At the snap, he took to the air, soaring over defensive and offensive linemen. Once Illinois' Elmer Hickman received the handoff, Arrington descended and brought the fullback with him to the ground.

"It's a classic situation when preparation meets opportunity," Arrington said. "I was prepared. I felt confident about what they were going to do based off of the tendencies that I studied on film review."

Following the footsteps

Penn State's third two-time All-American linebacker revered the Lions' 1980s teams. And as Conlan and D.J. Dozier were awarded

MVP honors of the 1987 Fiesta Bowl, it was the running back that he especially relished.

At North Hills High School, Arrington played both sides of the ball. Offensively, he followed in the footsteps of Dozier, and rushed for more than 4,000 yards in his high school career.

"If you can play linebacker from a running back's perspective, then I think you're ahead of the game," Arrington said.

Linebackers watch how blocks develop along the offensive line during run plays and feel their way to the ball carrier. As Arrington became accustomed to weaving his way through these holes as a running back, it improved his awareness as a defensive player.

When the high school Parade National Player of the Year arrived on campus in 1997, the coaching staff originally placed the athlete at safety. As Arrington showed a nose for the football and charged the line of scrimmage in practice, he moved to a new position.

Playing outside linebacker, Arrington teamed with All-American middle linebacker Brandon Short to form one of the most intimidating duos in collegiate football. And when they locked eyes with future Super Bowl-winning quarterbacks Tom Brady and Drew Brees during games, Arrington and Short were ready to lead the Penn State defense.

"We played against some very talented players," Arrington said. "You need to have more belief in what you're able to do and how you're going to dictate to them versus preparing how they're going to dictate to you."

Before game day, Arrington and the Penn State defense studied tendencies and identified opposing playmakers. No music played during practices. Instead, the thuds of shoulder pads sounded as players improved their craft. Once it was game time, No. 11 flew to the ball.

LaVar vs. Na'il

The Bednarik Award winner formed a rivalry against another Big Ten foe. When the Lions hosted Ohio State in 1999, Arrington and counterpart Na'il Diggs traded big plays and pounding hits.

"It was friendly between [Diggs and I]," Arrington said. "He was making the plays first, so he'd look over at me almost like 'I'm giving you the floor.' Then he'd run off and I started making plays. I looked at him, started laughing and put my hand up like, 'C'mon, c'mon, your turn.'"

LaVar Arrington hits Steve Bellesari Collegian File Photo

At the start of the second quarter, the floor belonged to Arrington. During one play, the outside linebacker came free off the edge. The only thing that stood between the Butkus Award winner and quarterback Steve Bellisari was the Ohio State running back. And once Arrington hurdled Jonathan Wells, he tossed Bellisari to the ground to complete the sack.

Penn State defeated Diggs and the Buckeyes, 23-10.

Arrington said no matter how talented another team's linebackers might be, "Linebacker U" will always belong to Penn State because that is where it was created. Similarly how no one could take "The U" away from Miami, nobody can strip "Linebacker U" away from Happy Valley.

Leaving a legacy

When Arrington played, fans filled the lower bowl and the second deck at Beaver Stadium to watch. But in the crowd of more than 90,000 people, a couple of loved ones stood out for the future No. 2 overall NFL draft pick.

"I would locate [my parents] before the game during warm ups," Arrington said. "As soon as we got to the sideline, I would locate my parents again. No matter where the game was, my mother, my father and I had a pregame ritual. I would always locate them and we would do our ritual, and then I knew it was time to play, like I knew it was OK."

In his final game as a Lion, Arrington was named Defensive MVP of the Alamo Bowl. He recorded 72 tackles, including 20 tackles for loss and nine sacks in his final collegiate season.

"I think the one component that makes every linebacker from Penn State is our desire to be everything we could possibly be," Arrington said. "I think it's our ability to lead but also be led. It's ultimately an innate sense of team and understanding of what we represent to our team."

The 1999 Games of the Season

PSU was invited to the Pigskin Classic and so #3 ranked Penn State began its season on August 28 at Beaver Stadium against #4 ranked Arizona. The Lions controlled the game and got the win W (41-7) before 97,168. On September 4, Akron took a try at the # 2 Lions at Beaver Stadium. PSU won in a high scoring game W (70-24).

Pittsburgh then played the #2 ranked Nittany Lions on September 11 at Beaver Stadium and Penn State won its third in a row W (20-17) to start the season. PSU then traveled to Miami before the summer was over to play the Hurricanes in the Orange Bowl. The Nittany Lions beat #8 Miami in a very close game W (27-23) and were now at 4 wins no losses for the season ranked at #2.

The Big Ten games began with Indiana on September 25 at home W 45-24). Next, on October 9 after a bye week was Iowa in Kinnick Stadium, Iowa City. Penn State triumphed again bring the season record to 6-0, and holding on to 2nd place. PSU played Purdue next on October 30 at Ross–Ade Stadium in West Lafayette, IN and won again W (31-25).

It was a very good year and the next week's game on October 30 at Illinois in Memorial Stadium • Champaign, IL, would add to #2 PSU's wins with a W (27-7) victory over the Fighting Illini. This was a special game, especially because of the hard play of Defensive End Courtney Brown which was simply outstanding.

For the third time in the last four weeks, a Nittany Lion—this time Courtney Brown—has been selected Big Ten Defensive Player of the Week, with defensive end. Courtney Brown earning the honor on October 30, 1999.

Brown was honored for his outstanding play in Penn State's 27-7 win at Illinois. The senior from Alvin, S.C. once again was sensational, surpassing his career-high with four sacks for minus-25 yards to become the school career leader with 32 sacks. Larry Kubin tallied 30 from 1977-80. A semifinalist for the Lombardi Award and a candidate for the Bronko Nagurski Trophy and Chuck Bednarik Award, Brown made eight tackles, second-highest of his career, forced a fumble and broke up a pass vs. the Illini.

A pre-season All-American, Brown has earned Big Ten Defensive honors four times in his career. A Penn Stater has earned the Conference's defensive honor five of the 10 weeks this season.

The Nittany Lion defense has been ferocious the last four weeks, including 24 sacks, with Brown one of the primary reasons for the unit's success. Against Illinois, Penn State allowed a touchdown, 113 yards and six first downs in the first quarter, but then virtually shut down the hosts, permitting only 135 yards, no points and six first downs over the final three quarters. The Illini gained 248 total yards and were 8 of 31 passing for 107 yards. In the second period, UI gained five yards on 12 plays and did not have a first down and in the third stanza, Illinois gained 29 yards on its first five possessions while the Lions were scoring 17 points to take a 24-7 lead.

The Lions recorded seven sacks for minus-42 yards vs. Illinois, second-highest of the season, and forced 13 punts, most for an opponent since Cincinnati had 13 in 1988. Ten of Illinois" 17 possessions ended in three plays and three others lasted only five. Following the Illini's first quarter touchdown, Penn State forced punts on 10 consecutive possessions.

This season, before the Illinois game, Brown had 37 stops, leading the Big Ten with 21 TFL (minus-119), 14 sacks (minus-97) and the team with his three forced fumbles. He needed just three more TFL to break the school single season record of 23 he then shared with Kubin. His four TFL vs. the Illini moved him into seventh place on the Big Ten career TFL chart with 62, needing five more to crack the top five. He got what he needed

Brown is one of the quietest greatest stars ever in defensive football. His career total of 33 sacks is also a Penn State record. That is impressive enough, but his tackles for loss mark that he got later this season indicates that the powerful defensive end was just as dominant against the run as he was against the pass -- which, quite frankly, the quiet star from South Carolina was for the Nittany Lions.

Only one college player in the last 11 years -- former Buffalo star Khalil Mack -- has compiled more career tackles for loss. Penn State's had some dynamic defenders over the years but Brown took playmaking to another level.

Against Purdue on October 23, the former Macedonia HS All-American added two more entries into his impressive resume by grabbing his first career interception and returning it 25 yards for his first collegiate score. The interception TD was the first for a PSU defensive lineman since Chris Mazyck did so against Ohio State in 1994.

Following the Purdue game, Brown received a ringing endorsement from Joe Paterno: "Courtney Brown is a great football player. I don't like to plug kids, but if he doesn't get the Lombardi Award there's something wrong with somebody."

The Rest of the 1999 Season

Penn State (9-0, 5-0) was ranked No. 2 and hosted Minnesota (5-3, 2-3) the following Saturday at 12:10 p.m. EST in an espn2 national telecast.

At eight and zero, Penn State was thinking championship but when Minnesota came to Penn State on November 6, the Gophers were thinking upset and they got it L (23-24) #16 Michigan added to #6 PSU's woes the following week at home in another close match L (27-31) Just five points separated PSU from an undefeated season at this point. Michigan State took the *special* out of this otherwise great season when it defeated the Lions at Spartan Stadium L (28-35) before 74,231.

#13 PSU was ready to play in the Alamo dome v #18 Texas A&M in the Alamo Bowl on December 28, and they won the game easily also made the season. It sure was not a bad season. In fact it was a very good season but with all the losses v Big Ten teams, PSU not only missed the National Championship but also the Big Ten Championship despite its fine (10-3) record (5-3 v Big Ten Conference teams).

Player Highlights Courtney Brown

All-American Selection: 1999

Courtney Brown was not your basic defensive end. He was a star player for Penn State. Hailing from Alvin, SC, Brown was an All American selection in 1999. He was selected by the Associated Press, Football Coaches, Football Writers, Walter Camp, The Sporting News and The Football News. He also was a finalist for the Bronko Nagurski Trophy, Rotary Lombardi Award and Chuck Bednarik Award. He was one powerful football player.

Brown shattered PSU long-time records for career tackles for loss (70) and sacks (33) and the season mark for team tackles for a loss TFL (29). He played three years as a starting DE. Most players in the Paterno system used their first year as a redshirt year for learning football. He was tied for third in Big Ten career TFL and was named 1999 Big Ten Defensive Player-of-the-Year.

He was the fourth Nittany Lion selected All-Big Ten three times, he finished his brilliant career by earning the Hall Foundation Award as the team's Senior MVP. He made 55 tackles (33 solo), with 29 TFL (minus-150), 13.5 sacks (minus-107), an interception (TD) and three forced fumbles.

At the Penn State pro day Brown measured 6'4⅞" 271-pounds; ran a 4.52 seconds forty-yard dash; had a vertical leap of 37" and bench-pressed 225 pounds 26 times. Brown was selected by the Cleveland Browns as their first overall pick of the 2000 National Football League Draft, making him the eleventh defensive lineman to be taken first overall in the 70-plus year history of the NFL Draft. He has played with the Browns (2000-04); the Denver Broncos (2005-06); and he signed with San Diego prior to the 2007 season.

Brown had a productive pro rookie season, recording 69 total tackles and 4.5 sacks. His second season was cut short due to injury, but Brown recorded 4.5 sacks in 5 games. Brown had problems staying healthy for the rest of his career, and struggled on the field because of injuries. From 2002-2004, Brown only played in 26 games and recorded just 8 sacks. He finished his professional football career with the Broncos in 2005. Brown lives in St. Stephen, S.C.

Player Highlights Brandon Short

Brandon Short was a great middle linebacker, from the PSU football class of 1999. The McKeesport, Pa football great was and All America Selection by the Associated Press, Football Writers and Walter Camp. He also was chosen a second-team All-American by The Sporting News and third-team by The Football News. Short was a finalist for the Butkus Award as the nation's top linebacker, he and LaVar Arrington were the first teammates to be finalists for the honor.

Chosen a team co-captain prior to the season, Short was a four-year starter and two-time first-team All-Big Ten pick. He concluded his superlative career second on the school's career tackles for loss list with 51, the 17th-best total in Big Ten annals. He also was sixth on the school career tackles list with 273.

He is just the 12th Nittany Lion to crack 100 tackles in a season with 10 or more stops six times in '99. Short led the Lions with 103 tackles (62 solo), including 12 TFL, four sacks, three pass breakups, a fumble recovery, an interception and a blocked kick. He was the North squad's Defensive MVP in the Senior Bowl.

Short was selected by the New York Giants in the fourth round of the 2000 National League Draft and played with the Giants (2000-03) and the Carolina Panthers in (2004-05). Short played 5 seasons for the New York Giants and two for the Carolina Panthers and then he re-signed with the Giants in 2006.

In his rookie year saw action in 11 regular season games and was inactive for five games because of an ankle injury. He appeared in all three of the Giants postseason contest, including Super Bowl XXXV.

Short unfortunately was involved in a 2002 training camp cafeteria fistfight with teammate Jeremy Shockey. The two players brawled after Shockey, a rookie, refused to sing his college fight song—a training camp hazing ritual.

Short made the news again after he broke New York Jets quarterback Chad Pennington's wrist during a tackle in the 2003 Giants-Jets preseason game. Pennington would miss the first six games of the 2003 season.

Short signed as a free agent with the Carolina Panthers in 2004, and appeared in all 32 games at strong side linebacker with Carolina in 2004 and 2005. He tallied 70 tackles and helped the Panther's defense collect 38 take-aways, which tied a team record. He returned to the New York Giants in April 2006, signing as a free agent.

Short spent time as an NFL analyst for Daily News Live, a current T.V. show with NY media panels who analyze NY sports on the SNY Network in NYC. He earned his MBA from Columbia Business School in 2010, and began working for Goldman Sachs that year. He moved to the firm's Dubai unit in 2012.

He left Goldman Sachs in April 2013 to co-found World Business Partners UAE, a Middle East lender specializing in loans for small- and medium-sized companies which comply with Islam's ban on interest, along with the religion's bans on investments in alcohol, firearms, and other products.

2000 Penn State Football Season Coach Joe Paterno

The 2000 Penn State Nittany Lions football team's head coach was Joe Paterno. This was another one of those building years (5-7 with 4-4 in the Big Ten). It was just the second losing season for Coach Peterno in his 35-year stint so far at Penn State. Long time defensive coordinator Jerry Sandusky retired before the season began and he was replaced by Defensive coach Tom Bradley.

Penn State, ranked #15 to begin the season agreed to be in the annual Kickoff Classic held at Giants Stadium on August 2th. The Opponent was #22 USC. The Nittany Lions lost the game L (5-29). PSU would lose to Toledo the following Saturday, September 2 at home L (6-24). It took 'til the third win to get a win and it was at home against Louisiana Tech as PSU prevailed in a blow-out 67-7. After two weeks of losses the win felt pretty good. The good feeling would not last long as PSU traveled to Pittsburgh's Three River Stadium and were beaten by the Panthers on September 16 L (0-12).

Unranked and playing with a at 1-3 record, Penn State faced off with Ohio State on September 23 in Columbus. The Buckeyes dominated the Nittany Lions L (6-45). Purdue, a tough team in its own right came to Beaver Stadium on September 30, and lost to the Nittany Lions in a close match W (22-20). On October 7, PSU traveled to the Hubert H. Humphrey Metrodome in Minneapolis, MN and were beaten by the Gophers L (16-25). The Fighting Illini were next at home on October 21, and PSU collected a win against Illinois W (39-25).

On October 28 at 7:00 PM at Indiana, PSU played a close game and beat the Hoosiers W (27–24). A determined Iowa team came to Beaver Stadium to play some tough football on November 4 and beat the Nittany Lions L (23-26) in double overtimes. As of 1996, there would be no more ties.
On November 11 unranked PSU played at Michigan Stadium (The Big House) before 110,803. The #20 Wolverines beat Penn State L (11-33). The following week, November 18, Michigan State played the Lions at Beaver Stadium. Penn State triumphed in a nice season ending win. W (42-23).

2001 Penn State Football Season Coach Joe Paterno

The 2001 Penn State Nittany Lions football team was coached by Joe Paterno in his 36th season with the Lions. Penn State did not play Big Ten teams Minnesota and Purdue this year. Also, due to the events of 9/11, the Virginia game was rescheduled from September 13, 2001, to December 1, 2001.

Much to Nittany Lions Fans chagrin, this would be the second of two-rebuilding seasons. This team had one less loss than the 2000 team, finishing at 5-6 (4-4 in the Big Ten). If you'll look ahead, the agony ends in 2002 as PSU works its way back into the top twenty. But, not this year.

In a Baptism of Fire, The Nittany Lions began the 2001 season on September 1, against a #2 ranked Miami team at home before a home crowd of 109,313 in the newly renovated and expanded Beaver Stadium. Miami came in ready to go and beat the Lions L (7-33).

Adam Taliaferro Rejoices

Those watching while it was happening and after the fact believe that the most emotional and electrifying moment of all-time occurred just before the Miami night game began. It was when Adam Taliaferro walked, then skipped through the south tunnel after suffering a paralyzing injury nearly a year earlier at Ohio State.

This record crowd in and expanded Beaver Stadium that now featured club and private suites gave Taliaferro a long standing ovation, but the joy ended soon as Miami coasted to victory en route to the national title.

After the break for the country to heal from the 9/11 2001 terrorist disaster, PSU resumed play on September 22 at home and were beaten by Wisconsin L (6-18). On September 29 at Kinnick Stadium Iowa City, IA, PSU lost its third straight game against no wins yet for the season. L (18-24). On October 20 at Northwestern, the Nittany Lions finally came alive and beat the Wildcats W (38-35) in a close shootout W (38-35).

The Big Ten overall had a bad year in 2001. #12 Illinois (7-1) won the Conference. #20 Michigan came in second at 6-2. They were the only ranked Big Ten Teams. I 2001. Ohio State was 5-3 in third place, and PSU was 4-4, tied with Purdue and Iowa.

On October 27, Ohio State played the Nittany Lions at Beaver Stadium before 108,327. Penn State would not say no and beat the Buckeyes in a very close game W (29-27). This went down as one of the best games ever at Beaver Stadium.

PSU v Ohio State Oct 27, 2001 PSU Win 29-27 --- Johnson makes catch

The Beaver Stadium faithful honored their legendary coach when the Nittany Lions rallied from a 9-27 deficit to beat the Buckeyes. With this win, Joe Paterno passed Alabama's Bear Bryant as the winningest coach in major college football with 324 victories. Write-ups of the event after the game note that the genuine love and heart-felt emotion that flowed between the coach and the fans in the post-game ceremonies will always be remembered by those who were there.

Let's look at the specifics of the game. Penn State first received the kickoff. Paterno decided to start Matt Senneca instead of Zack Mills and of course a few Lions fans were upset. Senneca may have been a bit shaky from his concussion. He struggled on the first drive. Ohio State wasted no time when they gained possession. Their quarterback, Steve Bellisari quickly threw a 66-yard post to WR Michael Jenkins behind the secondary for the score.

Hoping to come back quickly, JoePa took Senneca from the game and put in Mills on the second possession. Things immediately went Penn State's way. Bryant Johnson made a leaping catch for 30-yards. But, then Mills got pasted on an option pitch which saw RB Larry Johnson gaining 31-yards.

There was no more offense left once PSU got inside the ten but Robbie Gould brought in three points from 23-yards out to make the score 7-3.

The Lions held strong on the next series, but OSU punted a huge one and pinned PSU inside the 10. Mills took off on a 5 for 5 passing trek reaching Eric McCoo on a nice 35-yard touch. Again the drive stalled just outside the red zone, and Gould then hit his career-long field goal of 46 to bring PSU within one point.

DE Michael Haynes's got a sack on 3rd-down and this ended OSU's next effort. The Lions then went for broke. Mills threw a "to who?" pass under pressure and it was picked off by LB Cie Grant, who brought it back into PSU territory. Bellisari was effective running 18 yards, but the Buckeyes stalled.

Tressel opted for a field goal on 4th and 1, and Mike Nugent nailed a 28-yard field goal. OSU now had a 10-6 lead early in the second quarter.

PSU then put together a nice drive. It featured completions to TE John Gilmore and Bryant Johnson and the drive stalled again but Robbie Gould made a booming 46-yarder into the wind to bring the scoring difference to 1 point.

Ohio got one more possession in the first half, and they clicked. Bellisari hit Jenkins again on a post route for 68 yards and the Buckeyes were on the Penn State 2. The Nittany Lions defense again became a wall and Tressel's team from the end zone. The field goal was like an extra point and the Buckeyes lead 13-9 at the half.

The third quarter was dull with little action but that was after the second play for Ohio State when Jonathan Wells went like a dose of salt through the middle of the defense for a 65-yard touchdown. In just 57 seconds, the Buckeyes had a commanding 20-9 lead. Penn State continued its turnover problem just a few plays into their first drive. WR Eddie Drummond let a wide-open reception bounce off his helmet and into the hands of OSU's Derek Ross for a 45-yard touchdown return. The birds were booing as the 1-4 Lions fell behind by 27-9.

Senneca had watched Mills carry the team on his shoulders but there was always a show stopper. On the next PSU drive after the OSU touchdown, PSU executed an option run to the short side of the field, Mills saw a gap and leapt over his own downed lineman five yards down the field. The jump was unexpected by the safety and there was hesitation which permitted Mills to bounce off of tackle towards the sideline.

From there, the fleet-footed Mills trekked 69 yards with defenders almost catching up—but he got the score. The PSU attempt for two failed. Penn State and the boo-birds were now smiling and there appeared to be a change in momentum.

Lydell Ross fumbled in PSU territory and the Lions kept the momentum rolling. Mills rolled left and hit Bryant Johnson who dived for the 33-yard reception. One play later, Mills looked right and threw to the left, finding another Johnson—Tony, this time—just past the goal for a 26-yard score. The Lions were still down 27-22, but they could taste a difference in the game. Zack Mills had changed it all by taking the Nittany Lions 124 yards while chalking up 13 big points.

After the kickoff, Shawn Mayer and Anthony Adams sacked on Bellisari to force a Buckeye punt. Penn State was on the move again. On the first play of the fourth quarter, Mills did the impossible. When the snap sailed over his head, he picked it up on the bounce and ran from the rush. He spotted a wide-open FB R.J. Luke, and the young QB Mills hit him with a perfect pass.

Luke did his part by running thirty yards down the sideline. On the next snap, Mills tossed a strike to Eric McCoo on a wheel route for a 15-yard touchdown. After having given up two touchdowns in the first five minutes of the second half, Penn State scored three of their own in the next ten—29-27. Penn State had the lead with a whole fourth quarter to play.

Ohio State played back and forth ball with the Lions until late in the fourth quarter. Then, it got dangerous as OSU gained yardage each play down the field with impressive catches by WR Jenkins. All of Beaver Stadium including the boo-birds were holding their breath with just a two point lead.

With OSU heading for a score on the PSU 32, an offsides call on PSU forced the Lions to give the ball back after a second Israel interception and it enabled the Buckeyes to keep moving. The PSU defense was on alert. Michael Haynes banged in and got a sack on Bellisari again, and the defense forced an Ohio State field goal attempt. The kicker, OSU's Nugent had trouble with the kick but got it off with a low trajectory. DB Bryan Scott jumped way up for the game-saving block. Penn State then had to hold the lead for just 2:55 more.

Larry Johnson rushed for one first down, and then on the next third down, Mills scrambled for 35 yards and stayed in bounds at the end of the play. Tressel's had no more timeouts. Three rushing plays later and Penn State had won a thriller and Joe Paterno got his Gatorade and win #324 of his career.

After an emotional embrace between Joe and wife Sue at midfield, players carried their leader from the field, and Penn State unveiled a 7-foot bronze statue of Paterno to commemorate the milestone. This bitter PSU season was sweetened by this one record-setting Saturday in Happy Valley.

For the rest of the season, with Zack Mills at the helm, PSU looked like a much better team. The Nittany Lions won three of their last five, which included another great comeback effort at Michigan State. The two losses were heartbreaking nail-biters against Rose-Bowl bound Illinois and Virginia.

In one of the write-ups on this game the one from the nittanylionsden.com was a wonderful postscript to Joe Paterno and the contrast between the coaches and their travails.

"Success may have been Tressel's after 2002, but the man on the other side of the field from Tressel in 2001 gave him a blueprint for success with honor; Paterno never fell under NCAA investigation for academic, financial, or recruiting illegalities in all his years of coaching. Yet even while he did things the right way, without any stigma as a cheater, Paterno found his name at the top of all the coaching record books." Considering how JoePa's career ended in what for him was an 8-1 season gaining his 409th victory, beating Bear Bryant's record, brought an even brighter tribute.

On November 3 at home, PSU beat Southern Miss W (38-20). On November 10, it was off to Illinois, the Conference Champions and a close defeat at the hands of the Fighting Illini L (28-33). The Hoosiers were next to play on the huge new Beaver Stadium field on November 17. Penn State prevailed in this game W (28-14).

On November 24 PSU played Michigan State in Spartan Stadium East Lansing, MI and won a close one (W 42–37) bringing the record to 5-5 on the season. On December 1, the make-up game from the 9/11 cancellation was played against Virginia in Scott Stadium, Charlottesville, VA. Penn State lost to the Wahoos in the last game of the 2001 season L (14–20).

2002 Penn State Football Season Coach Joe Paterno

The 2002 Penn State Nittany Lions football team was coached by Joe Paterno in his thirty-seventh year as head coach. The team improved substantially over 2000 and 2001, finishing the full season at 9-4 (5-3 Big Ten) and #15 in the Coach's Poll and #16 in the AP. Ranked #10 at game time, PSU was invited to the Citrus Bowl against #19 Auburn. In a game played on January 1 2003, in which neither team showed much offense, Penn State scored just four points less than the Tigers and lost the Bowl game in Orlando, FL, L (9-13).

On August 31, Penn State began its season at home defeating Central Florida W (27-24). #8 Nebraska played the Nittany Lions on before 110,753 on September 14, W (40-7). n one of Beaver Stadium's treasure games the largest crowd of Penn Staters in Beaver Stadium history--110,753 were treated to a great football feast. The fans had to believe they were experiencing one of the greatest Nittany Lion games ever as No. 25 Penn State simply clobbered No. 8 Nebraska in a sizzling night time atmosphere weeks before the leaves would even begin to fall.

Like all routs, the game quickly lost its luster as the Nittany Lions pummeled a Nebraska team that went on to finish with its worst record (7-7) in 41 years. Regardless, all wins feel good.

On September 21, at home. Louisiana Tech was defeated by Penn State W (49-17). Before the game, the only tie-breaker game ever for PSU had been at Iowa and the Hawkeyes did it again on September 28 at Beaver Stadium—this time the tie was settled in just one controversial OT L (35-42). Let's look at this great PSU game though it ended in a loss, in some detail below:

PSU v IOWA, The Striped Shirts Won?
2. Iowa 42, Penn State 35, OT (2002)

At State College, this game was a heartbreaker for sure. Even though this game ended up in a PSU loss doesn't matter to the greatness of the game. It was full of fireworks, crazy drama, and an improbable comeback that almost was enough for the Nittany Lions.

The pundits agree that this outing against Penn State was the closest call a fine Iowa team had during what would be an undefeated Big Ten season. Yet, it looked like a rout early.

Brad Banks and Dallas Clark led the Hawkeyes to a 35-13 lead more than halfway through the fourth quarter. There is no way to find much sol ace in that score.

It had been 23-0 at one point and probably should have been 30-0 with six minutes still left in the second quarter. However, the Big Ten officiating crew blew a call while blowing dead Antwan Allen's strip of Larry Johnson and the resultant fumble return for a TD. The officials had not ended their impact on the game.

Iowa could have punched PSU in the face for a knockout on two other occasions but Clark botched a would-be TD catch that was picked off in the end zone for a touchback and the Hawkeyes later fumbled at the Penn State 1 yard line. Tough winning when the players are nervous or they do not produce.

Iowa had been completely dominating this year against the Lions before PSU quarterback Zack Mills found a way to get Penn State back in it against all odds. Mills and PSU were nothing short of spectacular. The quarterback finished with a school-record 399 yards passing and four TDs.

The pundits replay of the game say that Mills had gotten frustrated with the cumbersome play-calling system that had been routinely delivered signals from the sideline too late. So, he decided to call his own plays at the line and the Lions got on a big roll.

Twenty-two straight points later, a spree that included a 36-yard Mills-to-Larry Johnson TD pass that ignited the rally and an 8-yard TD pass to Bryant Johnson with 1:20 in regulation that capped it, the Lions had incredibly forced overtime against the almost toughest team in the nation.

That's when the officials stepped back in to ruin a few students playing a game of football. Iowa scored 6 and 1 on its first OT possession thanks partly to an 11-yard bobbled catch by Maurice Brown ruled complete. Then they striped guys ruled a second-down catch by Tony Johnson at the 2 out of bounds. Mills ended up missing Bryant Johnson on fourth down to end it. The milk was sour and the stripes had made it sour but PSU most often does not complain when it losses—just we the faithful. This time was different.

Even when the game was over, the action wasn't. An incensed 75-year-old Joe Paterno, rightfully sprinted down the field to head referee Dick Honig. He grabbed the ref to speak to him as he entered the south tunnel just to vent in his ear. This game and another one full of gaffes at Michigan two weeks later are generally credited with creating college replay review.

We all could do better but the striped guys need to have their own version of replays!

On October 5, the #20 ranked Lions then traveled to Camp Randall Stadium in Madison, WI and beat the #19 ranked Badgers in a close match W (34-21). Always tough #13 Michigan then beat the Nittany Lions by just three points L (24-27) at the Big House before 111,502. Paterno's teams most often won and when they lost, they rarely were taken prisoners. There are so many one point to one touchdown losses that it makes one wonder how great a coach Joe Paterno really was. I know I am more impressed reading his record post facto and I was already impressed.

On October 19 unranked Northwestern scheduled a Big 10 opportunity to take down the Lions at Beaver Stadium but the Wildcats were not wild enough. Before 108,853, Penn State shut out and blew-out the fire in Wildcats W (49-0). Somehow no matter who was the coach Ohio State had a great team. The Buckeyes almost always gave Paterno's teams a game if not a loss.

The story was the same on October 26 at Ohio Stadium in Columbus, OH for this long-time rivalry game. Ohio State at

#4 and PSU at #18 squared off for the defensive battle. The Buckeyes persevered and got the win by six points L (7-13).

On November 2, at home, PSU recovered and beat the Fighting Illini of Illinois, W (18-7) Two weeks later on November 16, Indiana played #16 Penn State on their home field in Bloomington and were beaten by the hard-charging defense and high scoring offense of the Nittany Lions W (58-25). In between on November 9 at home, Penn State beat Virginia W (35-14). Michigan State is nobody's pushover team but the determined #15 PSU Nittany Lions took on the Spartans at Beaver Stadium on November 23 and could not stop scoring W (61-7).

With a big win at Michigan State, and a five and a half week rest, some of the fire just was not there on January 1, 2003 at 1:00 PM when #10 PSU went against #19 Auburn in the Citrus Bowl at Orlando, FL (It was also called the Capital One Bowl. It was an exciting game for 66,334 fans and for a home ABC TV audience of millions. Everything was perfect but the outcome as Penn State's offense could not muster much L (9-13) in a 4-point loss.

Player Highlights Larry Johnson

Larry Johnson was an exciting Penn State football player at Tailback and he was accorded many honors for his great work. In 2002, he was selected by the Football Coaches, Associated Press, Football Writers, The Sporting News and Walter Camp. That is a lot of honors. He was also an All-American Selection for 2002.

Johnson also was the recipient of the Maxwell and Walter Camp Player-of-the-Year Awards and the Doak Walker Award, presented to the nation's top running back. He was third in balloting for the Heisman Trophy and was the Chevrolet National Offensive Player-of-the-Year.

Adding to the recognition for his great years was a unanimous first-team All-Big Ten selection.

Nebraska vs. Penn State 2002
Penn State's Larry Johnson pulls away from Nebraska defender

Johnson became just the ninth player in NCAA Division I-A history—and the first in the 107-year history of the Big Ten Conference -- to rush for more than 2,000 yards in the regular-season. He finished the season with 2,087 yards on 271 carries, for an outstanding 7.7 average, and 20 rushing touchdowns.

This effort put him on the top in the whole nation in rushing (160.5 ypg) and all-purpose yardage (204.2). He was fourth in scoring (10.8 ppg). He became the first Nittany Lion to lead the nation in rushing or all-purpose yardage and joined placekicker Matt Bahr (1978) as the only Penn Staters to lead the nation in two statistical categories in the same season.

Johnson shattered the Penn State game rushing record three times and blew by the 200-yard mark on four occasions, becoming the first Lion ever to post four 200-yard games in a season or career. His final record-breaking effort was a spectacular 327 yards at Indiana. He also tallied 279 yards against Illinois, 257 against Northwestern and 279 yards -- all in the first half -- in his home-finale with Michigan State.

Johnson posted eight 100-yard rushing games on the year and averaged an all-time Big Ten-best 8.8 yards per carry and 183.1 yards in eight conference games. His 2,655 all-purpose yards in 2002 shattered the Penn State record by more than 800 yards and were the fifth-highest total in NCAA history.

His 5,045 career all-purpose yards also were a school record. Chosen the Senior Bowl MVP, Johnson was selected by the Kansas City Chiefs in the first round of the 2003 National Football League Draft. He has played five seasons (2003-07) with the Chiefs and was selected All-Pro in 2005 and 2006. He set a National Football League record in 2006 for the most carries in a season. He had some issues with the Chiefs and did not play for a while.

From 2009, to 2011, Johnson met some good fortune and played with the Bengals, Redskins and the Dolphins at the end of his career, making at least twelve more $million and then he wrapped up his career in 2011.

2003 Penn State Football Season Coach Joe Paterno

The 2003 Penn State Nittany Lions football team's head coach was Joe Paterno in his thirty-eighth year. I bet JoePa in reflection would have still coached this year even though it was his worst ever. It was one of the worst seasons in PSU history. I guess if you bring home a lot of big ones, having a season in which there appears to be no harvest is expected. But, Penn State Fans get agitated when the W's are not there in the column. Realistically all home teams feel the same. Our coach is supposed to win. Wins rarely happened in 2003. In a word, the year stunk with a 3-9 record and the second worst record in the Big Ten (1-7). Illinois at 0-8, had to live with its season for some time to come.

After some season background information, let me get right to the scores Rather than take this sequentially and drag it out, let me first share the wins with you and then we'll run quickly through the losses. I'll just give you the scores without a lot of supporting information. But, please be forewarned, even I can't make it better than it was.

The offense returned just five starters, including quarterback Zack Mills, who was on pace for a record-shattering season before he injured his left throwing arm. Clearly with a seasoned QB, the season would have been different. Penn State was expected to do much better. Starting the season ranked No. 25 in the Coaches college football preseason poll and unranked in the AP college football preseason poll. Though coaches really matter, when the fundamental players are missing, it is tough to make up for lack of players with great grooming.

On August 30, at home, PSU beat Temple W (23-10). On September 20, PSU beat Kent State at home W (32-10). Then, as the season went on one loss after another finally, a game Indiana team came into Beaver Stadium and gave the Lions a spiritual lift on November 15 W (52-7). That's all the wins she wrote in 2003.

The loss column was huge in 2003. Let me write the date, home/away and the score below on all the losses so you and I can get through them quickly.

September 6 at home v Boston College L (14–27)
September 13 at #18 Nebraska L (10-18)
September 27 at home v #24 Minnesota L (14–20)
October 4 at home v Wisconsin L (23–30)
October 11 at #18 Purdue L (14–28)
October 25 at #16 Iowa L (14–26)
November 1 at home, v #8 Ohio State L (20–21)
November 8 at Northwestern L (7–17)
November 22 at Michigan State L (10–41)

And, that was the games of the 2003 season.

It is always nice to find something good in a season so bad. The name of nice in this case is Michael Robinson, a special athlete. Let's take another look at the Temple Game and Michael Robinson's performance to get back on an upbeat path.

The Temple Game Michael Robinson

After the 2003 Temple game, Penn State's Michael Robinson looked like he had just walked the gauntlet about 12 times and though beaten was still standing. He had a bruised left eye which was swollen shut. It was a gauntlet of sorts against Temple and the young man kept moving, gaining, and enduring. It was a pack of Owls responsible for his swollen eye. Robinson felt that even with his helmet, the area around his eye was getting whacked every play.

This was the big change for Robinson, once thought to be just the future QB at PSU. Such a great athlete could play anywhere. It was just the second time in his career he started at tailback, lining up at wide receiver and quarterback within two series, and of course he also took time to return some punts on the side.

Who says Robinson could not do everything. Before the game was over, He even snagged a tackle statistic when he bought down Zamir Cobb, who had converted Temple's fake punt.

From early in his career to his moving on to the pros, Robinson created a major dilemma for his coaches. It is a great problem but a dilemma nonetheless. The problem of course is not "whether," but "where" to play him. Penn State football coach Joe Paterno, never really minded the problem of figuring out where to play him. He was always just happy to have him on the team.

"Robinson's such a good athlete. The problem with Robinson is that he's got to practice at quarterback," Paterno said. "He's going out on some tailback plays, he's running a lot of other things, he's running back punts and if he wasn't as strong of an athlete as he is, he probably couldn't do it all. He's an easy guy to coach."

Robinson finished the afternoon as Penn State's leading rusher with 84 yards on nine carries, most of which came when he broke free down the right sideline for 53 yards before being brought down from behind early in the fourth quarter.

"Joe [Paterno] came to me on the sideline, and he said, 'give it to him and let him go,' " Robinson said." The offensive line did a great job, and I bounced it outside."

The only pass that Zack Mills completed in the first quarter was to Robinson on a six-yard screen pass. Robinson returned two punts for 18 yards.

Robinson is listed as a quarterback. But, on this day against Temple, he took just five snaps before replacing Mills in the closing minutes and he didn't throw a pass. He would play less and less QB and more and more RB throughout his outstanding PSU career

Robinson said that a couple times in the Temple game passes were called when he was lined up behind center, but that the Nittany Lions were forced to check out of them or a fumbled snap prevented him from passing. He did attempt two passes, but both fell incomplete. On both, he took a handoff from Mills. On the first one, his pass landed in-between wide receivers Kinta Palmer and Tony Johnson. On his second pass, he overthrew Mills, who ran a route after handing the ball off.

Robinson said he is having fun doing everything that he is doing, but that receiver is his favorite position other than quarterback.

"I enjoy playing receiver," Robinson said. "It reminds me of being in the backyard and going out, and going up to catch passes."

Most would believe that playing so many different positions would be extremely difficult, but it has not been that way for Robinson.

Fullback Sean McHugh said that being a quarterback by trade allows Robinson to play anywhere.

"The quarterback's job is to know what everyone on the field is doing," McHugh said. "It's definitely to his advantage, because he knows what everyone is doing and can fill in for anyone."

In 2003, Robinson still was spending most of the week with the quarterbacks. He said that he never attends the running back meetings or wide receiver meetings, and that he gets the same number of repetitions under center that Mills gets.

But when Robinson was coming out of Varina High School in Richmond, Va., he didn't expect at this stage of his college career to be playing so many spots on the field.

"I thought I'd be on my way out of here next year," Robinson said. "But I never expected to be returning punts or playing receiver, or the things I do right now. But I have done it in high school, so it's kind of easy for me."

On this particular Saturday against Temple, he did what he always does: Michael Robinson made everything look easy.

2004 Penn State Football Season Coach Joe Paterno

The 2004 Penn State Nittany Lions football team's head coach was Joe Paterno in his thirty-ninth year. The wonderful coach JoePa and the same wonderful man over the last two years has began to have trouble winning games in his later years of coaching. In 2004, he was 77 years old but still spry and he did have player issues.

If this were a mystery novel you'd have to wait until next years and the next to see how this comes out but it is not. It is real, it is fact based, and if you want to, you can look it up but soon, in the next ten pages or so, you will have all your answers about the Penn State record under Joe Paterno. He stopped coaching in his forty-sixth year and in 2002, it was his thirty-ninth. He was one heck of a coach!

As we approach the end of Coach's career, we will provide some more information about what he faced at the beginning of the season and what the prospects were for success, etc. One thing is for sure, as long as JoePa was the coach, he had the energy to run the field with the best of them—well into his eighties.

In the spring of 2004, there were changes made to the coaching staff. As you will see by this year's less than sterling 4-7 overall record overall (2-6 Big Ten), coupled with last year's (2003) 3-9 record, something was wrong.

The changes affected long-time offensive coordinator Fran Ganter, who signed up for the new Associate Athletic Director for Football Administration, after 37 years as a player and coach for Penn State. Former Penn State quarterback Galen Hall joined the coaching staff as the new offensive coordinator and running backs coach. Mike McQueary, another former Penn State quarterback, joined the staff as the wide receivers coach and also served as the recruiting coordinator.

In addition to the coaching changes, head coach Joe Paterno had his contract extended through the 2008 football season, despite having had three losing seasons out of the past four. Whenever a coach creates a bunch of potholes in his record, there are many who cry for his ouster. There was a major sentimentality for Coach Paterno but there was also a lot of rumbling under people's breaths.

Things that should improve only improve if there are ingredients of improvement. The 2003 second-leading receiver Maurice Humphrey, for example, was expelled from school and convicted of three counts of simple assault. He would not play another down for Penn State. His absence created a major void of experience at the wide receiver position. Senior Gerald Smith was the most experienced receiver, and he had limited action and just 15 catches in 2003. Zack Mills was healed and he and Derek Wake were elected team co-captains by their teammates. Because of the dubious future for 2004, PSU was unranked at the beginning of the season by both the AP and the Coaches.

Despite concerns for success, as the calendar ticked, the season began in September with Akron at Beaver Stadium W (48-10) On November 4, PSU made the trip to Alumni Stadium to play a determined, aggressive and never-quit though often over-manned Boston College. The Eagles beat Penn State in a tough match L (7-14).

Central Forida, a team that has kept getting better and better, came to Beaver Stadium on September 18 and were handily beaten by the Nittany Lions W (37-13) . Then, on September 25, it was off to Camp Randall Stadium •in Madison, WI for another PSU loss L (3-16).

On October 2, at the Hubert H. Humphrey Metrodome • in Minneapolis, MN   at #19 Minnesota, PSU succumbed to the badgers L 7-16). Always tough and always surprising, #10 Purdue knocked off the Lions at Beaver Stadium L 13-20). Iowa came to Penn State's homecoming and spoiled it in a close game L (4-6) before 108,062. Never to be taken lightly, PSU played OSU in Columbus and were beaten L (10-21)

On November 6, at Beaver Stadium, a confident Northwestern team beat Penn State L (7–14). Then, on November 13, at Indiana, PSU pulled out all stops and beat the Hoosiers in Bloomington W (22–18) before 24,092. On

November 20, an often great Michigan State team invaded Beaver Stadium in University Park, PA and were beaten by a full season experienced Nittany Lions squad W (37–130 before 101,486 to end the season.

2005 Penn State Football Season Coach Joe Paterno

The 2005 Penn State Nittany Lions football team for the fortieth year in a row were coached by the one and only JoePa (Joe Paterno) in another of many great winning seasons. Just when you think there is a systemic reason for losses that may involve coaching, the same Paterno formula again brings in more wins than anybody could ever expect and guys like me and perhaps you too, regardless of where we were in the dark losing years say, "Of course, that's JoePa. He's our coach."

This was Paterno's toughest mountain to climb. The Nittany Lions were coming off of back-to-back losing seasons, finishing 3–9 in 2003 and 4–7 in 2004, capping a stretch from late 1999 where Minnesota upset the #2 Nittany Lions with a late field goal until the goal line stand at Indiana. There were four of five seasons being losing seasons and the lone winning season in 2002 featuring many extremely frustrating close losses. You lived through the frustration in this book, and this is one of our chances to smile.

This stretch was called "The Dark Years", sometimes including 2002 as well. The team finished this sketchy 2004 season with wins over Indiana and Michigan State. As always, a strong finish helps springboard momentum into the next season (2005 in our case). So here we are with a great year, which we are about to discuss, having closed out 2004 with two nice wins, there was a ton of hope for continuance into the 2005 Nittany Lions season. It happened.

Instead of five starters in 2003, this year's team returned 18 starters from last year's squad. Eight starters returned on offense, led by starting quarterback Michael Robinson who also played at wide receiver, tailback, and punt returner during his first three years at Penn State. Robinson played exclusively under center after the graduation of Zack Mills. PSU heralded the fact that it had nine defensive starters return from a unit that did not allow more than 21 points in a game in 2004. Also returning was safety Chris Harrell who suffered a neck injury in 2003 and missed the 2004 season. It was time to play.

Michael Robinson, Alan Zemaitis, and Paul Posluszny were elected tri-captains of the football team in 2005. Posluszny was the first junior captain since 1968.

Penn State had made the pundits wary in their last four out of five tough seasons. So, they started the season unranked in both the AP and the Coaches college football preseason polls. Who can argue with an excellent # 3 finish in both polls and an 11-1 overall record as well as a 7-1 record in and co-championship in the Big Ten, Penn State had recovered and the prognosis for the patient was good.

On September 3, PSU began the season and the home season by beating South Florida at Beaver Stadium W (23–13). On September 10, the next week, a tough Cincinnati team was taken down by the Lions at Beaver Stadium in University Park, PA W (42–24). Finally winning, PSU next engaged Central Michigan at home on September 17 W (40–3). Then, on September 24 at Ryan Field in Evanston, IL, PSU defeated a scrappy Northwestern squad W (34–29).

On October 1, the still down by the press but tough on the field degraded Nittany Lions, unranked after four straight wins, played at home against the #18 Minnesota Gophers and showed the stuff from which they were made before 106,604 at Beaver Stadium and ABC TV. PSU won big W (44-14). Somebody had to notice that Penn State was again playing Nittany Lions Football.

Never giving up in the tough games, on October 8, a finally ranked #16 PSU hosted the Ohio State Buckeyes before 109,839 at home and outlasted the Ohio Squad W (17-10).

The Nittany Lions' win over the No. 6 Buckeyes before another frenzied night time "whiteout" crowd of 109,839 was an epic milestone, marking the return of Penn State to the college football elite. The Lions took the lead in the Big Ten Conference and went on to finish No. 3 in the polls with a BCS Orange Bowl win and their best record (11-1) in 11 years.

Ready to play anybody and win, the 2005 Nittany Lions finally met a team that could beat them. Unranked Michigan was a different team at home than away. The Wolverines hosted the game at Michigan Stadium in Ann Arbor, MI (aka, the Big House) before a huge crowd of 111,249. They barely beat Penn State (two-points) L (25-27) but they won nonetheless. This tough Michigan team was the single reason why the Nittany Lions were not undefeated and untied in 2005. In his fortieth year Paterno was still outclassing all coaches as they came by. What a record! Michigan somehow survived Paterno in 2005.

On October 22 at Illinois the #12 PSU Lions won big...very big against the Fighting Illini W (63-10). On October 29, on Homecoming, PSU beat Purdue at home W (33-15). On November 5, another Big Ten Tough team, Wisconsin were beaten by #10 Penn State at home W (35-14) before 109,865 electrified PSU fans and maybe a few others. On November 19, PSU took out its Michigan frustration against a guiltless Michigan State at Spartan Stadium in East Lansing, MI with a convincing win W (31–22).

At 11-1, On January 3, 2006 at 8:00 PM, #3 ranked Penn State won a shot at the Orange Bowl against nemesis #22 Florida State at Dolphin Stadium in Miami Gardens, FL (aka the Orange Bowl). After winning the opportunity to play during the season. PSU won the game in three overtime periods W (26-23).

Player Highlights Tamba Hali

Tamba Hali was a great PSU defensive end in 2005. He is from Teaneck, N.J., and gained lots of honors at PSU for football. He was selected by the American Football Coaches Association, Associated Press, Football Writers Association of America, The Sporting News and Walter Camp Football Foundation. Hali was also a finalist for the Nagurski Trophy, presented to the nation's top defensive player, and the Ted Hendricks Defensive End-of-the-Year Award.

Hali was a unanimous selection as the Big Ten Defensive Lineman-of-the-Year and first-team All-Big Ten. He led the conference with 11.0 sacks and 17.0 tackles for loss. Hali made 65 tackles, with 17 TFL (minus-86), 11 sacks (minus-79), four pass breakups and one huge forced fumble, which the Lions recovered in the waning minutes to preserve a 17-10 win over Ohio State.

Hali's season sack total is tied for sixth-best at Penn State and his 36 career TFL are tied for 10th-best.

The Kansas City Chiefs selected Hali in the first round of the 2006 National Draft. Hali is very proud of his selection and he still shows a ton of Penn State Pride as he recently chose not make himself available for free agency because he feels at home at Kansas City after ten years. He still plays like a kid with wonton enthusiasm for the game and a healthy respect for the Kansas City Chiefs.

He is now on most recent $22 million extension with the Chiefs which he thought about before saying no to free agency. He enjoys explaining that he has been a Chief for so long he couldn't imagine playing for anyone else. He has that old time loyalty that transcends cash. OK...$22 million is not peanuts but neither is $50 or $100 million for a great player.

He loves telling people that he was the last first-round draft pick of Chiefs founder Lamar Hunt, who died about seven months after the Chiefs selected Hali in the 2006 draft.

Moreover, he figures why learn a new way when he already loves the old way,

Hali said. "I couldn't imagine going somewhere else and needing to establish myself as a player again, especially being in the game this long...I wanted to end my career here. It's a family atmosphere here, and everything (general manager John) Dorsey, coach (Andy) Reid and the Hunt family stand for, everything they say, has been right on point."

Hali also made it clear that he's focused. He garnered his sixth Pro Bowl nod in 2015, finishing with 48 tackles and 6 ½ sacks for a Chiefs team that finally ended its playoff misery with a 30-0 wild-card win over the Houston Texans. It was the club's first playoff victory in 22 years and Hali's first in four tries.

The Chiefs think the world of this player who thinks the world of them:

"Tamba is one of the most passionate and competitive football players I've had the privilege to be around," GM Dorsey said in a statement announcing the deal. "His leadership and playing ability have been critical to our success defensively. He's a great teammate and a true professional. We are pleased he is staying in Kansas City."

"Well, as long as I love the game, as long as I continue to have the will to play at a high level and enjoy being around the guys, and there's no distraction that's leading to me exiting before I need to, I'll play as long as my body lets me," Hali said.

When things change, he'll move on. Until then with a great Penn State career behind him and with ten Kansas City years already under his belt and still at just 32 years old, Hali may be signing a lot of three year extensions if those knees keep doing the job for him.

Player Highlights Michael Robinson

Burton Michael Robinson, aka Michael Robinson, played quarterback and wide receiver for the Nittany Lions leading the team to a Big Ten Conference title in 2005 and being recognized as the Big Ten Offensive Player of the Year in 2005. He won the Chicago Tribune Silver Football as the Big Ten's MVP.

Quarterback Michael Robinson

During his first three years at Penn State Robinson had done some rushing and receiving, but very little throwing. Many fans saw his ascension to the starting role as more of a sign that prized sophomore Anthony Morelli was being protected than a sign that Penn State was about to win a Big Ten title.

In 2002, Robinson was being moved all the time from QB to RB to SB to SE or wherever because he is a great athlete. He started at tailback against Michigan and at slot back against Auburn in the Capital One Bowl. As the "Bob Aspromonte," of PSU somehow he had enough yardage to be the second leading rusher in 2002 with 263 yards and six touchdowns on 50 carries. He also caught nine passes for 44 yards.

In 2003 with the Nittany Lions, he still had not gotten the full nod. He did start eight games—three at quarterback and five at tailback. He completed 62-of-138 passes for 892 yards, five touchdowns, and five interceptions and finished second on the team with 396 yards and three scores on 107 carries.

In 2004, Robinson got his eight games again. He was second on the team with 33 receptions for 485 yards (14.7 avg) and three touchdowns. He completed 14-of-39 passes for 170 yards, a touchdown, and five interceptions. He was third on the squad with 172 yards on 49 carries.

Michael Robinson became a super hero in 2005, He had his best numbers of his college career. He was named Big Ten Conference Offensive Player of the Year by the league's coaches and was a consensus second-team All-Big Ten choice. He was named to the Maxwell Award watch list and was a semi-finalist for the Davey O'Brien Award, given to the nation's top passer. He completed 162 of 311 passes (52.1%) for 2,350 yards, seventeen touchdowns and ten interceptions.

His 2,350 passing yards at the time ranked fifth on the school season-record list, topped only by Zack Mills (2,417 in 2002), Tony Sacca (2,488 in 1991), Anthony Morelli (2,651 in 2007) and Kerry Collins (2,679 in 1994). He was second on the team with 163 carries for 806 yards (4.9 avg) and eleven touchdowns, becoming the first player in school history to throw for over 2,000 yards and rush for over 500 yards in the same season.

His 806 rushing yards set a school season-record for quarterbacks and he became the first quarterback in Penn State history to run for at least ten touchdowns in a season. His 28 touchdowns (17 passing, 11 rushing) was one shy of the school season-record of 29 (26 rushing, 3 catching) by Lydell Mitchell in 1971. Robinson also became the first Nittany Lion to throw three touchdown passes in three separate games during the same season since Todd Blackledge in 1982.

Robinson was captain of the 2005 team, one of Penn State's most competitive teams in years led by Coach Joe Paterno, winning the Big Ten championship and the over the Florida State Seminoles in a gut-wrenching triple-overtime victory. He also finished fifth in the voting.

Robinson's Pro Career

San Francisco 49ers (2006–2009)
Seattle Seahawks (2010–2013)

Michael Robinson was drafted in the 4th round of the 2006 NFL Draft by the San Francisco 49ers. The 49ers wasted no time converting the versatile athlete into a running back. 49ers head coach Mike Nolan was immediately impressed with Robinson's attitude and toughness during training camp. Robinson began his first season as a pro as the #2 back in the 49ers backfield.

After Robinson scored his first and second career touchdowns against the Philadelphia Eagles and veteran pro-bowl safety Brian Dawkins for one of them, knocking Dawkins out of the game, in week 3, Mike Nolan indicated that he intended to use Robinson more often in goal line situations. Unfortunately for PSU fans, Despite Nolan's statement, Robinson's playing time actually would decrease over the course of the season, and he did not score another touchdown. He finished with 38 carries for 116 yards, 9 receptions for 47 yards, and 2 touchdowns.

Michael Robinson was released by San Francisco on September 3, 2010 at the end of the 2010 preseason. He was signed September 6, 2010, by the Seattle Seahawks at the urging of first-year assistant special teams coach and former 49ers player,

On December 12, 2011, against the St. Louis Rams Michael returned his first career Special Teams Touchdown on a blocked punt. On January 19, 2012, Robinson made his first career Pro Bowl as an alternate, starting at fullback for the injured John Kuhn. Life in the pros is tough for sure. On August 30, 2013, Robinson was released by the Seahawks during final cuts, after the use of a prescription medication shut down his kidney and liver and caused him to lose 30 pounds. On October 22, the Seahawks re-signed him to a one-year deal after his health improved.

On February 2, 2014, Robinson caught a pass for 7 yards in Super Bowl XLVIII en route to a 43-8 win over the favored Denver Broncos. It would be the last game of his career, as he retired after the game. When he retired, Robinson became an analyst for the NFL Network. Robinson guest-starred as himself in a couple of episodes on The Young and the Restless, where he meets with Victor Newman.

2006 Penn State Football Season Coach Joe Paterno

The 2006 Penn State Nittany Lions football team's head coach was Joe Paterno in his forty-first year. As always, the Lions played its home games at Beaver Stadium in University Park, Pennsylvania. Though not as clean as 2005, PSU was making everybody take notice again with a season record of 9-4 (5-3 in the Big Ten). PSU had a winning in the Big Ten and against non-Big-Ten teams. Certainly there were better years but this signaled an escape from the Dark Years back into the top 25 with a Coaches ranking of 25 and an AP rank of 24.

The 2006 season began with the Nittany Lions ranked #19 in the AP and Coaches preseason polls. With losses to Notre Dame and Ohio State, the team dropped out of the rankings, but snuck back into the top 25 at season end.

Everybody had been looking for an unprecedented 2006 after Penn State had some major unexpected success in 2005 after two consecutive losing seasons. The 2005 team was a big part of the 2006 team. As you recall from last year's synopsis in this book. The team began 2005 unranked in any poll, and yet finished 11–1 and ranked third.

With only one loss, the team achieved a Big Ten co-championship with Ohio State. Some great players achieved great milestones with linebacker Paul Posluszny winning both the Chuck Bednarik and Dick Butkus Awards. Also, consensus All-American. Quarterback Michael Robinson finished fifth in the Heisman Trophy voting. It was a fine year but this is 2006 and the old saying, what are you going to do for me now comes into play.

Paul Posluszny and Levi Brown were elected co-captains of the football team for 2006. Posluszny became the team's first two-time captain since 1969. No matter which PSU game you watched in 2005 or 2006, you would hear Posluzny's name accoladed for his fine play.

In 2006, Pozlusny kept at his excellence and was also named the 2006 Big Ten and consensus national pre-season Defensive Player of the Year. The Nittany Lions team was ranked No. 19 in both the AP and Coaches college football preseason polls. They made the top 25 and came close to an even better season.

Before we go on with the games of the season, let's profiled Paul Posluzny as this was his senior year. Posluzny was one of the greatest linebackers in the greatest Linebacker school in the country, Linebacker U, aka PSU.

Player Highlights: Paul Posluzny,

In 2005, Paul Posluszny was a junior outside linebacker at Linebacker U and captain for Penn State. He had a great year as a junior with 82 tackles, ranking third in the Big Ten and 11th in the nation with 11.7 tackles per game. In 2005 and 2006, Posluzny was named a semifinalist for the 36th Rotary Lombardi Award, presented to the nation's top lineman or linebacker. In both years, the 6-2, 234-pound linebacker was one of 12 semifinalists up for the prestigious award and in 2005, he was one of only three non-seniors chosen. On November, 15, 2005 Posluszny was selected a finalist.

He was joined as a finalist by Louisville defensive end Elvis Dumervil, Ohio State linebacker A.J. Hawk and Texas defensive tackle Rod Wright. Ohio State's A.J. Hawk won the award but Paul Posluzny, just a junior in 2005, competing for the award by playing his brand of football, had turned a lot of heads. The award is presented to the nation's top lineman or linebacker.

In the football version of the never ending story, Penn State All-American Paul Posluszny, who did cleanly win the prestigious 2005 Butkus Award as a junior, was again selected a finalist for the 2006 honor, which is presented to the nation's top linebacker. A fellow Big-Ten player, LaMarr Woodley from Michigan was selected out of the top four. Clearly Posluzny's nomination as a finalist shows how toughness and the abilities of this great football player. As a new guy to sports journalism, I find it quite strange however that a school that has put out the best cadre of linebackers in America has had such a hard time having many of them gain this award.

In 1978, Bruce Clark received the award and then during a period in which PSU had many top linebackers, none made the cut until Carl Nassib got the award in 2015. Just saying! OK, I am saying even more. Would anybody off the street believe than Clark and Nassib were not linebackers? And, so Linebacker U has never won the award with a linebacker. Strange! Strange like all the undefeated season without a championship. OK, enough jawboning.

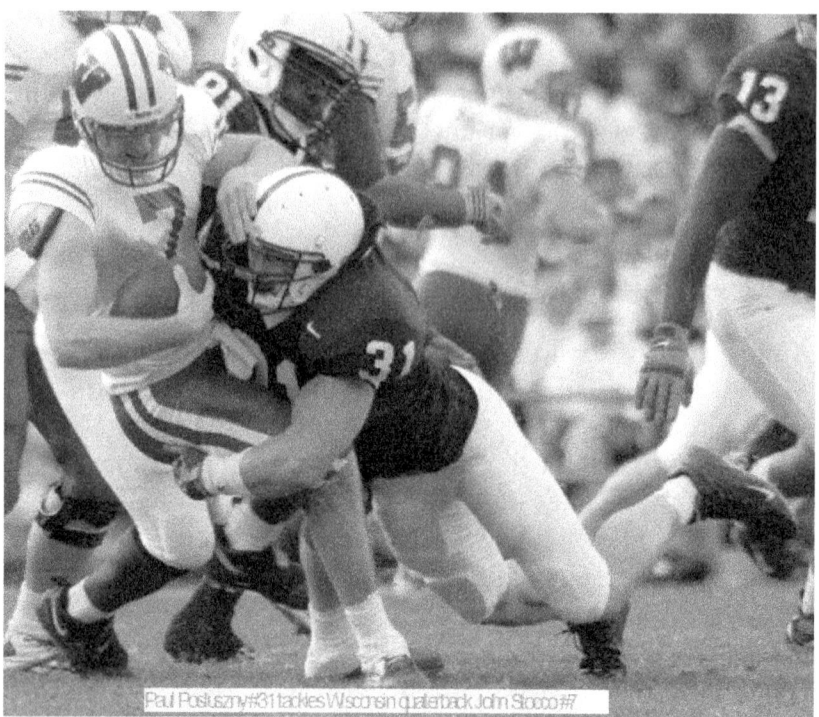
Paul Posluzny #31 tackles Wisconsin quarterback John Stocco #7

Posluzny started playing when he was six, back home in the Pittsburgh area. He recalls his dad asking if he wanted to do something new and play football. So he said sure and gave it a shot. He's been playing ever since. Paul Posluzny had a great high school career, was highly recruited, and he felt really comfortable coming to Penn State. He likes to say that one of his favorite notions about Penn State is that it is Linebacker U and he is a linebacker. He feels that anytime you play a position like linebacker at a school known for that, it's really an honor and a privilege. To Posluzny, it is something to try to uphold.

Baseball is his favorite other sport. Like many of us who are not seven foot tall, he once liked basketball. His major at PUS is finance, but he is not exactly sure how he picked it. Posluzny will need that finance degree in life to take care of his holding from being a star professional athlete.

The official skinny on POZ from Aliquippa, Pa is that he played outside linebacker for PSU in 2005-06. He received lots of awards and nominations including being selected by the Associated Press, Football Writers Association of America, The Sporting News and Walter Camp Football Foundation in 2005 and the AP and Walter Camp Football Foundation in 2006.

Posluszny became just the second two-time winner of the Chuck Bednarik Award, presented to the nation's top defensive player, in 2006. In 2005, he also won the Butkus Award, presented to the nation's top linebacker and was a finalist for the `06 honor.

He was the 13th Nittany Lion to be named a two-time first-team All-American, Posluszny also was a two-time finalist for the Rotary Lombardi Award.

He was selected Big Ten Defensive Player-of-the-Week a conference-record five times in his career. He served as The Nittany Lions' first two-time team captain since 1968-69. He set the record for Penn State career tackles with 372.

He was a starter in his last 37 games at PSU. He became the first Nittany Lion to lead the team in tackles three times and to post three 100-tackle seasons, recording 116 in 2006. Posluszny also was a two-time first-team ESPN--The Magazine Academic All-American, and was selected the 2006 Academic All-American-of-the-Year among Division I football players.

Posluzny has only good things to say about Joe Paterno: *"He teaches us about really just growing up and being a man,"* POZ once said. *"Besides the football, he's preparing us to be good men in life."*

He and Jeff Hartings (1994-95) are the only Nittany Lions to earn first-team All-America and Academic All-America honors twice. Posluszny graduated with a degree in finance in 3 1/2 years and was selected by the Buffalo Bills with the second pick of the second round in the 2007 NFL

Draft. He was later signed by Jacksonville as an unrestricted free agent on July 29, 2011.

As a Pro, this ninth-year LB started 101 career games and is now in his fifth season with the Jaguars. He has impressive stats with career totals including 1,079 tackles (764 solo), 12 INTs, 12.0 sacks, eight forced fumbles, three fumble recoveries and 32 passes defensed. He was voted to Pro Bowl in 2013.

As a former second-round pick of the Buffalo Bills in 2007, he joined the Jaguars as an unrestricted free agent in 2011 ... It was a good deal for the Jaguars. Pusluzny has produced 100-plus tackles in six of the last seven seasons including a career-high and single-season franchise record 231 stops in 2012. He owns two of the four highest tackle totals in Jaguars history as he compiled 192 tackles in 2011, the fourth-most for a season

He posted double-digit tackles in 40 of 56 games with the Jaguars including 15 of 16 games in 2012. When he played with the Bills he led the team in tackles his final two seasons including a then career-high 140 in 2010 ... Had then career-best three INTs in 2009. He had missed 13 games as a rookie with forearm injury and missed the final nine games in 2014 with a torn pectoral muscle.

Paul Posluzny was first Bills rookie to start the season-opener since 1987. He was the first player ever to record 100-plus tackles three times in a college career ... Two-time winner of Bednarik Award for best defensive player in the nation. Paul Posluzny is the real deal and he is a Penn Stater.

Penn State began the season at home against Akron on September 2, W (34-16). Notre Dame then hosted PSU on September 9 after not playing for many years. ND took advantage of home-game spirit and pummeled the Nittany Lions L 34-16) in a game that was not as close as its score. PSU would even the score v Notre Dame the following year at home. On September 16, PSU beat Youngstown State W (37-3). Then, on September 23, the #24 ranked Nittany Lions traveled to Ohio Stadium in Columbus, OH and were beaten by #1 Ohio State W(L 6–28) before 105,266.

On September 30, PSU beat Northwestern at Beaver Stadium in University Park, PA W (33–7) before 108,837. On October 7 at Minnesota's Hubert H. Humphrey Metrodome in Minneapolis, PSU beat the Badgers in Overtime W (28–27). On October 14 at home, PSU played #4 ranked Michigan and were defeated L (10–17) before a capacity crowd of 110,007. Homecoming featured Illinois and PSU won the game W (26-12). PSU then defeated Purdue at Ross–Ade Stadium • West Lafayette, IN W (12-0).

On November 4, PSU played at Camp Randall Stadium • Madison, WI, against Wisconsin and were defeated L (3-13). On November 11, Temple came to play PSU and the Lions won big W (47-0). Then, on November 18, Michigan State played a tough battle at Beaver Stadium but lost to Penn State W (17-13) before 108,607.

Penn State finished the regular season at 8-4, winning a berth to play on January 1 at 11:00 AM to play #17 Tennessee in the Outback Bowl in Raymond James Stadium, Tampa, FL. The unranked Nittany Lions triumphed in a nice game W (20-10) before 65,601. With its 9-4 record (5-3 in the Big Ten), PSU made its way into the top 25 with this win #25 and #24 in the Coach's poll and the AP respectively.

2007 Penn State Football Season Coach Joe Paterno

The 2007 Penn State Nittany Lions football team was coached by Joe Paterno in his 42nd year and played its home games in Beaver Stadium in University Park, Pennsylvania. Penn State was ranked #17 in the AP and #18 in the Coaches college football preseason polls.

On April 27, 2007, State College police announced that six members of the squad were charged with a range of criminal charges related to an altercation that occurred in an apartment in downtown State College earlier that month. Most of the charges were eventually dismissed or were whittled away by pleas agreements.

For his part, not confining the issue to just six players, Coach Paterno announced that, because of the incident, the entire football team will clean Beaver Stadium on Sundays after home games, a task usually handled by members of Penn State's club sports teams. The team began serving this punishment following their 59–0 victory over Florida International.

The Nittany Lions finished the season with the same record and same ranking as 2006 – 9-4, and #25 and #24 respectively in the two major polls

On September 1, #17 PSU defeated Florida International at Beaver Stadium W (59–0). Keeping their word, members of the squad cleaned the stadium on the Sunday after the game. On September 8, at Beaver Stadium, it was make-up time as Penn State thumped Notre Dame a good one before 110,078 W (31-10), one year after The Irish had delivered a similar blow to the Lions at home. On September 15, Buffalo made a rare appearance playing Penn State in a rout by PSU W (45-24). On September 22, a stubborn Michigan State handed PSU its first loss of the season at Beaver Stadium in a close match L (9-4). The second loss came quickly the following week on September 29 at Illinois L (20-27)

PSU picked itself up after two losses in a row and hosted Iowa in Beaver Stadium. The Nittany Lions got back on track with a win against the Hawkeyes W (27-7). PSU beat Wisconsin at Wisconsin the following week in a nice win W (38-7). PSU then played at Indiana and beat the Hoosiers W (36-31) On October 27 Jim Tressel brought his #1 ranked Ohio State team to Beaver Stadium and overpowered the #24

Lions L (17-37). Back at it again against Purdue on November 3 at home. PSU won a close one W (26-19)

On November 10, PSU shut out Temple W (31-0 at Lincoln Field in Philadelphia. Then on November 17 in Spartan Stadium, PSU lost to Michigan State in another close battle L (31-35).

Ranked 8-4 after the regular seasons the Nittany Lions got a shot at Texas A & M in the Alamo Bowl in the Alamo Dome in San Antonio, TX. The game was played on December 29 at 8:00 PM before 66,166 plus a naotionwide ESPN TV audience. In a close match, PSU prevailed W (24-17) and thus finished the season at 9-4 with rankings of #25 and # 24 in the Coaches and AP polls.

2008 Penn State Football Season Coach Joe Paterno

The 2008 Penn State Nittany Lions football team was coached by Joe Paterno in his forty-third year. Ranked #6, PSU had a great record of 11-1 going into the Rose Bowl v #5 USC L (24-38). The team finished with a great winning season of 11-2 and were ranked #8 in both polls.

In the good news and bad news category before the end of the previous-season, difference maker linebacker Sean Lee announced his plans to return for his senior season. Unfortunately, Lee, the mainstay on the defense, tore his anterior cruciate ligament in his right knee during practice and was sidelined for the entire season. Lee was permitted to use his redshirt and returned in 2009.

There was some bad news in Spring with five players being suspended prior to spring drills for their involvement in an October 7 fight at the HUB-Robeson Center during the previous season, including defensive tackle Chris Baker, linebacker NaVorro Bowman, defensive back Knowledge Timmons, defensive tackle Phil Taylor, and receiver Chris Bell. Tight end Andrew Quarless was also suspended after a

DUI incident in March. Later Bell was kicked off the team for brandishing a knife at a teammate.

Following spring workouts, Baker, Bowman, Quarless, Timmons and Taylor were allowed to rejoin and work out with the team. Baker was sentenced to two years' probation. When you are trying to be #1, it hurts when players off the field choose to not engage life as gentlemen. It hurts them, the university and the team. Good recruits are tough to find and experienced team members are even harder to find.

#22 ranked PSU started the season early on August 30 against Coastal California at home with a really big win W (66-10). On September 6, the next team to try their luck at the #19 Lions in Beaver Stadium was Oregon State. The Nittany Lions won by a large amount W (45-14)

Playing again at the Carrier Dome in Syracuse after eighteen years on September 13, #17 Penn State dominated long-time rival Syracuse W(55-13). On September 20, Temple lined up at Beaver Stadium and were beaten by #16 Penn State W (45-3). The #12 Nittany Lions were now 4-0 for the first time in years. #22 Illinois was next at Beaver Stadium and the Lions won W (38-24). On October 4, at Ross–Ade Stadium in West Lafayette, IN, #6 Penn State beat Purdue W (20–6).

The smell of a special season was again in the air as Joe Paterno had put together another great team. It was his forty-third season and after all that time to still be walloping great teams was a mark few coaches could ever achieve.

On October 11, at Wisconsin in Camp Randall Stadium, The Nittany Lions kept pouring it on W (48-7).

Michigan game – Say no more

On October 18, The Lions took on a very powerful Michigan team at Beaver Stadium, and were relentless in trouncing the always-tough Wolverines W (46-17).

The crowd went nuts after this long-sought victory. Huge carloads of exhilaration emanated from the first victory over Michigan after nine straight losses over 12 years. This bad record may fade from the mind in the future, but the 110,017 impassioned Homecoming fans thoroughly enjoyed the second half thrashing under the lights as Beaver Stadium rocked and rolled, and PSU picked up a fine W (46-17).

Like many other great PSU games at Beaver Stadium, there were thousands of white pompoms fluttering as 100,000 Penn State fans broke into a sing-along as the happy night fell on Beaver Stadium in the Happy Valley.

Joe Paterno had picked up many nemeses in this 60 years of coaching but they say his greatest nemesis was Michigan and its nasty, victory-seeking Wolverine football team. On this evening in October, these warriors from mid-America were about to be vanquished by a #3 ranked Nittany Lions and its

81-year-old coach. The post-game celebration would create the need for a bird's-eye view of party time in Happy Valley.

Though the season ended without a championship at the time, JoePa was getting a great look at some of the folks in his lineup that were about to make PSU a national championship contender.

Behind the running of Evan Royster and a few momentum-shifting plays by the defense and special teams, the PSU got the game going its way by withstanding the Wolverines' early moves and most importantly, the Nittany Lions worked as hard as they could to not only snap a nine-game losing streak to their Big Ten rivals, they whacked them a good one W (46-17) on this particular Saturday.

Paterno was limping and so he was not on the field to enjoy his record 380th victory. The outstanding master of the college coaching profession was relegated to working from the press box for a third consecutive week because of his sore hip and leg.

"My being upstairs -- it's funny, I'm not sure that's not the best place for a head coach," he said. "I mean you really get a view of things, I get a better view of football games from up there than I ever do on the sideline."

What Coach Paterno saw was a team that should be no worse than third in the BCS standings when it heads to Big Ten rival, and eternal powerhouse Ohio State next week.

"Am I starting to like it up there? I'll never like it, it doesn't mean that the team might be better off with me up there," Paterno said.

No team had ever won as many in a row against Penn State during Paterno's 43 seasons at the helm than Michigan. But if ever there was an opportunity for the Nittany Lions (8-0, 4-0) to break the streak it was 2008. The Wolverines at (2-5, 1-2) were struggling in their first season under coach Rich Rodriguez, but like many teams with new coaches, they expected things to get better as time went by. Nonetheless, they were a powerful team.

"It's a fact, you take it year by year, game by game, we lost to them last year, and coach has made a great point this week, that this Penn State team has not lost to this Michigan team," center A.Q. Shipley said.

Michigan came in the game as a 23 1/2-point underdog because they were not at prime under their new coach Rodriguez, for sure. The Wolverines were unaccustomed to being low in the odds maker's opinions.

Michigan looked like a good bet early with their spread offense clicking as they sped to a 17-7 lead early over Penn State in the second quarter. But the Lions (8-0, 4-0) soon deciphered the spread, and got its own high-powered version of Rodriguez's offense rolling. The lions delivered the knockout punch with a safety, a partially blocked punt and a forced fumble on consecutive second-half Michigan possessions. Michigan did not look good.

"Oh, we executed for a while and then we didn't," said Rodriguez, whose team needs to win four more games to avoid Michigan's first losing season since 1967. "That's what happened. We executed, we moved the ball a little, and when we didn't, we didn't."

Jared Odrick gave Penn State its first lead of the game at 19-17 when he dragged down backup quarterback Nick Sheridan in the end zone with 4:39 left in third quarter. The free kick set the Nittany Lions up at midfield, Royster's 21-yard run put them at the 1 and Daryll Clark sneaked in at 3:04 to make it 26-17.

Royster, one heck of an athlete, ran for 174 yards on 18 carries, with a 44-yard TD run in the first quarter.

A minute later, Nathan Stupar blocked Zoltan Mesko's punt deep in Michigan territory and Penn State turned the short kick into a Kevin Kelly 32-yard field goal on the first play of the fourth.

60 seconds or so after that, Aaron Maybin sacked Steven Threet, who fumbled, and the Lions took over at the Michigan 19. A sore elbow forced Threet to miss a few series.

Clark's second 1-yard sneak turned the final 12 minutes into a Beaver Stadium celebration bash, with Penn State fans singing along to "Sweet Caroline" and enjoying their team's first victory against Michigan since 1996. It was as Lawrence Welk would say, "Wunnerful!"

The Wolverines had surely tormented Paterno and his Nittany Lions over the prior 12 seasons, with too many lopsided losses and heartbreaking defeats. In 2005, the last time Penn State was in the hunt for a national title, it was Michigan that scored a touchdown on the final play to hand Paterno's team its only loss of the season.

This one couldn't have started better for Michigan but things that start well do not always end well. After a three-and-out for Penn State, Michigan put together its longest drive of the season. The 14-play, 86-yard march featured all the best of Rodriguez's spread offense. The option cleared running lanes for Threet and Brandon Minor, who surpassed his season high on the drive with 42 yards rushing.

Minor finished it off with a 5-yard TD run. "But we've been seeing little glimpses of that all season," Minor said.

A Penn State fumble led to a 27-yard field goal by K.C. Lopata and the Nittany Lions faced their largest deficit of the season.

Sometimes one cannot recognize a comeback until it is mostly finished. After Royster's 44-yard TD romp, Michigan went on the march again.

Another near-flawless drive by the Wolverines, this one 78 yards, was capped by Minor's 1-yard plunge and it was 17-7 early in the second quarter. Minor had 117 yards on 23 carries.

Pundits queried if it were possible that the mere sight of those winged helmets had their team mystified. The vaunted wolverines were ready to win at a moment's notice. But, the notice never came.

Michigan had 185 yards in the first quarter, but only 106 the rest of the way. Penn State's defense can be stacked up against the best in the land and it would win.

"We really stayed calm, we knew Michigan was going to come in and try to play us hard, they do it every year," Royster said. "We just needed to adjust to it."

With just 23 seconds left in the half, the game was being played at top speed. Clark found Jordan Norwood for a 3-yard touchdown pass to make it 17-14, it seemed as if Penn State had come through the worst of it and grabbed control of the game.

The second half would have its rewards for the Nittany Lions as they soundly beat the Wolverines W (46-17). And ain't that sweet!

After Michigan, It seemed nothing could beat the Lions. But, Ohio State was the next on October 25, week and #10 Ohio State always played its best at home and rarely lost to Penn State. Would this game, played at Ohio Stadium, with so much on the line be different? ..... Answer = Yes! This was a different Penn State team.

PSU won this important game W (13-6. Sometimes when a team triumphs over its biggest threat in a season, they relax a bit and the next tough team claims a victory. On November 8 at Iowa, Penn State lost its first game of the season in what would have been an undefeated championship season, to a really tough Iowa Team by just one point L (23-24).

#7 PSU came back on November 15 v Indiana and defeated the Hoosiers at Beaver Stadium W (34-7). On November 22, #17 Michigan State played the Lions at Beaver Stadium. Penn State had fully recovered from the Iowa loss and beat the Spartans in a blowout-shootout W (49-18.

On January 1, 2009, #6 Penn State had another shot at greatness as it took on #5 USC in the Rose Bowl. USC was always tough and this was a special year for the Nittany Lions. The setting was Pasadena California in the Rose Bowl Stadium. The game was televised by ABC and the attendance was 93,293. It was a great game. PSU lost by 12 points in a real determined battle L (24-38) PSU finished the season 11-2. It was a fine # 43 season for Coach Joe Paterno.

2009 Penn State Football Season Coach Joe Paterno

The 2009 Penn State Nittany Lions football team was coached by Joe Paterno in his forty-fourth year. The Nittany Lions continued to play home games in the newly massive Beaver Stadium in University Park, Pennsylvania. As an aside, for those concerned about academics and athletics, in 2009, Penn State University had the highest graduation rate among all of the teams on the Associated Press Top 25 poll with 89% of its 2002 enrollees graduating. Miami and Alabama tied for second place with a graduation rate of 75%.

2009 was also another great year for football, though the two losses were heartbreaking, coaches are paid gazillion dollars a year to achieve records such as PSU's 11-2 record this particular year. Though 82 years of age in the 2009 season, Paterno never weakened.

He was strong and the squad was strong. How can you argue with an 11-2 record? The Nittany Lions also won the Lambert-Meadowlands Trophy award to the best team in the ECAC for the 28th time and the second consecutive year. Penn State is an impressive team and Joe Paterno, even in his few losing seasons, was an impressive coach.

There are always a few personnel setbacks in preparing for a season. In December, 2008, for example, QB Pat Devlin decided to transfer from Penn State and did not play in the Rose Bowl. Devlin appeared in ten games for the Nittany Lions, passing for 459 yards, four touchdowns and no interceptions.

In January, redshirt sophomore defensive end Aaron Maybin announced that he was skipping his final two seasons of eligibility and declared for the 2009 NFL Draft. Junior defensive end Maurice Evans, also declared for the draft. On top of these three losses of key players, the defense lost its entire starting secondary to graduation. The good news was that all-everything linebacker Sean Lee had healed and returned to the line-up for his senior season. The offensive unit had its own woes losing three-fifths of the line to graduation. Despite the losses, the team still looked strong and performed very well.

Ranked #8 pre-season, on September 5, in the home opener, PSU defeated Akron W (31–7) for a fine start to the season. On September 12, Syracuse returned the favor and came to Beaver Stadium to be beaten by an on-cue # 5 ranked PSU Nittany Lions Team W (28-7). Next, on September 19, at home, PSU beat the Temple Owls W (31-6). Ranked #4 with a 3-0 record PSU was off to the races until IOWA stopped by on September 26. The Lions lost to Iowa L (10-21). Back on the Big ten schedule at Illinois, PSU defeated the Fighting Illini in Champaign on October 3 W (35-17).

On October 10, Eastern Illinois made a rare trip to Beaver Stadium and were beaten big by the Nittany Lions W (52-3).

Minnesota came to Beaver Stadium on October 17 and the Gophers were shut-out by the Nittany Lions W (20-0) PSU then traveled to the Big House in Ann Arbor Michigan and beat the Wolverines W (35-10). Staying on the road on October 13, PSU beat Northwestern W (34-13).

Always a nemesis and always tough, #10 ranked PSU played #12 ranked Ohio State at home on November 7, before 110,033 and lost this year's game L (7-24). At home again on November 14, The Nittany Lions beat Indiana W (31-20). Moving on to the Michigan State game, the Lions traveled to East Lansing and defeated the Spartans in a well-played game W (42-14).

Ranked #11 with a 10-2 record, Penn State got to play on New Year's Day in the Citrus Bowl—aka the Capital One Bowl—in Orlando at 1:00 PM, the best time for a January 1 football game IMHO. I saw the game on ABC TV and 63,025 saw the game live in Florida. The opponent was a tough #15 ranked LSU team who like PSU, were planning to win the game. I

It was a real close match but the Nittany Lions held tough and beat Louisiana State W (19-17). With an 11-2 record with the bowl win and a #8 rank in the Coach's Poll and #9 in the AP, it was a fine year indeed for PSU football and Coach Joe Paterno. It was a fine game to kick off the Master Coach's next to last full season.

Player Highligh Sean Lee

Sean Lee was in the on-deck circle at Linebacker U to be the Linebacker Apparent. He had been a three star recruit out of Pittsburgh but he broke into the Paterno lineup early. He made his Penn State debut as a true freshman in the 2005 classic whiteout win over Ohio State. He started every game as a true sophomore, ending the year third on the squad in tackles. He maybe had become a PSU Linebacker as in his junior season in 2007, he finished the year second in the whole Big Ten in tackles, and he was named second team All-Big Ten.

He would have had an even bigger 2008 when an ACL tear in spring practice crippled him while it was repairing after surgery. He sat on the sidelines wearing a head set during the games watching for things to report. Penn Staters were hoping that after such a nurturing Lee would be back at Beaver Stadium in 2009. It was not what it was expected to be.
During 2009, he simply was not the same player as in 2007. He just was not as strong physically as in 2007. He was forced to sit three games due to lingering injuries, but despite all that he did end the year with 86 tackles (39 solo) in the middle, right alongside NaVorro Bowman. He used his innate football sense and intensity and then he was drafted in the second round, 55th overall.

After being drafted by Dallas, Lee was still plagued by recurring injuries and he was susceptible to hard hits. It was his fifth year and it was a much better year. After the emergence of Rolando McClain at middle linebacker the previous year, Lee was moved to weakside linebacker to protect him from direct hits by the defensive line and take advantage of his playmaking abilities. In the second game against the Philadelphia Eagles, he had 16 tackles (2 for loss), two passes defended, an interception in the end zone, and sealed the 20–10 win with an onside kick recovery, although he also suffered a concussion.

His performance earned him NFC Defensive Player of the Week. On December 7 against the Washington Redskins, he posted 13 tackles, two tackles for loss and one sack.

He finished with 156 tackles (led the team), 2.5 sacks, 11 tackles for loss (led the team), 6 quarterback pressures, one interception and 5 passes defensed. He appeared in 14 games, missing one contest because of a hamstring injury and the other because of a concussion. Lee was named to his first Pro Bowl, as an injury replacement for Kansas City Chiefs

Player Highlights NaVarro Bowman

PSU star Linebacker NaVorro Roderick Bowman was born on May 28, 1988 in District Heights Maryland. From day one, he worked every day of his life to become a great football player. He was so good, nobody wanted to see him leave PSU but the pressure to change life status for players is very difficult to refuse. On January 4, 2010, after a great PSU career, Bowman's mother announced his decision to forgo his final year of NCAA eligibility and enter the 2010 NFL Draft.

On the second day of the Draft, Bowman's ticket was punched in the third round as the 91st overall pick. The San Francisco 49ers gained a powerful player for their roster. Bowman wears number # 53 for the 49ers.

Bowman was a standout player at Suitland High School in Forestville, Maryland. Despite missing his HS Senior year with a shoulder injury, his junior year was very impressive with 165 tackles, 9 sacks, and 3 fumble recoveries as a linebacker. A versatile athlete, Bowman also ran for 1,200 yards and 22 touchdowns as a running back. I dare you to bring him down. He became Maryland Defensive Player-of-the-Year, first-team All-State, Washington Post first-team All-Met and first-team All-Conference. He was recruited to Penn State by Larry Johnson, Sr.

He was redshirted in 2006; played nine games in 2007; thirteen games in 2008, and 9 games in 2009 before leaving a year early for the NFL.

After the redshirting season Navarro played every game in which he was physically capable. He missed 2 games in 2007 due to a sprained ankle suffered at Illinois. He had 16 tackles, with one sack, a forced fumble, a fumble recovery, a blocked kick, and a pass breakup that season.

He played a lot more in 2008, mostly because All-American Dan Connor moved to the NFL but also because of an injury to presumptive starter Sean Lee. Despite the attrition, however, Bowman kept the Nittany Lions ranked in the top ten among three primary defensive categories. Individually, Bowman led the Nittany Lions in total tackles (106), solos (61), and assisted tackles (45), was second in tackles for loss (16.5) and tied for third in sacks (4.0). He also forced two fumbles, recovered a fumble, grabbed an interception and had five pass breakups.

His first start came in week four versus Temple in which recorded 11 tackles, including five tackles for loss and three sacks, a forced fumble and an interception. He won his spot in the 45-3 win and he was named Big Ten Co-Defensive Player of the Week.

He finished the season with sadness and an outstanding performance in the bowl game. The game was played one day after his high school coach, Nick Lynch, was killed in an automobile accident in Maryland.

Bowman mauled Southern California in the 2009 Rose Bowl. He responded to the personal tragedy by breaking the Penn State bowl record with five tackles for loss (minus-21 yards), and tying the Rose Bowl record set by Ohio State's Andy Katzenmoyer in the 1997 game. He also recorded his fourth sack of the season among his eight tackles (seven solo) against the Trojans. For his superb efforts against USC, Bowman was selected to ESPN.com's 2008-09 All-Bowl team, one of two Big Ten players named to the squad.

When the season was over Bowman had gained a lot of great recognition:

- First-team All-Big Ten selection.
- Maryland Defensive PoY (2005)
- Maryland All-State (2005)

- Washington Post All-Met (2005)
- Big Ten Defensive PoY (9/20/2008), (11/14/2009)
- All-Big Ten (2008)

First year pro in 2010, he played in all 16 games, starting one in place of Patrick Willis. Willis was ruled out for Week 17 after undergoing a second surgery on his broken right hand. He finished his rookie year with 46 tackles.

In his second NFL season, Bowman became the starter at inside linebacker with the departure of Takeo Spikes to free agency. Starting alongside All-Pro linebacker Patrick Willis, Bowman made huge strides and finished the year with 143 tackles, 2 sacks, and 8 pass deflections. In addition, he was also the team leader in tackles, while finishing second in the NFL in solo tackles.

With the emergence in Bowman's play, he helped a top ranked 49ers defense set a NFL single season record of not allowing a rushing touchdown for 14 games. The previous record was held by the 1920 Decatur Staleys, who did not allow a rushing touchdown in a 13-game season. Starting all 16 games in 2011, Bowman finished the year with 143 tackles, 2 sacks, 8 passes defended, and 3 fumble recoveries. The 49ers finished with a 13-3 record for an NFC West pennant but lost to the eventual Super Bowl champ New York Giants 17-20 in the NFC Championship game in overtime.

Although he was not voted to the Pro Bowl for his stellar season, he was named to the First-Team All-Pro by the Associated Press. He was also voted No. 85 on NFL Network's Top 100 Players of 2012, which recognizes performance from the previous season.

2010 Penn State Football Season Coach Joe Paterno

The Penn State Nittany Lions football team was coached by Joe Paterno in his forty-fifth and last full season with Penn

State University. Team captains for the 2010 season were wide receiver Brett Brackett and defensive tackle Ollie Ogbu. After a number of great seasons in a row, especially the outstanding 2009 season, it was again time for some rebuilding. The Nittany Lions finished the season 7–6, with a 4–4 record in the Big Ten play. They qualified and they played in the Outback Bowl where they were defeated by Florida L (37-24). The bottom line is that it was another winning season.

As an aside, it was Ohio State that had big troubles with the NCAA this season. On July 8, 2011, long after the 2010 season had ended, in the wake of NCAA violations for improper benefits to student athletes and the subsequent cover, Ohio State vacated all of its victories, as well as the conference and Sugar Bowl championships, from the 2010 season as self-imposed sanctions. Since Penn State lost to Ohio State, the official record for the Lions is 7-5; not 7-6 for 2009.

On September 4, at Beaver Stadium in the season home opener, #14 PSU beat Youngstown State W (44–14). On the road again—this time at Bryant–Denny Stadium in Tuscaloosa, AL, on September 11, #14 ranked PSU lost to the #1 ranked Alabama Crimson Tide L (3–24). On September 18 Kent State came to Beaver Stadium to play the #20 Nittany Lions and the Lions Prevailed W (24–0). Temple played the Nittany Lions on September 25 and were beaten in a nice, close game W (22-13).

Penn State has had bad luck with Iowa since joining the Big Ten. October 2 was no different.as the Lions lost at Iowa City L to the Hawkeyes L (3-24). On October9, PSU lost to Illinois at home L (13-33). Then, on October 23, at Minneapolis Penn State won a nice match against the Gophers W (33-21). By the time Michigan came to Beaver Stadium, the Lions were hungry for the old winning days. PSU took care of business with Michigan W (41-31) before 108,539.

On November 6, PSU beat Northwestern at home W (35-21) and followed that up with a loss away at Columbus to the Ohio State Buckeyes L (14-38). This loss was vacated about a year later because of some issues with special favors for certain Ohio athletes. On November 20, PSU played Indiana at FedEx Field in Landover, MD and beat the Hoosiers W (41-24) On November 27, PSU wrapped up its season losing to #10 ranked Michigan State at home L (22-28).

Having had a winning Season (7-5), PSU played Florida in the Outback Bowl on January 1 at Raymond James Stadium in Tampa, FL and lost a tough battel L (24–37) in Joe Paterno's last bowl game as head coach.

Player Highlights Stefan Wisniewski

In 2008, Stefen Wisniewski was the first Nittany Lion true freshman offensive lineman to start a game since center Joe Iorio in 1999, Wisniewski was a starter in 12 games at guard in 2008, and a starter in 25 of the last 26 games.

Selected a 2010 first-team preseason All-American by Athlon, Lindy's, Sporting News and Phil Steele's College Football Previews, Wisniewski was a 2009 third-team All-America honoree by Collegefootballnews.com. Wisniewski became Penn State's first three-time Academic All-American

In 2009, his Junior Season, Wisniewski was shifted from guard to center prior to spring practice and emerged as one of the nation's top offensive linemen. Starting every game, he was selected first-team All-Big Ten by the coaches and media and was named a third-team All-American by Collegefootballnews.com.

Wisniewski and senior tackle Dennis Landolt anchored a line that had four different starting lineups in the first six games, but meshed well in the second half of the season. Wisniewski also was selected a first-team ESPN The Magazine Academic

All-American®, joining teammates Josh Hull and Andrew Pitz on the first-team.

In his 2007 Freshman PSU Season, Wisniewski played in eight games and was joined by linebacker Chris Colasanti as the only true freshmen to earn time on the field. He was named to The Sporting News Freshman All-Big Ten team. Wisniewski played in each of the last seven games, making his collegiate debut against Buffalo. One month later, he made his first career start in the 36-31 win at Indiana, getting the nod at right guard.

He became the first Penn State true freshman offensive lineman to start since center Joe Iorio in 1999. Wisniewski helped the Nittany Lions rush for 192 yards and pass for 197 in the important road win over Indiana. He saw action on 230 snaps, led by 42 in the Alamo Bowl win over Texas A&M, as he helped the Lions run for a season-high 270 yards. He compiled a perfect 4.0 grade-point average during the 2007 fall semester.

Stefen David Wisniewski is the son of Leo and Cindy Wisniewski and has one sister, Sarah. He comes from a deep football family. His father was a standout defensive lineman for the Lions, lettering from 1979-81 and serving as a tri-captain in 1981. He was selected by the Baltimore Colts in the second round of the 1982 NFL Draft and played four seasons with Baltimore/Indianapolis.

An uncle, Steve Wisniewski, was a two-time first-team All-America guard during his Penn State career (1985-88) and was selected All-Pro eight times in his 13 years with the Oakland/Los Angeles Raiders. In his free time, Stefen enjoys reading and working out. He is interested in pursuing a career in teaching and coaching or in the ministry. Wisniewski is one of the squad's premier students, compiling a perfect 4.0 grade-point average.

Stefen Wisniewski was taken with the 48th overall pick in the second round of the 2011 NFL Draft by the Oakland Raiders, and he signed with the Raiders shortly before the beginning of the 2011 training camp. Stating that he wished to create his own legacy, he declined to wear his uncle's old uniform #76 (which was available), opting for his college #61 instead.

At the beginning of the 2011 season, coach Hue Jackson named Wisniewski the Raiders' starting left guard, placed between Samson Satele at center and Jared Veldheer at left tackle. On opening day of the 2011 NFL season, the offensive line cleared the way for 190 rushing yards and a victory over the Denver Broncos.

Stefen Wisniewski was made to play football. He was immediately named the Pepsi NFL Rookie of the Week for Week 3 of the 2011 NFL season, after the Oakland offensive line cleared the way for 234 rushing yards and allowing only one sack against the New York Jets.

His lead block on a pivotal fourth-quarter touchdown run gave Oakland a two-score lead. In January 2012, Wisniewski was named to the Pro Football Weekly All-Rookie team for his outstanding rookie season as starting left guard.

Wisniewski helped pave the way for the NFL's 7th ranked rushing attack and anchored an offensive line that only allowed 25 sacks, tied for 3rd best in the NFL. With the departure of Samson Satele to the Indianapolis Colts in the 2012 offseason, Wisniewski became the Raiders' starting center. After a few more years, he moved to Jacksonville

Wisniewski signed a one-year contract with the Jacksonville Jaguars on April 18, 2015. On March 9th 2016, Wisniewski became a free agent.

He is now back in Pennsylvania with the Eagles. Welcome home, Stefen. On April 4, 2016, Wisniewski signed a one-year contract with the Philadelphia Eagles. Let's all hope the deal is mutually beneficial.

2011 Penn State Football Season Coach Joe Paterno

The 2011 Penn State Nittany Lions football team was coached by Joe Paterno in his forty-sixth and final year. Coach Paterno was the head coach for the first nine games of the year in what looked like it might be another championship season after the rebuilding year. As everybody knows there was a major scandal at Penn State and the Coach was fired in the wake of the devastating allegations involved.

Defensive coordinator Tom Bradley took over the team for Joe Paterno. Without discussing the merits of the case as this was well covered earlier in this book, and continued coverage is in the final chapters, it is certain that the firing of the head coach main stream was very disruptive to the season. The Nittany Lion players continued to work hard and they were clearly innocent victims of the situation and they continued to play but with heavy hearts.

Penn State finished the season 9–4, 6–2 in the Leaders Division of the Big Ten to be co–division champions with Wisconsin. Due to the head-to-head loss to Wisconsin, they did not represent the division in the inaugural Big Ten Championship Game. They were invited to the Ticket City Bowl where under Tom Bradley's best efforts as interim coach, they lost to Houston 14–30.

You may remember that Penn State began the season with an unsettled quarterback situation. There was a battel between sophomore Rob Bolden and one-time walk-on junior Matt McGloin split starting duties in the 2010 season. Rob Bolden was named the starter for the season opener against Indiana State, but things changed.

Matt McGloin was the first walk-on quarterback to start at Penn State since scholarships were reinstated in 1949. Prior to his college career, McGloin was a Pennsylvania all-state quarterback while attending West Scranton High School, a few miles from where I live. He became the starting quarterback for Penn State Nittany Lions football team and led the Lions from 2010 to 2012

The season began like any other on September 3 at Beaver Stadium v Indiana State. #25 ranked PSU defeated the Sycamores W (41-7). On September 10, the #20 ranked Paterno forces got their first setback of the season against #3 Alabama L (11-27). This would be the very last loss in Joe Paterno's excellent career. Penn State would win their last seven games coached by Paterno. When PSU played Nebraska in game 10, Tom Bradley would be the new interim head coach.

On September 17 PSU beat a tough Temple team at Lincoln Financial Field in Philadelphia, PAW (14-10). On September 24, the Paterno forces beat Eastern Michigan at Beaver Stadium W (34–6). PSU then traveled to Bloomington Indiana before 42,621 on October 1, and the Lions beat the Hoosiers W (16-10). When Iowa came to Beaver Stadium on October 8, Penn State finished them off in a close match W (13-3).

Purdue was the next win for the Lions at Beaver Stadium in October 15, W (23-18). These were all typical Paterno close matches where the defense does a yeoman job. On October 22, #21 ranked PSU then beat Northwestern at Ryan Field in Evanston, IL W (34-24). PSU then finished off Illinois in another close game at Beaver Stadium on October 29. The #19 Nittany Lions beat the Fighting Illini W (10-7).

The Illinois game at Beaver Stadium was the end of Joe Paterno's season and the end of Joe Paterno's 45+ year head coaching career with Penn State. He finished his part of the season with another great record at 8-1, losing only to #3 ranked Alabama. When he gave up the team to Tom Bradley, to play Nebraska, Paterno's nine-game season Penn State team was ranked # 12.

Tom Bradley's shot at being coach came shortly after the November 4 grand jury report was released on Friday, November 4. There was no game Saturday. On November 9, Joe Paterno offered to retire at the end of the season, which was going pretty good for the players at the time. PSU officials instead fired Paterno and the University president on November 9, and appointed Bradley interim coach just three days before one of the toughest games of the season—#19 ranked Nebraska

On November 12, Tom Bradley's team, clearly upset by the week's happenings lost at home to the Nebraska Cornhuskers in a close game L (14-17). Having regained some composure by November 19 at Columbus Ohio, the #21 PSU squad beat Ohio State in a close game W (20-14). The #19 Nittany Lions finished off the season with a big loss at #12 Wisconsin L (7-45).

Tom Bradley led the disenchanted PSU Nittany Lions to the Cotton Bowl and PSU lost L (14-30). From the Nebraska game on, nothing seemed real as the whole football program was in disarray.

Player Highlights Michael Mauti

Michael Mauti had no clue his 2011 season would be abbreviated by injury. He was a Linebacker U Linebacker all over the field making the big plays for the first three games of 2011 season. He was earning recognition and would have surely gotten the plaudits with a completed senior season. But it was not to be.

He suffered a torn anterior cruciate ligament in his left knee. Before his injury, Mauti had recorded 21 tackles, with 3.0

tackles for loss, one interception and three pass breakups in three-plus games. In the meeting with an ever tough No. 2 Alabama, Mauti led the team with a career-high 13 tackles and had two pass breakups. If there were more Mauti's on the team, the outcome would have been different.

He was superb in helping the Nittany Lions hold Temple to 10 points, recording six tackles (all solos), including a career-tying three for a loss (minus-eight). In the fourth quarter, he made a diving interception, the first of his career, to set up Penn State's final touchdown drive at Lincoln Financial Field. Mauti saw action on 182 snaps, topped by 76 against Alabama.

Mauti's junior season ended abruptly in the first quarter against Eastern Michigan with a torn anterior cruciate ligament in his left knee. These are tough injuries and tough to fully recover. Mauti did not play the rest of last season, but he continued as a leader at practice and on the sideline during games. His continual presence permitted him to maintain his slot on the team's 70-man roster for away games. He worked very hard in his rehabilitation and he was in the forefront during winter strength and conditioning sessions. He showed his leadership by example and his warrior mentality.

He worked out in spring in selected drills was expected to be 100 percent in time for the season. He was a likely Butkus Award and post-season honors candidate. Michael Mauti is a fierce competitor, and without a doubt, one of the team's hardest workers and when engaged, he is a sure tacker. Few escape his clutches. He is the consummate linebacker with the proper balance of acumen and athleticism and speed to chase down a ball carrier or blanket a running back or tight end in pass coverage.

After all the prep work, this intense and focused fifth-year senior started the first four games last season and had 11 career starts. After game four, he had 21 tackles, with 3.0

tackles for loss, one interception and three pass breakups in three-plus games in 2011 prior to his second injury.

The former Mandeville High School All-American graduated in December 2011 and is on schedule to earn a second degree, in labor and employment relations, in December. Mauti and his older brother, Patrick (2005-09) have combined with their father, Rich, to join the long line of fathers-son tandems to play at Penn State over the past 50 years.

In his junior season, he played in 11 games, with seven starts. He garnered 5.5 tackles for loss (minus-18), with two sacks and a pass breakup. Mauti rewrote his career-high in tackles in three consecutive games during the season.

He was selected Big Ten Co-Defensive Player-of-the-Week against Northwestern, after making a career-high 11 tackles and a career-best 3.0 TFL in the historic comeback win. In his first game since the 2009 Rose Bowl due to a serious knee injury, Mauti made five tackles against Youngstown State.

He recorded six hits at No. 1 Alabama in his first career start. Mauti tied his then-career-high with seven tackles in the 24-0 win over Kent State. He recorded seven tackles in the win over Temple, with five hits in the second half, helping the Nittany Lions hold the Owls to 71 yards and no points in the final two quarters. His seven tackles tied for the team-high.

He made six tackles, including four solos, in the Big Ten-opener at Iowa and recorded his first career sack, taking down quarterback Ricky Stanzi for a five-yard loss. Mauti did not see action in the Big Ten home-opener with Illinois due to a sprained ankle. He broke his career-high in tackles at Minnesota, leading the line backing corps with eight stops, including five solos and 0.5 TFL for a loss of two yards.

Mauti rewrote his career-best in hits for the second consecutive week, totaling a team-high 10 in the primetime win over Michigan. For the third straight game, Mauti broke his career-high in tackles, recording 11 against Northwestern to share Big Ten Defensive Player-of-the-Week honors. He made a career-best three tackles for minus-eight yards in helping Penn State rally from a 21-0 deficit to post a 35-21 decision for Joe Paterno's 400th win.

Mauti made one tackle at Ohio State, but left the game in the second quarter with a shoulder injury, which sidelined him against Indiana. In limited action against No. 10 Michigan State, he recorded two tackles. Mauti compiled four stops against Florida in the Outback Bowl, with 0.5 tackles for loss. He saw action on 476 snaps, topped by 59 against Florida and 58 in the wins over Minnesota and Northwestern.

It was in his sophomore season that he first injured his anterior cruciate ligament in his right knee during an August practice, sidelining him for the entire season. He took a medical redshirt season.

Big and strong and wise enough to play as a freshman, Michael Mauti came out of the blocks ready to play. He was an immediate asset for the defense and special teams after graduating from high school early and enrolling in the University in January 2008.

One of three true freshmen to play in every game, he made 26 tackles, with one minus-yardage stop and a fumble hit. He made a season-high seven tackles against Michigan, including one for a two-yard loss. He delivered one of the biggest hits of the season when he leveled Wolverine Sam McGuffie on a kickoff return, forcing a fumble.

The Wolverines did recover the ball, Mauti's hit charged the Nittany Lion defense and faithful in erasing a 10-0 deficit to win the game, 46-17. His own play carried with it tons of emotion for others. He also made three stops each in the wins over Indiana and Michigan State and had two hits in four other games. The freshman saw action on 249 snaps, led by

33 against the Wolverines and 30 against Southern California in the Rose Bowl. He made four tackles in the 2009 Blue-White game and was the recipient of the Jim O'Hora Award, presented to the defense's most improved player during spring practice.

Mauti came from a great football high school, Mandeville HS, playing the position of hard-hitting linebacker for Coach Guy LeCompte. He was selected to the 2008 U.S. Army All-American Bowl. He finished his HS senior season with 121 tackles, 24 for loss, with four sacks. He also caused four turnovers, including two forced fumbles and two interceptions, which he returned for touchdowns. He was ranked among the ESPN.com Top 150 recruits in the nation and was rated a Top 20 inside linebacker by Rivals.com.

Mauti is from a football family of Penn Staters. He is the son of Rich and Nancy Mauti. He has an older brother, Patrick, and sister, Rachel. Patrick was a wide receiver for the Nittany Lions from 2005-09. Their father was a letterman at Penn State in 1975 and '76 as a wide receiver and played for the National Football League New Orleans Saints (1977-83) and Washington Redskins (1984). Michael is majored in crime, law and justice. Born January 19, 1990 in New Orleans, La.

Mauti's pro career began when he was drafted by the Minnesota Vikings in the seventh round, 213th overall of the 2013 Draft. The Vikings also selected fellow Penn State linebacker Gerald Hodges in the fourth round, reuniting the teammates in the NFL. He played for the Vikings for two years, primarily on special teams, before being cut at the end of training camp in 2015.

The New Orleans Saints claimed Mauti off waivers after Minnesota released him. On October 15, 2015, in a Thursday Night Football game v the Atlanta Falcons, Mauti blocked a Matt Bosher punt and returned it for a touchdown. The block was widely compared to a famous punt block made by Saints safety Steve Gleason in a 2006 game against Atlanta, in the

Saints' first home game after a year of wandering after Hurricane Katrina. This was more special as Gleason was present and received an award at the 2015 game, while Mauti himself had attended the 2006 game in person.

Michael Mauti is one of the good guys in football and in life and he is a key element in many PSU pundits best of PSU football lists. He always occupies a nice spot.

Mauti, as many other PSU players enjoyed Penn State; enjoyed PSu Football, and enjoyed playing for the most decorated coach who has ever lived—Joe Paterno!

Chapter 22 — The Bill O'Brien Era From 2012 to 2013

Coach # 15

2012 Bill O'Brien 8-4   (6-2 Big Ten)
2013 Bill O'Brien 7-5   (4-4 Big Ten)

Penn State head coach Bill O'Brien leads his team onto the field at Beaver Stadium for an NCAA college football game against Navy in State College, Pa.,...

2012 Penn State Football Season Coach Bill O'Brien

After over 60 years of coaching at Penn State (15 as assistant and 46 as head coach), Coach Joe Paterno passed away from Lung Cancer on January 22, 2012. This disease was once diagnosed as very treatable. Many of us who admire his work and who admired the man in life and in death believe that the consensus thought of this good man being fired and not having done enough to help others was more than enough to kill him, or deplete his desire to live, hastening his death.

So many fans and pundits and alumni who could have simply suggested that they did not buy into his major involvement at all in the scandal, as I would have, stayed silent. Joe Paterno died not a hero as he should have passed out of life. Surely, our merciful Lord has him slotted properly.

Unfortunately, the greatest figure in Penn Satte Football from the day football was invented, died as a potential reprobate instead of a great hero. That, in my opinion killed him as much as lung cancer from a very treatable disease in January, 2012. His fortitude if he felt it was worth it, would have given us the man who could speak about so many great seasons and so many great players, and how to live life.

How did the decisions made by non-football people help PSU or sports in general? These decisions were all off-base and so they did not. It did not.

Unlike the last forty-six years, at the beginning of the 2012 Penn State Nittany Lions football season, the PSU team needed a new coach. It would be Bill O'Brian, a good man. PSU was coached in 2012 by Bill O'Brien, and not Joe Paterno or Tom Bradley. It was O'Brien's, first season and so as had been the accustomed venue for his team, the Lions played home games in Beaver Stadium in University Park, Pennsylvania, US.

PSU continued as a member of the Big Ten Conference and the team played in the Leaders Division. Due to NCAA sanctions, Penn State was ineligible to play in a bowl game for the 2012 season. The NCAA hurriedly had placed Penn State in the toilet before the verdict had been drawn properly on the 2011 scandal.

O'Brien was hired as Penn State's 15th head football coach, replacing Hall of Fame coach, Joe Paterno. He was introduced as the head coach at a press conference on January 7, 2012. The team added player names to the back of their jerseys to recognize the players who stayed with the program despite adversity, and they also wore a blue ribbon to support child abuse victims. Football issues were not as important as human issues. PSU was right there offering thoughts of redemption. But, no redemption was to be offered to Joe Paterno despite his contrition.

After losing its first two games, the Nittany Lions finished their season winning eight of their final 10 to finish with a record of eight wins and four losses (8–4). They were not eligible to participate in a bowl game despite their winning record. Many PSU fans were wondering why the team and players were suffering as their playing football with encumbrances seemed to be punishing the wrong people. The student athletes were punished. The state of Pennsylvania was punished. Coach Paterno was punished unmercifully while there was only one accused

There seems to be those in the media ready to attack great institutions such as the Catholic Church, and Penn State University, while giving a pass to others that they would prefer to protect.

CBS News reports the following:

> *Hofstra University researcher Charol Shakeshaft looked into the problem, and the first thing that came to her mind when Education Week reported on the study were the daily headlines about the Catholic Church.*

"Think the Catholic Church has a problem?" she said. "The physical sexual abuse of students in schools is likely more than 100 times the abuse by priests."

So, in order to better protect children, did media outlets start hounding the worse menace of the school systems, with headlines about a "Nationwide Teacher Molestation Cover-up" and by asking "Are Ed Schools Producing Pedophiles?"

> No, they didn't. That treatment was reserved for the Catholic Church, [and now Penn State University] while the greater problem in the schools was ignored altogether.
>
> As the National Catholic Register's reporter Wayne Laugesenpoints out, the federal report said 422,000 California public-school students would be victims before graduation — a number that dwarfs the state's entire Catholic-school enrollment of 143,000.

Protestants are worried as they know no institution is without its perpetrators. They feel lucky to an extent that they have not been called as has the Catholic Church and now of course Penn State University

I am not trying to create a controversy here between Catholics and protestants and K-12 public school teachers but the high-handed treatment of Penn State's innocent student body and athletes and State College as well as the defamation of Coach Paterno without a trial seems out of step with how the media and the pundits handle situations in other institutions.

> There is an extensive report by Kathryn Joyce, from Prospect.org called "The Next Christian Sex Abuse Scandal." It is an eye opener to the extent of the sexual abuse epidemic in many Protestant Churches and schools. By this article, we do not want to undermine Catholic abuses by Catholic priests whom we feel should also be burned at the stake, but it is time to fess up, and before we pull the plank out of the eye in our Catholic brothers, Protestants should first see the plank in their eye."

I have a number of concluding chapters in which I look at Joe Paterno as a human being and as a major asset to the Pennsylvania State University, and as a person who helped the University achieve its greatness.

The damage to children in the Penn State sexual abuse situation cannot be minimized. That is not my issue, but a witch hunt intended to defame Penn State and Joe Paterno and the football program, is not an appropriate response to the problem. Jerry Sandusky has been found guilty. The facts have apparently spoken and unless we plan to close down every public school and fire every principal whose charges went off on their own, then destroying the value of a Penn State experience and a Penn State education should be off the table.

Now, let's get off the subject of why Bill O'Brien became the coach and concentrate on his first season. In this

Games of the 2012 PSU Football Season

On September 1, at Beaver Stadium, the Nittany Lions unexpectedly lost to the Ohio University Bobcats L (14-24) as the Lions were trying to recover from a bad dream. The Bobcats obviously were not the same old pushover Bobcats.

They had changed under the guidance of Frank Solich. The whole Ohio football program enjoyed a return to national prominence in 2006, and in 2012 they beat Penn State and won their next six games. Tough to take the loss but a worthy opponent nonetheless.

On September 8, PSU traveled to Scott Stadium in Charlottesville, VA and were beaten by Virginia in a nailbiter L 16–17) Bill O'Brien's team was 0-2 when Navy came into Beaver Stadium on September 15. The Lions became the new Nittany Lions on this day as they beat Navy W (34–7).

Bill O'Brien recorded his first victory as Penn State's head coach when the Nittany Lions defeated Navy, 34-7, at Beaver Stadium on September 15, 2012.

On September 22, a toughening Temple Owls team came to play the Lions at home and were beaten back in a tough game W (24-13). Penn State under Bill O'Brian had gotten its edge back and was playing good football.

On September 29, The Nittany Lions traveled to Memorial Stadium in Champaign, IL and beat the Fighting Illini W (35–7). On October 6, Northwestern arrived at Beaver Stadium ready for a tough game and they got one. PSU beat the Wildcats in a close match W (39-28). The team had begun to gel after all the coaching changes. Next on October 20 at Iowa's Kinnick Stadium in Iowa City, IA, Penn State beat a tough Hawkeyes team W (38–14). PSU was on a roll but the next game on October 27 at home against #9 ranked Ohio State L (23-35) was a setback but it did not stop O'Brien's team from moving to the next victory against Purdue.

On November 3 at Ross-Ade Stadium • in West Lafayette, IN, PSU defeated the Boilermakers in a nice game W (34–9). On November 10, PSU played #18 Nebraska and did all it could to win but it was not enough as the Cornhuskers squeaked out a win against the Lions L (23-32). When Indiana came to town on November 17, PSU was finished losing for the season and the Nittany Lions beat the Hoosiers W (45-22). On November 24, it was Wisconsin at Beaver Stadium. In an overtime game, the determined Nittany Lions pulled out a fine victory making the season very respectable at 8-4. PSU was not eligible because of NCAA four year sanctions from playing Bowl Games.

2013 Penn State Football Season Coach Bill O'Brien

The 2013 Penn State Nittany Lions football team was coached by Bill O'Brien and they were a member of the Big Ten Conference and its Leaders Division. Penn State was ineligible to play in a bowl game for the 2013 season, the second season of a four-year ban, due to NCAA sanctions imposed in the wake of the Jerry Sandusky sex abuse scandal.

Before the season, Penn State needed to find a starting quarterback. They had an open competition between true freshman Christian Hackenberg won and started all 12 games for the Nittany Lions. Hackenberg had been ESPN's top-rated passer of the 2013 class. He beat out junior college quarterback Tyler Ferguson for the job

Despite sanctions, PSU still was able to recruit some stars though many chose to stake their fortunes elsewhere. Hackenberg headlined the 2013 recruiting class, which also featured tight end Adam Breneman. Breneman of course had a nice 2013 as a true freshman but injured himself as a sophomore, missed the 2014 season completely, and never really was able to play right again. After achieving his degree, he retired from football following the season due to a chronic knee injury.

John Butler was named Penn State's new defensive coordinator upon the departure of Ted Roof. Most predicted Penn State would have a similar season to that of the 2012 team, which won eight games and lost four, but there was uncertainty, as injuries were a big part of the season. PSU was thin in many positions because of the sanctions including offensive line and linebacker.

The Nittany Lions started well by opening the season with two non-conference wins, but lost to the UCF Knights, who ultimately went on to a BCS bowl, the Fiesta, in their third game. Entering Big Ten play, the Nittany Lions were 3–1, and in their first conference game they lost to Indiana before defeating Michigan in a quadruple-overtime thriller. They alternated losses and wins for the remainder of the season, losing to Ohio State, Minnesota, and Nebraska, and defeating Illinois, Purdue, and Wisconsin.

At the end of the season, Coach O'Brien, who did his best with two NCAA handicapped PSU teams accepted the head coaching position with the Houston Texans, leaving the Nittany Lions after two seasons. Early in 2014, the Nittany Lions hired James Franklin to replace O'Brien as head coach for the 2014 season.

Bill O'Brien was one of those special coaches that only are discovered every so often. Despite NCAA sanctions including limited scholarships and a bowl ban, He and his recruiting team retained their top recruit: quarterback Christian Hackenberg. Additional, PSU finished with the 24th ranked recruiting class according to ESPN, who cited retention of top prospects Hackenberg and tight end Adam Breneman, as well as adding depth in the secondary, overall giving them a "B" rating. Not bad for a team that many had completely minimized.

Coming off an 8–4 season during which attrition took its toll on overall prospects as nobody can win National Championships without well-gifted backup players, many college football pundits and analysts expected the Nittany Lions to perform similarly in 2013. There was the realization that since they were running thin on talent at the start, the season outlook could change quickly if the team was hampered by injuries. Then again, PSU could surprise everyone and win more games than they did in 2012. The results are in and it was more former than latter.

On August 31 PSU and Syracuse met at Met Life Stadium East Rutherford, NJ before 61,202 and the unranked Nittany Lions won the game W (23-17). On September 7, PSU played Eastern Michigan at Beaver Stadium and beat the Eagles handily W (45-7). On September 24, a tough Central Florida team beat the Nittany Lions in a nail biter at Beaver Stadium L (31-34). Kent State was next Sept. 21 as the Nittany Lions shut out the Golden Flashes at Beaver Stadium W (34-0). On October 5   at Indiana's Memorial Stadium in Bloomington, IN. PSU lost to the Hoosiers L (24–44) before 42,125.

Allen Robinson (8) catches the ball at the one yard line to set up the game tying touchdown at the end of the fourth quarter of a game against Michigan at Beaver Stadium on Saturday, Oct. 12, 2013 Penn State beat Michigan in quadruple overtime, 43-40.

On October 12, at home, PSU beat a stubborn Michigan Team in 4 OT periods, W (43-40).

Then, after a bye week, PSU was soundly beaten on October 26 by #4 Ohio State at Ohio Stadium in Columbus, OH. L (14–63) before 105,889. PSU had some luck in the tie games this year. Again, on November 2, the Nittany Lions tied and then beat Illinois in OT at home W (24–17).

On November 9 at the customary Noon start time, PSU lost to Minnesota at TCF Bank Stadium in Minneapolis, MN L (10–24) before 48,123. The following week on November 16, at home Purdue was on the short end of the score W (45-21) before 96,491at Beaver Stadium. Since Paterno's departure the crowds at Beaver Stadium were not at max. On November 23 at home, Penn State lost its OT charm after it tied Nebraska. The Cornhuskers won in single overtime L (20–23) in OT before 98,517. On

November 30 in the season finale and Coach O'Brien's swan song, PSU beat #14 Wisconsin at Camp Randall Stadium in Madison, WI W (31–24) before 78,064

November 9, 2013, facts taken from report by Mike Dawson, mdawson@centredaily.com

Player Highlights Allen Robinson

Allen Robinson is quite a football player with a knack for making things look easy on the football field. He has what it takes plus a lot of heart. He has great size, speed and strong hands.

In the 2012 season, Robinson busted onto the scene with nine catches for 97 yards in the high-octane Bill O'Brien-led offense. With his confidence confirmed by the breakout season-opener, Robinson never looked back en route to racing into the record books during a dominant sophomore season. The awards in 2012 and 2013 piled up for the athletic and vastly talented wideout, who was selected the 2012 Big

Ten Richter-Howard Receiver-of-the-Year and first-team All-Big Ten by the coaches, media, BTN.com and ESPN.com.

Robinson was named an All-American by The Sporting News and Phil Steele named Robinson to his second-team All-America squad. Robinson shattered the Penn State season receptions record with 77 catches, besting the previous record of 63 held by All-Americans O.J. McDuffie (1992) and Bobby Engram (1995).

He also obliterated the season mark for a sophomore that had been held by Engram (48, 1993) and Deon Butler (48, 2006). Robinson's 1,013 yards marked just the third 1,000-yard receiving season in school history, joining Engram (twice) as the only 1,000-yard season receivers to wear the blue and white.

Having made three catches for 29 yards as a freshman, Robinson led the Big Ten in catches, receptions per game, receiving yards and touchdown catches in 2012. His 11 touchdown grabs were tied for second-highest in a season at Penn State (Engram, 1995).

Robinson's 6-3 frame and leaping ability makes him a big target in the red zone, and he enters the year tied for ninth on the career touchdown receptions chart after two seasons. The former Orchard Lake St. Mary's Prep standout has breakaway speed and has always been elusive in the open field.

Other happenings at PSU in 2013

Mike Dawson - mdawson@centredaily.com, wrote a piece in 2013 titled: Penn State trustees, Freeh blasted at Franco Harris forum. I used it as a fact basis for my own piece which is below. Here it is with some poetic license. Opinions are mine.

It is not over. The outrage at Joe Paterno's take-down will continue for a long time to come, and in my opinion, the people's verdict will exonerate the famed coach. More than 250 people turned out on a November 2013 Saturday night to listen to supporters of Coach Joe Paterno admonish Penn State for its firing of the legendary coach exactly two years before, as well as bringing forth a number of other points regarding the fallout from the Jerry Sandusky scandal.

It helps to remember this was not the Joe Paterno scandal. It was and is the Jerry Sandusky scandal. If it weren't for the big prize money, maybe it would not even be the Sandusky scandal. I am not accusing anybody…just supposing. I know I do not know for sure. But, for sure, Sandusky's behavior was observed and documented as being at a minimum a little flaky. Where is the truth?

The event moniker, "Upon Further Review," did exactly what it was supposed to do. Presenters roasted Mike McQueary, the board of trustees and the quick-to-blame media. This was a long process while it was happening and it is tough to know exactly what was happening when so the presentations were necessarily complex and contained a lot of analyses of the data. Nonetheless, the message was simple: these PSU and Paterno supporters believe the truth is the major missing ingredient from the scandal.

Co-organizer of the event, Ray Blehar, who is no longer held in high regard by those pro-Paterno forces that want just the truth offered these comments:

"Those investigations will hopefully get to the truth…if they don't, we will continue to press on."

The event was sponsored by Nittany Lion great Franco Harris, and in addition to Blehar, it featured presentations by Eileen Morgan and John Ziegler, a filmmaker who released the documentary "The Framing of Joe Paterno" in 2011. Zieglar has made some changes to the documentary since then as some of the information received from Blehar did not meet the smell test.

"We can't forget what they did to Penn State," said Harris, one of the most visible and loyal Paterno supporters over the past two years. "We have to find the truth, and that's what's really important." Morgan prefaced her remarks by saying she wasn't criticizing or judging McQueary.

She said that parts of McQueary's first three descriptions of the shower incident in 2001 are different from the last three, and she pointed out revelations that he made on the stand during a preliminary hearing for ex-administrators Graham Spanier, Tim Curley and Gary Schultz over the summer.

That's when McQueary said he had a conversation with Paterno in which the coach told him Nov. 9, 2011, that Old Main would make him the "scapegoat." Old Main is another term for the main Building at Penn State and is used often to refer to the entire University Structure.

Eileen Morgan also said the grand jury presentation that put forth the charges against Sandusky did not get it all right. There was a huge error of omission according to Morgan as there was nothing about what the McQueary family friend Jonathan Dranov had told the grand jury.

Blehar pulled no punches while blasting the board of trustees, and suggesting that former trustee John Surma had a vendetta against Paterno and subsequently wanted Paterno fired. Blehar noted that he does not believe that some trustees have said they didn't see news reports in March 2011 about the investigation and weren't aware of the allegations until the grand jury presentment came out.

Admittedly, it is tough to believe that the Board could be so blind to what is happening at their own institution.

As for the Freeh investigation, Blehar was very vocal noting that it was a "fake," and that former FBI director Louis Freeh "was hired to deceive the public into believing an independent investigation would be done." These are major accusations and from my own research, Blehar is not the only person with that opinion.

Ziegler, who produced the documentary conducted prison interviews with Sandusky. His take is that the message that the media has put out is wrong about the nature of Sandusky's crimes: *"I believe that the nature of his crimes are vastly different from the public perception," he said. "Gun to my head, I do not believe Jerry Sandusky had a sex act with a boy." That is a bold statement for sure while Sandusky is rotting in prison and Paterno is dead.*

Ziegler also showed no love for the media's handling of the circumstances, and he had no problem bashing national news reporters and anchors for saying that Sandusky had raped boys. The event also put forth a panel discussion following the presentations by Morgan, Blehar and Ziegler.

Another tidbit revealed is that the Harrisburg lawyer Rob Tribeck said the grand jury that heard McQueary's testimony was not the same grand jury that was empaneled when the presentment was issued. The 30th statewide grand jury was first empaneled, and the 33rd grand jury was empaneled when the presentment was released. Tribeck offered that the grand jury had found that McQueary's testimony was credible while that of Curley and Schultz was not found to be credible.

His take was that the grand jury presentment was written by a prosecutor to "incite the public." The media did little independent work and instead followed the presentment said "like sheep."

Ryan Bagwell, a panelist and a Penn State alumnus said he had set up a fund to help offset the costs to pursue his open-records cases that are before the state's Open Records Office. He's facing a challenge from Penn State to keep private email correspondence that former state education secretary and ex-trustee Ron Tomalis had with Freeh. One day, perhaps the truth will all come out but along the way a lot of damage has been done to some pretty good people.

Read more here:
http://www.centredaily.com/news/local/education/penn-state/jerry-sandusky/article42834075.html#storylink=cpy

Chapter 23 — The James Franklin Era From 2014 to 2016 +...

Coach # 16

2014 James Franklin 7-6   (2-6 Big Ten)
2015 James Franklin 7-6   (4-4 Big Ten)
2016 James Franklin

Penn State head coach James Franklin, center, leads his team onto the field at Beaver Stadium before an NCAA college football game against Akron.

2014 Penn State Football Season Coach James Franklin

The 2014 Penn State Nittany Lions football team was led by first year head-coach James Franklin and played its home games in Beaver Stadium in University Park, Pennsylvania. It continued as a member of the Big Ten Conference and played in the newly organized East Division. As in 2011 through 2013, Penn State was ineligible to play in a bowl game due to NCAA sanctions. However, on September 8, 2014, the NCAA announced that Penn State would again be eligible for post-season games, effective immediately.

The Nittany Lions had a 7-6 overall record for the season with a 2-6 Big Ten mark, placing sixth in the Big Ten East Division. The Nittany Lions respectably concluded the season with a victory in the Pinstripe Bowl over Boston

The 2014 season began on August 30, in Croke Park, Dublin Ireland in the Croke Park Classic. The Lions and another American team, UCF, played in the "old sod." Coach Franklin had to travel quite a ways for his first win W (26-24) in a very close game before 53,304.

On September 6 PSU played at home v Akron and beat the Zips W (21-3). A toughened Rutgers team invited PSU to play at High Point Solutions Stadium in Piscataway, NJ. The Nittany Lions got their third win of the young season W (13-10). On September 20, PSU played Massachusetts at Beaver Stadium before 99,155 and collected a blow-out win over the UMass Minutemen. W (48-7).

On September 27, the Big ten started to appear on the PSU schedule and the Nittany Lions 4-0 record was about ready to leave the perfect stage. Northwestern started it off by beating Penn State at Beaver Stadium L (6-29). On October 11 in a night game at Michigan, PSU kept the game close but the Wolverines won in the end W (13-18). On October 25, #12 Ohio state was next to get a piece of the Nittany Lions in a one touchdown game at Beaver Stadium L (24-31) On November 1, new Big Ten Team Maryland played PSU at Beaver Stadium and just eked out a win L (19-20)

On November 8 at Indiana, PSU finally had enough determination to win a close one W (13-7). On November 15, Temple came to Beaver Stadium and the Lions beat the Owls W (30-13). The following week, on November 22 at Illinois, the Lions lost another very close game L (14-16). For want of a few points here and there it would have been a different season. The final regular season game was on November 29 against #10 Michigan State at Beaver Stadium. PSU lost this game by a much wider spread than the others L (10-34).

Penn State qualified for one of the new Bowl games after Bowl Sancions were lifted. On December 27 at 4:30 PM, Penn State played a feisty Boston College team in Yankee Stadium in the Bronx, NY and beat the Eagles in OT W (31-30). The game was also aired on ESPN. Overall, at 7-6, a recovering Penn State program had not yet gone negative without JoePa.

2015 Penn State Football Season Coach James Franklin

The 2015 Penn State Nittany Lions football team was led by second year head-coach James Franklin The Nittany Lions finished the season 7–6; (4–4 in Big Ten) to finish in fourth place in the East Division of the Big Ten. They were invited to the TaxSlayer Bowl where the Lions lost to Georgia in a close battle L (17-24).

On September 5, PSU lost decisively to Temple in the season opener at Lincoln Financial Field in Philadelphia. Temple had decided it was no longer a push-over team under coach Fran Dunphy L (10–27). The game attendance was 69,176. On September 12, Buffalo played the Lions tough but PSU came away with a win at Beaver Stadium against the Bulls W (27-14).

Beaver Stadium would be a busy place for another four weeks with Rutgers being the first visitor on September 19. The Lions won W (28-3) San Diego State was next on September 26, W 37-21) Then, on October 3, Army came in to steal away some PSU pride but failed W (20-14). Attendance was picking up with this game total at 107,387. Then, on October 10, Indiana challenged the Nittany Lions but the Lions beat the Hoosiers W (20-14).

It was the Nittany Lions time to travel and first it was to Ohio Stadium in Columbus, OH on October 17. The #1 Ohio Buckeyes, coached by "take no prisoners" Urban Meyer defeated Penn State this day quite decisively L (10-38) before

108,423. On October 24, PSU traveled to Maryland's M&T Bank Stadium, Baltimore, MD where the Lions pulled out a real nailbiter victory W (31-30).

Back at home on October 31, PSU defeated Illinois in a shutout W (39-0). On November 7 PSU was back on the road again against Northwestern in Ryan Field Evanston, IL. The Wildcats pulled off the squeaker this time L (21-23) Then on November 21 an always tough #14 Michigan played the Lions at Beaver Stadium in University Park, PA. The game was also broadcast on ABC. Michigan defeated Penn State on this day, L (16–28) before a nice crowd of 107,418.

Back to back Michigan teams were on this year's schedule. This time on November 28, PSU was on the road to play #6 Michigan State at Spartan Stadium in East Lansing, MI. Michigan State could not be stopped and the Nittany Lions took one of its worst losses ever L (16-55).

Penn State was offered a January 2 Bowl game appearance against a trough Georgia team in the TaxSlayer Bowl at noon at EverBank Field • Jacksonville, FL. The game was televised on ESPN and the attendance at the game was 58,212. Georgia just about beat the Nittany Lions L (17–24).

Penn State under James Franklin had two identical 7-6 seasons counting this bowl loss. There was a difference however, in that this year, PSU did 100% better when playing conference games (4-4).

With Joe Paterno having just one really dark period—even during his worst period, he would come back after rebuilding and pound the opposition. The fans are looking for James Franklin to pull a JoePa in 2016.

2016 Penn State Football Season Schedule Coach Franklin

The 2016 Penn State Nittany Lions football team will be led by third year head-coach James Franklin and play its home games in Beaver Stadium in University Park, Pennsylvania.

The Penn State Nittany Lions are a member of the East Division of the Big Ten Conference.

Penn State announced its 2016 football schedule on July 11, 2013. The 2016 schedule consists of 7 home and 5 away games in the regular season. The Nittany Lions will host Big Ten foes Iowa, Maryland, Michigan State, Minnesota, and Ohio State, and will travel to Indiana, Michigan, Purdue, and Rutgers.

The team will host two of the three non–conference games which are against the Kent State Golden Flashes from the Mid-American Conference (MAC), Pittsburgh Panthers from the Atlantic Coast Conference (ACC), and the Temple Owls from the American Athletic Conference (AAC).

Date	Opponent	Site
September 3	Kent State*	Beaver Stadium •
September 10	at Pittsburgh	Heinz Field •
September 17	Temple	Beaver Stadium •
September 24	…at Michigan	Michigan Stadium •
October 1	Minnesota	Beaver Stadium •
October 8	Maryland	Beaver Stadium •
October 22	Ohio State	Beaver Stadium •
October 29	at Purdue	Ross–Ade Stadium •
November 5	Iowa	Beaver Stadium •
November 12	at Indiana	Memorial Stadium •
November 19	at Rutgers	High Point Solutions
November 26	Michigan State	Beaver Stadium •

Chapter 24 — Joe Paterno: The Fine Man, the Great Coach, and the Legend!

Only one Joe Paterno was ever built by God!

Before 2004 game: Penn State football coach Joe Paterno leads his team onto the field

We all know Joe Paterno as the inimitable and accomplished head football coach at Pennsylvania State University. He was without a doubt one of the most successful coaches, if not simply the most successful coach in the history of collegiate football. Paterno is well known for his quotes to help others succeed such as the following:

"Believe deep down in your heart that you're destined to do great things."

"The will to win is important, but the will to prepare is vital."

"Success without honor is an unseasoned dish; it will satisfy your hunger, but it won't taste good."

Joe Paterno had substantial success and great success and he had his success with honor. He was always a great man. He never changed to fit the times. His greatness and his legacy of respect for humankind will only increase as time goes by. Joe Paterno was not superhuman, god-like, or all-seeing, and he spent his time coaching football.

Contrary to popular belief, Joe Paterno was not born a coach in a manger. As a new born, little baby Joe knew that few colleges would hire him to coach their great football teams if he needed his mom and dad to take him to the practice field and to the games. But, this would soon change.

Like all of us, Paterno was born of regular parents who happened to be Italian. They pressed upon him early the importance of education and Joe, a quick learner, never forgot his parent's lesson. His date and place of birth is December 21, 1926, in Brooklyn, New York. Brooklyn was in his accent and he never lost that special voice.

Before he turned to college, Paterno was already turning heads. As a high school senior, Joe Paterno and his younger brother George, then a junior, gained notoriety throughout the New York metropolitan area for their exploits on the football field and basketball court. Hard as it to believe, neither were close to six foot tall.

BORO GRID STARS—George and Joseph Paterno, Brooklyn brothers, out for Spring football practice at Brown University, were former stars at Brooklyn Prep. They are hopefuls for regular backfield posts with Rip Engle's

The "Gold Dust Twins," as they were known, had led Brooklyn Prep to an 8-1 season in 1943, with the only loss against St. Cecilia's School in Englewood, N.J. At the time, St. Cecilia School was coached by none other than Vince Lombardi, who would go on to become a Hall of Fame coach with the Green Bay Packers.

After his HS graduation, Paterno attended and graduated from Brown University in 1950, where he played football both ways as the quarterback and a cornerback. It was not easy getting to Brown as dad wanted both boys, Joe, and George, to attend the same college together. The boys were small but star athletes nonetheless.

The Paterno brothers - George 1950 and Joe 1950

Finally, a wealthy alumnus from Brown University offered to pay for both Joe and George to attend the Providence, R.I., school -- in 1944, it was legal for donors to pay for player scholarships. Like Ed Kelly, my dad would have said if an alumnus from King's College had offered me such a deal, "Stop thinking…take the deal!"

JoePa had a great career at Brown. He was inducted into Brown's Athletic Hall of Fame in 1977. His former Brown coach, Charles ("Rip") Engle, became head coach at Pennsylvania State University (Penn State) and hired the 23-year old Paterno as an assistant coach. That just about ended dad's hope for his son Joe to become an attorney. After 16 years as his assistant, Paterno succeeded Rip Engle as Penn State's head coach in 1966.

He was nothing less than phenomenal as a head coach in his very late thirties right from the start. Paterno led Penn State to consecutive undefeated seasons in 1968 and 1969 and another undefeated season in 1973. He had to wake up the pundits and the other coaches to ever gain in the rankings. He did.

Like many of his time period, Joe Paterno served in the U.S. Army during World War II. After the war, Paterno went to Brown, where as noted, he dominated the gridiron as the school's quarterback and led his team to an 8-1 season in his senior year. He graduated from Brown in 1950, and after settling down at Penn State, he married Suzanne Pohland in 1962. The couple had five children together, all of whom later became graduates of Penn State.

None of these fine people, who know their dad and husband like no other people know him, will let his legacy, or the legacy of the football program at Penn State University remain tarnished because of the rash judgment of a board of directors that had read a book about how to get monkeys off backs.

PSU Head Coach Paterno

In 1966, as noted, Coach Paterno became the head football coach of Penn State University. His first season was a draw, with 5 wins and 5 losses, but he worked especially hard to build up the school's football program. Before long, Paterno racked up impressive scores, including coaching the team to two undefeated regular seasons in 1968 and 1969. Over his 61 years as assistant and as head coach, Joe Paterno became not just a revered coach but he also became a beloved figure at the university. Of course he became known for his trademark thick, square-shaped glasses and for his leadership skills.

He was always in shape and ran with the team onto the field for football games. He had a revered nickname "Joe Pa," which stuck with him from the first time it was used. He dedicated himself to his team, the Nittany Lions. Joe Paterno could have made a lot more money and could have coached anywhere he wanted. He even turned down a chance to coach professional football with Pittsburgh and with the New England Patriots in 1973.

Though PSU was not awarded National Championship status for the many perfect records (undefeated and untied) that Paterno accumulated with Penn State, he did lead the Lions to two National Championships—in 1982 and in 1986. Both of these are consensus and unquestioned. In recognition of his contributions to his winning team, he earned the Sportsman of the Year honor from Sports Illustrated in 1986.

Overall, Paterno had an impressive record as the Nittany Lions' coach. In 46 seasons, he led his team to 37 bowl appearances with 24 Bowl wins. In October 2011, Paterno set a major record of his own when Penn State defeated Illinois. This victory marked his 409th career win, making him the leader in career wins for Division I coaches. Think of all the greats that coached in Division I.

Those who know Joe Paterno or had any dealings with the man or the coach know one thing among many. Coach Paterno was as honest as the day is long. When he was notified about the allegations, he did something about it. He did not sit like a doofus wringing his hands as the corrupt press would have you believe.

He explained it in his own words: "I didn't know exactly how to handle it," referring to allegations of sexual abuse against Sandusky. "So I backed away and turned it over to some other people, people I thought would have a little more expertise than I did. It didn't turn out that way."

Jerry Sandusky was not a Paterno enemy but never a close friend of Paterno. He was just a talented defensive coach and Paterno was his boss. They did not go out drinking together! When Sandusky asked for access to training and workout facilities, before allegations, Paterno balked. He said that the kids should certainly not be permitted to use the facilities, period—but apparently he was overridden by AD Curley, who was Paterno's boss.

After leaving Penn State in that terrible time in 2011, Joe Paterno began suffering major health problems.

RIP Joe Paterno

He was diagnosed with lung cancer in late 2011. While it was initially thought to be treatable, Paterno succumbed to this illness just two months later, on January 22, 2012. At Mount Nittany Medical Center in State College, Pennsylvania, he passed on into eternal life. Many of his former players believe he dies of a broken heart.

I am sure he is helping fill in the details for many in heaven for those who missed some of the greatest games of his career. He is missed by us all but mostly for sure by his devoted family.

Joe Paterno is survived by his wife, five children, and 17 grandchildren. In a statement, his family said: "He died as he lived. He fought hard until the end, stayed positive, thought only of others and constantly reminded everyone of how blessed his life had been ... He was a man devoted to his family, his university, his players and his community."

USA Today wrote a nice story several days after Joe Paterno's death and funeral that captures a lot of the goodness of the man and the good feelings he projected with friends and especially family.

They first relate how right before his death, his son, Jay Paterno leaned over his dying father, gave him a kiss, and whispered in his ear. "Dad, you won," he said. "You did all you could do. You've done enough. We all love you. We won. You can go home now." Coach Paterno died that Sunday, January 22, of lung cancer at age 85.

Millions would have been at the memorial service if they could have been accommodated. About 12,000 attended the Thursday event which was held in the Penn State basketball arena. Jay Paterno, who was also a coach at Penn State working for his dad, reflected on what he called the "magnificent daylight" of his legendary father's life.

Son Jay took the opportunity to defend the Joe Paterno legacy against criticism that he failed to do more when told about an alleged child sexual assault involving one of his former assistants. Bravo to the courage of the Paterno family.

Joe Paterno had a lot of friends which he knew and he had a lot of friends about which he did not know. Nike founder and CEO Phil Knight asked for time at the funeral celebration of life, and offered his thoughts which mirror those of many of us. Knight won a thunderous standing ovation when he defended Paterno's handling of the 2002 allegations against former defensive coordinator Jerry Sandusky. Paterno, he hinted, had been made a scapegoat. Knight said:

"If there is a villain in this tragedy, it lies in that investigation and not in Joe Paterno's response,"

Joe Paterno's widow, Sue, was among those rising to their feet in accord with Knight's well-needed words. The memorial service capped off three days of mourning on campus. Besides Knight and Jay Paterno, the 2-hour ceremony was filled with many who offered lavish praise for the man we all called "JoePa."

We all know the 409 legacy that the NCAA temporarily had taken away from the coach and the university. JoePa had racked up more wins — 409 — than any other major-college football coach. He led his team to two national championships, and his mantra was always "success with honor." He insisted his athletes focus on academics as a requisite for playing football for Penn State. His 409 represents our 409 and all are good wins.

From The Collegian
Joe Paterno put education before all else
By Joe McIntyre
Jan 23, 2012

Joe Paterno was always more than just a coach. I have copied this article which I feel the reader will enjoy, from the University's student newspaper, the Collegian which tells a story about how Joe Paterno, who happened to be a Full College Professor, had a deep love for education:

> *As he walked into Chuck Benjamin's home in Cresskill, N.J., to recruit the then-high school senior, Joe Paterno happened to notice a book his prospective athlete was reading.*

It was "Crime and Punishment" by Fyodor Dostoyevsky, a novel filled with difficult-to-pronounce Russian names such as Raskolnikov, Marmeladova and Zarnitsyn. But Paterno knew their pronunciations. He had read it before. He remembered the characters. He spoke with Benjamin about his high school studies and discussed why he was reading Dostoyevsky's piece.

Before Paterno's visit, Benjamin had visited and received scholarship offers from not only a few "big-time" football institutions, but a number of Ivy League schools, as well. The defensive tackle was a bright kid, earned solid marks in school.

But what made his decision to choose Penn State and deny a university like Dartmouth easy was Paterno's knowledge of the arts and the importance he put on his athletes' education.

"I said to myself, 'Goodness, there is no other coach in the world who is such a Renaissance man, in my mind, as Joe Paterno, He knows football. He knows literature. He knows politics. He was just incredible. So much for going to Dartmouth, I ended up saying that this is where I wanted to go.'"

When the coach recruited players, football always remained on the backburner. Sure, these high school stars had aspirations of playing football for the Nittany Lions, but in Paterno's eyes that shouldn't be why they chose Penn State.

Paterno promised parents that their sons were going to come to Penn State to get an education, and he reiterated to players that that's what they were going to get. They were going to have a great college experience, earn a degree and maybe play a little football, too.

He didn't care whether it meant he would lose players on Saturdays or skip recruiting a player in general. If a player didn't take his education seriously, Paterno wouldn't think twice about punishing him or looking him over, a philosophy that few other coaches subscribed to.

That's the way he always was. When he recruited Rich Mauti in the early '70s to when he recruited Mauti's two sons, former Lion Patrick and current Lion Michael, Paterno's recruiting bits may as well have been prerecorded routines. His three important aspects of the decision to attend Penn State were in the same order for Rich Mauti's parents as they were to him when his sons were recruited. First was education, second was college experience and third was football.

Nothing has changed.

"It's never wavered. That's been his way," Mauti said. "Incredibly, he's been able over the years to translate that into an incredibly successful football program. Again, there's so much beyond football. Football is so shallow relative to what this man has done. To call him a football coach is not justifiable. It really isn't."

During Paterno's time with the Lions, Penn State has had 47 Academic All-Americans in football, with 37 earning first team honors. The Lions' all-time total of 49 Academic All-America football players ranks third among all FBS institutions and leads all Big Ten institutions.

In the 25 years they have been eligible (all within Paterno's tenure), the Lions have been recognized by the American Football Coaches Association (AFCA) 21 times, including 2011, in their annual Academic Achievement Award survey. Only Note Dame and Virginia (22) have more honorable mention citations.

In 2011, the Lions also earned the top spot in the fifth-annual Academic BCS rankings, as determined by New America Foundation's Higher Ed Watch with 117 points, followed by Boise State (107), TCU (101) and Stanford (100).
During Paterno's tenure, the Lions have turned out highly successful physicians, cardiologists, orthopedic surgeons and lawyers. The coach was a part of molding young boys into

high-profile business executives, real estate CEOs, politicians, professors, teachers and stockbrokers.
Had it not been for Paterno, Benjamin may not be in New Jersey practicing his 31st year of law. It took a suggestion from his coach for the then-senior to even look into law school.

Like Paterno's father questioned of him after his playing days were over, Benjamin was asked by Joe Paterno nearly the identical question Angelo Paterno posed to his son back in 1950.

"Joe said, 'Well, what are you going to do now?'" Benjamin remembers.
And after Benjamin stayed at Penn State for a year as a graduate assistant, like Angelo, Joe offered law school as an option to Benjamin.

But unlike Joe, his player took up the advice.

"When he talked to me about law, and the way you can apply so much of what you have learned as an English literature major in the practice of law, I had never thought about it before," Benjamin said. "No one in my family had ever gone into law, so he was kind of the person who steered me in that direction."

Still, it wasn't only the standout student Paterno focused on. If a player slacked off in the classroom, he didn't play. If during freshman year he skipped mandatory study hall, his uniform would stay clean. If a player was struggling to keep up with his studies, he'd be sure to get the tutoring he needed or else it meant the bench.

"His grand experiment worked," Mauti said. "You'll see it today, even this past year. Some kids got into academic troubles, and they just don't play. There's no gray area. You go to school. You're coming here to get an education."

When former players returned to Happy Valley to see a football game and got the chance to visit with Paterno, the coach would always remember what they were up to. He would ask Benjamin how his career in law was progressing.

"The fact that he remembered so many things about all of us was just unbelievable," Benjamin said. "He had such a mind. The fact that he could remember so much about literally thousands of people who went through Penn State playing for him was incredible."

He never forgot what was important. He never forgot what he preached and what he taught. He never forgot that all else came second to school.

"Education first" was the Joe Paterno mantra. And he lived by it.

"He talked on a daily basis about how every day is a special day and go to class," Benjamin remembers.

"He said, 'Look this is all there for you. It's up to you to seize it and make the most of it.'

Paterno Biography Commissioned

A year or so before his death, Joe Paterno agreed to open the internal book in his mind about his personal life to former Sports Illustrated writer Joe Posnanski. At the time, of course neither could have expected where their respective journeys would end. Posnanski more than likely hoped for a best-seller, and Paterno was hoping to squeeze a few national championships into the book before the final period (.) came about. I am one of the proud owners of the book called PATERNO.

The book was released on August 21, 2012, and it has sold reasonably well. I would recommend it for your Penn State Football Library. It would make a nice read. Joe Posnanski lived in State College, Pennsylvania through the final tough months of Paterno's life and was with him and his family as the scandal that eventually consumed him unfolded. Posnanski has since added a new afterword to the book to capture it all.

His book delves deep into the life of Joe Paterno, going back to his childhood days in Brooklyn and his college days at Brown. It is an honest look and therefore a positive look at Joe Paterno through the eyes of the young men he coached. It is also a portrait that goes beyond the daily headlines and into the life of a great man whose mettle included being a stubborn idealist, a teacher, and a flawed but principled human being who, to the very end, loved to coach.

Lou Prato offered his thoughts on the book prior to its 2012 arrival. Prato is a bona fide Penn State football historian. Mr. Prato expected that the Posnanski biography would reveal a lot of inside information from Paterno's life. He guessed right. Prato said: "For the publishers to make their money back and for him to make more money, it better be good."

In an interview with USA Today, Posnanski offered comments about the grueling task of chronicling Paterno. He used these comments as a Preface for his book.

"Every few minutes, it seemed, there were new details, rumors, accusations, defenses, truths, lies, so many it was hard to see straight," he writes. "I suspect I will never have a more difficult task as a writer — I've been told by several authors that no biographer in American history has had a book change so drastically in the course of reporting."

Posnanski began writing a book in which Paterno's underwhelming vices would have turned some heads. Now, Paterno's virtues will do that. Joe Paterno was a regular guy with an awful lot of skill and compassion. When you heard him speak right in front of you, you would be in awe of the man, his accomplishments, and how normal he seemed. And his sense of humor was as good as the best comedian out there.

The Collegian did a piece on the Posnanski work when it was released. The comments to the Collegian article about the book are profound and I include them here because they tell the story as most of us see it. Joe Paterno was a good guy who did what he thought was right but was punished nonetheless.

Robert Harris commented on September 6, 2012

> *"Having casually followed US college football for a number of years -- including my time playing in Canada during the early 80's -- I was a semi-informed but highly motivated reader. I had a vague notion of Paterno's characteristics but few details, so this fascinating portrait really filled in the gaps for me. And it was done in a well-paced, approachable and intelligent manner. Overall, an excellent read.*
>
> *"On the matter of Paterno's culpability, with respect to properly reporting his knowledge of Sandusky, I found myself flipping back and forth emotionally. At one point my reaction was the author was cutting Joe Pa the maximum allowable slack -- but then as I read more closely I found maybe that bias was more of my own as I was tainted going in by the press stories which expressed unfettered outrage. In addition, I must say I appreciated the fact the author took a risk and briefly included his personal response to Paterno's question about "what do you think of all this?" It was appropriate and illuminated other aspects of the text nicely.*
>
> *"Paterno lived a rich and authentic life. While his blind spots unfortunately led to his downfall, I believe, as the emotion subsides, the everyday fan will have a more balanced view of his entire legacy."*

Chapter 24—Joe Paterno: Fine Man; Great Coach, and the Legend

Briana commented on September 8, 2012

> "This is an unbiased, truthful story of a great coach, and a great man who made a mistake that caused him to lose everything he'd worked 61 years for. Even Paterno said that all his life he'd worked to make a name for himself, now it's all gone. That was one of my favorite quotes from the book, along with this one: "They really think that if I knew someone was hurting kids, I wouldn't stop it? Don't they know me? Don't they know what my life has been about?" He said himself he regrets not following up, but he had done what he was supposed to do, he did not know all the circumstances and details, and thought it was taken care of. I think the fault lies with the ones he reported to who did not go directly to the police. Truthfully, yes Paterno should have followed up, but the book says repeatedly that at that point in his life, he wanted nothing to do with detail, only to coach his team. I think other things that came along were far from his mind, especially because he didn't know details about this situation.
>
> "It's evident in his career that he was not out to make money, or cover up child molesters to make Penn State a great football program. If that was the case, he would have worked to keep Sandusky on staff, even after the 1998 incident, as defensive coordinator because the team suffered some of their worst seasons after Sandusky left. And if he was out for fame and money, he would have taken the numerous offers for a head coaching position in the NFL. The New England Patriots offer him 1.3 million and part ownership when he was making $30,000 for a cow field college team and he turns it down, but all he cares about are wins, fame, and glory? Come on.
>
> "Fact is, he made a mistake and he was the face of Penn State. People give him credit for having way more power than he actually has (he even said this numerous times in the book) and he took the fall because of his moral responsibility to follow through. It's too bad that his legacy will forever be tainted for this. And the media has made things so much worse. Facts are skewed and people jump to conclusions

without finding out the truth. This book is a truthful rendition of the man's entire life's work and the mistake that took away all of the good he had done."

Phen Andrews commented on August 21, 2012

"Posnanski's book needs to be read by those that prior to November 2011 only knew Joe Paterno as a football coach. A lot of favorite vignettes of Paterno's legacy are here, including stories of his childhood in Brooklyn and the disappointment of his father upon Paterno's decision to shirk law school to instead coach at Brown University. Posnanski outlines Paterno's rise and explains how he etched out a special place in many Penn Staters hearts, but the author also holds no punches in his criticism of Paterno's handling (or mishandling) of the Sandusky saga. Posnanski has stated on the record that the Paterno estate has had zero input on his final draft, making this the most unbiased and most thoroughly researched biography of Joseph Paterno.

"If your intention is to read this book to learn more dirt about Paterno's role in the Sandusky scandal, you will walk away disappointed. If you care to learn more about the man that millions idolized and attempt to understand his legacy and fallout, then you must read this book."

Bymatt Thomason commented on October 22, 2015

"Fair warning, I am a PSU grad as is my son. This appears to be a fair treatment of Joe's career. No one will ever know what happened with Sandusky because Joe is deceased. Joe was undoubtedly by far the greatest division one college coach ever. Not only did he win more games than anyone else, almost every single player graduated and he would only take the best kids. He passed up on lots of kids that became starts for other colleges simply because they didn't fit the Penn State mold either in terms of character or academics. All the other well-known college coaches had a lot of kids playing for them that

could barely read and write and some were borderline criminals. However, even I have my doubts whether he should have done more than he did to keep Sandusky away from PSU. There is zero chance he knew about problem and looked the other way."

Lou Prato, PSU Historian

Lou Prato is the unofficial if not official PSU historian with all of the historical books he has written about Penn State. He is typically at the center of solving any historical controversy in Penn State. For my money, Prato needs to inject himself into the innocuous discussion I had with my neighbor John Anstett, and his cousin Aldo Casseri of New Orleans—both, like me, avid Penn State Football Fans. John found information that the nickname "JoePa" was coined by an eight year old girl in 1963. Now he can't find the link nor can I. I defer this to Mr. Prato when he has the time.

Another example of Prato coming to the rescue was in his 1999 Town and Gown article in which he researched the source of the "We Are Penn State!" cheer known so well today. He discovered the source was a connection to the cheerleaders of the late 1970s / early 1980s but did not narrow it down to a specific year. At one time it was thought that the cheer came about from Penn State standing up to racism in the well-publicized events of the Cotton Bowl and the 1947-48 football team / season.

Prato describes a deep and detailed history of how the cheerleaders created the cheer over the course of several seasons. The cheerleaders felt they had no beat-all and end-all cheers as did other teams such as Ohio State and USC. Prato cites articles that are subsequent to the late 1970s/early 1980s in which the phrase is mentioned in multiple Collegians and other University documents. In none of these references to

"We Are Penn State!" was the 1947/1948 time period or the racial stand brought forth.

Thank you Mr. Prato for more fine work on our behalf.

We certainly are Penn State, and as Pennsylvanians, friends, alumni, etc. we are very proud of our State University. For most of us who have been around for the sixty plus years that Joe Paterno coached, first with Rip Engle and then as the Head Coach of the Nittany Lions, Joe Paterno was and in many ways still is Penn State. Sixty years is a lifetime for sure. JoePa is Penn State to many of us and even more so, JoePa is Penn State Football. No matter what has transpired, this has not changed. It is undeniable. Joe Paterno is Penn State Football. And, that is not a bad thing at all!

I met Joe Paterno once in my life and I liked him an awful lot. I bet others also met him once or perhaps never met him and liked him an awful lot. I bet people close to him liked him an awful lot and loved him an awful lot more. Joe Paterno spread that kind of contagion... a very good kind of contagion from a very good man.

He spoke to a group of IBM Systems Engineers from Pennsylvania at the Hershey Resorts on the 25th anniversary of the Systems Engineering Profession within IBM. His message was on point. His jokes were perfect. And, the master coach stayed around to chat with the folks after his speech.

Everybody at the event loved him and could not wait to shake his hand and say hello and share some Joe with Joe. IBM people have never been known for congeniality as an overriding characteristic per se but a Joe Paterno was able to bring out the best of this assemblage of stodgy and mostly boring systems curmudgeons from IBM. It was a great day thanks to Joe Paterno.

On January 27, 2012, just a few days after Coach Paterno's death, Bruce Adams—(BAdams@MainLineMediaNews.com) interviewed a number of main-line coaches in various college sports and these comments from St. Joseph's University men's basketball coach Phil Martelli were typical of his peers reaction to his life and his death:

St. Joseph's University men's basketball coach Phil Martelli once received a phone call from Paterno during his first year as head coach of the Hawks. It is a neat story and typical of Joe Paterno:

"When I was just starting at St. Joe's, a reporter asked me who my coaching heroes were, and I said that I had no heroes who were coaches, but, as people, there were three individuals [in sports] that I admired—Magic Johnson, Chris Evert-Lloyd and Joe Paterno," said Martelli, who never met Joe Pa. "The reporter mentioned it to Joe, and [Paterno] called me. We talked about what it was like coaching at a Catholic school, and coaching in the Atlantic 10, which Penn State had just left. I was blown away – it was like talking to my Dad or an uncle."

Asked what Paterno's legacy will be, Martelli replied, "I think his legacy will be perfect. I think the whole [Jerry Sandusky] thing has humanized him - he made errors in judgment, but don't we all make mistakes in our lives. His legacy will be that of a good human being who made mistakes, made errors, like we all do."

More information on Joe Paterno's life is available here: www.biography.com/people/joe-paterno-9434584)

http://www.framingpaterno.com/betrayal-joe-paterno-chapter-ten-conclusions,

My thank you to the author for permitting this excerpt of the Conclusions on Joe Patern's involvement the Sandusky case.

"The Betrayal of Joe Paterno" Chapter Ten: Conclusions

Submitted by jzadmin on Mon, 07/08/2013 - 08:5

The media has been out to destroy Joe Paterno from day one of the Sandusky scandal. At this point, most Americans are fully tuned-in to the staggering dishonesty and reality twisting that the mainstream, corporate news media engages in on a daily basis. For example an April 2016 poll shows that just 6 percent of Americans say they have a lot of confidence in the media. This puts the news industry about equal to Congress and well below the public's view of other institutions. Basically, Americans believe that the media has a big problem with the truth. Why should we believe the drivel they print about Joe Paterno?

Too often when a story like Sandusky and Paterno hit the papers, since it is, for the most part, our only opportunity to get the scoop. Consequently we often buy the stories at first at least as if they are fact. But, then we realize this is the same lying media that never tells the truth. Why should anybody believe the negative media slant on Joe Paterno? And, so more and more Penn Staters and Americans at large are realizing that the media has not told the truth about Joe Paterno and they are not about to tell the truth about Joe Paterno.

The Board of Trustees (BOT) fired Joe Paterno and Graham Spanier without a hearing and without them even being in the same room. The American people have this thing about the establishment and the BOT is the epitomy of the establishment at PSU. They are the elite and just like members of both political parties today, this elite establishment vote to protect itself from harm.

On November 9, 2011 the BOT did not care what was best for the university. They should have shown courage and fired themselves. The establishment BOT are the top dogs. They run the institution. Joe Paterno and Graham Spanier were just employees. By the way, most of the BOT that made the Paterno decision have been fired by being unelected in recent BOT elections. The PSU BOT is no longer very well respected.

My point is that we cannot believe the media about this incident and we surely cannot believe the self serving Board of Trustees who in fact are the establishment. Why should we believe the media in this case; and why should we believe the PSU establishment that was willing to do handstands so they would not be implicated. The answer is we cannot believe either. Therefore, we must begin to look at this situation with open eyes and without their prejudice spoon fed to us by the self-serving media and the self-serving Board of Trustees.

Betrayal of Joe Paterno Chapter Ten Conclusions

One year after the release of the Freeh Report, this is what seems to be reality of the aftermath of the Sandusky scandal and its impact on the State College community:

Joe Paterno's reputation and legacy have been completely destroyed, the Penn State football program has been crippled, and the university's reputation has been badly besmirched. Many lives have been greatly damaged, money has been lost, friendships have been severed, and wonderful memories have been painfully erased. The public battle to tell the real truth of what happened here has been badly lost and, thanks to the media shutting down the investigation, there is no chance of that dramatically changing anytime in the near future. The only current hope for justice hangs on two very different court cases, neither of which may ever even reach the point of an actual verdict.

What caused this seemingly dire set of circumstances? Well, in my view it all comes down to lots of cowardice, stupidity and back luck (most of it flowing directly from the "Original Sin" of this story, the decision of the Penn State Board of Trustees to effectively fire Joe Paterno and Graham Spanier, thus creating in the media/public's mind an irreversible "guilty" plea). The media and most of the public somehow bought into a scenario which makes absolutely no sense and for which there is shockingly little evidence. Think about it. Joe Paterno, a man without a major ethical blemish in a half century long career of swimming (and winning) in the shark-infested waters of college football, decided to actively protect a child molester who used to work for him, whom he never liked, and who had open disdain for him? Why? To avoid bad publicity, something about which he never previously cared and which would have been highly unlikely to come his direction anyway?

Wow. That is quite a story.

It has always baffled me that that there is absolutely no proportionality in this case when it comes to what we have been asked to believe and the nature of the evidence to justify that scenario. As someone who has a dim view of humanity in general I acknowledge that of course it is possible that Joe Paterno was a complete fraud for 50 years, or that he nonsensically decided to throw away his reputation at the end of his life for no apparent reason. But if you are going to convince me of something that outrageous you better at least bring some damn evidence to the table.

Take for instance the O.J. Simpson case. Was it absurd to think that someone like Simpson would kill two people for no seemingly logical reason? Of course it was. But the evidence that he indeed did do that was not only sufficient; it was overwhelming (though sadly, to the criminal jury, a videotape of the crime literally would not have been enough evidence to overcome the absurd burden of proof in that case). In comparison to the proof against Simpson, the evidence against Paterno is like the plains of Texas measured against Mt. Everest (and frankly the evidence of Simpson's guilt was also stronger than what currently exists against even Sandusky).

And yet, incredibly, the media is still completely convinced that Paterno is guilty of at least grave moral weakness and potentially criminally running a cover-up to purposefully protect a person he knew to be a pedophile (and yet those who believe in the former scenario seems to have no issue with Paterno being punished based on the very different latter circumstances). The strangest part of their certitude on this issue is their universal unwillingness to debate me or anyone else on the actual facts here. You would think that if you were really so confident in yourself that you would enjoy humiliating someone like me by showing the world how utterly wrong I am. And yet the opposite has been the case. No matter how much money I offer to charity (since they all seem to say that it is the "victims" who matter most) I have never gotten anyone in the media to debate me other than for a few minor bouts on Twitter before they inevitably quickly run away realizing that they are overmatched.

If I ever did get the chance to fairly debate any of these frauds, here are just some of the questions which need to be answered in order to believe that Joe Paterno is indeed "guilty" as charged. Despite enormous efforts to do so, I have never had even one media member even try to sufficiently answer any of them.

How do you have a cover-up without Mike McQueary, the only witness, being intimately involved?

Why is McQueary not even alleging being part of a cover-up in his lawsuit against Penn State?

Why was McQueary not given the open wide receivers job until three years after the incident?

Why was McQueary not prevented from testifying by Paterno or at least told to tone his story down?

Why did Joe Paterno testify in a way which actually partly backed up McQueary, even in his final interview with the AG's office when he had to know that his "cover up" was falling apart?

Why, when all the principles knew that McQueary had testified almost a year before the story broke was none of the "evidence" destroyed and why were they seemingly completely unprepared for what hit them?

Why did Curley, Schultz and Spanier not even bother to hire their own attorneys and why did Paterno only "hire" his son Scott?

Why did Curley and Schultz not even try to get their stories remotely straight?

Why have Curley, Schultz and Spanier not flipped on each other for a plea bargain?

How is it that Spanier could even be theoretically involved when that would have either required it being his idea (in which case Curley and Schultz would have thrown him under the bus immediately), or that Curley and Schultz nonsensically told their boss that they were going to engage in a cover-up of a pedophile?

Why, if Paterno led a cover-up which destroyed his career/life did Curley release a statement praising his "honor and integrity" when he died?

Why would they cover up the crimes of someone who was an ex-coach who no one liked and who had disdain for Paterno?

Why did Paterno follow up with McQueary to ask him if he was okay with how things were being handled and why did Mike say that he was?

Why has not one person come forward to say that they knew all along that Sandusky was a pedophile?

If they knew Sandusky was a pedophile, why did Penn State football elect to maintain a close relationship with the Second Mile charity long after he left, and even after the 2001 episode?

How was Joe Paterno supposed to know that Sandusky was a pedophile when Jerry's own wife and several of his kids are still convinced, even after his trial, that he is totally innocent?

What exactly was Joe Paterno supposed to do differently and exactly when was he supposed to do it in order to have not done "wrong" here?

Why did Paterno allow writer Joe Posnanski to follow him around and allow him to maintain access during a year which he had to know (if there really was a cover-up) that it was all going to come collapsing down after McQueary testified in late 2010?

Why did Posnanski not find even one significant piece of evidence implicating Paterno?

Why was Paterno, a guilt-prone and ardent Catholic, smiling and waving publicly after he was just fired for protecting a pedophile and had to know that his cover-up was going to become public?

Why was there not one shred of consciousness of guilt shown by anyone who was supposedly part of the cover-up?

Unfortunately, I have very little confidence that any of these vital questions will ever be answered satisfactorily, mostly because they can't be without a giant hole being blown out of the media's conventional wisdom about what really happened here.

The Paterno rebuttal makes more sense than the Freeh Report

There was a major injustice done in the Freeh Report, which was taken by the press and the NCAA as the gospel truth, though it was fraught with inaccuracies. The NCAA chose not to use its own protocol and instead lashed out at everybody it could find to assure that the NCAA itself was not found guilty or implicated for not admonishing its member school properly. The NCAA did not mind taking skins while saving its own skin! They could have done lots better just as they claim JoePa could have.

The PSU Board of Directors must have been AWOL during Paterno's 61 years of excellence for the University. Was it Notre Dame or Alabama or Pitt officials that insisted the statue of JoePa be erected as a monument to such a great coach? Why could the Board not have taken a few extra minutes to look through a Penn State Nittany Lions Lens rather than the lens of a hungry to indict media.

Why would nobody in the official PSU chamber stand up to defend a great man, a great coach, and the very person who had brought the University so much fame? Why were elite establishment officials with power so willing to hurt anybody else, including the State College community and the university itself to help protect themselves? Is it no wonder why Penn State supporters are upset?

When a mother or father does not support a son or daughter who has not yet been declared guilty of a crime, why would that be? Why would PSU not ask for more time before taking action? Why was the NCAA so anxious to avoid its own stringent protocols so that they could pronounce a "Guilty" verdict on Joe Paterno and the University that he loved? Who is the bad guy here?

The Paterno family rightfully has been fighting to restore the legacy of former Penn State football coach Joe Paterno, flatly denying the allegations in the report by former FBI Director Louis Freeh that the legendary coach was complicit in a cover-up of child sexual abuse by a former assistant coach.

Most PSU fans have come around to supporting the Paterno family in this quest for justice rather than giving credence to a biased report that was given full acceptance by people who should know better. These people include the Board of Directors of Penn State University, the corrupt media, and the NCAA.

"The Critique of the Freeh Report: The Rush to Injustice Regarding Joe Paterno," the report prepared by King & Spalding is available on paterno.com. This is an appropriate title for an objective analysis of the Freeh Report which finds everybody guilty almost at the same level as the convicted perpetrator of the acts, Jerry Sandusky. It simply is not fair. But, those who have saved their skins do not care.

The Paterno family has been understandably trying to protect the reputation of the family patriarch Joe Paterno for sure, but PSU had a major stake in the game also as the damage done to the university is severe. Why did PSU's BOT not take the same approach as the Paternos? How do you erase almost half of a storied football program and remain the same. Alumni and students, professors and the community have been harmed by a rush to injustice as portrayed in the Freeh report. Where is the university advocate?

The critique is described as an attempt to set the record straight with independent expert analysis examining the "most glaring errors on which the Freeh report is based." I have read the report and I think the team did a fine job in constructing this rebuttal. Joe Paterno had been convicted and sentenced and in fact he had been hung, without ever having gone to trial. That simply is not the American way.

"The Freeh report reflects an improper 'rush to injustice,'" the 238-page critique says. "There is no evidence that Joe Paterno deliberately covered up known incidents of child molestation by Jerry Sandusky to protect Penn State football or for any other reason; the contrary statements in the Freeh report are unsupported and unworthy of belief."

In their critique of the Freeh report, former U.S. Attorney General Dick Thornburgh and experts Jim Clemente and Fred Berlin examined the Freeh report and found that it is "deeply flawed and that key conclusions regarding Joe Paterno are unsubstantiated and unfair."

According to the critique, the Freeh report "uncovers little new factual information as to Joe Paterno and does very little to advance the truth regarding his knowledge, or more accurately lack of knowledge, of Jerry Sandusky's molestation of children."

Because the 2011 scandal has become the most negative parts of the Penn State Legacy, one cannot hide from it. And, so, I have included the summation of the report below as we come close to wrapping up a book about great moments in Penn State football.

The report commissioned by the Paterno Family and so ably completed is one of those great moments in Penn State as it gives an honest account of what happened and it refutes the clear rush to injustice that had been perpetrated against a mostly innocent Penn State community. Thank you for selecting this book for your personal reading.

Rather than leave you all with the retort to the Freeh report as your last taste of Penn State and Joe Paterno in this book, I have included several other chapters to add more clarity and then we finish the book on a positive note by higlinghting Penn State's best linebackers and running backs.

We all miss Coach Paterno and wish he could make a comeback some-day soon. At least one day, we'll get that fine statue back where it belongs.

To show the aura of the proceedings, let me show the beginning of the documetns prepared by those looking for relief for Joe Paterno on a new page. It is an impressive packof dignitaries and whet they have to say in their report, makes a lot of sense... much more than the Freeh report which had a scent of politics on it.

KING & SPALDING

1700 PENNSYLVANIA AVENUE, NW
WASHINGTON, DC 20006-4707
202.737.0500

CRITIQUE OF THE FREEH REPORT:
THE RUSH TO INJUSTICE REGARDING JOE PATERNO

KING & SPALDING: **FEBRUARY 2013**
    WICK SOLLERS
    MARK JENSEN
    ALAN DIAL
    DREW CRAWFORD

CONTAINING INDEPENDENT EXPERT REPORTS BY:

    DICK THORNBURGH, LLB. FORMER ATTORNEY GENERAL OF THE UNITED STATES

    JIM CLEMENTE, J.D. FORMER FBI PROFILER, PROSECUTOR, AND CHILD SEX CRIMES EXPERT

    FRED BERLIN, M.D., PH.D. PHYSICIAN, PSYCHIATRIST, AND PSYCHOLOGIST AT THE JOHNS HOPKINS HOSPITAL AND SCHOOL OF MEDICINE AND EXPERT IN PUBLIC HEALTH APPROACHES TO CHILD SEX ABUSE

CRITIQUE OF THE FREEH REPORT:
THE RUSH TO INJUSTICE REGARDING JOE PATERNO

After the Freeh Group, which had been retained as Special Investigative Counsel ("SIC") by the Penn State Board of

Chapter 24—Joe Paterno: Fine Man; Great Coach, and the Legend 541

Trustees to investigate the Jerry Sandusky child sex abuse scandal, released its report in July 2012, the Paterno family asked King & Spalding to conduct a comprehensive review of both the report and Joe Paterno's conduct. They authorized us to engage preeminent experts and to obtain their independent analyses as an essential part of that review.

This Critique of the Freeh report, which incorporates and attaches those independent analyses in full, sets the record straight. We conclude that the observations as to Joe Paterno in the Freeh report are unfounded, and have done a disservice not only to Joe Paterno and to the Penn State University community, but also to the victims of Jerry Sandusky and the critical mission of educating the public on the dangers of child sexual victimization.

Dick Thornburgh, former Attorney General of the United States, and experts Jim Clemente and Fred Berlin, have each carefully examined the July 12, 2012 report prepared by Louis Freeh, and have each determined that the report is deeply flawed and that key conclusions regarding Joe Paterno are unsubstantiated and unfair.

This Critique summarizes their expert conclusions and describes the most glaring errors on which the Freeh report is based. As Dick Thornburgh explains, the Freeh report reflects an improper "rush to injustice." There is no evidence that Joe Paterno deliberately covered up known incidents of child molestation by Jerry Sandusky to protect Penn State football or for any other reason; the contrary statements in the Freeh report are unsupported and unworthy of belief.

As described in more detail below, there is no reason to believe that Joe Paterno understood the threat posed by Jerry Sandusky better than qualified child welfare and law enforcement professionals. There is no evidence that Joe Paterno conspired with Penn State officials to suppress information because of publicity concerns. And Joe Paterno's testimony before the grand jury in 2011 was truthful. As Messrs. Thornburgh and Clemente and Dr. Berlin have each concluded, the full story behind the tragic events involving Jerry Sandusky is not the one told by the Freeh report.

SUMMARY OF KEY POINTS

Joe Paterno's last written words before his death focused on the victims of Jerry Sandusky. In a handwritten note, Joe Paterno emphasized: "Good side of scandal - it has brought about more enlightenment of a situation (sexual abuse of young people) in the country."

The Paterno family directed King & Spalding to seek independent opinions of the Freeh report by experts in identifying and investigating child victimization and pedophilia, as well as by experts in conducting independent and reliable internal investigations. Those independent experts include the former top legal officer of the United States, Attorney General Dick Thornburgh; former FBI profiler and child molestation and behavioral expert, Jim Clemente; and The Johns Hopkins Hospital and School of Medicine physician and psychologist, Fred Berlin.

King & Spalding's Critique of the Freeh report, which incorporates the independent analyses of these three prominent experts, concludes that the Freeh report is deeply flawed and that its conclusions as to Joe Paterno are unfair and unsupported.

Each one of the Freeh report's main observations about Joe Paterno is wrong: each is either contradicted or unsubstantiated by the evidence. The authors of the Freeh report chose not to present alternative, more plausible, conclusions regarding Joe Paterno's role in the events involving Jerry Sandusky.

This Critique concludes, based on our interviews, including of Coach Paterno before his death, based on our review of documents and testimony, and, importantly, based on information from our access to the lawyers for other Penn State administrators, that (1) Joe Paterno never asked or told anyone not to investigate fully the allegations in 2001, (2) Joe Paterno never asked or told anyone, including Dr. Spanier and Messrs. Curley and Schultz, not to report the 2001 incident, and (3) Joe Paterno never asked or told anyone not to discuss or to hide in any way the information reported by Mr. McQueary. Joe Paterno reported the information to his superior(s) pursuant to his understanding of University protocol and relied upon them to investigate and report as appropriate.

Former Attorney General Thornburgh is an expert in conducting effective fact investigations. He has reviewed the Freeh report and concluded that its investigative methodology is flawed, that its factual findings are limited and incomplete, and that its observations as to Joe Paterno are unreliable and unfounded. In the former Attorney General's own words, he concluded:

> "The lack of factual support for the SIC's inaccurate and unfounded findings related to Mr. Paterno and its numerous process-oriented deficiencies was a rush to injustice and calls into question the credibility of the entire Report."
>
> "In my opinion, the Freeh Report is seriously flawed, both with respect to the process of the SIC's investigation and its findings related to Mr. Paterno."
>
> "When considered in the context of investigation 'best practices,' it is evident that the Freeh Report and many of its findings as they relate to Mr. Paterno are not accurate, thorough, fair or credible. The process of the SIC's investigation was deficient in numerous ways, including the failure to

> interview virtually all of the key witnesses and the reliance upon limited, ambiguous documents."
>
> "Perhaps most significantly, the findings in the Freeh Report about Mr. Paterno concerning his alleged knowledge of the 1998 incident and purported concealment of the 2001 incident were not properly supported."
>
> "This lack of evidence supporting the Report's most scathing findings and the serious flaws with respect to the process of the SIC's investigation cause me to conclude that the Report's findings concerning Mr. Paterno are unjust and wrong."

The Freeh report was oversold to the public. Penn State officials, the NCAA, and other bodies detrimentally relied on the Freeh report in a rush to judgment about Joe Paterno. The limitations of the investigation, which were numerous and fatal to fundamental fairness, were not adequately explained or understood before that rush to injustice solidified the false public narrative about Joe Paterno.

The Freeh report missed a critical opportunity to educate the public on the identification of child sexual victimization, and instead used the platform created by this scandal to sensationalize the blaming of Joe Paterno. The Freeh report ignored decades of expert research and behavioral analysis regarding the appropriate way to understand and investigate a child sexual victimization case. Mr. Jim Clemente is one of the leading former FBI profilers of child sex offenders, and himself a survivor of childhood sexual victimization. As Mr. Clemente bluntly put it:

> "The SIC failed to properly factor the dynamics of acquaintance child sexual victimization cases into their investigation. Consequently, the SIC

misinterpreted evidence and behavior and reached erroneous conclusions. Any investigation will reach the wrong result by using the wrong approach and by interpreting the facts through the wrong filter."

"There is no other way to say it: on the most critical aspects of the Sandusky investigation, the SIC report is a failure. It does a tremendous disservice to Penn State, Joe Paterno, and the victims of Jerry Sandusky."

Expert analysis shows that Jerry Sandusky was a "skilled and masterful manipulator," who deceived an entire community to obscure the signs of child abuse, using a variety of proven techniques. Those techniques included: perpetuating an image as a playful "nice guy" who was a foster and adoptive parent with kids around him at all hours in all types of capacities, leveraging his position as a respected member of the community, and creating a children's charity to legitimize his credibility in interacting with kids.

Expert analysis shows that Jerry Sandusky fooled qualified child welfare professionals and law enforcement, as well as laymen inexperienced and untrained in child sexual victimization like Joe Paterno. Sandusky's techniques as a pillar of the community created a proven psychological and cognitive impediment for them to recognize the red flags and other signs that Sandusky was a child molester.

Joe Paterno himself knew very little about Jerry Sandusky's personal life and did not know private details about Sandusky or his victims. For decades, Joe Paterno respected Sandusky's talent as a coach and professional colleague and recognized Sandusky's widely-stated passion for helping kids, but the Freeh report missed that they disliked each other personally, had very little in common outside work, and did not interact much if at all socially.

Expert analysis shows that while signs of Jerry Sandusky's child molestation existed with the benefit of hindsight, at the time of the 2001 shower incident reported by graduate assistant Mike McQueary, information was conveyed to Joe Paterno in terms that were too general and vague for him to disregard decades of contrary experience with Sandusky and to conclude that Sandusky was a child predator. As summarized in former FBI profiler Jim Clemente's own words:

> "Given my 30 years of education, training and experience working, evaluating and assessing child sex crimes investigations around the world, it is my expert opinion that Paterno did not know, or even believe in the possibility, that Sandusky was capable of sexually assaulting boys. At worst, he believed that Sandusky was a touchy-feely guy who had boundary issues. This fact is clear from his repeated statements before he died."

> "[Paterno] did what he believed was reasonable and necessary to address the situation based on his understanding of the facts, and his position at the time. Paterno did what most people who cared about children would have done in the same situation. More than a decade later, and in hindsight, Paterno showed his concern for the victims when he stated he, 'wished [he] had done more.'"

> "Paterno, like everyone else who knew Sandusky, simply fell victim to effective 'grooming.' [Grooming is a dynamic process of seemingly innocent, positive public behaviors by the offender, aimed at gaining the trust of the targeted child, parents and the community.] As an expert

behavioral analyst and based on my review of the evidence, Paterno did not believe that the information he received from McQueary amounted to Sandusky being a predatory child sex offender."

The Freeh report is uniformly biased against Joe Paterno. For the authors of the report, there are no gray areas. They ascribe motives to people they never met or interviewed, and interpret ambiguous documents with a clarity and decisiveness that is impossible to justify.

None of the experts found any support for the Freeh report's assertion that Joe Paterno, along with three other Penn State administrators, including the President, conspired to conceal Jerry Sandusky's actions because they wanted to avoid bad publicity. That core "conclusion" by Mr. Freeh was entirely unfounded and has resulted in a great disservice to everyone involved in this tragedy.

Mr. Freeh irresponsibly blamed Joe Paterno in this scandal, and violated the most basic notions of due process by offering a flawed, one-sided viewpoint without affording any meaningful opportunity for Joe Paterno, his representatives, or any neutral third party to assess or even respond to Mr. Freeh's opinions before he announced them as proven at a national press conference.

Mr. Freeh generated a rapid domino effect of negative coverage that immediately and unfairly tainted perceptions of Joe Paterno by the media, the Penn State community, the NCAA, and the public.

The timing of Mr. Freeh's press conference and report ensured that the rush to judgment occurred without any meaningful review of the Freeh report itself. The Freeh report, which was 267 pages and included 702 endnotes and 105 pages of appendices, was released only an hour before his press conference. The virtually instantaneous and uniformly negative reporting after his press conference perpetuated his many unproven assertions and opinion-based conclusions, without any evaluation or analysis by the news outlets that adopted Mr. Freeh's wide-ranging and unchallenged proclamations.

The NCAA improperly relied on the Freeh report in compelling Penn State to enter into a "consent" decree and accept draconian penalties. Only eleven days after the release of the Freeh report, and without conducting any factual investigation of its own, the NCAA announced severe sanctions that deeply impacted the University and the community.

The NCAA circumvented its established enforcement mechanisms and violated its own due process rules. It never identified a single infraction of NCAA rules based on Sandusky's crimes, much less an infraction by Penn State that implicated the NCAA's jurisdiction and core mission of ensuring competitive balance in amateur athletics.

The Freeh report is full of errors, unsupported personal opinions, improper allegations and biased assertions. Despite the Freeh report's claim to the contrary, access to vital documents and critical witnesses was severely limited. Those limitations, which were understated or ignored in the report, call into question the report's legitimacy.

Despite reportedly reviewing millions of documents and interviewing hundreds of witnesses, the Freeh report relies primarily on a handful of emails, none of which Joe Paterno authored or received, to make assertions about Joe Paterno, and shockingly does so even though Mr. Freeh never interviewed the actual authors of the emails. This Critique of the Freeh report addresses seven of the most egregious, unfounded, and unfair conclusions about Joe Paterno; the three other expert reports attached to this Critique combine to expose and address many more.

The facts establish that Joe Paterno acted honestly and in good faith throughout the Sandusky scandal, from the moment he received Mr. McQueary's 2001 report, through his grand jury testimony, until the day of his death in January 2012.

Dr. Fred Berlin, a preeminent physician and psychologist from The Johns Hopkins Hospital and School of Medicine, studied and reviewed the evidence in this case, and he assessed Joe Paterno's life more broadly. Dr. Berlin concluded:

> "I have not seen evidence supporting a conclusion that Joe Paterno had acted in bad faith, nor have I seen evidence supporting a conclusion that he has ever been a man who lacked a genuine concern about the wellbeing of others — including the wellbeing of children."
>
> "In my professional opinion, there is absolutely nothing about the way in which Mr. Paterno had led his life, or about his characterological makeup, that would support the unsupported inference that 'in order to avoid the consequences of bad publicity,' he had been one of the 'powerful leaders' at Penn State who had 'repeatedly concealed critical facts related to Sandusky's child abuse from the authorities, the University's Board of Trustees, the Penn State community, and the public at large.'"

In any fair courtroom or truly independent investigation, the target of an inquiry rightfully would expect all the facts, including the full scope of his life, to be considered when assessing his culpability. In this instance, however, the Freeh report ignores Joe

Paterno's lifetime record of moral conduct and altruism as if it were irrelevant to the case. Experts in the behavioral dynamics of child sexual victimization, as well as experts in conducting sensitive investigations, have concluded that such an omission was a serious flaw that undermines the credibility of the report. That conclusion is captured by Dr. Berlin:

> "Joe Paterno had known very little about the extent of the acts for which Mr. Sandusky had subsequently been convicted. In my judgment, given his history of a life well led, and of good character, and in light of the unsubstantiated nature of the inferences against him, to conclude that for any reason he would have been unconcerned about the wellbeing of children, would require turning a blind eye to the values that he had consistently demonstrated, and to the essence of what his life had been all about."

Joe Paterno died just over a year ago concerned for the victims, determined that the full truth should be revealed, and hopeful that these events could raise consciousness of child abuse detection more broadly and prevent its recurrence. As in his life, Joe Paterno remained committed to helping others at his death.

Sue Paterno and her family remain deeply committed to that mission and will continue supporting significant steps, and making more contributions financially and emotionally, to increase child abuse awareness, identification and education in this country. This effort is one important chapter in that journey.

* * * * *

-- End of report summation --

JoePa made his mark

You can read all of the books about Joe Paterno and of Penn State Football, and you still will not know all about JoePa. I am convinced there are so many great facts that you can discover that are not well known if known at all, that are not written about at all. You can find so much new stuff that you can write your own book about this great man and this great university all by yourself.

Joe Paterno's last three months and his death upset the entire nation in much the same way as Knute Rockne's sudden death in a plane crash in March, 1931. Both were well after their respective seasons had ended. In both accounts, the community at large was filled with shock. Both coaches were beloved by all. Joe Paterno was so beloved in State College that for a long time after his death, full-size cardboard cutouts of him were common sights around town. Even an ice cream flavor, "Peachy Paterno," was named after him.

In college football's fraternity, the folks knew him simply as "JoePa."

Former Nebraska Coach Tom Osborne, who won three national titles in the 1990s, suspects the scandal took a toll on Paterno's health and detracted from his otherwise stellar career. Many of us feel the same.

"His longevity over time and his impact on college football is remarkable," Osborne said in a statement: "Anybody who knew Joe feels badly about the circumstances. I suspect the emotional turmoil of the last few weeks might have played into it."

Only days after he issued a tempered response to the initial Sandusky allegations, Paterno expressed heartfelt remorse over what had happened on his watch. "I am absolutely devastated by the developments in this case," Paterno said in a statement released hours before he was fired abruptly—a bit too abruptly! "I grieve for the children and their families, and I pray for their comfort and relief." He vowed to "spend the rest of my life doing everything I can to help this university."

The end of the Paterno Era at Penn State came less than two weeks after he recorded his 409th career victory, which moved him past former Grambling Coach Eddie Robinson on major college football's all-time list. Thanks in part to the anti-Freeh report and people finally speaking up, all of those 409 wins are back on the official Penn State and the official Paterno records.

Joe Paterno was a five-time national coach of the year, won two national titles, fielded five unbeaten teams and was the first major college coach to eclipse Bear Bryant's victory record of 323. Bear Bryant was Joe Paterno before Joe Paterno appeared on the football scene.

Paterno ended his career as the all-time leader in bowl appearances (37) and bowl victories (24) and in 2006, he was inducted into the College Football Hall of Fame by acclamation. He is the only coach to have won all four of college football's major bowls: Rose, Fiesta, Orange and Sugar.

Voted into the same Hall of Fame class, Paterno and Florida State Coach Bobby Bowden spent years jostling with each other for the all-time major college win record. Just as Joe Paterno. Bobby Bowden was also a great and well respected coach.

"History will say he's one of the greatest," Bowden commented after the Coach's death. "Who's coached longer, who's coached better, who's won more games, who's been more successful than Joe? Who's done more for his university than Joe?"

During Paterno's tenure, Penn State produced 79 first-team All-America players, 33 first-round NFL draft picks and 16 National Football Foundation scholar-athletes. This is the record of a football coach; not a university.

Most universities do not have statistics like that for all their years of football. Penn State officials owe Joe Paterno through his family a debt of gratitude for his support of the school.

Besides great athletes, Joe Paterno helped produce great scholars. He wanted his team's players to have the full experience of an education at Penn State, including graduation. He was the best in the country at providing that.

The NCAA's annual study of institutions nationwide revealed that Penn State student-athletes at the University

Park campus had a Graduation Success Rate (GSR) of 87 percent compared to a 77 percent average for all Division I-A institutions. Could that have been achieved with a disinterested coach?

The list of those who played for Paterno includes Jack Ham, John Cappelletti, Franco Harris, Lydell Mitchell, Curt Warner, Shane Conlin, Matt Millen, Todd Blackledge, Kyle Brady, LaVar Arrington, Larry Johnson, Courtney Brown and Kerry Collins. I bet you can name ten or more--more!

Paterno's teams were known for their toughness and selflessness. The school's blue-and-white uniforms were famously nondescript — lacking player names, decorations or logos — a Brand X quality that came to symbolize the program's team-first image.

An English literature major at Brown University in Rhode Island, Paterno was a voracious reader whose favorite sayings included Robert Browning's "Ah, but a man's reach should exceed his grasp, or what's a heaven for?"

Rest in Peace (RIP) Dear Coach Paterno! We sure do miss you!

Chapter 25   The First Family of Nittany Lion Football

Paternos and Suheys had been very close

They are so close, they should figure out how to reconcile

Jay Paterno, who was always close to his father both on the football field and off, in many ways has taken the lead as the de-facto spokesman for the Paterno family in the wake of the Sandusky scandal. Just as if it were your dad, the Paterno's have a lot at stake. They think there dad was a good guy! That's what their beef is all about. Where would you be if the issue were about your dad?

One of the unintended consequences of the Sandusky scandal is that a crack formed in the once close knit cordial relationship, which the Paternos enjoyed with the Suheys The Suhey family of course are memorialized as the First Family of Nittany Lions Football. The love affair goes back many generations and it is real. The Suheys and the Paternos have been a Nittany Lion legacy of true friendship and kindness and love to each other over the ages!

I asked the Suhey family, and I asked Jay Paterno to contribute a chapter to this book about the controversy from their personal perspective. I promised not to edit the content. Neither chose to do so. I have never met either so I understand. Neither agreed.

Dr. Paul Suhey, Sr. was a member of the BOT (Board of Trustees) who voted against Joe Paterno. It is my understanding that he had always been a friend to the

Paterno family. The Suheys don't talk much about it but it seems that Paul has an opposite stance on JoePa from the rest of the Suhey family for his own reasons.

Paul Suhey played linebacker for Jay's dad, Joe Paternal and had lots of contact with the Paternos while a player and afterwards as a member of the PSU Board of Directors. Paul Suhey is singled out in this chapter only because he voted with the Board *to fire Joe Paterno*. As a Suhey, guys like me who live far away from Beaver Stadium, have a tough time reconciling his vote to the JoePa that we have come to love and revere over the years. Paul Suhey has explained his reasons and his vote was not an accident.

And that in my opinion is the rub today between the Suhey family and the Paterno family. Paul Suhey sided with his Board compadres in the PSU establishment over Joe Paterno and the Paterno Family. It is that simple. But, I bet underneath it all, it is more complicated than simple. Maybe Paul Suhey knew something that nobody else knew and he was unable to say. Who Knows?

Many Penn Staters and friends of both families are hoping for a reconciliation but we all know it will not be coming as long as hard heads prevail. The solution for the rest of us of course, while this family brawl continues, will come about as we pray for contrition and redemption and we also pray for the spirit of forgiveness. Harboring ill will not lead to a solution. Yet, it is very understandable that there is anger.

Paul Suhey had lots of contact with the Paternos while a PSU player and afterwards as a member of the PSU Board (aka BOT). Paul Suhey, Sr. picked what may have been the only option available to him to remain in good stead on the BOT. From my vantage point, he chose the easy way out and voted with the Board to fire Joe Paterno. Sorry Paul, speak out if this is not true!

I like to personalize things such as a long-term family relationship. How about you? What if someone, who was a long-time friend voted to fire your heartsick dad? What if your dad was so heartsick that it killed him? I think that's where we are in the big matter. No Suhey will give up their guy and no Paterno is ready to suggest that Joe Paterno's record is a fraud that he permitted children to be sent to Sandusky's Second Mile to be used for things we would rather not discuss.

On the evening of the big decision of the BOT, like all the other trustees, Paul Suhey, a family friend of the Paternos, chose to have nothing to say when Joe Paterno was fired. He uttered no words against JoePa and he provided no words of support for his long time mentor, and close family friend.

As a member of the BOT, Paul Suhey had become a small-time politician. He had a choice. He could have said something positive for the record but he chose not to say a word. Paul Suhey may have had to vote by conscience as he did but does he really think Paterno's legacy sould be damned forever?

Penn State President Graham Spanier, left, and Joe Paterno's tenure at Penn State came to an abrupt end Wednesday night. By MARK VIERA NOV. 9, 2011

The default decision was already spelled out according to the chairman of the board. On that fateful evening Graham Spanier and Joe Paterno would be fired. Joe Paterno had not digested this whole situation, nor even his evening meal before the board had him out of PSU for good. Paul Suhey may not have been OK with that but he went along to get along. Many other friends of Penn State were not OK with Paul Suhey on that matter for sure!

Having a love for Penn State and admiration for the Paterno and Suhey families without knowing either personally is a situation in which most Penn Staters now find ourselves. Not only do we have the scandal and its terrible effect on the children (victims), Joe Paterno, Happy Valley, and a host of others but the first Family of the Nittany Lions and the Family of Joe Paterno are not talking to each other. Contrition, Redemption, Forgiveness and prayer are sorely needed.

When I first fully realized that the source of the rift was Paul Suhey's vote against JoePa in the major board hearing out of which JoePa was fired; I figured it had to be a mistake. I gave Paul Suhey the benefit of the doubt. I figured he had done what he did but he did not mean to do what in fact he had done. Sometimes when faced with the consequences of our actions, we dig in to justify them, rather than dig deep to find out if we acted properly.

Paul Suhey was a respected JoePa football player and friend and surely, if not pressed by powerful forces on the BOT would have called for more time rather than a rush to judgment and actions that are irreversible. He did not do so. Paul Suhey was as quiet as a church mouse along with 31 other mice who did not want to be in the big hotel room that night. I do not like using pejoratives but it sure seems that there were 32 cowards plus a cowardly governor. Only if Ben Franklin himself showed up would the room have shown one person with courage.

Since the decision night, I expected Paul Suhey's family and friends, to have had a few cold ones with Paul to encourage him to do what he thinks is the right thing. Unfortunately, if that session has happened, it has caused Paul Suhey to dig in more on his silent default position. He did come out with a statement that in my opinion does not help matters. Like many, I am looking for a real reconciliation of Paternos and Suheys with contrition, redemption, and forgiveness. That's how it is done.

Paul Suhey used the values of the coach whose values he questions when he explained his posture on the "thumbs down on Joe" vote. Suhey said that it was values learned in part from Joe Paterno that led him to his highly-criticized decision to support the board's surprising dismissal of the legendary head football coach on November 9, 2011. Said less surgically, Paul Suhey voted to decapitate Joe Paterno, while he was still alive. All of us know that Paul did not mean it that way!

Sometimes we just feel we are repeating ourselves as we put forth our spew about what we feel about issue A and issue B. And so, I found a few paragraphs that do a great job about what I am trying to say about this situation.

I would love the Paternos and the Suheys to be friendly again. However they must accommodate that. JoePa and Bob Higgins would love it too! These notions about JoePa are from the new book called

"The Betrayal of Joe Paterno" Chapter Five: The Firing. This item was submitted online by jzadmin on Tue, 07/09/2013 - 23:23

[Please read this excerpt as it helps in understanding what Paterno endured when everybody who loved him had abandoned him. Not that Joe Paterno is or ever was Christ in anyway, but the notion of abandonment is so strong here that we cannot help but get the notion the bad guys were in charge of bringing down Joe Paterno. It was as if to save the Phariseesand Sadducees. You make the call:]

Read the book to find out what other powerful thoughts can be explored!

"Of all the countless acts of extreme stupidity and cowardice that have been a part of this incredibly sad story, the moment of the Paterno firing really stands out for special condemnation.

Forget for an instant that there is a very good chance that Joe Paterno did nothing remotely wrong here. The notion that 32 people (all of whom knew him, many of them extremely well) could be on that conference call and not one of them even say a word in response to the proposal to fire him is probably the most stupefying act of human weakness that I can immediately recall.

These were all highly educated and successful people. Most of them had already made their way in the world. Some were untouchable financially or professionally. A few had extensive legal backgrounds. And yet somehow not even one of them found the "courage" to even ask, "Does anyone think we ought to at least ask Joe what the heck happened before we do this based on presumptions made because of a 23-page, inherently one-sided, grand jury presentment which doesn't even charge Joe with a crime?"

Maybe even more amazing is that, regardless of what the impact would be on Paterno himself, not one of the board members seemingly grasped the full implications of what they were doing to their university as a whole.

Familiarity often breeds contempt and so over 50 years as head coach Paterno himself had lost enormous personal capital with members of the board (for instance, in addition to having offended the Surmas, Paterno coached four members of the Suhey family, but it apparently only took one of them to feel snubbed by the coach for trustee Paul Suhey to turn on him). But regardless of how the trustees felt personally about Paterno and whether he had hung on way too long to the job, a remotely rational look at the situation would have made it obvious that firing him at that moment was the very worst thing for the school to do for its own self-interest.

While it seems pretty obvious that the board foolishly thought that by firing Paterno they were somehow separating themselves from the story and "moving on," the reality is that what they were really doing is branding the Sandusky scandal, for all time, a "Penn State Scandal." After all, they fired the great Joe Paterno and, effectively, the school president over this. That meant that they, and by extension, the school itself had to be "guilty" (this "self-verdict" would of course also be devastating to any chance of Paterno ever getting a fair hearing, especially when it was assumed by many that the board had "inside info" on what really happened, even though John Surma admitted at his infamous press conference that they did not).

In the face of overt terroristic threats by the media, essentially what the Penn State Board of Trustees decided to do was something like this: condemn to death the face of their school without the hint of due process, inform him of their decision by cell phone, and then order his assassination via a circular firing squad made up of horrendous shooters. All of that was then followed by a tone-deaf press conference perfectly timed for maximum unrest to ensue in the aftermath of their breathtaking stupidity and cowardice.

For those who may say, "What else could they possibly have done?" I suggest that under this kind of thinking we would all be speaking German or Japanese right now because this country certainly would never have won World War II if such spinelessness had dictated our response then to tyranny and injustice.

Jay Paterno has a new book out in which he singles out six board members who should have at least given his dad the initial benefit of the doubt. Here is what Jay Paterno thinks of them:

Those singled out in a rare outpouring of personal, delayed outrage in a chapter evoking Shakespearean tragedy that is entitled "The Firing, Tempest, and Et Tu Brute," include the following:

Anne Riley. Jay recalls an episode from his own childhood in which Riley's father, Ridge, collapsed in the Paterno's kitchen during a visit to work on a history of Penn State football. In young Jay's memory, his father was trying to resuscitate the elder Riley while an ambulance was called.

"In her father's moment of greatest need, my mother and father tried to save his life," Jay writes. 'In my father's hour of greatest need, where was she?"

Paul Suhey. Jay remembered his father going to Jacksonville, Fla. to speak to high school athletic directors and coaches for Suhey, a former Penn State player who had just started a sports medicine clinic there.

Suhey's mother, Ginger, had been Jay's godmother.

"In this critical moment, where was that family loyalty?"

Jesse Arnelle. A man Joe Paterno had helped recruit to Penn State 60 years earlier, and who had gone on to become a successful attorney.
"Couldn't he see that due process, a core American legal value, was being violated here?" Jay Paterno writes.

Ed Hintz. Described as a longtime family friend. Jay Paterno recalled Hintz's silence and evasion when his sister, Mary, had tried to reach him on the telephone the day before, when rumors about Joe Paterno's possible firing were starting to escalate.
"
Did he say to my sister that he would go to the wall for my father? No."

John Surma. Surma, then the chief executive officer of United States Steel Corp., announced the firing to the world that night.

Surma's brother, Vic, played for the Nittany Lions in the late 1960s and early 1970s. But to the Paternos' mind, he had turned on Joe when his own son walked on to Penn State and didn't get a scholarship.

"I am sure John Surma heard his brother's complaints and the constant harping about Joe," Jay wrote.

Steve Garban. The titular chair of the board at the time, and previously the school's senior vice president for business and finance.

"In his administrative career at Penn State, Garban could always count on Joe Paterno to run a football program that was successful on and off the field... and that did not waste money.

"For the decades of service, faithful to the end, what did Joe Paterno get from Steve Garban? Silence. He sat there as John Surma read the words."
Of the six trustees so named, only Hintz, a part of the board's business and industry delegation, remains on the current board.

Anyone not with me is against me!

In Matthew 12:30, we get some insights into the pain and the justification for the hurt in the Paterno family over the Sandusky scandal and the board's handling of it. Joe Paterno, once known as a good guy in regular circles, all of a sudden went from common hero of many to a common criminal according to the media. How could that happen without design?

The Lord said: "Anyone who isn't with me opposes me, and anyone who isn't working with me is actually working against me." As much as I would like to assign some special absolution to Paul Suhey for the violation of his friendship and trust with Joe Paterno and his family, which comes before all allegiances, I have nothing to offer. Paul Suhey must live with what he did. Let him speak for himself.

When Paul Suhey remained silent among the 32 silent trustees who used their silence to sentence Joe Paterno to a living death before his death shortly after his sentence, he turned his back on reality and focused on the binding relationships of the prestigious and noble in the establishment circles at PSU.

I would like to say that I admire the Suhey / Higgins family and I do but I regret to say that Paul Suhey and the entire board should have taken the figurative seppuku Samurai Sword before called upon to do so. In other words, without being asked, they should have all tendered their resignations. They created more problems than they solved by staying on. They were the head of the hydra!

The Paterno's and the Suheys always seemed to have a good relationship. Along the way to the end of Joe Paterno's career in 2011, there seemed to be no issues of consequence between the first family of Penn State Football and the God-like Octogenarian coach and his family.

Over the years Paul Suhey had gotten elected to the board and until he lost his Trustee reelection bid recently, he had put in 15 years of dedicated service to the university as one of the top board members.

As news leaked out about who in the University hierarchy might have to be sacrificed to appease the media, and to save the BOT, the two top officials to be fired on a unanimous secretive "everybody's list," were President Graham Spanier and Head Coach Joe Paterno.

There are still thirty two members of the Board at PSU and so the table in the Hotel had to be huge. They met as did the Sanhedrin to find fault with Christ; not to exonerate Joe Paterno. They sat at this rectangular table at the Penn Stater Hotel while Gov. Tom Corbett of Pennsylvania was on the speaker phone.

Other trustees were present, many emotionally spent. They all could have done a lot better if they all were not thinking about how their decisions about the fate of others would affect their own lives personally! Selfishness, not selflessness for PSU drove this group of cowards to vote against Penn State itself.

The board made more than two decisions during this period but the Penn State Community has found two of the decisions to be especially repugnant. The two board decisions that took the brunt of the criticism from the Penn State community are unquestionably clear — the unanimous choice to remove Joe Paterno as head coach and the unwillingness to refute the Freeh report, which resulted in significant collateral damage to the university such as the NCAA sanctions. If there were a brave man on the PSU BOT, his or her voice was not heard on the night of the slaying of Joe Paterno.

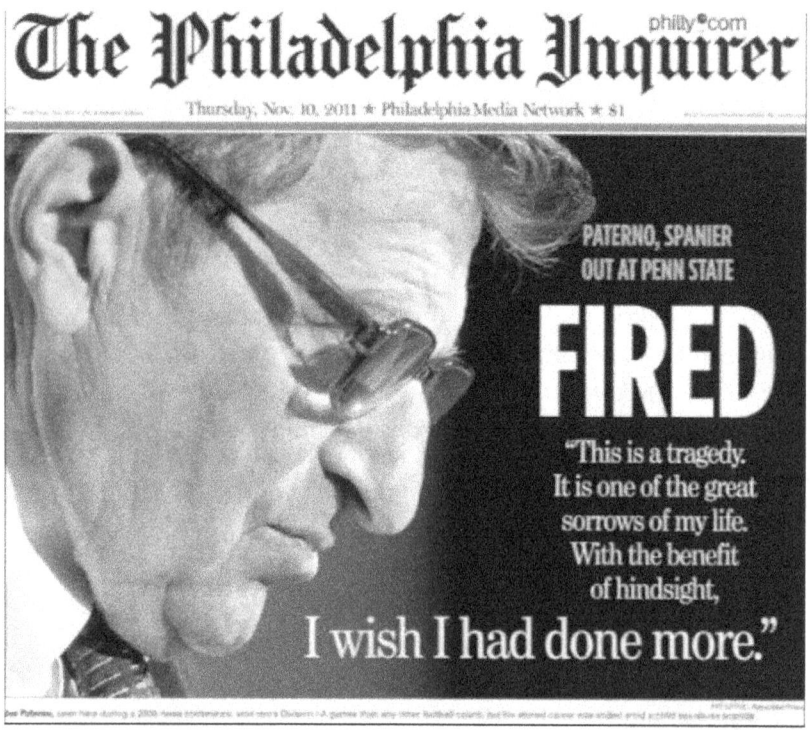

By trade, at IBM for 23 years prior to becoming a college professor, I was a Senior Systems Engineer. It was my job to design solutions and to analyze problems in order to solve them. The folks who held my position in IBM at the time were known as problem solvers. I was a problem solver for IBM and let me tell you that I can't let it go. The PSU debacle is a problem waiting for a solution. I have the solution for this problem but nobody would like it.

Start talking to me about an issue that needs a solution, and I will be thinking of a solution. I solved many problems while at IBM. I brought the problems into my dreams and often solved them when I was asleep. There might be many ways to solve particular problems and my job at IBM was to come up with one, make sure it was a good one, and make sure it would work. I solve problems at home the same way; but my wife, who is the uncontested boss of the family, often finds my solutions substandard to her thinking. Hah! But true!

Before I learned how President Spanier and Coach Paterno's heads were so quickly placed on the table, I questioned why the thirty-two heads of the top ruling body, The Board of Trustees, BOT, had been spared. Why were there no board members at fault? Seems like a fair question?

Governor Corbett had the luxury of having a number of fine state-sponsored Academic Institutions such as Bloomsburg, and East Stroudsburg, etc. from which he could have empaneled a "Blue Ribbon Group of the best administrators." They could have run PSU while it was getting its act together. How was it fair that the BOT got to determine whether the BOT needed to be admonished or not?

Those on the deciding body of "jurors," surely were not about to convict themselves or the one next to them even if bowth were 100% guilty. It is human nature that the BOT would find the BOT harmless. The BOT should not have had that option.

Surely this thought of mine had to be prevalent on the minds of all the members of the board. None wanted any blame for a part-time, though seemingly important activity in their lives. They wanted no credit nor blame for Paterno's fate. So, they sheepishly let their "boss" make the decision and they acceded in silence as cowards so often do.

The First and most appropriate thing an empowered Blue Ribbon Panel from let's say East Stroudsburg could have done would be to fire every board member and evaluate who was on their firing lists. The most essential board members according to the officials at ESU could then be asked to stay temporarily to help in a predefined way before accepting their fate. They would all be fired nonetheless.

An incomplete purge with the head of the Hydra intact would offer no solution and at PSU, since November 2011, we know that this hydra has not offered a solution. Those with a vote have taken it upon themselves to purge the guilty board one election at a time.

It should have been done day one before any functionaries were fired. If ESU or Bloomsburg officials had to run PSU while a great new board was being constituted, so what? The functionaries at PSU such as Spanier could have been left in place, while the new temporary Lords watched their moves very closely.

This would have been the action of a body of governors who were not fearful of their own expulsion. Better yet, before anybody fired them, to repeat, the entire board should have taken the sword as bravehearts and resigned. If this were such a big deal and it was, why stop at those who report to others. Go to the top. Cut off the head and start from scratch. But the head should have removed itself. But, the head was the head of a body made of cowards!

The board was scrambling to address the child sexual abuse scandal involving the university and its football program. All of the elite BOT members "knew" that Graham B. Spanier would be removed as president. But, what about Joe Paterno? In this huge room with the huge table and the Governor on the phone in symbolic harmony with the seventh house and the moon, and the mystics of the seventh rebellion, the tension in the room mounted. This board was unprepared for tough duty. The members just wated the pain to go away.

None of the cowards wanted the decision about Paterno to be laid at their feet. They did not want the public backlash. If the BOT could have fired a maintenance man or a parking lot attendant and have their prestige spared that night, it would have been done, and they would have rejoiced that they got it over that night.

These cowards, who did not have the courage to resign as would have been proper, would have had no problem firing anybody to save their own skins. If needed, they would have taken the perpetrator and had him hung on the closest tree just to get it over with permanently so they could move on with their own preciously more important lives

Yet, it was Joe Paterno, not the maintenance man nor the parking lot attendant whose fate would be determined. Paterno eventually made it to the agenda as the last item to be discussed and determined by the board before they could all go home. But, it was too distasteful for the board to discuss openly, and have the discussion recorded, especially if their words for or against Paterno would be traceable through posterity. Cowards die a thousand times before their death. The valiant never taste of death but once!

The top dog on the Board, Surma, announced that a secret agreement appeared to have been reached to fire Paterno — the trustees having determined that he had failed to take adequate action when he was told that one of his longtime assistants had been seen molesting a 10-year-old boy in Paterno's football facility. Amazing how bad things can be done so cleanly!

Surma, those present recalled, surveyed the other trustees — there were 32 — for their opinions and emotions before asking one last question: "Does anyone have any objections?

If you have an objection, we're open to it." Wow! That was it and Paterno was out clean as a knife through butter!

Let me repeat that simple question since it asked people to think about a lot without telling anybody what to think about. In different terms that he Surma would not have used, the question could have been posed this way:

"Does anybody have any objections to slamming a man against a wall of no return—a man who worked from 1950, before most of us were born, to today (November 9, 2011), a mere 61 + years of service, with no trial, on an issue that is yet unproven, about which all of us are perplexed but would like to be relieved and exonerated. If we are sure that this man, who we all know and have loved, who has brought our institution so much goodness and acclaim acted knowingly to harm children or permit them to be harmed, then we have no choice but to fry him good so we ourselves can never be tried or fired...

"But then again there are no accusations by the authorities against this man. After all, it is possible that Coach Paterno is just as innocent as we the board. So, with that said, if you have no objections to stoning him and taking away his dignity and his life even though we have no idea what the heck he might have done, or what we are doing in this matter, if you can come up with anything—we're open to it"

No one in the huge room with the huge table and all the important people spoke a word. The accused two, Spanier and Paterno, once known as good guys, clearly unworthy to be among the elite, were not in the esteemed chamber with the BOT at the time. There was silence from all including the phone speakers. Paterno's 46-year tenure as head coach of one of the country's storied college football programs was over, and the gravity of the action began to sink in.

"It was hard for us to want to get to the point where we were going to say that," said Ira M. Lubert, a board member who works in private equity. "I was lying in bed that night shaking. And I couldn't sleep — thinking: We just terminated Joe Paterno."

Mr. Lubert, I know you. You are a good man from when you worked with me at IBM, but you and your cohorts should have been thinking before you had to start shaking. It was a railroad job on Joe Paterno and Graham Spanier. Everything was designed to preserve the board and to heck with all other principals and principles in the issue.

The truth did not matter and apparently to many, it still does not matter. The preservation of the board, which in today's world would be seen as the preservation of the PSU establishment, was foremost and paramount. Nobody had the time to care about "the little guys" when the board itself was under fire?

I have never met any of the Suhey's but for years I have heard about them. I do not know Paul Suhey, other than that I know he is Steve and Ginger Suhey's son. He is of a fine and famous PSU family. Paul Suhey did not speak against coach Paterno. He did not speak at all. Silence in this case was the vote to fire the 84-year old coach. How did all 32 members become OK with a silent default decision to terminate?

I believe the board had some great coaching in the BOT room. Somebody had their ear. How else could they unanimously agree to fire Joe Paterno without hearing anything from anybody present? A good man named Paul Suhey and another good man named Ira Lubert silently gave up Joe Paterno. I do not know who; but somebody had to be coaching the group of 32 and their arguments must have been very persuasive.

How else could 32 intelligent beings become fully convinced that the correct decision was to abandon Joe Paterno? Without a rush to judgment and the greasing of the skids, a better decision would surely have been rendered. Nothing the board did that night helped the institution but it did assure the sustenance of the board.

It does not make sense that the thought patterns of 32 BOTs were all magically aligned so that they all came to the same conclusion. Somebody made it seem to them that to save their own skins, they had only one choice. None of the 32 were brave enough to challenge that somebody!

Somebody convinced them all that without the BOT, PSU would be damned or they all would be damned. Ira Lubert, a great man, a great business man, never thought any of his board decisions would affect Joe Paterno's legacy. Ask him! He is still sick over this decision.

This chapter will not sell many copies of this book to PSU board members. That's OK. I write it as I see it. It is my contention that the BOT conclusions were reached with the help of a powerful manipulator. The individuals on the board were thus convinced to create fiction out of truth much to the detriment of Penn State and to State College, and to all of us out here who simply love the truth.

This decision cannot stand the test of time. The Penn State establishment—the BOT, must step down or be fired and the truth brought forth. I commend Jay Paterno and others who have made that their mission.

My recommendation for Paul Suhey of course and for any board member wishing to start fresh consists of three elements: contrition, redemption and forgiveness. Give your deepest regrets; tell the truth, and let's all be done with this sad chapter in PSU history.

Let's herald the Suhey Family like they would surely herald the Paternos.

The Suheys and the Higgins's

Virginia H. "Ginger" Suhey, the matriarch of Penn State football's first family of football spanning four generations, passed away on November 23, 2011 just a few weeks after the JoePa scandal broke loose. She was 84. Her husband Steve had preceded her in death on Jan. 8, 1977. The Suheys 'and the Paternos thus in a few month period both lost the leaders of their respective families.

Born Virginia "Ginger" Higgins on July 3, 1927 in Clarksburg, W.Va. She was the daughter of the late and great PSU long-time football coach Robert A. Higgins and Virginia Gaylord Higgins. On March 3, 1949 Ginger married Steven J. Suhey. Mr. Suhey had the pleasure of marrying the daughter of his collegiate coach, Bob Higgins.

Ginger was a life-long resident of State College. She was a 1944 graduate of State College Area High School, and a 1948 graduate of Penn State University. Upon graduation, she taught physical education at Juniata College. Ginger and Steve were very proud of their seven children, sons Stephen, Paul, Matthew and Larry; daughters Kathy, Betsey and Nancy; 11 grandchildren. Ginger had two sisters Mary Ann Higgins Lyford and Nancy Higgins Dooley.

After the death of her husband, Ginger took over his business, LG Balfour Co., with her son Larry. She was an active member of Kappa Alpha Theta Sorority, Penn State Nittany Lion Club and St. Andrews Episcopal Church.

All American guard Steve Suhey was born on Jan. 8, 1922 in Jamesville, N.Y., He enrolled in 1941 at PSU. Because of the war, he had to postpone both college and football. Suhey was quite a football player and he loved Penn State University and its football program. Suhey played Guard on Bob Higgins 9-0-1 undefeated 1947 Penn State football team which, by the way tied SMU 13-13 in the 1948 Cotton Bowl.

Steve played one year prior to his active duty period and after three years of service in the Pacific with the Army Air Corps, he returned in 1946, safe, and in good shape, and ready to continue as a standout football player.

When he completed his tenure as a player at Penn State, Steve Suhey did not have enough credits to graduate. He completed his degree post facto while playing two years with Pittsburgh in the National Football League. At 27 years of age, he retired from professional football. It got him his degree. Suhey married Ginger at 27 years of age, and then coached high school football before joining the family business, L.G. Balfour Company.

Steve Suhey was inducted into the National Football Foundation College Football Hall of Fame in 1985. He had earned All-America honors as a member of the unbeaten 1947 Penn State team coached by Bob Higgins. He later coached at Waynesboro (Pa.) High School before putting the oval ball down and becoming a salesman for the L.G. Balfour Company until his death in 1977 exactly on his 55th birthday.

Steve and Ginger Suhey had seven children as noted previously, including Larry, Paul and Matt. These three were all playing football for PSU when their dad passed away in 1977. All had different football gifts, yet all three boys gained multiple letters at Penn State during the 1975-1979 period.

The Suhey and Higgins family have a relationship that is almost as old as Penn State itself and it is one that includes the Paternos. Ginger's dad, Bob Higgins is in this book as one of PSU's finest and longest term coaches. Ginger Suhey, Paul Suhey's mom, was Jay Paterno's godmother. Coach Higgins also played his football at Penn State from 1914 to 1916, at which time he made All-American in 1915. After spending WWI in the service, Higgins came back to captain Penn State's Football Team, earning All-America honors again in 1919.

Everybody has a best day. In a 20–0 victory over Pittsburgh, PSU's staunchest rival, that season, Higgins caught a pass from Walter Hess and turned it into a thrilling 92-yard touchdown that was so impressive that it was immortalized in Knute Rockne's "Great Football Plays."

The Bob Higgins coaching story at PSU is told in this book in Chapter 17. Before coming back to Penn State, Higgins coached four seasons at West Virginia Wesleyan (1920, 1922–1924), and he coached three seasons at Washington University in St. Louis. He returned to Penn State in 1928, first as an assistant coach, before becoming head coach in 1930.

He served as head coach of the Penn State Nittany Lions for the next 19 seasons. He was a terrific coach. He led the Nittany Lions to only the second unbeaten season in the school's history, culminating in a tie versus Southern Methodist University in the 1948 Cotton Bowl Classic. It was just the second time that Penn State had ever played in a bowl game.

Higgins retired after the 1948 season, but he remained at Penn State as a special assistant in the Physical Education Department until his full retirement in November 1951. He had a great coaching record of 123–83–16. Considering the many years that he had to go without scholarship players, Bob Higgins' record is even more impressive.

The Suhey family ties thus go back three generations. Well, not exactly! Steve and Ginger Suhey's two grandsons, Kevin Suhey, who played from 2005 to 2007, and Joe Suhey, a fifth-year running back for the Nittany Lion football team in 2011 are fourth generation Higgins / Suhey family members.

As noted, Ginger's late husband, Steve, was a key player and All-America selection on Penn State's 1947 squad that went 9-0-1. Sons Larry, Paul and Matt all played football for State

College Area High School and Penn State. At State High, they were standout players on Little Lion teams that were considered among the best in Pennsylvania in the 1970s. Paul lettered for the Penn State football team in 1975-78, Larry in 1975-76 and Matt in 1976-79.

The Nebraska game on November 12, 2011 was the first game after Joe Paterno was fired by the board. Joe Suhey, Matt's son had played that afternoon for the Nittany Lions. Along with former PSU teammates and alums from other eras, Matt Suhey the ten year Chicago Bears pro (PSU 1980) was obliged to pose for pictures on Senior Day. It was tough duty after Paterno having just been fired.

Smiles were pasted on and the pain was real. It was not the way the Suheys envisioned their son Joe, a fifth-year senior who already had his degree, would be saying goodbye to a stadium that's been home to so many in the family.

When queried at the game, Matt Suhey, wished not to elaborate on his range of emotions or details related to charges involving former Penn State defensive coordinator Jerry Sandusky. But Suhey did make a point to praise Paterno, who decades ago once temporarily lived with Suhey's parents and Joe Paterno is Matt Suhey's sister's godfather.

"He has been nothing but extraordinary for me and our family and he has nothing but my support," said Suhey, who played for Paterno from 1976-79 before becoming Walter Payton's lead blocker and a great Chicago Bear himself. "It's hard for me to put it into words so I'd just as soon not."

Paul Suhey, Matt's older brother, is a respected orthopedic surgeon based in State College, and had been a member of the Penn State Board of Trustees until the recent election. As noted, Matt played for 10 years with the Chicago Bears in the National Football League. He is a member of the Pennsylvania football all-century team.

At Penn State, Ginger's father, Bob Higgins, who passed away in 1969, lettered in football, baseball, boxing and wrestling. He was succeeded for one season by Joe Bedenk as coach of the Lions, who was then followed by Rip Engle (1950-1965) and then Joe Paterno (1966-2011).

According to "Road to Number One," a history of Penn State football written by the late Ridge Riley, Paterno lived for a year with Ginger and Steve Suhey when he came to Penn State from Brown, and was a first-year Nittany Lion assistant coach. The Paternos and the Suheys loved each other like family.

"Sunny (Rip's wife) and their son, Chip, hadn't arrived at the house Rip had already bought on Woodland Drive," Riley wrote, "and there was no furniture, but Joe slept for two weeks in a cot until he moved in with Steve and Ginger Suhey for the first year, and then with the Jim O'Hora family." Al Browning, from the Tuscaloosa news wrote this piece about Joe Paterno from when the Coach just came to Penn State. Not everybody in life starts out with a silver soon but good people and good friends let them use their spoons until they can use their own.

By AL BROWNING
News Sports Editor

NEW ORLEANS — At age 24, Joe Paterno was lonely, practically broke and en route to farm-dotted woods from a concrete jungle.

The streets of Brooklyn had made him wise, but State College, Pa., offered strange surroundings. There were no Dodgers to watch on Saturday afternoons, no sidewalk bums to dodge and very little night life.

Paterno admits he was scared the night he arrived at Penn State University to begin his career as a college football coach. His salary was $3,200 a year — just enough money for spaghetti and Spanish Rice, as it turned out — and he was in bad need of a place to hang his coat.

Then the door opened at the house owned by Steve and Virginia Suhey, who were to produce three sons who would play for Paterno after he became head coach at Penn State.

The two surviving principals of that story — Paterno and Virginia Suhey — were caught rehashing those trying first days at Penn State here Thursday afternoon.

Two of the sons watched in the background, before joining their Penn State teammates at practice in preparation for a Monday afternoon Sugar Bowl game against Alabama. The gleams in the eyes of running back Matt Suhey and linebacker Paul Suhey indicated they were proud of the hospitality their family had shown a stranger who would later become one of the coaching elite of college football.

"Joe shared our two-bedroom apartment," said Virginia (Ginger) Suhey. "It was a difficult time for him, a young man in new surroundings. He enjoyed meeting our young friends and we enjoyed having a thoughtful, intelligent person in the house. We played bridge by the hours, which is what you did when you did not have a lot of money to socialize, and we ate Spanish Rice.

"He ate so much of that rice back then, I doubt he can look at it today."

The year was 1950,

Chapter 25—The First Family of Nittany Lion Football

Joe Paterno in 1950 arriving at Penn State Looking Sharp!

Like most of us, the Suheys are tough people once they set their sights on a notion. Paul Suhey has not had it easy with his own family, the Paterno family, or even his own PSU teammates. Yet, he is seemingly undaunted. He clearly believes that he had *right* on his side and he chose to test his opinion of *right* by recently running for a sixth three-year term on the PSU board. It was not so easy.

He did not make it. That may mean that more people think he was more off base than on target. That may mean that a lot of people think Paul Suhey is wrong. Hopefully, over time, his stubbornness will ease up so the Suhey and Paterno families can reconcile. That's what we all would like.

Fellow members of the PSU Letterman's Club were quite descriptive in their rancor about the BOT action v Joe Paterno without a trial. They labeled the former PSU linebacker under Paterno as a *traitor*. For a guy who never met Paul Suhey, I did not see him give the presumption of innocence to Joe Paterno. He went along with a board who had the Coach declared guilty from moment one.

Even though there were no charges and in fact, none were ever specified. The board found Joe Paterno guilty but they were not sure of what he was guilty! Guilt was never specified.

Paul Suhey was not the leader but he was a complicit follower. He and his band of 31 other PSU establishment board members had tar and feathered their once revered coach before the coach even knew the tar was being warmed. Suhey's teammates did not like that at all.

Overwhelmingly the Lettermen forecasted their intent and then voted Paul Suhey down from the Board of Directors. Dr. Suhey will long be remembered as one of the guys who could have helped but instead he assured that Joe Paterno was fired. Instead of being the hero, who when he had the opportunity, sought the truth in the Sandusky scandal, Paul Suhey went along with his BOT cronies to get along. Big difference!

The former players in the Letterman group repeated the mantra of many in the Penn State alumni community. The word for Pro-Penn Staters is that the board effectively and unfairly made Paterno the scapegoat for all of Sandusky's sins, without even providing the appearance of a trial and without caring about the meaning of the word, fair. Nobody is saying children were not hurt but casting spurious stones at some who may be innocent is no way to find the truth.

The press had been stirring the pot from the first time it smelled blood. They wanted somebody big to go down for better stories. They kept trying to find more dirt in the Sandusky scandal even if the dirt was gone.

The press seemed pleased when they spotted the lightest implication of Joe Paterno. The press had an agenda and it was not the truth. There is still much bitterness about Paul Suhey's betrayal of his coach and this will be reconciled only when he addresses this in full with his peers.

IMHO, Suhey must show some level of contrition hoping for redemption, while asking for forgiveness. Otherwise, the scenario will continue to play out with the same nastiness and bitterness as the below letter, which was circulated by his football peers to prevent Paul Suhey from regaining his seat on the BOT in 2016.

A group of football lettermen sent out this note to their peers, urging them to oppose Suhey in the BOT election, because of the BOT role and Suhey's role in particular in the firing of Joe Paterno as coach following the Jerry Sandusky grand jury report in November 2011. Suhey, a State College native and former star linebacker under Paterno, had been on the board for 15 years.

Paul Suhey Lettermen Letter
SUCCESS WITH HONOR

March 28, 2013

Dear Fellow Lettermen,

We write to you about a matter of great importance to our University. As fellow Lettermen and alumni of the Pennsylvania State University we, like the rest of the Nation, were horrified by the actions of Jerry Sandusky. No words that we or anyone else can say will ever heal Sandusky's victims, their families or the damage that he caused other than to say our thoughts and prayers remain with them.

Also horrifying has been the ensuing damage inflicted to the standing of our University due in large part to the failure of the Board of Trustees. It is for this reason that we are compelled to step forward and oppose Paul Suhey's re-election to the Board. We take this action with the full understanding of the division this may cause amongst us. It is not a role we relish but, it is one we believe is necessary to prevent any further damage to our University.

At nearly every turn over the past sixteen months, the Board of Trustees has failed miserably to exercise the necessary leadership and responsibility to guide our University. No greater illustration is the Board's handling of Joe and the Freeh Report. While admittedly not knowing all of the facts, the Board unanimously rushed to judgment and fired Joe after 61 years of service to the University without ever once talking with him. Similarly, the Board to this very day has failed to discuss the substance of the Freeh report let alone question its evidentiary basis or lack thereof. The consequences of these actions have severely tarnished the reputation and legacy of Coach Paterno and have brought great harm upon the University, our beloved program and the innocent players and coaches who now occupy our locker room.

In the coming days, you will no doubt hear how Paul Suhey disagreed with these actions but cannot tell "his side" for legal reasons or how he knew Joe as "Uncle Joe". To this we say nonsense! Actions speak louder than words and if Suhey disagreed with the actions the Board was taking he had both an obligation and a duty to speak up and cast his vote accordingly. The fact that he failed to do so only underscores the point that he is not fit to serve on the board a day longer. The choice is for everyone to make but, for us it could not be any clearer — retire Paul Suhey, like he claimed to retire Joe, by not re-electing him.

Todd Blackledge '82; Robert Capretto '67; Tom Donchez '74; Franco Harris '72; Justin Ingram '00; Christian Marrone '97; Brian Masella '74; Lydell Mitchell '72; Michael Robinson '04; Steve Smear '69; Brandon Short '99;

Telling Joe the Bad News

Joe Paterno always had time to show up in person. He recruited in person. He gave speeches in person. He showed up for parental sessions with players in person. Yet, after a zillion personal appearances on behalf of Penn State University and others, the final insult and another sign of BOT cowardice was that this set of trustees were too impatient to address the matter in a personal meeting with Coach Paterno.

Instead, they first rushed to judgment. When they had the unanimity they demanded, they immediately went for the kill. But, they forgot about protocol. Instead, they just wanted their personal pain to end by giving Paterno a life-ending pain from which he could never recover and about which he could never fully understand.

Their best explanation for their poor work was a strong desire to "put this behind them," no matter the cost, as if choosing to accept the blame when none was due, would lessen the ill effects. How could such a group of business leaders and politicians have such a collective lack of backbone or sense of reason and purpose? Was there not one brave man among them?

In the final rush moment of the rush job decision, the board had to inform Joe Paterno of its decision. They had to make sure that the 61-year dedicated football coach knew that in no uncertain terms that he had been fired before their board meeting had even concluded. Technology was prevalent but even technology could not superimpose the full board into a Star-Trek transporter and materialize it in Paterno's living room for the final discussion. Surma had declared that no discussions were deemed necessary.

This important body of Penn State's finest establishmentarians could not wait until morning to contact the 61-year coach. So, they decided that a phone call at 10:00 PM was the right technology and all that was technically needed to end 61 years of dedication from the most honored employee PSU had ever had and ever will have.

Isn't it hard to fathom that with 32 real people on the board, supposedly the finest in the community, not a one spoke up once to give Paterno the benefit of the doubt after 61 years. Can you imagine what they would do for a one-month employee if the press were demanding answers?

Why the rush? They wanted it OVER! Plain and Simple! It was about them. It was not about justice or Joe Paterno of Graham Spanier. They had no idea what to do so they simply wanted it all OVER! They wanted life to continue tomorrow but they had enough for today for sure! Too bad if Spanier and Paterno got hurt as long as they got their eight hours! Whoever said BOT members should have to work OT?

For this group of lazy cowards, it was not about Paterno or his family, nor about Penn State as a university and it was not about all the great supporters or about the folks in State College who bend over backwards to support the university every day. It was about the selfish board itself, and their deep wish to be free from this terrible burden of making a decision that might have their names associated with it.

It did not matter to them that they would be killing other people's careers. They knew that if they did not fire all the big fish, guilty or innocent, this travesty might not end until the next day or the next and then what about golf? What about the fun planned for the weekend?

This "exercise," which was for real, had already taxed these poor souls on the board, who had agreed to take a fluff position at PSU for their own benefit not for their potential disrobement. They were not looking for anything negative to come out of their arrival as members of the royal PSU establishment.

When they were counting mice and men in the hotel that day, there was a lot of chirping and teeth gnashing but the supposed men in the chamber were all quiet. They had been advised to say nothing...but by whom?

Were there no friends of Paterno on the board? If the coach had thrown a lit cigarette from his car window, in front of the gendarme, he would have had a fighting chance though clearly guilty. Would the board have put him down for the lit cigarette offense? Maybe? Maybe they simply did not like Joe Paterno? Were they waiting for something and when they got something that smelled like deadly blood, they could not let go?

Nobody on the board had the guts to even visit Joe Paterno at home or worse yet, invite him into the inquisition, and so this notion of a phone call became the approved method of contact to relay the eminent board's final decree: "Joe, you're fired! I am surprised this board did not simply tell the Press: "Joe's fired...you tell him!"

All the cowards on the BOT had agreed it was the appropriate method of contact. Nobody would get dirty. It was nice and sanitary. Someone who would remain anonymous for the good of the university would make the phone call so it would be all over in minutes and the whole 32 sugarplums could dance in their own fine night's sleep. Sleeping well was so important because firing Paterno was such an important, yet potentially sleepless decision!

The brave constabulary did not even call Joe Paterno up from their meeting room with the governor still on the line to make it official to tell JoePa that he was fired. Nice touch! But, no, they did not. They used a trick reserved for Weasels: Paterno had to make the phone call himself in order to get fired:

Ironically, Joe Paterno was accused of no wrong-doing. In fact, the proper authorities said he had fulfilled his legal obligations by reporting what he knew to his superiors. Nevertheless, the university Board of Trustees summarily dismissed him with a late-night phone call four days after Sandusky's arrest. They knew better than the police!

At about 10 p.m., Joe Paterno and Sue were getting ready for bed when the doorbell at their home rang. All thirty two BOT members were at the door so they could each speak to the coach. Well, not exactly! An assistant athletic director was sent by the BOT to the door, and he or she wordlessly handed Sue a slip of paper. It was a silent written handoff that had emanated from a silent decision of thirty-two trustees.

There was nothing on the note but the name of the vice chairman of trustees, John Surma, with a phone number. The two Paternos, Sue, and Joe, stood frozen by their bedside in their nightclothes, Sue in a robe and Paterno in pajamas and a Penn State sweatshirt. Paterno dialed the number.

Surma told Paterno, "In the best interests of the university, you are terminated." Paterno hung up and repeated the words to his wife. She grabbed the phone and redialed. "After 61 years he deserved better," she snapped. "He deserved better." Hey those ten words at least had reached double digits.

There was no hearing and there were no rebuttals. It was fait accompli. It was a done deal. What a low-class lot! A strong governor would have fired them all and if he had fired them all immediately instead of cowering along with them, he might still even be the governor today... or at least Pennsylvanians would be wishing he could be the guy.

Paul Suhey and his ilk felt that they had won one for the establishment. The Penn State fancy hierarchy is not what Penn Staters and fans from across the world see when we think of Penn State Football. Suhey should have known better. He knew JoePa from eye contact.

I had the pleasure of being on the faculty of PSU for a Semester while a member of another faculty and I rooted for Penn State football as a Pennsylvanian all my life—as did many others. Everybody loves the university, the football team and the coach. How could the board sell us all out so conveniently?

The lettermen who signed a letter about Suhey making the board or not in 2016, at the time offering their lack of support for Suhey, were all one-time good-guy gumbas of Paul Suhey. They loved Paul Suhey. He did not see the situation as they saw it and he they had given him the power. He took an opposite stance on their Coach as they preferred. For participating in the firing debacle, they asked unanimously for Paul Suhey to be voted off the board in the alumni balloting which opened on April 10.

Their word stood and Suhey was not reelected. Suhey still has chosen not to relent in any way. He never mused that he may not have done everything rightly. He did not see firing Joe Paterno as a mistake. In fact, he affirmed his position. Jay Paterno found it distasteful that Mr. Suhey used the coach's own words to justify his actions.

Paul Suhey offered that among the life lessons he learned from Paterno as a player and captain of the 1979 team were integrity, and that "good leaders can't be afraid of doing the right thing because it's unpopular." Suhey also noted as a board member at Penn State "my responsibility is to do what I think is right for the university that I love. I had to make what I knew would be a stunningly unpopular decision but I believed then, as I believe now for many reasons, that it was the right decision…I understand that there are many people who believe it was the wrong decision, as much as I believe it was the right one," Suhey concluded in his statement. "I am

OK with that and I respect the opinions of others who disagree with me."

I have said this a few times in this chapter. Paul Suhey has taken a hard line. The Suhey family and the Paternos are not interested in the hard line. It is time that Penn State begins again to respect Joe Paterno. Those who voted against JoePa need to ask us all for contrition so that we Penn Staters can give those who took the wrong stance the redemption they seek. When we are convinced they are sorry, and they are contrite of heart, we will forgive them all for sure, and the Suhey / Paterno lovefest can begin again. The sooner, the better!

Amen!

Chapter 26 Joe Paterno: A Life - He was Penn State

No man can do everything 100% well

My deepest expression of thanks to Penn Live for Permission to reprint this fine article, the epitaph of Joe Paterno by Bob Flounders. It ran on Penn Live on Jan. 24, 2012 at 3:53 PM. I have applied some poetic license.

Joe Paterno; Great man; Great coach.
Even JoePa could not do it all

He [Joe Paterno] was a relatively small man by physical standards.

He preferred the quiet life in many respects.

The reality, though, was that most everything about Joseph Vincent Paterno was large and loud, two traits not typically associated with life in bucolic Happy Valley.

Penn State's sports icon passed away Sunday morning at the age of 85 after a two-month fight with lung cancer. [Though he was made of iron, he was not a kid when he died and unlike the Pope, he was not infallible]

He was known to most simply as "JoePa" but he was a complex man.

You had the Paterno who lived in a modest State College ranch house on McKee Street, within walking distance of Beaver Stadium. Paterno would know - he frequently made the walk.

You had the Paterno who guarded his team's privacy and insisted they practice away from the media spotlight.

You had the leader who was adamant that his Nittany Lions wear unassuming blue-and-white uniforms.

You had that Joe Paterno.

Then there was the man that became a college football legend. A coach who won two national championships and produced five perfect seasons. A coach who amassed 409 wins, the most ever by a major college coach.

Chapter 26 Joe Paterno—A Life. He was Penn State

There was the man who built a university and, some would argue, a town. A man who built a football machine, starting from scratch.

At Joe Paterno's first game as head coach, on Sept. 17, 1966, the Lions beat Maryland 15-7 in front of a Beaver Stadium crowd of 40,911.

During Paterno's final season, on Sept. 10 of 2011, eventual national champ Alabama beat Penn State 27-11 at Beaver Stadium in front of a sellout crowd of 107,846.

So there was that Paterno.

...

The Sandusky name was a heavy anchor around Paterno's neck as he began to slip in recent weeks. So much so that when asked about Sandusky, Paterno said: "It is one of the great sorrows of my life. With the benefit of hindsight, I wish I had done more." [Of course!]

Paterno is gone now, but his tale is still unfinished.

"I hope there isn't a rush to complete Joe's story, because I think there is a lot more to this story that's going to come out," said one of his celebrated former players, TV football analyst Matt Millen, the day after his death. "Eventually, it will come out and we have to be patient. We're always in a rush these days."

Millen visited with Paterno and his wife, Sue, in their home last month. They talked about many things and the subject of Sandusky came up.

"I was honest with Joe," Millen said. "I said, 'Coach, I think it's going to get worse before it gets better.' And it could get worse."

Paterno entered his final season at Penn State as a man above reproach. A coach. A father. A teacher. A leader.

In the final two months of his life, he proved to be all too human as the details of the Sandusky investigation became public. But before that – for 61 years – Paterno also proved to be extraordinary.

Stories will continue to be written about the man and his accomplishments. Speeches will be given. There will be books about his life and his career.

None of them will completely capture him.

None of them will capture the excitement that Penn State fans felt as this modest-looking man from Brooklyn, with thick glasses and white socks led his team out of the tunnel on a crisp fall afternoon.

None of them will capture the pride they felt for a leader who somehow managed to combine victory and integrity.

None of them will capture the love they felt for a grandfather of 17 who became a surrogate grandfather to hundreds of thousands.

And, yes, none of them will capture the sense of anger and disappointment at how the final 79 days of his life unfolded.

...

How do you sum up that life? Here is one way:

- *Two national championships.*
- *Five perfect seasons.*

- Dozens of first-team All-Americans.
- A superb graduation rate.
- Twenty-four bowl victories.
- And a very rare induction into The College Football Hall of Fame as an active coach.

Here is another way:

The plain blue-and-white jerseys with no names remain to this day. Because it was never supposed to be about individual glory.

"The main thing that will always stick with me about Joe is how he did things, how he did things his way and how he did things the right way,' " said Dallas Cowboys linebacker Sean Lee, who left the PSU program in 2009.

"Joe wanted to win but what concerned him more was how he won. It had to be with his guys – guys that were disciplined, guys that went to class, and guys that continued to get better."

"There were no shortcuts."

That was how Joe Paterno coached and it was how he lived.

Paterno hated it when reporters would ask about him instead of the team.

He stuck with the same university for 61 years — praised it, fought for it, and gave to it generously even after he had been fired in disgrace.

And, more telling still, alone among all those caught up in the Jerry Sandusky scandal — from university leaders and trustees to Sandusky himself — Paterno joined his own critics. While all the others insisted that they had done absolutely nothing wrong, Joe admitted that he should have done more.

While others did nothing but justify their own actions, Joe alone confessed, "I'm sick about it."

But the final, tumultuous, heart-wrenching weeks of Joe Paterno's life did not wipe out the historic career that preceded them.

THE PATERNO WAY

Paterno's life could easily have turned in another direction. But if it had, we probably wouldn't be writing odes about his greatness as a defense attorney, would we?

That was the choice he faced more than 60 years ago: coaching or law school.

Shortly after leaving Brown University in the spring of 1950, the former quarterback received a surprise call from former Brown coach Rip Engle, who was moving to State College to overhaul the Lions program.

Engle was permitted to bring along one assistant.

He wanted his former quarterback, Paterno — a slow-footed, matchstick-thick winner who had guided Brown to a 9-1 mark a year earlier.

The 23-year-old Brooklyn native needed money before heading to Boston University Law School. He jumped at the offer.

Paterno expected his coaching career to be brief. His dad, Angelo Paterno, who earned his own law degree at 44, wanted his oldest son to follow his lead.

"Everything was set," Paterno said.

But when he got to quiet State College, the New York City kid embraced small-town life. More importantly, he was bitten by the coaching bug.

A short time later, Paterno met with his father and explained that law school wasn't for him. He wanted to coach football.

"My father told me if that's what I wanted to do, just make sure you make a difference," JoePa said.

Paterno coached in State College a dozen years before settling down. He married the former Suzanne Pohland in 1962. She had graduated from Penn State earlier that year.

Paterno, a legendary perfectionist in the fall, was known to arrive home late from the practice field, but his daughter, Mary Kay Hort, said that when the Paterno children were still young, her mother would hold dinner to make sure the family ate together.

There was no question about the 49-year love affair between Joe and Sue Paterno.

"There is a lot of love going in both directions between those two," former Penn State President Bryce Jordan once said.

Paterno succeeded Rip Engle as head coach in 1966. His first team won its first game, 15-7 over Maryland, but bogged down that season to 5-5.

Clearly, there was an adjustment period.

Engle did it his way. Paterno claimed that he stayed within Rip's framework but he had his own methods. More intense methods.

On game days and especially on the practice field, Paterno's motor always ran hot. His players learned early on: Paterno was unafraid to break a player down before slowly building him up.

Some of Paterno's players from the earlier years sought out his assistants, begging them to tell the head coach to lighten up.

Instead, the players changed. They stayed the course, and by November they were simply playing harder than the opposition.

Soon, the results would be spectacular.

But Paterno's players had to cut it in the classroom, too. Or they weren't going to play. In a world where many college athletes were students in name only, Paterno insisted on a marriage of academic and athletic excellence. Without exception.

JoePa called it the Grand Experiment, and Sue Paterno played a part as well. She would tutor Lions players, sometimes at their State College home and sometimes at the team's study hall.

It worked.

Paterno's 2011 team ranked first in the Academic Bowl Championship Series rankings, which measures academic progress and graduation rates among all of the teams in the BCS rankings.

In the rankings among teams in The Associated Press Top 25, which were announced in December, Penn State was tied with Stanford with a Graduation Success Rate of 87 percent.

Said Millen: "My first thoughts about Joe are not as a coach because he was well beyond that. He was an educator and a teacher. He taught lessons — some about football, mostly about life."

TO THE TOP

It didn't take long for Paterno's coaching career to take off. In fact, it took exactly one year.

After a 5-5 first season in 1966, the 1967 season brought an 8-2-1 mark and a Gator Bowl appearance. It was also the start of The Streak.

Penn State played 31 consecutive games, from Oct. 14, 1967, to Sept. 26, 1970, without losing. Here's a number to chew on: 30-0-1.

By the end of 1968, PSU was No. 3 in the country, a distinction the Lions earned after rallying past Kansas 15-14 in the final minute of the Orange Bowl.

The 1968 season was also significant because of Paterno's decision to sprinkle his defense with a number of talented sophomores. One of them was a linebacker named Jack Ham, who eventually played his way into All-America status.

Paterno followed an unbeaten 1968 with an unbeaten 1969. Identical 11-0 marks. But the end of 1969 infuriated the head coach — PSU, a 10-3 victor over Missouri in the Orange Bowl, had to settle for No. 2.

In 1973, Paterno produced his third unbeaten season in eight years and his first and only Heisman Trophy winner.

Hard-charging tailback John Cappelletti galloped for 1,522 yards and 17 touchdowns to lead an unheralded PSU team — unranked at the start of the season — to a No. 5 finish.

Paterno went 56-16 during the remainder of the 1970s, and he would have one more frustrating brush with a first national championship.

His 1978 team, led by quarterback Chuck Fusina, fullback Paul Suhey and defensive stalwarts Millen and Bruce Clark, brutalized its way to an 11-0 regular season. Eight times, the Lions held opponents to 10 points or less.

Armed with a No. 1 ranking, the Lions headed to New Orleans to play No. 2 Alabama in the Sugar Bowl against Paul "Bear" Bryant and Alabama.

In one of the most savage games a Paterno team ever played, PSU dropped a 14-7 decision, thanks to a late goal-line stand by the Crimson Tide. On fourth-and-goal from the 1-yard line, Alabama linebacker Barry Krauss dove over a pile to stop running back Mike Guman from the tying TD.

The finish to Paterno's 13th season proved to be unfortunate. PSU was clearly the best team in the East in the 1960s and 1970s, but remained one step away from greatness. As the 1980s arrived, the gap between Paterno's teams and perennial champions such as USC, Oklahoma and Alabama continued to narrow.

The 1981 squad fielded a typically bruising defense, with an overpowering offensive line led by Mike Munchak and Sean Farrell. And never before was there a quarterback-running back-wideout troika like Todd Blackledge, Curt Warner and Kenny Jackson — all future first-round NFL picks.

Ironically, on Jan. 22 – the day Joe Paterno died – Curt Warner's son, Jonathan Warner, a wide-out from the state of Washington, visited the campus and verbally committed to play for new Penn State coach Bill O'Brien in 2012.

In 1981, midseason losses to Miami and Alabama dropped PSU to 7-2, but the Lions finished strong and came roaring back in 1982.

Paterno's time had come. No team came within nine points of the Lions in their final six regular-season games. PSU worked its way up to No. 2 and secured a Sugar Bowl pairing opposite top-ranked Georgia on New Year's Day, 1983.

This time, Penn State and Paterno didn't misfire. Finally, they were No. 1.

Four years later, Penn State climbed the mountain again. The 1986 squad was vastly different than the 1982 team. Defense and special teams were the calling cards.

During Penn State's 11-game regular season in 1986, the Lions played only one team ranked in the top 20. But in late October, the sixth-ranked Lions visited No. 2 Alabama.

Penn State's defense, an ornery bunch led by All-America linebacker Shane Conlan, was poised to make a statement. The Lions tormented Alabama's offense and won a 23-3 victory that pushed Paterno's team to No. 2.

PSU went up against No. 1 Miami in the Fiesta Bowl.

The brash Hurricanes, coached by Jimmy Johnson, were solid favorites. Miami's defense had speed and its offense featured Heisman Trophy quarterback Vinny Testaverde.

The Hurricanes gained 445 yards but turned the ball over seven times. Penn State's defenses were tough, turning Testaverde away at the Lions' 1-yard line with a game-clinching interception by linebacker Pete Giftopoulos.

Penn State was national champs again. This time, a lot of the credit went to the defense led by one of Paterno's top assistant coaches, Sandusky.

Paterno was named the American Football Coaches Association Coach of the Year for the fourth time and Sportsman of the Year by Sports Illustrated.
Paterno's popularity was growing. So was his impact off the field.

Two years after PSU's second title run, Paterno seconded the nomination of George H.W. Bush at the 1988 Republican National Convention.

HARD YEARS

The Lions' intense practices under Paterno were legendary. Some players from the 1960s and 1970s insist that PSU practices were often more difficult than the games.

Paterno was a yeller. Make that a screamer. And he rarely played favorites. The Lions' best players were treated the same as third- and fourth-teamers: roughly.

"He can't stand mediocrity," former PSU radio announcer Fran Fisher said years ago.

"He can't stand anybody or anything that doesn't strive to be the ultimate. It drives him crazy that somebody with talent or somebody with potential doesn't pursue it to its 'nth' degree. It just drives him nuts."

Paterno's Brooklyn bark dominated PSU practice sessions. No one was safe. No mistakes were tolerated. The man saw everything.

"No matter what time of year — practice, spring ball, preseason practice — you always kind of had to have your head on a swivel, like Linda Blair, to try and figure out where Joe Paterno was," Jack Ham said. "Because he was everywhere.

"I always remember a mistake [Ham's teammate and later offensive coordinator] Fran Ganter made. Joe was about 50 yards away, and he just came running."

The 1982 and 1986 national championships were JoePa's signature seasons and moments on the field.

There would be many more great moments and some very good teams, including the 1994 squad – an offensive juggernaut led by future first-round NFL picks Kerry Collins (quarterback), Ki-Jana Carter (tailback) and Kyle Brady (tight end) – that finished 12-0 and No. 2 in the country.

But there would be no more championships

And at the start of the 21st century, Paterno's teams began to fade. Penn State had joined the Big Ten in the 1993 season, and the yearly battles against Ohio State, Michigan and others were taking their toll.

The Lions' recruiting also began to suffer. There was a definite lack of talent on some of PSU's teams in 2000, 2001, 2003 and 2004 – in the latter two seasons combined, the Nittany Lions were just 7-16.

Paterno, nearing 80 years old, was on the hot seat. Many fans clamored for him to step down or be replaced for 2005.

Paterno promised a turnaround. And aided by young talents such as Derrick Williams and Justin King, the Lions delivered. Penn State finished 11-1 in 2005, won the Big Ten and beat Florida State in the Orange Bowl.

Paterno had survived his roughest stretch on the sideline.

But during his last six years, Paterno would have to deal with repeated health issues – he broke his left leg in 2006 and had his right hip replaced in 2008 – and then he would have to deal with Jerry Sandusky.

The painful bodily injuries were the easy part.

SHOCKING

Jerry Sandusky is a former Penn State player and he was regarded as a defensive genius. The man who built Penn State football's reputation as "Linebacker U."

On Nov. 5, [2011] Sandusky was arrested and indicted on 50 counts of sexually assaulting 10 boys.

The news turned the sports world upside down. The prominence of Sandusky, as well as two top Penn State officials who were charged with perjury. The horrible allegations and graphic details in the attorney general's report.

Above all, the fact that it happened on Joe Paterno's watch. Many of the incidents were alleged to have taken place in the Penn State football locker room, both before and after Sandusky's retirement as a coach in 1999.

But it was an alleged incident in 2002, more than any other, that brought about Paterno's downfall.

Mike McQueary said that, in 2002, he witnessed Sandusky [and a 10-year old boy in the locker room showers. One time McQuery said he witnessed a rape and in testimony four other times, he was not sure exactly].

When he reported it to Paterno, the coach ...reported it to his own superior, then-Athletic Director Tim Curley...

In mid-January, with his 85-year-old body frail and his condition deteriorating, Paterno conducted one final interview, with The Washington Post.

He sat in a wheelchair at the family kitchen table, surrounded by his wife, Sue, sons Scott, Jay and David, and daughter Mary Kay. He talked about his response in 2002 when McQueary came to him.

"I didn't know exactly how to handle it." He said. "So I backed away...I'm sick about it."
...
Joe Paterno won more games than any coach in major college football and he did it his way, the right way.

His players went to class and Paterno made sure they graduated.

He was a humanitarian. A father figure. A teacher. A leader. A role model. And he should be remembered that way.

In the end, everyone who idolized him also knew that Joe Paterno was deeply human. He was capable of making serious mistakes.

But at the end of his life, he was also human enough to admit it.

Chapter 27—Penn State's Best Linebackers from 1965 to 2015

Twelve Top Linebackers at Linebacker U

- Dennis Onkotz 1967 – 1969
- Jack Ham 1968 – 1969
- Greg Buttle 1973 – 1975
- Shane Conlan 1983 – 1986
- Andre Collins 1986 – 1989
- Brian Gelzheiser 1991 – 1994
- Brandon Short 1996 – 1999
- Lavar Arrington 1997 – 1999
- Paul Posluszny 2003 – 2006
- Pete Giftopoulis – 1985-1987
- Dan Connor 2004 – 2007
- Novarro Bowman 2006-2009

Source: Our thanks to
http://www.blackshoediaries.com/2007/6/10/214341/999

Dennis Onkotz was a two time first team All American on the great Penn State teams of 1968 and 1969. Both teams went 11-0 with Orange Bowl wins over Kansas and Missouri. Amazingly, neither team was awarded the national championship. Onkotz started all three years (freshmen didn't play back then) and finished his career as Penn State's all-time leading tackler with 287 tackles. He led the team in tackles in 1967 and 1969 with 71 and 97 respectively.

His tackling record would be passed by three guys later on, but two of them had the benefit of playing as freshmen and having additional regular season games. Onkotz still holds

the record for interceptions by a Nittany Lion linebacker with 11, and three of those he returned for touchdowns. He was such a gifted athlete that he also returned 47 punts for an average return of over 13 yards as Penn State's primary punt returner.

After Penn State Onkotz was a third round pick by the New York Jets. An injury in his rookie season ended his playing career. In 1995 Onkotz was selected to the College Football Hall of Fame.

Jack Ham was not highly recruited out of high school. He almost went to the Virginia Military Institute before Penn State offered him their last scholarship in 1966. He went on to team up with Dennis Onkotz and Jim Kates in 1968 and 1969 to lay the foundation for the legacy that would go on to become known as Linebacker U. Ham was a three year starter and was selected a first team All American in 1970 after registering 91 tackles and four interceptions as a team captain.

He ended his career with 251 tackles which was good enough for second on the all-time list back then second only to Onkotz. Today he is thirteenth on the all-time list, but again, back then freshmen didn't play and the regular season was only 10 games until 1971. He also blocked three punts during his career, a school record that would stand until it was tied in 1989. During his playing career Penn State amassed a record of 29-3 with two undefeated seasons.

After college, Ham was a second round pick by the Pittsburgh Steelers. He started as a rookie and went on to be a key member of their Super Bowl dynasty of the 1970's. He was inducted into the Professional Football Hall of Fame in 1988 and joined the College Football Hall of Fame in 1990. In 2000 Ham joined the Penn State Radio Network and calls the games with Steve Jones.

Greg Buttle was one of the most colorful players to ever wear the Blue and White. His jovial nature often drew the ire of a then young Joe Paterno. His junior and senior year statistics are simply mind blowing. 165 tackles as a junior and 140 tackles as a senior. Again, he didn't have the benefit of 12 regular season games or even playing as a freshman back then. Buttle still holds the single season tackle record as well as the record for tackles in a single game (24). His 343 career tackles were a school record until it was passed by Paul Posluszny in 2006. Buttle was honored as a consensus All American in 1975. During his playing career Penn State only lost five games and went undefeated in 1973.

In 2001 he was awarded the Silver Anniversary Butkus Award for the 1975 season.

After college Buttle played nine seasons for the New York Jets in the NFL and is a member of their All Time Jets team.

Shane Conlan ...Many Penn State fans consider Shane Conlan to be the prototypical linebacker by which all other linebackers are judged. He was an unknown prospect coming out of high school, but would go on to become a two time First Team All American that led his defensive squad to appearances in two National Championship games. The 1986 defense was one of the greatest of all time not allowing any opponents to score more than 19 points. In the Fiesta Bowl Conlan had eight tackles and two interceptions in leading Penn State to their second National Championship over the Miami Hurricanes. He ended his Penn State career with 274 tackles which is still good enough for fifth all time.

Conlan was a first round draft pick of the Buffalo Bills (8th overall) in 1987 and went on to claim the NFL Rookie of the Year award. He was named to the Pro Bowl in three straight seasons from 1990 to 1992. The Bills went to the Super Bowl each of those seasons, but couldn't win the game. Conlan joined the Los Angeles/St. Louis Rams in 1993 and played a few more years before retiring in 1995.

Andre Collins...After playing on a National Championship team his freshman year, Collins endured some disappointing seasons the rest of his Penn State career. None-the-less, he was a shining star on the defense. Collins broke 100 tackles in each of his junior and senior seasons, one of only five Nittany Lions to achieve the feat. In 1989 Collins was named a First Team All American and a Butkus Award Finalist. He finished his Penn State career ninth in all time tackles.

Collins went on to play 10 years in the NFL for the Washington Redskins. He was a starting linebacker for the team that won Super Bowl XXVI. Today he serves as Director of Retired Players for the NFL Players Association.

Brian Gelzheiser wasn't a very flashy linebacker. He didn't win All American Awards. He wasn't named as a finalist for the Lombardi or Butkus Awards. But he was a steady performer that showed up week in and week out. He was a starter and key member of the 1994 team that went undefeated in winning Penn State's first Big Ten Championship. He tore the medial collateral ligament in his knee in August before his senior year. He sat out week one, but suited up against USC in week two. Not only did he play, he recorded 10 tackles. Gelzheiser also recorded 100 tackles in junior and senior years and finished his Penn State career as the second all-time leading tackler. Today he is still number three on the list.

Gelzheiser was a sixth round selection by the Indianapolis Colts in the NFL draft. His NFL career never amounted to much. After a brief stint in the NFL Gelzheiser went into sales in the Pittsburgh area.

Brandon Short On any other team, Brandon Short would have been the best player on the defense. But when you line up next to Lavar Arrington, people tend to call you "the other guy". Short started all four years at Penn State (Played at defensive end his freshman year). Short led the team in tackles his senior year with 103. He was named a First Team All American and a Butkus Award finalist along with Arrington.

Short was a fourth round pick for the New York Giants in the 2000 NFL draft and appeared in Super Bowl XXXV as a rookie. He signed with the Carolina Panthers for the 2004-2005 seasons before rejoining the Giants in 2006.

Lavar Arrington is easily the most physically gifted linebacker to every play at Penn State. He was big enough to take on offensive linemen yet fast enough to cover wide receivers in man coverage.

His playing style could best be described as "chaos", as he often went outside of the system by abandoning his assignment. Although he was undisciplined, he made several spectacular plays by simply following his instincts.

No play epitomized Lavar's style more than The Lavar Leap. In his junior season he was named a First Team All American and won both the Bednarik and Butkus Awards. He didn't rack up an overwhelming number of tackles, but he wreaked all kind of havoc in the backfield with 19 career sacks and 39 TFL good enough for eight and ninth all time respectively.

Arrington was the number two pick overall by the Washington Redskins in the 2000 NFL draft. He made three consecutive Pro Bowls from 2001-2003 until he suffered a season ending knee injury in 2004. After a very public feud with head coach Joe Gibbs, Arrington was released and signed with the New York Giants. He appeared to be regaining his old form before an ankle injury ended his season in week seven of 2006.

Paul Posluszny. Known simply as "Poz", Paul Posluszny embodied the Joe Paterno image of the student athlete. Hall of Famer Jack Ham once called him "the greatest linebacker to ever play at Penn State." His work ethic on and off the field were unsurpassed. He was named team captain both his junior and senior seasons, a rarity in the Joe Paterno era. Poz was a key member of the 11-1 team that beat Florida State in the Orange Bowl and finished ranked #3 in the country. He recorded 116 tackles in both his junior and senior seasons. He's the only Penn State linebacker to ever record 100 tackles in three consecutive seasons (2004-2006). Poz won the Dick Butkus Award in 2005 and won the Chuck Bednarik Award in 2005 and 2006. He was also named a First Team All American in 2005 and 2006. Poz is Penn State's all-time leading tackler with 372.

Posluszny was drafted in the second round of the NFL draft by the Buffalo Bills. 2007 will be his rookie season.

Pete Giftopoulos: 1985-1987. He was starting inside linebacker for the Nittany Lions. 'At Penn State, Pete Giftopoulos learned to speak the language of his coach Joe Paterno since Pete loves football and JoePa loves football. Pete had a successful career at Penn State followed by an eight-year stint with the Hamilton TigerCats in the Canadian Football League. Pete loves football.

Perhaps best known for his game-saving interception in the end zone against Vinny Testaverde and the Miami Hurricanes in the 1987 Fiesta Bowl, which brought the Lions their second national championship in five years, Giftopoulos was part of a strong linebacking corps that also featured Shane Conlan and Trey Bauer.

He tried out for the NFL (Pittsburgh) and did not make it. Just because he was not in the NFL, it didn't mean his football career was over. While he was trying out with the Steelers, he was also drafted by the Saskatchewan Roughriders in the first round of the CFL entry draft. Because Canadian teams in the CFL (there are American teams as well) have to have 20 Canadian players on their roster, Giftopoulos was a valuable commodity up north. The Tiger-Cats knew this as well, so they traded a first round draft pick and future considerations for him. Eight years later, Pete G. is a definite success.

Dan Connor... Dan Connor could have gone pro after his junior season in 2006. If he had he would definitely have been be on the list. He is one of the best ever. Connor cracked the starting lineup as a true freshman in 2004 and set a freshman record for tackles with 85. In 2006 and

2007 Connor was named First Team All American and finished second in the Bednarik Award voting in 2006 to his teammate, Paul Posluszny. In 2007, he gained the award.

He is currently eighth on the all-time tackle list and will most likely be the leader by the end of his career.

Even though he could have gone pro after his junior season, Dan Connor returned for his senior year in 2007. He switched from outside linebacker to middle linebacker in 2007. He was a top prospect for the Lombardi, Butkus, and Bednarik awards, winning the Bednarik Award in 2007. He was. He was predicted to be a first round draft pick in the NFL when his Penn State career was done but as good fortune had it, he was chosen in the third round by Carolina, where he plays football today. For a short while he was traded to the Giants and the Cowboys were he played. Now, he is back with the Panthers

Navorro Bowman: 6'1", 232 lbs; Projected 40 Time: 4.6-4.7 sec.

His 2009 Penn State Stats: 93 tackles (52 solo), 17-60 TFL, Sacks 3.0-15, 2 INT, 2 FR.

Bowman was a redshirt freshman on special teams in 2007. He was a physical player with speed and tenacity in pursuing the ball and bringing down the ball carrier. In limited duty due to a stacked depth chart with upper classmen like Dan Connor and Sean Lee, Bowman managed 16 tackles to go with a sack and 2.5 TFL. His season was cut short by a few games after he was involved in an on campus altercation and suspended from the team for the rest of the 2007 season.

Bowman returned in 2008, and thanks to a depleted linebacker unit from Connor's graduation and Sean Lee's knee injury, Bowman got the chance to start in week four of the season and never looked back. Though many don't remember, Bowman had a significant role in Penn State's biggest win of the year against Ohio State. Everyone remembers Mark Rubin knocking the ball out of the hands of Terrelle Pryor on a 3rd and 1 quarterback sneak.

But as the ball was bouncing around out of control with bodies flying everywhere, it was Bowman who jumped in the pile to cradle the ball giving Penn State the huge momentum swing that propelled them to victory. He went on that season to lead the team in tackles with 106, and recorded 17.5 TFL, 4.0 sacks, and 1 INT to go with it.

His efforts earned him First Team All-Big Ten honors from the media and coaches.

Chapter 28 Penn State's Greatest Running Backs from 1909-2012

Our sincere thank yours to BSD@mhubbell on May 13, 2007, 10:11p.
http://www.blackshoediaries.com/2007/5/13/221130/292

I have written ninety percent of this book but as I find nice stuff that is appropriate for the reader, now that I am packaging the book and preparing its publishing, I sometimes decide to include it. That may mean that this version of the book is the most inclusive ever available. I may be forced to pare thirty to fifty pages from its ranks if demanded by the attributed authors of the pieces as I am not as judicious as I am approaching press time.

That is why I try to give all sources attribution. For some that may not be enough. When I write, I want the world to read it. Those that don't care whether their work is read or not in all the right places, can have a beer on me or tell me the exact pages from this printed book and I promise your stuff will be gone post haste...with no looking back and no returns.

My biggest concern is that somebody someplace is going to say, "But what about that nice Jimmy Cefalo guy from Pittston... isn't he from up your way in WB? He was great. Why is he not in the book? Was it because hist Pittston team beat your Meyers team the year he played? Then, why not?

Well, if that is your question and you can wait for a response here it is:

Jimmy Cefalo was the best football player that I ever saw play in high school at Meyers Stadium (Wilkes-Barre

Stadium) against Meyers, my alma mater. By then, I had long graduated and was comfortable in the seats eating the Nardone Pizza they serve at the games.

I loved watching football in Meyers Stadium and watching Jimmy Cefalo was like watching a pro playing against high school wannabees. I did not know that a young man from Pittston could grow such huge muscular thighs that could enable him to mow down every lineman he encountered.

Cefalo was that impressive as a high schooler. Penn State's Jimmy Cefalo was Pittston's Jimmy Cefalo even before he was Miami's Jimmy Cefalo. Yep, same guy. Great ball player! I never saw a better athlete, period! He did well and I always rooted for him. He was one of ours!

James Carmen "Jimmy" Cefalo

When the stork arrived at Cefalo Haven some place tucked within the inner surrounds of Pittston, PA, it was October 6, 1956. The young man being carried was at his smallest and weakest point in life. Yet, over time he was able to become an American Journalist, news broadcaster and sports broadcaster, radio talk show host, and of course like Curt Gowdy and the Phillies, he is now the Voice of the Miami Dolphins, He is also a businessman, wine enthusiast and former professional American football wide receiver and game show host.

As noted previously, I met Jimmy Cefalo him from a distance as I was watching a football game when I was about 24 years old and he was about 18. It seems like yesterday. He more than likely would not recognize me even though I was not wearing a protective helmet in the stands during the game.

I observed the talented Cefalo when he was a kid at Pittston High. Even though I am a football enthusiast, and I went to a ton of high school games, I had never seen anybody play so well... ever.

Jimmy Cefalo is the real deal and he ripped into every defense in the Wyoming Valley right from the line. He held nothing back and his team won. He got banged and bruised but he always won the yards even with no blockers. He became an adept pass receiver and maybe even one of the greatest. I knew he could outskirt the DBs but I was always hoping one of those huge collegiate linemen had to deal with a pair of Cefalo thighs on a running play. It would have been awesome.

I thought the readers of this book might enjoy a local press release from the Wyoming Valley from which I hail.

YATESVILLE — Former Pittston Area great Jimmy Cefalo returned to his alma mater Friday night to present the school with a "golden football" during the game against Abington Heights.

Cefalo, in conjunction with the Super Bowl, the National Football League, and athletic company Wilson, presented longtime Pittston Area head football coach Bob Barbieri with the football. Barbieri accepted the football on Pittston Area's behalf.

Footballs were given to all former Super Bowl participants and were to be presented to programs that show character and perseverance.

Cefalo, who played for Penn State and won Super Bowl XIX with the Miami Dolphins, said this was the first time he's been back to the field since his final high school game.

"It's a great honor to be back here," he said.

"The National Football League's program is an important program and I'm glad to be part of it."

The former Patriot is a member of the Pennsylvania Football News All-Century team and was a standout at Penn State from 1974 to 1977. He was named MVP of the 1976 Gator Bowl.

A third-round pick of the Miami Dolphins, Cefalo appeared in two Super Bowls and caught a 76-yard pass against the Washington Redskins, one of the longest in Super Bowl history.

In 1984, Cefalo caught the Dan Marino pass that broke the record for most touchdown passes in a season.

A meet-and-greet was held for Cefalo prior to the game at the Red Mill in Pittston. Cefalo then spoke to current Pittston Area players before the game. Cefalo was also an honorary captain and was part of the coin toss.

When asked about what Cefalo remembers most about his time playing high school, college and professional football, he came back to his roots.

"Most of my shining moments were on this field," he said. "That's where it all started. Here, it was special. It was with my friends and the guys on the playground. I think this is the shining moment."

How can we not all agree!

Jimmy Cefalo, not heralded as much at Penn State because of all the talent was clearly the most talented player that non-coaches, and real coaches ever saw come from Wyoming valley because it was right in front of us.

I herald Jimmy Cefalo of Penn State. Despite his greatness, he never uttered a negative word.

OK, let's now look at the other guys on the running back list one at a time.

J. Lester "Pete" Mauthe 1909-1912

Mauthe was a four year letterman as a fullback for the Nittany Lions in 1909-1912. During his playing years Penn State amassed a record of 26-2-4 including a stellar record of 8-0-1 in 1911. His senior year in 1912 he was elected captain and led Penn State to an 8-0 perfect season. In addition to being the team's fullback, Mauthe was also the team's punter and place kicker.

After graduation he became the head football coach at Gettysburg College where he coached one season for a 3-6-1 record. He later went on to become a successful CEO at a Youngstown steel company and served on the board of trustees at Youngtown State University and Penn State. In 1957 he was elected into the College Football Hall of Fame.

Lenny Moore 1953-1955

Joe Paterno has often suggested that Lenny Moore is the greatest football player to ever play for Penn State. Moore starred as a halfback as the Nittany Lions went 18-9 during his playing days. He led the team in rushing in 1954 with a then school record of 1082 yards in nine games on just 136 carries for a whopping 8.0 yards per carry average. Moore was twice named to the All American team in 1954 and 1955. When he graduated he owned the school career rushing record with 2380 yards which is currently 12th on the all-time list. His stats are surely impressive considering freshmen were not permitted to play in those days. His signature high-stepping running style made him popular with the fans and sports writers. The fact that he was a great player was just more gravy.

Moore went on to star in the NFL playing 12 years for the Baltimore Colts and winning two NFL championships. He was a first round (9th overall) pick for the Colts and went on to be named Rookie of the Year in 1956. During his career he was selected to play in seven Pro Bowls. He was named league MVP and Comeback Player of the Year in 1964. He scored a touchdown in 18 consecutive games from 1963-1965, a record that stood for 40 years until broken by LaDainian Tomlinson in 2005.

Lydell Mitchell
1969-1971

In his day, Mitchell was the most prolific running back the college football world had ever seen. During his playing days Penn State amassed a record of 29-4 including an undefeated 11-0 season in 1969.

After two years of sharing running back duties with Franco Harris, Mitchell exploded in his senior year for 1567 yards and 29 touchdowns (26 rushing) in 1971. Both marks shattered single season school records and the 29 total touchdowns and 174 points set new NCAA marks. He also graduated as Penn State's all-time leading rusher with 2934 yards, still good enough for seventh on the all-time list. Still need evidence of Mitchell's greatness? Because of Mitchell, future Heisman winning running back John Cappelletti had to play on defense in 1971.

After Penn State, Mitchell went on to be drafted 48th overall by the Baltimore Colts. He was a key member of the Baltimore Colts-Miami Dolphins rivalry of the 1970's leading the Colts to three consecutive AFC East Division Championships. He had three consecutive 1000 yard seasons from 1975-1977 and went to the pro bowl all three years. He later went on to play for the San Diego Chargers and Los Angeles Rams before retiring in 1980. After his playing days Mitchell went on to become CEO of a sausage company in Baltimore Maryland. Today he lectures youths about the dangers of drugs and alcohol abuse. In 2004 Mitchell was elected to the College Football Hall of Fame.

Franco Harris 1969-1971

Franco never broke 700 yards in one season but still played on some great Penn State teams. He teamed with Lydell Mitchell to form the best 1-2 punch in the nation. Although he shared carries with Mitchell his entire career, Harris still finished fourth on the all-time career rushing list with 2002 yards, good enough for 16th all-time today.

After Penn State Franco Harris went on to star for 13 seasons in the NFL, 12 of them with the Pittsburgh Steelers. Harris was a key member of four Super Bowl Championship teams and was named MVP of the 1974 Super Bowl. He will forever be remembered for the "Immaculate Reception" in a 1972 playoff game against the Oakland Raiders. During his NFL career Harris was named Rookie of the Year in 1972 and went to nine consecutive Pro Bowls from 1972-1980. He was elected to the Pro Football Hall of Fame in 1990. After football Harris once again teamed up with Lydell Mitchell in purchasing the Parks Sausage Company. More recently he became owner and CEO of Super Bakery Inc.

John "Cappy" Cappelletti 1971-1973

Like all freshmen back then, Cappy didn't play his first year at Penn State. In his second year the offensive backfield was crowded with Mitchell and Harris sharing the load, so Cappelletti had to settle for playing on defense.

It wasn't until his junior year he was made a running back. He broke 1000 yards in his junior and senior year. As far as I can tell he was the first Nittany Lion to accomplish the feat. He exploded in 1973 for 1522 yards and 17 TD. He won the Maxwell Award and was a unanimous All-American. And of course he was awarded the prestigious Heisman Trophy.

He is the only Penn State player to ever win the Heisman Trophy award. He finished his career second to Mitchell on the all-time career rushing list for Penn State with 2639 yards and 29 career touchdowns. Amazingly Penn State only lost three games during his playing years and went undefeated in 1973.

Cappelletti will forever be remembered for his Heisman acceptance speech in which he dedicated the trophy to his younger brother, Joey, who was diagnosed with leukemia. After Penn State, Cappy went on to play in the NFL for ten years with the Los Angeles Rams and San Diego Chargers. John was elected to the College Football Hall of Fame in

1993. Today he is a successful business man and father of four, living in California.

Curt Warner
1979-1982

Curt Warner led Penn State to a 39-9 record during his playing days. He was the starting running back for the 1982 team that defeated Georgia in the Sugar Bowl to win Joe Paterno's first National Championship.

In 1981 he rushed for a school record 256 yards in one game against Syracuse, a record that would stand for over 20 years. Warner was twice selected a first team All American. To this day he still holds the career rushing record for Penn State with 3398 yards.

After Penn State Warner was a first round draft pick for the Seattle Seahawks, where he led the AFC in rushing his rookie year. He tore his ACL his second year in the league, but still went on to be a highly productive player. Warner went on to play for seven years and make three Pro Bowls with the Seahawks before retiring in 1990. Currently he owns and runs a Chevrolet dealership in Vancouver, Washington.

D.J. Dozier
1983-1986

D.J. Dozier won the hearts of Nittany Nation when he rushed for 1000 yards in his freshman year. Unfortunately, he played on some pretty disappointing teams in 1983 and 1984. But he was a major part of the teams that won 23 games and played in two National Championship games in 1985 and 1986. He played on some terrible offenses that were incapable of moving the ball through the air.

So much like Tony Hunt in 2006, Dozier faced eight and nine men in the box all day and kept chugging ahead four yards at a time. The image above of Dozier kneeling in the endzone after putting Penn State on top of Miami 14-10 in the 1987 Fiesta Bowl will forever live in the minds of Penn State fans as one of the greatest moments in our 100-plus year history. He was named a first team All American his senior year and finished his career as the second leading career rusher for Penn State only behind Warner.

Dozier was a first round draft pick by the Minnesota Vikings. Unfortunately his NFL career never really took off. He played four seasons with the Vikings and one year with Detroit before hanging it up to pursue a professional baseball career. He signed as an amateur free agent with the New York Mets and played two seasons in the minors before making his Major League debut on May 6, 1992. He was traded in October of that year and played his final game on October 4, 1992.

Blair Thomas
1985-1989

The debate has raged for decades among Penn State fans. Who was the better cutback runner? Warner or Thomas? Blair Thomas was the first player to rush for 1400 yards in two seasons earning All American honors in 1987 and 1989. He finished in the top five for the Heisman in 1989 and earned MVP honors in the Holiday and Senior Bowls. He ended his career the second all-time rusher for Penn State only 97 yards behind Curt Warner and stayed in second until Tony Hunt passed him in 2006.

After Penn State Thomas was selected by the New York Jets as the second pick of the first round. Unfortunately he played on some horrible Jets teams for six seasons and couldn't get much going in the NFL. He joined on with several teams over the next few years before he retired in 1995. After his playing days Thomas coached the running backs for Temple University before he gave that up in 2005. Today he lives with his wife and three children in King of Prussia, PA.

Ki-Jana Carter 1992-1994

Many Penn State fans consider Ki-Jana Carter to be the standard by which all other Penn State tailbacks are judged. He started out as a platoon player sharing carries with Mike Archie and Stephen Pitts, but he exploded in his junior year to claim the job all to himself. Carter was a key member of the 1994 team that went undefeated in claiming Penn State's first conference title in the Big Ten.

The 1994 offense featured several players that would go on to play in the NFL including Kerry Collins, Kyle Brady, Jeff Hartings, Marco Rivera, and Bobby Engram. In 1994 Carter rushed for 1539 yards and scored 23 touchdowns. The 1539 yards was the second highest total ever achieved by a Penn State tailback in a single season. The scary thing is he could have easily broken 2000 yards had the Penn State offense been so good. Paterno often sat Carter the entire second half when Penn State was up by several touchdowns. In 1994 Carter was named a first team All American and finished second in the Heisman voting.

Having earned his degree after the 1994 season, Carter decided not to return for the 1995 season. He finished his

Penn State career as the number 5 Penn State rusher of all time. Today he still sits at number 8.

After college Carter was picked #1 overall by the Cincinnati Bengals in the NFL draft. An unfortunate knee injury in the preseason of his rookie year forced him to have surgery and go through extensive rehab. He was never the same running back again. He moved from team to team for several years before officially retiring from the NFL in 2004.

Curtis Enis
1995-1997

Curtis Enis was a big physical running back that could run around you or run over you. He showed off his potential after he rushed for 683 yards as a freshman. With the starting job his in 1996, Enis pounded his way for 1210 yards and 13 TD. He came back his junior year and ran for 1363 yards and 19 TD and was named a first team All American. The 1997 team had high aspirations entering the season ranked #1 in the country.

A late season loss to Michigan led the team into a tailspin that ended with back to back losses to Michigan State and Florida in the Citrus Bowl. With less than 200 yards separating him from Curt Warner on the all-time rushing list, Enis could have returned for his senior year to get the record and he would have been a serious Heisman contender. There was speculation he was thinking of going pro, and then it was discovered he accepted gifts from an agent and his career ended in scandal.

Enis went on to be the fifth overall pick of the 1998 NFL draft. He played three uneventful seasons for the Chicago Bears before being cut and retiring.

Larry Johnson 1999-2002

Larry Johnson was an enigma his first three years at Penn State. He rode the bench mostly only getting carries when the game was in hand. When Penn State struggled in 2000 and 2001 he grumbled publicly to the press about the play calling and his playing time, a major no-no on a Joe Paterno team. After spending three years in and out of the doghouse he finally got to be "the man" in 2002, and he set out determined to show Paterno and everyone they made a mistake by not playing him sooner.

Johnson had the most prolific single season ever by a Penn State tailback rushing for 2087 yards and 20 TD with an amazing 7.7 ypc average. In 2002 LJ broke the school record for single game rushing yards three times and still holds the record today with his 327 yards against Indiana. In 2002 Johnson was named first team All American and won the Maxwell, Doak Walker, and Walter Camp awards and finished in the top five in the Heisman voting. He finished his Penn State career as the fifth leading rusher.

After college Johnson was drafted in the first round by the Kansas City Chiefs. Like his Penn State career, Johnson started out riding the bench and making noise in the press. When he finally got a chance to play Johnson rushed for 1750 yards in 2005 in only nine starts. He followed it up with 1789 yards in 2006 and has made the Pro Bowl each of the last two years.

Tony Hunt
2003-2006

Tony Hunt started his career as "the other guy". He was part of a recruiting class that featured the highly touted Austin Scott. He set to work the best he could and would end his career the second all-time rusher at Penn State. His straight ahead workhorse running style endeared him with the fans. As a sophomore in 2004 Hunt was the leading receiver on the team.

He was a key member of the 2005 offense that featured Michael Robinson and Derrick Williams. Hunt never won any awards. He was never named an All American. He never had any amazing runs. But yet he in many ways symbolized Penn State. Hard working. No nonsense. Straight ahead. Four yards and a cloud of dust. In his final game against Tennessee in the Outback Bowl, Penn State clung to a 17-10 lead in the fourth quarter, Tony Hunt put the team on his back like he did so many other times. Hunt ran the ball on seven consecutive plays gaining three first downs. The drive allowed Penn State to kill five minutes off the clock and put the Lions in position to kick a field goal and put the game out of reach. That was Tony Hunt.

Hunt was drafted in the third round of the NFL draft by the Philadelphia Eagles

That's All Folks!

We hope to bring out another version in about five years that focuses on PSU Football and removes or alters the stories about the scandal. PSU is much more than that. Thank you for choosing this book among the many that are in your option list. I sincerely appreciate it!

LETS GO PUBLISH! Books by Brian W. Kelly
www.letsgopublish.com; Sold at

www.bookhawkers.com
Email info@ letsgopublish.com for specific ordering info. Our titles include the following:

Great Moments in Penn State Football The story about the beginning of US football and Penn State football in the US as well as the great moments and great PSU coaches and players over the years.

I Had a Dream IBM Could Be #1 Again The story of how IBM can again hist the top as the #1 IT company in the world

Whatever Happened to the IBM AS/400? The story of the AS/400 and how and why it disappeared.

Great Moments in Notre Dame Football The story about the beginning of US football and ND football in the US as well as the great moments and great ND coaches and players over the years.

Thank You IBM The story of how IBM helped today's technology millionaires and billionaires gain their vast fortunes

WineDiets.Com PresentsThe Wine Diet Learn how to lose weight while having fun. Four specific diets and some great anecdotes fill this book with fun.

Wilkes-Barre, PA; Return to Glory Wilkes-Barre City's return to glory begins with dreams and ideas. Along with plans and actions, this equals leadership.

The Lifetime Guest Plan. This is a plan which if deployed today would immediately solve the problem of 60 million illegal aliens in the United States.

Geoffrey Parsons' Epoch... The Land of Fair Play Better than the original. The greatest re-mastering of the greatest book ever written on American Civics. It was built for all Americans as the best govt. design in the history of the world.

The Bill of Rights 4 Dummmies This is the best book to learn about your rights. Be the first, to have a "Rights Fest" on your block. You will win for sure!

Sol Bloom's Epoch ...Story of the Constitution This work by Sol Bloom was written to commemorate the Sesquicentennial celebration of the Constitution. It has been remastered by Lets Go Publish! – an excellent read!

The Constitution 4 Dummmies This is the best book to learn about the Constitution. Learn all about the fundamental laws of America.

America for Dummmies!
All Americans should read to learn about this great country.

Just Say No to Chris Christie for President!
Discusses the reasons why Chris Christie is a poor choice for US President

The Federalist Papers by Hamilton, Jay, Madison w/ intro by Brian Kelly
Complete unabridged, easier to read version of the original Federalist Papers

Bring On the American Party!
Demonstrates how Americans can be free from Parties of wimps by starting our own national party called the American Party.

Saving America
This how-to book is about saving our country using strong mercantilist principles. These are the same principles that helped the country from its founding.

RRR:
A unique plan for economic recovery and job creation

Kill the EPA
The EPA seems to hate mankind and love nature. They are also making it tough for asthmatics to breathe and for those with malaria to live. It's time they go.

Taxation Without Representation Second Edition
At the time of the Boston Tea Party, there was no representation. Now, there is no representation again but there are "representatives."

Healthcare Accountability
Who should pay for your healthcare? Whose healthcare should you pay for? Is it a lifetime free ride on others or should those once in need of help have to pay it back when their lives improve?

Jobs! Jobs! Jobs!
Where have all the American Jobs gone and how can we get them back?

IBM I Technical Books

The All Everything Operating System:
The story about IBM's finest operating system, its facilities, and how it came to be.

The All-Everything Machine
The story about IBM's finest computer server.

Chip Wars
The story of the ongoing war between Intel and AMD and the upcoming was between Intel and IBM. This book may cause you to buy or sell somebody's stock.

Can the AS/400 Survive IBM?
Exciting book about the AS/400 in an System i5 World.

The IBM i Pocket SQL Guide.
Complete Pocket Guide to SQL as implemented on System i5. A must have for SQL developers new to System i5. It is very compact yet very comprehensive and it is example driven. Written in a part tutorial and part reference style, this book has tons of SQL coding samples, from the simple to the sublime.

The IBM i Pocket Query Guide.
If you have been spending money for years educating your Query users, and you find you are still spending, or you've given up, this book is right for you. This one QuikCourse covers all Query options.

The IBM I Pocket RPG & RPG IV Guide.
Comprehensive RPG & RPGIV Textbook -- Over 900 pages. This is the one RPG book to have if you are not having more than one. All areas of the language covered smartly in a convenient sized book Annotated PowerPoint's available for self-study (extra fee for self-study package)

www.ingramcontent.com/pod-product-compliance
Lightning Source LLC
Chambersburg PA
CBHW050246170426
43202CB00011B/1578